Formal Refinement for Operating System Kernels

Iain D. Craig

Formal Refinement for Operating System Kernels

Springer

Iain Craig, MA, PhD, FBCF, CITP

British Library Cataloguing in Publication Data
A catalogue record for this book is available from the British Library

ISBN 978-1-84996-689-4 e-ISBN 978-1-84628-967-5

Printed on acid-free paper.

9 8 7 6 5 4 3 2 1

springer.com

To my Father at 75

Preface

This book was written as a companion to my book on modelling operating system kernels. It is intended to demonstrate that the formal derivation of kernels is possible (and, actually, quite easy, or so I have found *thus far*).

It is important for the reader to understand that the refinements contained in this book are not the only ones I have performed of microkernels. To date, I have refined four microkernels down to executable code and have now produced a kit of formally specified components that can be composed to form kernels. The first kernel included in this book is just one example of this work. The second kernel, the Separation Kernel, is new and was partly constructed out of the kit of parts (and the reader will see reuse in its specification and refinement) and was included for specific reasons that will become clear anon. Both kernels took less than three months' working time to produce (the actual time is rather hard to calculate because of frequent interruptions). Previous experience in refining kernels also paid off in the sense that there was little revision involved in their specification or refinement; the usual process of yo-yoing between levels of the derivation was absent. This appears to be an inevitable consequence of experience.

The time factor has been important in the production of the various kernels that I have derived. The micro kernel helps in no little way by imposing the rule that the kernel should be as small as possible. This is not to say that I would not be interested or willing to refine a kernel such as the second one I modelled in [4]. Such an exercise would be extremely interesting and one I would very much like to undertake; however, it would require time (and I am quite willing to put it in) and would require financial support. In today's climate, one would probably also have to ask what the point of such an exercise would be.

It is necessary to position this book. Mainly, I believe it to be an essay in formal methods software engineering and in operating systems. It can be argued that this book is a contribution to refinement, in particular, to refinement *in the large.* There is nothing in the literature on the scale of the refinements that are the subject of this book, as far as I am aware.

The Separation Kernel was included for specific reasons. First, there is at least one document from the US National Security Agency (NSA) recommending the Separation Kernel as the cryptographic kernel *par excellence*. In their documents, the NSA also states that the formal specification of a Separation Kernel would be highly desirable. Having looked at the various documents, the original paper by Rushby [11] in particular, the structure and functioning of the Separation Kernel appeared to be fairly simple. This would appear to have been one of the goals that Rushby had in mind when defining the architecture in the first place—it is another good example of how simplicity wins every time (Less *is* more.) As a result, I wondered what a specification would look like. What I found was what I expected. The result was quite easy to specify and to refine.

The reader will observe that there is little or nothing about bootstrapping or hardware-specific initialisation. This is because we do not consider these matters to be part of the kernel; they belong to the *environment* within which the kernel executes.

I think it necessary to make a couple of observations about the refinement itself. In the Z literature, two kinds of refinement are described: one relational, one functional. The relational refinement is the worst-case scenario. The functional refinement is, in my experience, the usual case. Indeed, in more than twenty years' experience refining specifications, I have found that the relationship between the abstract and concrete statements is almost always an identity. This experience is not restricted to kernels (of course) for a great deal of the code I have produced during that time has had at least some formally specified component (usually the components that are the hardest to understand). The code has included virtual machines and parts of compilers, so it is quite varied. For this reason, the fact that the abstraction relations in this book are identities does not cause me any concern. (Steve Schumann reports in a private communication the same experience.) I decided that proofs, which are strictly unnecessary when using a functional abstraction relation, should be included in the book. This was to show how they enter the refinement process and to show that they are relatively simple (given the prevalence of identity relationships, proofs of similar complexity are to be expected and that is a level of complexity that can easily be handled). Furthermore, I wanted to counter the claims that either the proofs could not be done or that they were too complicated; neither is the case. In the case of the Separation Kernel, a number of proofs are omitted (this was also for the reason that space was getting short and devoting much more space to such a simple system did not appear warranted). This is particularly the case with operations defined over conjunctions of state spaces. The proofs and preconditions of the components are given, as are the abstraction relations, so the production of the required proofs is a straightforward matter and can be produced in a relatively short period. In each case, the compound operation was checked against the components and short (i.e., outline or sketch) proofs produced as a safety device.

The purely textual parts of this book were written using voice-input software because my daily typing time was severely restricted on medical advice. Using voice-input software for the first time was an interesting and sometimes frustrating experience. The frustrations were mostly due to my being so used to typing and I found that having to *speak* rather than compose on the keyboard sometimes confusingly difficult. In particular, initially, I found it quite hard to navigate back and forth using just voice commands. (It led to the occasional and unwanted inclusion of expletives in the text and I hope that I have removed them all!) With greater experience, it turned out to be an effective method for producing text. It is worth trying!

A Note on Interrupts

When I started out, it was conventional wisdom that interrupts should be disabled for as short a period as possible. The reader will note that the space between disabling and enabling interrupts in the specifications and refinements that follow can be rather large. In some case (e.g., the interface routines at the end of Chapter 3), the reason for this is that I wanted to emphasise the fact that interrupts should be disabled for some part of the operation (for reasons that will become clear in a second, without necessarily being forced into saying *which* parts). Some processors have pipelines that might affect the exact time at which the interrupt operation is performed; this cannot be taken into account until the processor is known, so the safe option was chosen. In addition, the period during which interrupts are disabled can be extended when the desired response time of the system is known (here, we have no such knowledge). In such a case, the interrupt operations can be moved using the distributive law ($p \vee (q \wedge r) \Leftrightarrow (p \wedge q) \vee (p \wedge r)$) and the idempotent laws ($p \wedge p \Leftrightarrow p$ and $p \vee p \Leftrightarrow p$). In the other cases, the change to the interrupt flag (or whatever mechanism is used on the implementation platform) might have some interaction with another part of the system (e.g., on the IA32, if the *INT* bit in the *EFLAGS* register is not the same value as the processor interrupt flag, the system will crash); again, without knowing the exact hardware, precise location of the interrupt operationsis impossible.

Acknowledgements

First of all, I would like to thank Beverley Ford for agreeing to publish this book. Thanks are due in equal measure to Helen Desmond for making the process of producing this book as painless as possible. They have jointly performed the proof and copy editing stages of the test in order to expedite its publication. I would like to thank Steve Schuman for reading the manuscript while it was in sketch and in a more developed form and for a number of extremely interesting discussions on the refinement process (any errors are, naturally, my own fault). Considerable thanks are due to my brother, Adam. Once again, he drew the figures for me; in addition, he patiently typed those parts from my dictation that could not easily be done using voice-input software. Without his dedicated effort, the text of this book could not have been completed. As for the others who have helped (the regulars), as always, I offer my thanks.

Iain Craig
North Warwickshire
April, 2007

Contents

List of Figures

1

Introduction

This book is a follow-up to our earlier one on the modelling of operating system kernels [4]. The aim of that book was to argue that formal specification of kernels was possible in the sense that formal modelling could be undertaken and then followed by a specification, a design and then refinement to running code. The first part of this was the subject of [4]. This book is concerned entirely with the specification, design and refinement to executable code of two operating system kernels. One kernel is of the kind found in small systems, while the other is intended for use in cryptographic and other secure systems. The book does not contain reasoning about models and concentrates on refinement. The refinements are from abstract or high-level specifications to a level at which programming language code can be immediately derived by obvious translation from the last stage of the refinement process.

In [4], it was our aim to show that detailed models were useful. This allows designers to identify properties of their designs without the need to construct a system. This could well have economic advantages and might spark new and necessary work in the general area of operating systems. It was also argued in that book that the *post hoc* verification of systems, particularly critical systems and components such as kernels, was not a good solution to the problem of reliability; instead, we argued that a synthetic method was superior.

The main purpose of the book is to demonstrate that the refinement of formal specifications of (micro) kernels is possible and, moreover, quite tractable. This should be obvious, given the fact that it is possible to model a (micro) kernel formally. The refinement is a process of documentation, as well as proof and justification, so it is worthwhile to record it, thus adding weight to the argument at the start of [4].

A secondary purpose is to give examples of refinements that are larger than those we have found in the literature. There are issues raised by the refinement process that are never considered in the standard literature:

- How many refinements should complex operations receive?

- When should implicit preconditions be used?
- When is it worth relying on the properties of functional abstraction relations?

Some might now argue that this is not a complete specification and refinement because we have not included device drivers and low-level device-interface code. Some might even go as far as to claim that this is not possible because, for example, it involves bitmasks; it also requires processes to wait for flags to change state. It is our opinion that the formal specification of such things is possible; this opinion is based upon experience with small examples and with the specification of low-level operations (for example, the bitmap that is used as the basis for the semaphore table in the first refinement below; we also specified some generic device-handlers while writing [4] but they had to be omitted for reasons of time and space).

In any case, at this point, we cannot specify the actual pieces of hardware that might be controlled by this book's systems. For this reason, we have to be as generic as possible, so we have concentrated on the specification of portable systems. This does mean that we have ignored low-level issues. On the contrary, we felt it essential that context switches and other essential kernel operations should be included in the specification. The approach we have taken is that the hardware and instruction set is a given and cannot be further refined. One aim of the work reported here was to reduce the assembly language programming to the level of triviality, thus making it possible to encapsulate the assembly language in a couple of operations[1].

As can be seen from the specifications, interrupt-driven architectures are assumed, thus rendering the interface between the software and hardware specifications as small as possible. The context switch is thus reduced to a single instruction, one which raises an interrupt. The major part of the hardware specification is as generic as this. For the hardware architecture we have in mind, this is quite adequate and represents a reasonable specification of it; for other architectures (e.g., MIPS), it might be necessary to refine, perhaps, the high-level operations defined here.

By the publication of this book, we have shown that it is possible (and relatively easy) to specify small kernels and refine them to running code. What we have *not* done is try to specify a monolithic kernel such as the one used by Linux. One reason for this is that we do not care very much for the monolithic kernel for the reasons that it is too tempting just to add a feature to such a kernel on the grounds that there is nowhere else to put it (i.e., it is tempting not to solve a problem, just to throw things into the kernel); that is, the monolithic kernel does not require a clear separation of kernel versus non-kernel functionality. This lack of distinction has many implications for the performance of the resulting system. Instead, we prefer a smaller kernel that

[1] We write this as if assembly language were some kind of toxic material. There is no *a priori* reason why one cannot formally specify assembly-language programs, even though it is rarely done.

includes only those functions that are necessary. We prefer not to engage in further justification of our position; like many such debates, it is based upon a combination of technical and æsthetic factors.

1.1 Reasons for Selecting the Examples

This book contains the specification and refinement of two kernels:

1. A small and simple kernel.
2. A microkernel for cryptographic and other secure applications. This kernel is an instance of the *Separation Kernel* concept of Rushby [11].

The first kernel is related to the μC/OS kernel of Labrosse [8], a kernel that has been employed in a number of real-time and embedded systems. The kernel specified and refined in this book is also a close relative of the first kernel model in our [4][2].

Another reviewer complained that the specification we gave in another paper was too simple to be of any use in real systems. We need to address this point because it could be levelled by the same reviewer of this work. The small kernel that is refined in this book is similar to μC/OS and other kernels for small systems. We have read the code of such systems, and also used them, over the period of a good many years. The kernels that we have looked at are not undergraduate exercises or simplified versions, they are *real* kernels that are used in *real* applications. The initial design of the small kernel is based upon this experience. It was intended that the level of functionality be such that it could be used with only minor modification (context switch and interrupt enable/disable operations) in a *real* application. The modifications expected require only minor modifications to the formal specification; the remainder would remain the same.

It is true that we have not included sophisticated real-time scheduling methods. However, the kernels that we have inspected and used do not contain them, either; to claim that we have an unrealistic, over-simplified system because it lacks some particular real-time scheduling algorithm appears unreasonable. It is also true that we have not included alarm timers. The reasons for this are that they are not always provided by the kernels that we have

[2] A reviewer of a paper we wrote on this kernel strongly objected to the use of the adjective (they said "term") "real-time" in connection with this model. They claimed that the model could not be of a "real-time" system because it does not contain any temporal operators. There is a number of replies to this: (i) C and Ada are "real-time" programming languages but they do not contain temporal operators (and their formal semantics do not required them); (ii) there is a considerable number of small kernels similar to ours, μC/OS being one example, that are used in the development of "real-time" systems. We have read the descriptions, specifications and code of quite a few of these systems and have failed to locate a single temporal operator.

examined or used and that they are not particularly difficult to specify and, therefore, to refine to code using the formal method. If we extend the small kernel, asynchronous events such as alarms will constitute the first extension.

In brief, the kernel is composed of the following components.

- A process representation (the process table).
- A scheduler based on a priority queue.
- Semaphores in a global semaphore table.
- A simple synchronous message-passing system.
- A mechanism for putting processes to sleep for a specified period of time. (There is no alarm mechanism in this kernel, however).
- A set of initialisation and interface routines so that user-supplied code can call kernel operations (i.e., perform system calls).

User processes execute in the same address space as the kernel. To produce a working system, the code for user processes is linked to that of the kernel and the result bootstrapped somehow (this is considered outside of the specification, being, really, a processor-specific matter). Storage must be allocated by the user. This implies that they must define a memory map when designing their system.

It seemed appropciate to select this kernel as the first example refinement because

- It is a relatively simple example of a kernel. It contains no storage management, device drivers or Interrupt-Service Routines (ISRs).
- It makes few assumptions about the hardware upon which it runs. Indeed, it is quite portable; only a relatively few lines of code need be changed when porting to another processor.

On the other hand, the very simplicity of this first kernel is a problem *precisely* because it is processor-independent. In particular, there are no device drivers and ISRs to specify (other than the simple one for the clock). The specification and refinements employ a hardware model that is relatively general and portable; indeed, it can be employed on a number of processors. However, the interrupt mechanisms of processors vary considerably, so the specification included here is tailored to the Intel IA32 architecture[3].

We could have included specific hardware devices into the specification and its refinement just to show that it is possible. This was not done because we want this kernel to be portable and the inclusion of a specific device might have suggested that we were not being portable. In addition, we had already encountered space problems with this book and the inclusion of the description of a hardware device, its interface and the specification of its ISR

[3] The MIPS has also been considered and would have been used. However, we found problems with the GNU C compiler for the simulated MIPS that we intended to use.

and driver would have caused us to omit the Separation Kernel's specification, something we preferred not to do. We hope to specify a device's support software elsewhere in the near future.

The second example is the Separation Kernel introduced by Rushby in 1981 [11] for secure systems. The Separation Kernel derives its name from the fact that user processes are separated from each other both in space and in time. This implies that the address spaces of all user processes are disjoint and that the time during which one process executes can be identified as being different from that during which any other user process executes. The Separation Kernel is intended as a simulation of a distributed system. In a distributed system, in theory, all processes execute on their own processor, thus affording disjointness of address space. In addition, the execution of one process occurs on a processor during a particular time but does not affect the execution of other processes on other processors. Thus, one can say that process P_1 executes on processor p_1 during the period $t_1 \,..\, t_n$, while process P_2 executes on processor p_2 during the period $t_i \,..\, t_m$.

The problem is to translate this scheme to uniprocessor systems. This can be done by ensuring that all address spaces are disjoint, say by means of segmentation. Temporal separation can be had by ensuring that only one process executes at any point in time. Temporal separation is easy to arrange on a sequential processor (indeed, it is so obvious a property that it can be a little hard to explain convincingly).

The reasons for including the Separation Kernel are as follows:

- It is a little-known architecture and its specification and refinement are novel.
- It is a simple architecture and is, thus, easy to specify and refine in a few pages.
- It is an architecture that was explicitly defined for applications that should demand a formal approach to software development. Indeed, the US National Security Agency has stated [10] that the formal specification of Separation Kernels is highly desirable.

The specification and refinement in this book follow the recommendations of the National Security Agency's document [10]. The Separation Kernel proper is a microkernel that is formally specified. Upon the microkernel, there is a layer of so-called "trusted" code, principally device drivers and associated code. This trusted layer need not be formally specified but its specification, design and construction is carefully monitored so that it cannot engage in activities that would compromise the security of the system. Above this layer comes user-supplied code. This code is completely untrusted and can perform any activity and might be compromised in some way; although one might want this layer to be formally specified and tightly controlled, it is unlikely that it will be, at least in the near term. The overall architecture is depicted in Figure 1.1.

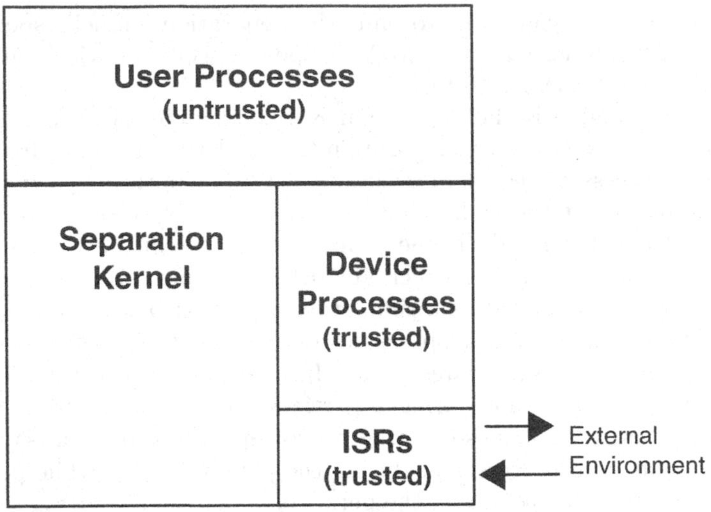

Fig. 1.1. *The NSA cryptographic architecture.*

The Separation Kernel itself is organised as follows (the reader will see that it is a simple structure):

- A process representation.
- A round-robin scheduler.
- Asynchronous inter-process message passing.
- Storage allocation mechanisms.

In addition, the specification includes:

- An interface for system calls from user processes.
- A collection of operations to support the construction of ISRs and device drivers.

These two last items are added so that the security of the system can be enhanced.

Our specification assumes that the processor upon which the microkernel executes supports segmentation. It was decided that virtual storage would not be included for the following reasons:

- Virtual storage requires some form of external store for page swapping. This would commit the specification to a particular hardware configuration, which was considered undesirable.
- It is possible in principle that external virtual storage can be attacked by malicious persons (e.g., corrupting or replacing pages). This was also considered undesirable.

It was, therefore, assumed that all user processes would reside in main storage and that they would be composed of two memory segments (the GNU C compiler generates two segments); they would be, in any case, memory resident. The kernel would also be memory resident. It would reside in segments that are disjoint from all others. Device drivers and ISRs are trusted code, so can be stored in the same segments as the kernel. This is more of an optimisation than anything else because it was considered that the time required to perform an address-space switch would not be tolerable for device-related code. Since this kind of code is trusted, it can be assumed that it will not interfere with the operations of the kernel (which is, in any case, an opaque chunk of code as far as they are concerned). The loading of user-process images into main store is something that we do not consider here (it is a matter that depends upon the hardware configuration); indeed, we have it in mind that the Separation Kernel would probably run on a co-processor. Finally, it was assumed that the processor would provide some mechanism for detecting illegal cross-segment references (segmentation errors) and that an ISR could be written to handle such references.

The assumptions of segmentation and cross-segment reference detection are reasonable. There are many processors supporting these features. The Intel IA32 and IA64 series of processors support them, for example.

For a full security kernel, it is necessary to write a formal security policy. This is an abstract model of the system that shows how violations of temporal and spatial separation are handled. This model has not been included in this book for the reason that it is not strictly relevant to the current task. However, readers should note that such a model for this specification is in the process of being documented and the relevant proofs are being undertaken.

1.2 Refinement Method

The method adopted in this book follows the conventional approach as defined by Spivery [12] and Woodcock and Davies [13].

First, an abstract specification is created, then a refined version (the *concrete* version) is created; the two are then related by the definition of an *abstraction relation.* Proofs are then undertaken to show that concrete operations represent abstract ones correctly. The concept of correctness reduces to showing the following two properties. First, the states in which an abstract operation can start are also, modulo the abstraction relation, those states in which the concrete one can start. Second, it is shown that if the abstract operation terminates in a state, s, then the concrete operation terminates in a state, s_c, that is related to s by the abstraction relation. In addition, a theorem is proved that the initialisation of the two state spaces are equivalent.

Once this has been completed, what was the concrete version becomes the new abstract version. A new concrete representation and abstraction relation are defined and the process iterates.

For the specifications in this book, some modules required no refinement, while others required two steps. In some cases, therefore, a state space was defined that does not require refinement; this is done when the state space consists of simple variables that are just updated by simple assignments. Example cases are the clock in the first refinement, parts of the scheduler in both refinements and the semaphore counter component in the first specification. In contrast, there are modules that required three refinement steps. It could be argued that two steps could be used instead. The reduction to two steps would, in our opinion, have made the refinement process less clear and clarity is an essential aspect of system design as well as documentation. The *PROCESSQUEUE* and *PRIOQUEUE* types both require two refinement steps: one from an abstract specification to an array-based representation and then to a representation based on the *next* attribute in the process table. The reader could try to refine the top-level specification to the one using *next*; it is certainly possible but, we consider, less clear than the three-step version.

In addition, the abstraction relation is an identity[4]. This makes proofs particularly simple. Indeed, because identity is a functional relation, the refinement process can be modified slightly, as outlined in [13]. Woodcock *et al.* show how the operation schemata can be calculated from the abstract specification and the abstraction relation. This has the implication that the proofs listed above need not be undertaken because they are guaranteed by the abstraction relation.

In this book, particularly in the first part, proofs are included; in the refinement of the separation kernel, some proofs are given but not others. In both exercises, the reader will see that the abstraction relations are all identities. We could have omitted the proofs in the refinement of the first kernel. We preferred not to do this for a number of reasons. First, we wanted to show how the full method operates on a scale somewhat larger than those usually found in the published literature. Second, we wanted to include proofs to counter the claim that they were either impossible, unintelligible or excessively complex; they are none of these and are all quite straightforward. In another of the kernel refinements that we have performed (but not published), some proofs did cause problems which were eventually resolved. Third, we also wanted to show how proofs are still possible even when working on conjoined state spaces. Fourth, undertaking a proof is a good way to gain a better understanding of the operation and it is also useful as a way of checking the abstract and concrete operation specifications as well as the abstraction relation. In another piece of work, we defined a concrete operation in a way that looked entirely sensible but it was found that it caused a revision of the abstraction relation which, it turned out, had not been properly thought out. Such errors or misconceptions should not be a cause for censure. Instead, they are valuable.

---

[4] This is something that we have found in almost every refinement we have done over the last twenty-odd years.

In the refinement of the Separation Kernel, proofs of individual modules have been included. The two proofs associated with many of the complex operations (those defined over conjunctions of state spaces) are not included, even though they have been undertaken and recorded. One reason for this is space (the book would become excessively long); another is that too many obvious proofs become rather tedious and would put the reader off continuing. Finally, there is the reason that the proofs are not required because the abstraction relations are identities; the proofs of the components are given, so those of the complex operations can be derived in an obvious fashion.

Finally, as always, there is the matter of hardware. As in [4], we have treated the hardware as a given. For the purposes of refinement, this implies that it is a state space and set of operations that cannot be further refined. This does mean that the specification can appear a little low-level in places but, as usual, appropriate abstract operations are defined over the hardware state space (context switch, half context switch, raise interrupt and so on), so some measure of abstraction can be had. The approach adopted is, in any case, akin to that one must adopt when specifying software that interfaces to a pre-existant library or subsystem; the software external to the specification can only be treated as a given. In the case of system models, this implies that the properties of the external entity must be inferred. In the case of refinements, it implies that no further refinement can be undertaken (in any case, one has no control over pre-existant entities).

1.3 Code Production

This book does not contain any code that can be executed. There are examples of the translation between final refinements and Dijkstra's Guarded Command Language [6]. These translations are included to show just how close to a programming notation the refinements reach.

There is no C or Ada. The complete code is not included. The reason for this is that there is no space.

We are, at the time of writing, translating the final refinements of the simple kernel into code so that it can be executed. The first refinement is has been translated to GNU C compiler. The target hardware is the Intel IA32 Pentium processor. The translation is a simple matter given the detail of the final refinement. Once translated into C, the result is tested and is, in this case, fairly exhaustive. It is pleasing to report that the code passed all of the tests. Testing, we believe, should be a confidence-building part of the method; we are making relatively exhaustive tests in this case because of the nature and size of the problem. All modules have passed their tests first time, so the refinement process can be argued to have worked. The low-level operations included in the specification are coded in assembly language; this is, again, a relatively simple activity. At the time of writing, the implementation has yet to be completed.

1.4 Organisation of this Book

This book naturally falls into four main sections:

1. This introduction (Chapter 1).
2. The specification and formal refinement of a small kernel (Chapters 2 and 3).
3. The specification and formal refinement of a Separation Kernel (Chapters 4 and 5).
4. Concluding remarks (Chapter 6).

The two refinements are also accompanied by a short, informal, introduction that outlines the organisation of each kernel in high-level terms. The refinements are annotated in English; the main concern is to justify the decisions made in the face of alternatives.

1.5 Relationship to Other Work

It has been pointed out that other workers have produced models of operating systems. This was a fact known to us when [4] was written. What made us continue with that book was the fact that it was intended that proofs of many properties, some obvious, some less so would be included in the book. Comparing what we wanted to do with the published literature, we found that published material either lacked proofs altogether or did not contain the range that we intended to produce (typically the former); we also wanted to work in a framework that was not based upon temporal logic.

As far as we are aware, there is nothing in the literature on the formal refinement of operating system kernel code from a formal specification.

In the case of verification, if one single bit in the code is altered, the entire system must be re-verified. Furthermore, verification often involves taking an informally specified object and reconstructing a formal specification from it. Unless the original designers are part of the exercise, it does not appear possible to determine whether the result of verification really does conform to the design. This must be true even when design documents are available for, as is often stated, a natural-language specification leaves a considerable amount unspecified because of our understanding of language. On the other hand, and this is another frequently made point, formal specification captures specifications unambiguously. The formal specification and refinement process requires that everything be captured in documents. It is clear that, should a single bit of a formally specified program be altered, the program no longer conforms to the specification. Unlike verification, it is possible, in this case, to determine whether the change is significant or not. It is also possible to propagate design decisions through a formal specification without requiring the production of code (by its very nature, verification depends upon the existence of code).

2

The Simple Kernel's Organisation

The purpose of this chapter is to describe in informal terms the organisation and purpose of the "simple" kernel that is specified in the remainder of this chapter.

As noted in Chapter 1, the kernel specified in this chapter is intended for use, actual or otherwise, as the kernel of embedded and simple real-time systems. The kernel is similar to Labrosse's μC/OS [8] and the first kernel modelled in [4]. This kernel was deliberately chosen as a link back to [4] and because we consider it important to demonstrate that this class of kernel can be formally specified and refined to working code.

In this kernel, each process has a unique identifier that is assigned to it by the kernel from a fixed set in a purely sequential fashion. The first process to be allocated is the *idle process*, the process that runs when no other processes are ready for execution; the second to be allocated will usually be the *initial process*, the process that creates all the other processes in the system (the model is *not* related to the one employed by Unix, it should be noted). Thereafter, the identifiers are allocated to processes in order of creation.

At present, each process has to make an explicit system call to obtain its identifier and there is no facility for determining, at runtime, the identifier of other processes (unless they, too, have determined their identity by means of the same system call). An obvious extension would be to make process identifiers available in a more usable way. Meanwhile, the mechanism specified here is workable.

The process representation is a set of mappings that are refined to vectors (one-dimensional arrays). The collection of these mappings is equivalent to the process table in other systems and we will refer to this collection of mappings as the *process table* or *PTAB* (this is the name of the state representation in the specification). The mappings are keyed by the identifier of the process and each mapping represents a different piece of information about the process.

In this kernel, the representation of processes is uniform in the sense that all processes are associated with the same kinds of information (in the other kernel specified in this book, there is a distinction imposed between different types of process). In this kernel, processes are represented by the following information:

- *Stack pointer.* This is a pointer to the top of the process' stack. It is used when performing a context switch.
- *Priority.* This is a small integer value. Small negative values represent high priorities, while small positive values represent low priorities. The default value is 0. The priority is used to sort the scheduler's *ready queue* and is also used to determine whether or not to cause a context switch.
- *State.* This is an enumeration type. The value associated with each process denotes the current state of the process. The state is used by the scheduler when determining whether a context switch can be performed. It is also used to document the process; an extension to the system is the inclusion of an operation that obtains the states of all the processes in the system (an operation similar to the Unix `ps` operation).
- *Incoming Message.* Processes can communicate using synchronous messages. This mapping is used to hold the latest message that has been sent to each process. When there is no message to be received or a message has just been read by its receiver, the value of the mapping is *nullmsg*.
- *Waking Time.* Processes can perform a system call that makes them wait for a specified period of time. The process specifies the duration of its sleeping time. The value stored in this mapping is the sum of the current time and the time at which the process should wake up. When a process wakes up, it is returned to the scheduler's ready queue and can be executed at some subsequent time.

In many kernels, processes are represented by structures or blocks of storage; the Linux kernel [2], on the other hand, employs an array-based representation similar to the one adopted here. A block/structure-based representation can be specified in Z and would use promotion to include the structure in the containing table. This approach separates the refinement of the structure from that of the table. The refinement process employed here combines the refinement of the mappings.

There are arguments for and against the benefits of these representations. As far as we are can see, the arguments balance out and what is left is personal preference. In other kernel specifications, we have adopted the other representation to good effect; in the end, though, we just like the mapping- or vector-based implementation of the process table.

In addition, the process table contains a state variable, *used.* This contains the identifiers of those processes that have been allocated. If a process identifier is not in this set, it does not represent a process that currently exists in the system. This variable is refined to the *freechain.* The freechain is a chain of elements in a vector called *next.* If an element is in the freechain, it denotes a process that is not in the system; the identifier of the process is the index of the element in *next.*

The next major component is the scheduler. The scheduling régime is based on a simple priority queue with highest priority at the head. We refer to this queue as the *ready* queue. When a process is added to this queue, its priority is used to determine where it should be inserted.

The priority queue is first specified as a separate module, whose elements are in a variable called *pq*. For the specification of the scheduler proper, promotion is used so the refinement of the priority queue can proceed independently of that of the rest of the scheduler.

The priority queue is refined to a chain through the *next* PTAB map. This removes the need to allocate additional storage inside the kernel. The complexity of the chain operations is a little higher than those on a simple one-dimensional vector but it was employed here for the following reasons:

- It shows that such chaining can be handled formally.
- Chaining, as noted above, uses no more space in the kernel.

The scheduler proper contains three variables in addition to the ready queue. One variable contains the identifier of the *null process* so that it can be easily accessed when the scheduler determines that there is nothing to do.

The null process is included explicitly as a process for the following reasons:

- It can be removed in other versions of the system.
- Its behaviour can be altered from a completely null behaviour (an infinite loop with no body) to something else.

These modifications require trivial respecifications of the system.

The other variables contain the identifier of the process that is currently executing and that of the process that ran immediately before the current one. The identifier of the currently executing process is required by the scheduler when performing a rescheduler operation, as follows. A slightly simplified account of the scheduler's conditions for rescheduling are as follows. If a reschedule is to be performed and the following conditions are satisfied, the scheduler schedules another process and performs a context switch:

- There are processes in the ready queue.
- The priority of the current process is lower than that on the head of the ready queue.
- The state of the current process is not marked as *ready* or *running*.

If there are no processes in the ready queue, the idle process is run. If either of the other conditions is not satisfied, the current process is continued and no context switch is performed.

Keeping the current and previous process identifiers is also useful when performing the context switch because it allows the switching code to access process data. It is also useful when testing systems built using the kernel. In the current version, it allows the scheduler to access the stacks of the two processes.

The scheduler provides the following operations:

- An operation to initialise the various data structures. This is called on system start-up.
- An operation to schedule the next process (*SchedNext*).
- An operation that suspends its caller and schedules the next process. If there are no other processes in the ready queue, the idle process is run. The operation forces a context switch.

Processes can synchronise using semaphores. The kernel contains a single table that holds all the semaphores that can be used by processes. The size of the table is a compile-time constant. It is organised as a bit map. The semaphores held in the table are *counting* semaphores; this is no restriction upon the semaphores' behaviour because the semaphore type contains an initialisation variable that can be set to 1 for binary semaphores.

Semaphores are defined as a separate type. Semaphore operations are promoted by the table type. There are three operations provided by semaphores:

1. Initialise.
2. Allocate a semaphore if possible (if not, an error is reported).
3. Free a semaphore[1].
4. Signal (the V operation).
5. Wait (the P operation).

The refinement of the semaphore table to bit maps was performed in order to demonstrate that structures requiring "bit banging" can be specified formally[2].

Semaphores are implemented using promotion. The semaphore proper contains a counter and a FIFO queue. The queue is defined as a separate type and its operations are promoted by the semaphore, thus simplifying the refinement. The FIFO is, like the priority queue, refined to a chain through the *next* map in the process table. In this case, chaining was considered essential. This is because there could be many semaphores in the system. Each semaphore contains its own, independent, FIFO queue. If the FIFO were implemented as a vector, this would mean allocation of a vector of suitable size for each semaphore. The scheme adopted here has the advantages that the space is allocated once and that each FIFO can be of arbitrary length.

Processes can also communicate by the synchronous exchange of messages. When a process is ready to receive a message, it executes a system primitive and enters the *psreceiving* state and is suspended. It remains in that state

[1] No check on ownership is performed, so freeing someone else's semaphore is a neat way to cause trouble! In a more secure version, recording the ownership of resources would be a good idea.

[2] In other work, we have also attempted the specification of the kinds of operations required, for example, in controlling hardware devices. Device controllers typically require bits to be set and unset by controlling software; they are often cited as a problem for the formal approach. After a little thought, we found that there is no such problem—provided, that is, one thinks clearly about it.

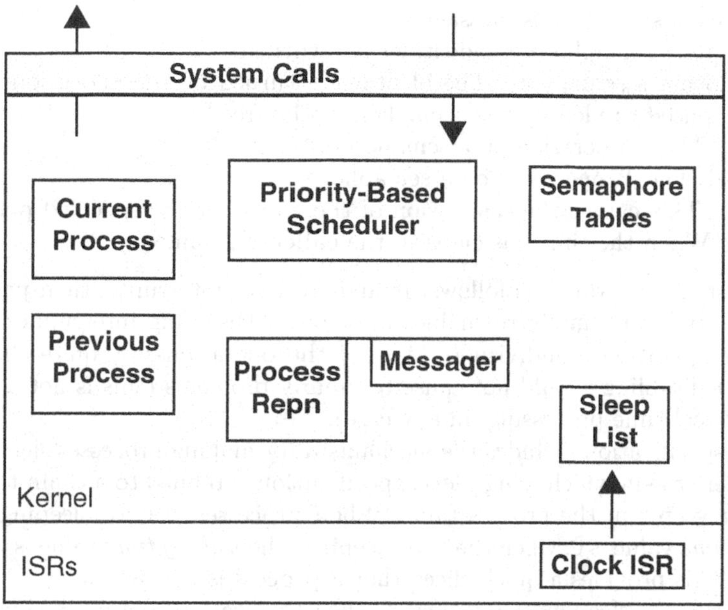

Fig. 2.1. *Organisation of the simple kernel.*

until another process sends a message to it. When the message is received, the receiver's state is set to *psready* and it is put back into the scheduler's ready queue. If a process sends a message to a process that is not blocked in the *psreceiving* state, the system reports the fact and the sender must try again (this rather crude approach could be hidden inside a library routine).

The organisation of this kernel is shown in Figure 2.1.

The interface to the system's facilities are made as simple and direct as possible so that the result is reasonably fast. In addition, the kernel assumes that the code implementing processes is linked with the kernel to form a single, loadable image. Storage is allocated by the programmer; the kernel, as it stands, does not contain any storage-allocation code. Storage can be allocated as data structures in C or assembly code or can be allocated as part of the linkage process.

The specification defines system calls for many of the operations mentioned above. Included in the calls are the following:

- Create process.
- Terminate. This operation is used when a process needs to terminate itself (it should be the last operation performed by all processes except the initial one). The operation works by killing the currently active process.
- Get process identifier.
- Send a synchronous message.

- Receive a synchronous message.
- Allocate a semaphore; an identifier is returned.
- Deallocate a semaphore. The identifier returned by the allocation operation is used to identify the semaphore to be freed.
- Wait. The P operation on a semaphore.
- Signal. The V operation on a semaphore.
- Sleep. This causes the suspension of the caller for the specified period of time. When the time has elapsed, the caller is resumed.

Each system call works as follows. It first disables interrupts, then performs the operation and finally re-enables interrupts. Disabling interrupts ensures that the operation is indivisible. Most of the operations are quite short, so interrupt disabling should not cause too many problems (this is not a kernel for hard real-time processing, in any case).

The specification includes the mechanism for making processes sleep. This is another case in which a high-level specification is refined to a chain through the *next* vector in the process table. When processes are not sleeping, their *waking time* value is 0; when they are sleeping, the *waking time* value is greater than 0. This provides a quick check that a process is not asleep.

To make the sleep mechanism work, the specification contains a clock. The clock is intended to be implemented as an *Interrupt Service Routine* (*ISR*) or *interrupt handler*.

The clock should work as follows. On every interrupt from the real hardware clock, the clock ISR increments a *tick* variable. If there are t ticks each second, when $tick = t$, the time in seconds since boot time is incremented by one, as is a second variable that records the number of ticks since boot time. If the number of seconds since boot is $0 \bmod 60$, the minute counter is incremented by one; if the minute counter is $0 \bmod 60$, the hour counter is incremented by one. In the current version, the actual clock time is not recorded (this could be included with relatively little work but could involve a hardware dependency).

If the clock used by the processor ticks at a rate such as once every 100msec, the above scheme can be used. Unfortunately, some processors do not have such accommodating clocks. The Intel IA32, for example, has a clock that has a cycle of something like 18.4MHz, a rate that is not all that helpful for keeping the time. For the IA32, the clock ISR is activated on every clock interrupt, as usual. When activated, the ISR increments an activation counter. When the activation counter reaches a certain value, the *tick* counter is incremented, as above. The IA32 clock's rate is doubly awkward because it does not divide the second exactly, so either a little clock drift has to be tolerated or a correction must be made from time to time. In the specification here, drift is tolerated (it is an example, after all!)

Now, many readers will be wondering about the real hardware issues. In particular, how context switches are performed. Furthermore, nothing has been said about processor registers—the process context, in other words.

The answer is that we prefer to have as little as possible to do with the processor's low-level details! One reason for this is that it makes the kernel more portable (all the hardware-specific operations are firmly delineated). The low-level operations required are:

- Enable and disable interrupts. These operations are usually performed by one instruction each.
- A return from interrupt (*IRET*) is also required to terminate ISRs. This is also frequently implemented as one or two instructions (usually one but, on the MIPS, for example, interrupts must be re-enabled and the return has to be performed explicitly).
- A context switch. The scheme adopted in this specification is that the registers are stored on the top of the process stack. This has the advantage that there is no permanent store allocated in the process table for the register set; this also implies that it is not necessary, *a priori* to fix the number of registers in the process table.
- A "half-context switch". This is used to set up the intial process' registers when creating it. This operation pushes one value (0) onto the initial process' stack when it is created. The reason for this is explained immediately below.

The context-switching scheme is also a fairly standard one. When the scheduler requires a context switch, it raises an interrupt. This interrupt is handled by an ISR that pushes the outgoing process' registers onto its stack and then pops the incoming process' registers from the stack. The ISR then immediately executes an IRET instruction and the incoming process is switched in.

Because the incoming process has been suspended using an interrupt, it will have the registers needed by the IRET instruction on its stack immediately below its other registers. This is clearly impossible if the process has never been interrupted, as is the case with the initial process. In this case, the stack must be set up so that the processor finds all the information it requires. To do this, dummy values are pushed onto the stack when creating the inital process. The IRET instruction needs to have an address to which control should be returned. Usually, this is the address of the instruction that was interrupted. In the case of the initial process, the address has to be its entry point.

On an Intel IA32, the above scheme is extremely easy to implement. The hardware pushes the return address and the flags register onto the interrupted process' stack when an interrupt occurs. The `pushad` instruction pushes the general-purpose registers onto the stack and the `popad` instruction pops them back. If the kernel executes within a single address space (as this one does), there is no problem with the scheme outlined above (the Separation Kernel in Chapter 5 uses multiple address spaces, so another approach is required).

On a MIPS, the scheme outlined above can still be used. However, it is up to the implementer to push and pop the registers. In addition, the return-from-interrupt operation must be implemented as a macro. First, the interrupt flag is reset; next, the instruction pointer in force when the interrupt occurred must be fetched from a co-processor register and incremented by four (four bytes, i.e.) and stored in a register; finally, a jump-on-register instruction is executed, citing the register in which the old instruction pointer is stored.

Although a bit longer, the MIPS sequence is still comparatively simple. It is clear that it can be represented in Z with a little work. Because we are aiming our refinements and implementation at the IA32/64 (simply because we have them available), we have omitted a detailed specification of the context-switching operation. A specification for the MIPS (or any other processor like it, for that matter) would include the specification of the registers and the operations required to implement the push and pop operations, as well as the return-from-interrupt operation. This is not difficult; indeed, we undertook it when examining a refinement of this kernel to the MIPS processor[3].

With this general outline of the kernel and the refinement out of the way, it is possible to progress to the specification and refinement proper. Both top-level specification and the various refinements are accompanied by a commentary to aid the reader's understanding.

[3] We did this as an exercise in refining to a RISC machine to determine what the problems, if any, might be; as with the IA32/64, we were pleased to find that it was straightforward. Unfortunately, we do not have a MIPS or other RISC available so that we can run the result—perhaps, one day!

3

A Simple Kernel

The first specification and refinement is of a small kernel of the type often used in embedded and real-time systems. The kernel resembles Labrosse's μC/OS [8] and the kernel of Chapter 3 of our [4].

The structure of the chapter is as follows. First, the types that are used throughout the specification and the refinement are defined.

Second, a specification of the hardware is given. This specification is at a relatively high level but could be refined to a lower one. The specification is aimed at an Intel IA32 implementation but should be sufficiently general to change to another architecture.

Third comes the specification and refinement of the kernel proper. This part occupies the vast majority of the chapter. Each major component is specified and then refined; this constitutes a section of the chapter. Refinements constitute a subsection and usually consist of the refined state space and operations followed by the abstraction relation; in some cases, where it seems more appropriate, the abstraction relation comes before the refined operations. The relevant proofs come at the end of each section. In a couple of cases, proofs are included within the statement of the refined operations.

3.1 Types

In this section, the major types are defined. As noted above, the types defined here are used throughout the rest of this chapter.

First, the *PID* and *GPID* types are defined. These types are used to name processes. The *PID* type is a subrange type with range *minpid* to *maxpid*, while *GPID* extends *PID* by the addition of the *nullpid*. The *nullpid* is defined below and represents the null process. The *null* process should not be confused with the *idle* process; the former is intended to be a null reference, while the latter merely does nothing while it executes—it is executed when the processor has nothing to do. The *idle* process has a normal process identifier (an element of *PID*) and is allocated at system startup time.

$PID \mathrel{\widehat=} minpid \mathrel{..} maxpid$
$GPID \mathrel{\widehat=} \{nullpid\} \cup PID$

$$\begin{array}{|l}
nullpid : \mathbb{N} \\
\hline
\forall p : PID \bullet \\
\qquad p < nullpid
\end{array}$$

The null value is usually the least element or somewhere in the middle. However, in a implementation using C vectors, indexing is zero-based, so the natural choice of zero is not available. The actual choice of value for *nullpid* is, in any case, arbitrary; what must be ensured is that there is no way in which *nullpid* can be confused with a valid value.

The *PSTATE* type is defined next.

$$\begin{array}{lll}
PSTATE & ::= & psterm \\
& | & psrunning \\
& | & psready \\
& | & pswaitsema \\
& | & pssleeping \\
& | & pssending \\
& | & psreceiving
\end{array}$$

This type represents the state of processes. A process can be in exactly one state at any time. The names denote states:

- State *psterm* denotes the *terminated* state.
- State *psrunning* is the state of a process that is currently executing.
- State *psready* is the state of a process that is ready to execute but not yet executing.
- State *pswaitsema* is the state of a process that is waiting on a semaphore.
- State *pssleeping* is the state of a process that is in a sleeping state (i.e., is waiting for a timer to expire before it can resume execution).
- State *pssending* is the state of a process that is sending a message (this might involve the process being suspended before the message can be exchanged).
- State *psreceiving* is the state of a process that is ready to receive a message.

The next definitions concern process priorities. Priorities are defined in terms of the range *maxprio* .. *minprio*, with smaller values denoting higher priorities.

$$\begin{array}{|l}
minprio, maxprio : \mathbb{Z}
\end{array}$$

The type denoting process priorities is *PPRIO*.

$PPRIO == maxprio \mathrel{..} minprio$

The type representing messages is, for simplicity, defined as atomic.

$[MSG]$

The MSG type includes a value denoting the null message:

$$nullmsg : MSG$$

It will be necessary to access components of elements of MSG. It is common, for checking purposes, to require access to the sender ($msgsrc$) and destination ($msgdest$) of a message; in addition, the $msgsize$ function returns the size of a message

$$\begin{array}{l} msgsrc : MSG \rightarrow PID \\ msgdest : MSG \rightarrow PID \\ msgsize : MSG \rightarrow \mathbb{N} \end{array}$$

The $WORD$ type denotes the contents of a word of storage.

$[WORD]$

Addresses in the store are represented by the $ADDR$ type.

$$ADDR == nulladdr \mathinner{..} maxaddr$$

Addresses are defined in terms of a range. The lower bound, $nulladdr$ is address zero.

$$\begin{array}{l} nulladdr : \mathbb{N} \\ maxaddr : \mathbb{N} \\ \hline nulladdr = 0 \\ nulladdr < maxaddr \end{array}$$

A representation is also required for time. This representation is called $TIME$. It is defined as a synonym for the naturals. Time can be assumed, for now, to start when the system is started.

$$TIME == \mathbb{N}$$

Finally, the $SYSERR$ type is defined. This type defines the values of the error variable set by various system components. When all is well, the error variable is set to $sysok$; when an error has occurred, the variable is set to another value.

$$\begin{array}{rcl} SYSERR & ::= & sysok \\ & | & pdinuse \\ & | & unusedpd \\ & | & ptabfull \end{array}$$

| *emptyqueue*
| *schedqfull*
| *schedqempty*
| *alreadyasleep*
| *toomanysleepers*
| *notallocsema*
| *nofreesemas*
| *procalreadyhasmsg*
| *destinationnotrcving*
| *badmsgdestination*
| *nomsg*

The interpretation of the values are:

- Value *pdinuse* denotes the state in which a process descriptor (process identifier) is already in use;
- Value *unusedpd* denotes the state in which a reference has been made to a process descriptor that is not in use.
- Value *ptabfull* denotes the state in which no more process descriptors can be allocated.
- Value *emptyqueue* denotes the state in which a queue of processes is empty and an attempt to dequeue a process has taken place.
- Value *schedqfull* denotes the state in which the scheduler's ready queue is full.
- Value *schedqempty* denotes the state in which the scheduler's ready queue is empty.
- Vaue *alreadyasleep* denotes the state in which an attempt is made by a process to enter a sleep state but that process is already marked as being asleep.
- Value *toomanysleepers* denotes the state in which there are too many processes in the sleep list.
- Value *notallocsema* denotes the state in which an attempt has been made to access a semaphore that has not been allocated.
- Value *nofreesemas* denotes the state in which no more semaphores can be allocated.
- Value *procalreadyhasmsg* denotes the state in which a receiving process already has an incoming message but has not yet processed it (thereby freeing its incoming-message slot).
- Value *destinationnotrcving* denotes the state in which the intended destination of a message is not currently in the state to receive it. The sender should wait until later.
- Value *badmsgdestination* denotes the state in which the destination process of a message does not exist.
- Value *nomsg* denotes the state in which there is no message in the incoming-message slot when an attempt to receive a message is made.

This section concludes with the definition of three schemata that are used in generic error situations.

When all is well, the *SysOk* schema sets the error variable, *serr*!, to *sysok*.

SysOk

$serr! : SYSERR$

$serr! = sysok$

The following operation tests *err* to determine whether it is *sysok*.

IsSysOk

$err : SYSERR$

$err = sysok$

This operation is used to re-direct the value of *serr*!. It is intended that *terr*? should be renamed when using this schema.

ReturnSysError

$terr? : SYSERR$
$serr! : SYSERR$

$serr! = terr?$

3.2 Hardware

The reader is warned that this section is heavily influenced by the Intel IA32/64 architecture.

First, a type is defined to denote the values *on* and *off*. This type is to be the value of the interrupt status flag (the "interrupt flag").

$ONOFF ::= off \mid on$

The processor implements a finite number of interrupt types, each denoted by a small integer in the range *minintno* to *maxintno*.

$minintno, maxintno : \mathbb{N}$

$minintno < maxintno$

A type, *INTRPTNO* is defined to represent the interrupt number.

$INTRPTNO == minintno \mathrel{..} maxintno$

The hardware state is represented by the following schema.

$$\begin{array}{|l}
\hline
\textit{HARDWARE} \\
\hline
genregs : REGID \rightarrow WORD \\
intflg : ONOFF \\
intno : INTRPTNO \\
\hline
\end{array}$$

The hardware has a set of general-purpose registers, *genregs*, an interrupt flag, *intflg* and a number denoting the current interrupt (if there is one), *intno*. In a fuller model, *intno* would be used to activate the appropriate interrupt service routine. Here, it is used just to provide a parameter to the operation that raises software interrupts. The general-purpose registers, *genregs*, is a function from register identifier, *REGID*, to a value (represented as a single word).

First of all, we need operations to enable and disable interrupts. First, the operation to enable interrupts is defined.

$$\begin{array}{|l}
\hline
\textit{EnableInts} \\
\hline
\Delta HARDWARE \\
\hline
intflg' = on \\
\hline
\end{array}$$

Next, the operation that disables interrupts is defined.

$$\begin{array}{|l}
\hline
\textit{DisableInts} \\
\hline
\Delta HARDWARE \\
\hline
intflg' = off \\
\hline
\end{array}$$

Since these operations do not refer to the before state, their precondition is *true*.

The above operations merely operate on the interrupt flag in the simplified hardware models.

A *Return From Interrupt* instruction is assumed. On many processors, this operation corresponds to a single instruction, often called `rti`. Amongst other things, this operation disables interrupts, increments the program counter so that it points to the instruction after the one that caused the interrupt and restores it to the hardware so that execution can continue. Since much of this is internal to the processor, we only specify it in outline.

$$ReturnFromInterrupt \mathrel{\widehat=}$$
$$\quad \ldots$$
$$\quad \fatsemi EnableInts$$

The process table, *PTAB*, is the structure maintained by the kernel to represent processes. Processes are represented as a collection of data items that collectively represent a process. As far as the hardware is concerned, it is necessary for each process' current stack top pointer to be stored in the process table. The reason for this is that, between activations, the values of the registers belonging to a process are stored on top of the stack.

$$
\begin{array}{|l}
\multicolumn{1}{l}{\_\_ \mathit{PTAB} \_\_\_\_\_\_\_\_\_\_\_\_\_\_\_\_} \\
\vdots \\
\mathit{stacktop} : \mathit{PID} \pfun \mathit{ADDR} \\
\vdots \\
\hline
\vdots \\
\mathrm{dom}\ \mathit{stacktop} = \mathit{used} \\
\vdots \\
\hline
\end{array}
$$

When a context switch occurs, the registers belonging to the outgoing process are pushed onto its stack. Then the registers of the incoming process are popped off its stack.

$$
\begin{array}{|l}
\multicolumn{1}{l}{\_\_ \mathit{ContextSwitch} \_\_\_\_\_\_\_\_\_\_\_\_\_\_\_\_} \\
\Delta \mathit{HARDWARE} \\
\Xi \mathit{PTAB} \\
\mathit{inpid?}, \mathit{outpid?} : \mathit{PID} \\
\hline
\mathit{pushregs}(\mathit{stacks}(\mathit{outpid?})) \\
\fatsemi \mathit{popregs}(\mathit{stacks}(\mathit{inpid?})) \\
\hline
\end{array}
$$

where *pushregs* is an operation that pushes all (necessary) registers onto the stack pointed to by $\mathit{stacks}(\mathit{outpid?})$ and *popregs* pops the equivalent registers from the stack pointed to by $\mathit{stacks}(\mathit{inpid?})$. This is an old technique for storing registers; it has the enormous advantage that it does not require storage in the process table. It has another advantage: the registers are always in an easily accessible location and access to them is relatively cheap.

Because of the architecture of most processors, we are compelled to assume that there will always be sufficient space on the outgoing process' stack to hold all the necessary registers. This is, however, a matter for the programmer. Furthermore, nowhere is the size limit for the stack saved, so it is not possible to determine whether there is any space available; even if there were, the test might be too expensive to apply, so we are left where we began.

The precondition of *ContextSwitch* could be *true* or it could be

$$\mathrm{pre}\ \mathit{ContextSwitch} \mathrel{\widehat=} \{\mathit{inpid?}, \mathit{outpid?}\} \subseteq \mathit{used}$$

The process is only partially complete at this point. When the first process is executed, where do the outgoing registers come from? To solve this problem, we define the following operation

$$\begin{array}{|l}
\hline
\textit{HalfContextSwitch} \\
\Delta HARDWARE \\
\Xi PTAB \\
inproc? : PID \\
\hline
pushregszero(stacks(inproc?)) \\
\hline
\end{array}$$

where *pushregszero* is a function that pushes one zero on the stack pointed to by *stacks*(*inproc*?) for every register that must be used by the process *inproc*?.

Finally, it is assumed that when a context switch is to occur, an interrupt is raised. On many processors, when an interrupt is raised, the program counter of the interrupting process is stored on the stack. On other processors, the program counter is stored in a well-defined location, usually in a designated register (as it is on MIPS processors). In order to complete the specification of the context switch, it is necessary to define an operation that raises the interrupt (*RaiseInterrupt*).

$$\begin{array}{|l}
\hline
\textit{RaiseInterrupt} \\
\Delta HARDWARE \\
ino? : INTRPTNO \\
\hline
intno' = ino? \\
\hline
\end{array}$$

Note that we say nothing about how the hardware responds to this. The precondition of this operation is *true*, as the following calculation shows. First,

$$\begin{array}{l}
\exists\, HARDWARE' \bullet \\
\quad intno' = ino?
\end{array}$$

This then becomes

$$\begin{array}{l}
\exists\, genregs' : REGID \rightarrow WORD;\ intflg' : ONOFF;\ intno' : INTRPTNO \bullet \\
\quad intno' = ino? \land \\
\quad genregs' = genregs \land \\
\quad intflg' = intflg
\end{array}$$

Using the one-point rule, this simplifies to

$$\begin{array}{l}
\exists\, genregs' : REGID \rightarrow WORD;\ intflg' : ONOFF;\ intno' : INTRPTNO \bullet \\
\quad ino? = ino? \land \\
\quad genregs = genregs \land \\
\quad intflg = intflg
\end{array}$$

This is clearly equivalent to *true*, so we can state

$$\text{pre } RaiseInterrupt \mathrel{\widehat=} true$$

To cause a context-switching interrupt, the following operation is invoked

$CTXTSW \mathrel{\widehat=}$
$\quad \exists\, ino : INTRPTNO \mid ino = context\_switch \bullet$
$\quad\quad RaiseInterrupt[ino/ino?]$

This expands into

$$\begin{array}{|l}
\multicolumn{1}{l}{_\ CTXTSW\ ____} \\
\Delta HARDWARE \\
\hline
intno' = context_switch \\
\hline
\end{array}$$

In this case, too, the precondition is

$\mathrm{pre}\ CTXTSW \mathrel{\widehat=} true$

This fact saves a good deal of work when defining the scheduler's main operation.

When the interrupt occurs, the ISR performs the following operations

$CTXTSWISR \mathrel{\widehat=}$
$\quad ContextSwitch \mathbin{⨾} ReturnFromInterrupt$

This operation calls the context switch to push the outgoing process' registers onto its stack. The outgoing process was the one that was executing before the context switch occurred, so its program counter will be pushed onto the stack by the *CTXTSW* operation. The incoming process will have had its stack organised by the *CTXTSW* operation, so we can expect its stack to have its registers at the top and its program counter underneath. By popping the registers, the stack is left in the state required by the *ReturnFromInterrupt*. In this case, however, control is passed to the incoming process, not to the one that caused the interrupt.

Although the principle of the above is quite general, it assumes that there is a `rti` instruction and that the stack contains the program counter on interrupt. These assumptions are not universal. There are processors that only push the interrupted process' program counter on the stack; there are processors that store the interrupting process' program counter in a register. MIPS does this and MIPS requires the programmer to increment the program counter themselves; its equivalent of the `rti` instruction just clears the interrupt flag. In the case of MIPS, therefore, a little more work must be done than we have outlined here.

The ISR for the half context switch also needs to find a program counter on the incoming process' stack. Since the process has not executed yet, so the stack has to be pre-loaded with program counter and default values for the other data that is pushed by the raise interrupt operation. The program counter value will be the entry point of the first process.

In a similar fashion, when a process is run for the first time, there is no program counter for it. In this case also, the program counter's value should be the entry point to the main procedure in the process.

3.3 The Process Table

In the last section, reference was made to the *Process Table*, a data structure maintained by the kernel to represent the processes it currently contains. Here, the process table, *PTAB*, and the operations required to support it, are defined.

First, the error schemata are defined.

The first operation is used to set the error flag when a process descriptor is unused and something wants to operate on it.

$$
\begin{array}{|l}
\textit{UnusedPD} \\
\hline
serr! : SYSERR \\
\hline
serr! = unusedpd \\
\hline
\end{array}
$$

The next schema represents the operation that records the error state when a process descriptor is in use and an attempt to allocate it again is made.

$$
\begin{array}{|l}
\textit{PDInUse} \\
\hline
serr! : SYSERR \\
\hline
serr! = pdinuse \\
\hline
\end{array}
$$

The final schema represents the operation to set the error value when the process table is full.

$$
\begin{array}{|l}
\textit{PTABFull} \\
\hline
serr! : SYSERR \\
\hline
serr! = ptabfull \\
\hline
\end{array}
$$

3.3.1 Top Level

Now, the state schema for the process table is defined.

$$
\begin{array}{|l}
\textit{PTAB} \\
\hline
used : \mathbb{F}\, PID \\
prio : PID \nrightarrow PPRIO \\
state : PID \nrightarrow PSTATE \\
stacktop : PID \nrightarrow ADDR \\
smsg : PID \nrightarrow MSG \\
wakingtime : PID \nrightarrow TIME \\
\hline
used = \mathrm{dom}\, prio \\
\mathrm{dom}\, prio = \mathrm{dom}\, state \\
\mathrm{dom}\, prio = \mathrm{dom}\, smsg \\
\mathrm{dom}\, prio = \mathrm{dom}\, wakingtime \\
\mathrm{dom}\, prio = \mathrm{dom}\, stacktop \\
\hline
\end{array}
$$

The *used* variable records the identifiers of those processes currently in the system. Each process in *used* has a priority that is represented by *prio* and a state that is represented by *state*. A pointer to the top of each process' stack is represented by *stacktop*. Processes are permitted to communicate using messages, following a synchronous régime, and messages, when received, are stored in *smsg*. Processes are each associated with a value that denotes the period, expressed in seconds, that it is to be suspended on a timer queue; when the period expires, the process is made ready for execution. By default, a process that is not sleeping is assigned a *wakingtime* value of 0 (zero).

When allocating process identifiers, it is useful to know which identifiers are free and which are used. Since *PID* is finite and $used \subseteq PID$, we can define *free* as:

$$PID \setminus used = free$$

This definition will make refinement considerably easier. It will also help in reasoning about the process table.

The process table is initialised by the following operation. Initialisation consists simply of setting *used* to empty. Since the domains of the partial functions comprising the rest of the *PTAB* schema are identical to *used*, this implies that the domains of these functions is also $\varnothing$.

```
┌─ PTABInit ──────────────────────────
│ PTAB'
├──────────
│ used' = ∅
└─────────────────────────────────────
```

The *UsedPID* schema defines an operation that is true when the input, $p?$, is an element of *used*. When this is the case, $p?$ refers to a known process (i.e., one that is present in the system).

```
┌─ UsedPID ───────────────────────────
│ ΞPTAB
│ p? : PID
├──────────
│ p? ∈ used
└─────────────────────────────────────
```

The next operation is true when there are process identifiers that can be allocated.

```
┌─ GotFreePIDs ───────────────────────
│ ΞPTAB
├──────────
│ used ⊂ PID
└─────────────────────────────────────
```

Note that $\varnothing \subset PID$. In this case, there are no allocated *PID*s. If $used = PID$, then $used \subset PID$ is false and there are no free elements of *PID*. This scheme is used because process identifiers are cycled in the sense that a single identifier can be allocated (i.e., denoting some process) at one time and unallocated (i.e., denoting no process) at another time. This is similar to the cycling indices when process identifiers are represented by array indices. The operation to allocate a process identifier is the following:

$$
\begin{array}{l}
\textit{AllocPID} \\
\hline
\Delta PTAB \\
p! : PID \\
\hline
p! \notin used \\
used' = used \cup \{p!\}
\end{array}
$$

By the definition of *free*, $p! \notin free$ follows from the predicate of *AllocPID*'s schema.

When deallocating or freeing a process identifier, the *FreePID* operation is employed.

$$
\begin{array}{l}
\textit{FreePID} \\
\hline
\Delta PTAB \\
p? : PID \\
\hline
used' = used \setminus \{p?\}
\end{array}
$$

The definition of *free* permits the inference from the schema of *FreePID* that $p? \in free'$, or that $p?$ is an element of *free* in the after state of this operation.

The lowest level of process descriptor allocation is the creation of the initial representation of the process. When a process is created, an identifier is allocated and some basic information about it is recorded in the process table. This second part of the operation is captured by *AddPDESC*.

$$
\begin{array}{l}
\textit{AddPDESC} \\
\hline
\Delta PTAB \\
p? : PID \\
st? : PSTATE \\
pr? : PPRIO \\
\hline
prio' = prio \cup \{p? \mapsto pr?\} \\
state' = state \cup \{p? \mapsto st?\} \\
smsg' = smsg \cup \{p? \mapsto nullmsg\} \\
wakingtime' = wakingtime \cup \{p? \mapsto 0\}
\end{array}
$$

It is clear that $p? \in used$ is required. It can also be seen that the default value for *wakingtime* is used to denote the fact that $p?$ is not currently sleeping.

The full operation to create a representation of a process within the process table is the following.

$$
\begin{aligned}
&\mathit{AddPD} \mathrel{\widehat=} \\
&\quad ((\mathit{GotFreePIDs} \land \mathit{AllocPID}) \mathbin{;} \\
&\qquad (\lnot\ \mathit{UsedPID}[p!/p?] \land \mathit{AddPDESC}[p!/p?] \land \mathit{SysOk}) \\
&\qquad \lor \mathit{PDInUse}) \\
&\quad \lor \mathit{PTABFull}
\end{aligned}
$$

First, a test is performed to determine that the process table is not empty. If this is the case, a process identifier is allocated and a check is made to determine whether the newly allocated identifier is currently in use (if it is, something serious has gone wrong, perhaps an attack—we do not deal with such matters in this system but we do record the fact). If all is well, basic information about the process is recorded in the process table and *sysok* is returned.

This expands into:

$$
\begin{aligned}
&\textbf{AddPD} \\
&\Delta \mathit{PTAB} \\
&p! : \mathit{PID} \\
&pr? : \mathit{PPRIO} \\
&st? : \mathit{PSTATE} \\
&serr! : \mathit{SYSERR} \\
\hline
&((\mathit{used} \subset \mathit{PID} \land \\
&\qquad p! \notin \mathit{used} \land \mathit{used}' = \mathit{used} \cup \{p!\} \land \\
&\qquad p! \in \mathit{used}' \land \mathit{prio}' = \mathit{prio} \cup \{p! \mapsto pr?\} \land \\
&\qquad \mathit{state}' = \mathit{state} \cup \{p! \mapsto st?\} \land \mathit{smsg}' = \mathit{smsg} \cup \{p! \mapsto \mathit{nullmsg}\} \land \\
&\qquad \mathit{wakingtime}' = \mathit{wakingtime} \cup \{p! \mapsto 0\} \land \\
&\qquad serr! = \mathit{sysok}) \\
&\lor serr! = \mathit{pdinuse}) \\
&\lor serr! = \mathit{ptabful}
\end{aligned}
$$

For the purposes of refinement, it is necessary to calculate the precondition of this operation. It is

$$
\begin{aligned}
&\mathrm{pre}\ \mathit{AddPD} \mathrel{\widehat=} \\
&\quad \mathit{used} \subset \mathit{PID}
\end{aligned}
$$

It is equivalent to

$$\mathit{PID} \setminus \mathit{used} \neq \varnothing$$

and to

$$\mathit{used} \neq \mathit{PID}$$

When a process terminates, its descriptor must be removed from the system. The *DelPD* operation does this.

$$DelPD \mathrel{\widehat=} (UsedPID \land FreePID \land SysOk) \lor UnusedPD$$

The deletion of process descriptors is simplified by the fact that the domain of each of the maps that constitute its representation is identical to *used*. Therefore, by deleting the process identifier from *used*, it is also removed from the other domains.

The *DelPD* operation expands into:

DelPD

$\Delta PTAB$
$p? : PID$
$serr! : SYSERR$

$(p? \in used \land$
$\quad used' = used \setminus \{p?\} \land$
$\quad serr! = sysok)$
$\lor\ serr! = unusedpd$

The precondition of *DelPD* is given by

$$\text{pre}\ DelPD \mathrel{\widehat=} \exists\, PTAB' \bullet p? \in used$$

The next few operations are required to read and write the attributes that comprise the representation of a process. The attributes of interest here are *prio*, *state* and *wakingtime*. In the case of *state*, there are operations that set the state to specific values; later in this specification, there will be other such operations defined. The structure of the operations is very much as one would expect, given the definition of the types in question. For this reason, little is said about the details.

ProcPrio

$\Xi PTAB$
$p? : PID$
$pr! : PPRIO$

$pr! = prio(p?)$

SetProcPrio

$\Delta PTAB$
$p? : PID$
$pr? : PPRIO$

$prio' = prio \oplus \{p? \mapsto pr?\}$

$$
\begin{array}{|l}
\hline
\textit{ProcState} \\
\Xi PTAB \\
p? : PID \\
st! : PSTATE \\
\hline
st! = state(p?) \\
\hline
\end{array}
$$

$$
\begin{array}{|l}
\hline
\textit{SetProcState} \\
\Delta PTAB \\
p? : PID \\
st? : PSTATE \\
\hline
state' = state \oplus \{p? \mapsto st?\} \\
\hline
\end{array}
$$

It is useful to have operations that set the value of *state*. The most useful is the one that sets the state to *psready* (this operation is applied when a process enters the scheduler's ready queue).

$$
\begin{array}{l}
SetProcessStateToReady \mathrel{\widehat=} \\
\quad \exists\, st : PSTATE \mid st = psready \bullet \\
\qquad SetProcState[st/st?]
\end{array}
$$

It expands into

$$
\begin{array}{|l}
\hline
\textit{SetProcessStateToReady} \\
\Delta PTAB \\
p? : PID \\
\hline
state' = state \oplus \{p? \mapsto psready\} \\
\hline
\end{array}
$$

$$
\begin{array}{|l}
\hline
\textit{SetWaitingTime} \\
\Delta PTAB \\
p? : PID \\
t? : TIME \\
\hline
wakingtime' = wakingtime \oplus \{p? \mapsto t?\} \\
\hline
\end{array}
$$

$$
\begin{array}{|l}
\hline
\textit{WaitingTime} \\
\Xi PTAB \\
p? : PID \\
t! : TIME \\
\hline
t! = wakingtime(p?) \\
\hline
\end{array}
$$

3.3.2 Refinement One

In this refinement, a free chain of process descriptors is introduced. This is used to allocate and free descriptors. At present, the free chain is defined in terms of an additional function, *freech*; in the next subsection, the free chain is refined to the *next* chain that forms part of $PTAB$.

The state representation for the refined process table, $PTAB1$, is as follows.

$$
\begin{array}{l}
\textbf{PTAB1} \\
\hline
hdfree, endfree : GPID \\
freech : PID \rightarrowtail\!\!\!\!\!\!\nrightarrow GPID \\
prio1 : PID \rightarrow PPRIO \\
state1 : PID \rightarrow PSTATE \\
smsg1 : PID \rightarrow MSG \\
stacktop1 : PID \rightarrow ADDR \\
wakingtime1 : PID \rightarrow TIME \\
\hline
hdfree = nullpid \Leftrightarrow endfree = nullpid \\
hdfree = nullpid \Leftrightarrow \mathrm{dom}\, freech = \varnothing \\
hdfree \neq nullpid \Leftrightarrow \mathrm{dom}\, freech \neq \varnothing \\
hdfree \neq nullpid \Leftrightarrow hdfree \in \mathrm{dom}\, freech \\
hdfree \neq nullpid \Leftrightarrow endfree \in \mathrm{dom}\, freech \\
hdfree \neq nullpid \Leftrightarrow freech(endfree) = nullpid)
\end{array}
$$

First, it should be noted that *prio*1, *state*1 and *wakingtime*1 are similar to those in $PTAB$; in $PTAB$, these variables are partial functions, while here they are total functions. This clearly has implications for the domain constraint on them that was used so successfully in the specification of $PTAB$.

The other point of interest is the representation of the free chain. We use two variables, *hdfree* and *endfree* to denote the first and last elements of the chain. So that an empty chain can be represented, these variables are of type $GPID$, so can be assigned to the value *nullpid*. The main part of the chain is represented by the (finite) partial injection *freech*. For the reason that *freech* is an injection, it follows immediately that it is 1-1; for the reason that *freech* is partial, it allows some elements of PID to be absent from its domain. When the freechain is empty, $\mathrm{dom}\, freech = \varnothing$. An empty free chain implies that there are no more process identifiers to allocate. This is the central point of the initialisation operation for $PTAB1$:

$$
\begin{array}{l}
\textbf{PTAB1Init} \\
\hline
PTAB1' \\
\hline
hdfree' = minpid \land endfree' = maxpid \\
\forall p : PID \bullet \\
\quad (p = maxpid \Rightarrow freech'(p) = nullpid) \land (p < maxpid \Rightarrow freech'(p) = p + 1)
\end{array}
$$

This operation merely sets *freech* to map to the next process identifier (second conjunct). The last proper process identifier is mapped to *nullpid* by the first conjunct.

The following operation corresponds to *UsedPID*. It employs the same logic as in the case of *PTAB*: a process identifier is used iff it is not free. Here, free is equivalent to being in the free chain, or, more precisely, in the domain of the *freech*.

$$
\begin{array}{l}
\textit{UsedPID1} \\
\hline
\Xi PTAB1 \\
p? : PID \\
\hline
p? \notin \operatorname{dom} \mathit{freech}
\end{array}
$$

The next operation could be defined in terms of dom *freech*. However, it is somewhat more useful to use *hdfree*. The invariant of *PTAB*1 states that $hdfree = nullpid \Leftrightarrow endfree = nullpid$, and that $hdfree = nullpid \Leftrightarrow \operatorname{dom} freech = \varnothing$. This permits a good deal of simplification so that the following schema is obtained.

$$
\begin{array}{l}
\textit{GotFreePIDs1} \\
\hline
\Xi PTAB1 \\
\hline
hdfree \neq nullpid
\end{array}
$$

Using the invariant, the predicate of this schema implies that $endfree = nullpid$ and $\operatorname{dom} freech = \varnothing$, so there can be no free identifiers.

The next operation allocates a new process identifier from the free chain.

$$
\begin{array}{l}
\textit{AllocPID1} \\
\hline
\Delta PTAB1 \\
p! : PID \\
\hline
p! = hdfree \\
freech' = freech \lhd \{p!\} \\
hdfree' = freech(hdfree)
\end{array}
$$

First, the next free identifier is the value of *hdfree*, so it can be made the output variable, $p!$. The value of *hdfree* must be updated to $freech(hdfree)$, so that $hdfree'$ is the successor of *hdfree* in *freech*. It is also necessary to remove *hdfree* or $p!$ from *freech*; $p!$ is a domain element of *freech*, so the $\lhd$ operation suffices to remove it from *freech*. It should be noted that, since $p!$ is *hdfree*, it can only occur in the domain of *freech*, so the domain subtraction operation is adequate and there is no requirement to remove $p!$ from the codomain.

This operation corresponds to *AddPDESC*. The correspondence should be clear.

$$\begin{array}{l}
\underline{\quad AddPDESC1 \quad}\\
\Delta PTAB1\\
p? : PID\\
pr? : PPRIO\\
st? : PSTATE\\
\hline
prio1' = prio1 \oplus \{p? \mapsto pr?\}\\
state1' = state1 \oplus \{p? \mapsto st?\}\\
wakingtime1' = wakingtime1 \oplus \{p? \mapsto 0\}
\end{array}$$

The following operation corresponds to *AddPD*.

$$\begin{array}{l}
AddPD1 \mathrel{\widehat=}\\
\quad ((GotFreePIDs1 \land AllocPID1)\\
\qquad \mathbin{;}(UsedPID1[p!/p?] \land AddPDESC1[p!/p?]) \land SysOk)\\
\qquad \lor PDInUse\\
\quad \lor PTABFull
\end{array}$$

This expands into:

$$\begin{array}{l}
\underline{\quad AddPD1 \quad}\\
\Delta PTAB1\\
p! : PID\\
serr! : SYSERR\\
\hline
((hdfree \neq nullpid \land\\
\qquad p! = hdfree \land freech' = freech \ndres \{p!\} \land\\
\qquad hdfree' = freech(hdfree)) \land\\
\qquad (p! \notin \operatorname{dom} freech' \land\\
\qquad\qquad prio1' = prio1 \oplus \{p! \mapsto pr?\} \land\\
\qquad\qquad state1' = state1 \oplus \{p! \mapsto st?\}) \land\\
\qquad\qquad smsg1' = smsg1 \oplus \{p! \mapsto nullpid\} \land\\
\qquad\qquad wakingtime1' = wakingtime1 \oplus \{p! \mapsto 0\} \land\\
\qquad\qquad serr! = sysok)\\
\qquad \lor serr! = pdinuse\\
\lor serr! = ptabfull
\end{array}$$

Using the fact that $\operatorname{pre}(A \lor B) \Leftrightarrow \operatorname{pre} A \lor \operatorname{pre} B$, we can omit $serr! = ptabfull$ immediately. In addition, the assignments $serr! = unusedpd$ and $serr! = sysok$ contribute nothing to the precondition and can also be omitted.

The precondition of *AddPD1* is required so that refinement proofs can be undertaken.

$$
\begin{array}{l}
\mathrm{pre}\ AddPD1 \mathrel{\widehat{=}} \\
\quad \exists\, PTAB1';\ p! : PID \bullet \\
\qquad hdfree \neq nullpid \land \\
\qquad p! = hdfree \land \\
\qquad freech' = freech \lhd \{p!\} \land \\
\qquad hdfree' = freech(hdfree)) \land \\
\qquad (p! \notin \mathrm{dom}\, freech' \land \\
\qquad\quad prio1' = prio1 \oplus \{p! \mapsto pr?\} \land \\
\qquad\quad state1' = state1 \oplus \{p! \mapsto st?\})
\end{array}
$$

This simplifies to:

$$
\begin{array}{l}
\mathrm{pre}\ AddPD1 \mathrel{\widehat{=}} \\
\quad hdfree \neq nullpid \land \\
\quad hdfree \notin \mathrm{dom}(freech \lhd \{hdfree\} \land
\end{array}
$$

It is equivalent to

$$hdfree \neq nullpid$$

The next few schemata define operations over the free chain. The purpose of defining these operations is to make manipulation of the free chain somewhat easier.

The first schema defines a predicate that is true when the free chain is empty.

EmptyFreeChain1

$$
\begin{array}{l}
\Xi PTAB1 \\
\hline
\mathrm{dom}\, freech = \varnothing
\end{array}
$$

The next schema defines an operation that adds an element to the end of the free chain.

AddNewLastFreechain

$$
\begin{array}{l}
\Delta PTAB1 \\
p? : PID \\
\hline
freech' = freech \oplus \{endfree \mapsto p?\}
\end{array}
$$

The next schema defines an operation that maps the last element of the free chain to *nullpid*.

AddFreechainLast

$$
\begin{array}{l}
\Delta PTAB1 \\
p? : PID \\
\hline
freech' = freech \cup \{p? \mapsto nullpid\}
\end{array}
$$

The *SetFCHead* operation sets the value of *hdfree*.

$$
\begin{array}{|l}
\multicolumn{1}{l}{\textit{SetFCHead}} \\
\Delta PTAB1 \\
p? : PID \\
\hline
hdfree' = p?
\end{array}
$$

Analogously, *SetFCLast* sets the value of *endfree*.

$$
\begin{array}{|l}
\multicolumn{1}{l}{\textit{SetFCLast}} \\
\Delta PTAB1 \\
p? : PID \\
\hline
endfree' = p?
\end{array}
$$

Using the schemata just defined, the operation to deallocate a process identifier can be defined. The freeing operation is initially defined as follows:

$$
\begin{array}{l}
FreePID1 \mathrel{\widehat{=}} \\
\quad (UsedPID1 \land \\
\qquad (((EmptyFreeChain1 \land AddFreechainLast \land \\
\qquad\quad SetFCLast \land SetFCHead) \\
\qquad \lor (UsedPID1 \land \\
\qquad\quad (AddNewLastFreechain \fatsemi AddFreechainLast) \land \\
\qquad\quad SetFCLast)) \land \\
\qquad SysOk)) \\
\quad \lor UnusedPID
\end{array}
$$

This version is adequate but not very good. In particular, if *EmptyFreeChain*1 is true, this fact implies that *UsedPID*1 is also true. That is, $\mathrm{dom}\, freech = \varnothing$ implies that $p? \notin \mathrm{dom}\, freech$. By omitting *UsedPID*1, the following is obtained:

$$
\begin{array}{l}
FreePID1 \mathrel{\widehat{=}} \\
\quad (((EmptyFreeChain1 \land \\
\qquad\quad AddFreechainLast \land SetFCLast \land SetFCHead) \\
\quad \lor (UsedPID1 \land \\
\qquad\quad (AddNewLastFreechain \fatsemi AddFreechainLast) \land SetFCLast)) \land \\
\qquad SysOk) \\
\quad \lor UnusedPID
\end{array}
$$

This can be transformed by distribution of *SysOk*. The transformation is justified by the propositional calculus theorem $(p \lor q) \land r \Leftrightarrow (p \land r) \lor (q \land r)$. The use of this theorem occurs frequently and can be used both to expand a schema by producing copies of conjuncts and to contract them by reducing multiple occurrences of a conjunct to a single one.

$$
\begin{array}{l}
FreePID1 \mathrel{\widehat=} \\
\quad ((EmptyFreeChain1 \land \\
\qquad\qquad AddFreechainLast \land SetFCLast \land SetFCHead \land SysOk) \\
\quad \lor (UsedPID1 \land \\
\qquad (AddNewLastFreechain \mathbin{;} AddFreechainLast) \land SetFCLast \land SysOk)) \\
\quad \lor UnusedPID1
\end{array}
$$

This definition can then be expanded into the schema that follows. A little simplification has been performed on the schema, it should be noted. Very often, when expanding definitions into schemata, we will take the opportunity to engage in some simplification; we will, though, outline the transformations employed unless they are obvious.

$$
\begin{array}{|l}
\hline
FreePID1 \\
\hline
\Delta PTAB1 \\
p? : PID \\
serr! : SYSERR \\
\hline
((\mathrm{dom}\, freech = \varnothing \land \\
\qquad freech' = freech \cup \{p? \mapsto nullpid\} \land \\
\qquad endfree' = p? \land \\
\qquad hdfree' = p? \land \\
\qquad serr! = sysok) \\
\lor (p? \notin \mathrm{dom}\, freech \land \\
\qquad freech' = (freech \oplus \{endfree \mapsto p?\}) \cup \{p? \mapsto nullpid\} \land \\
\qquad endfree' = p? \land \\
\qquad serr! = sysok)) \\
\lor serr! = usedpd \\
\hline
\end{array}
$$

In order to prove that *FreePID*1 is a correct refinement of *FreePID*, the precondition of *FreePID*1 is required. It is calculated as follows.

$$
\begin{array}{l}
\mathrm{pre}\, FreePID1 \mathrel{\widehat=} \\
\quad \exists PTAB1' \bullet \\
\qquad (\mathrm{dom}\, freech = \varnothing \land \\
\qquad\qquad freech' = freech \cup \{p? \mapsto nullpid\} \land \\
\qquad\qquad endfree' = p? \land \\
\qquad\qquad hdfree' = p?) \\
\quad \lor (p? \notin \mathrm{dom}\, freech \land \\
\qquad freech' = (freech \oplus \{endfree \mapsto p?\}) \cup \{p? \mapsto nullpid\} \land \\
\qquad endfree' = p?)
\end{array}
$$

This simplifies to

$$\begin{array}{l}
\text{pre}\ \mathit{FreePID1} \mathrel{\widehat=} \\
\quad \exists\, PTAB1' \bullet \\
\qquad ((\operatorname{dom} \mathit{freech} = \varnothing \land \\
\qquad\quad \mathit{freech} \cup \{p? \mapsto \mathit{nullpid}\} = \mathit{freech} \cup \{p? \mapsto \mathit{nullpid}\} \land \\
\qquad\quad p? = p? \land p? = p?) \\
\quad \lor (p? \notin \operatorname{dom} \mathit{freech} \land \\
\qquad (\mathit{freech} \oplus \{\mathit{endfree} \mapsto p?\}) \cup \{p? \mapsto \mathit{nullpid}\}) = \\
\qquad\qquad (\mathit{freech} \oplus \{\mathit{endfree} \mapsto p?\}) \cup \{p? \mapsto \mathit{nullpid}\}) \land \\
\qquad p? = p?)
\end{array}$$

and again to

$$\begin{array}{l}
\text{pre}\ \mathit{FreePID1} \mathrel{\widehat=} \\
\quad \operatorname{dom} \mathit{freech} = \varnothing \land \\
\quad \lor\ p? \notin \operatorname{dom} \mathit{freech}
\end{array}$$

It is equivalent to

$$p? \notin \operatorname{dom} \mathit{freech}$$

This is justified as follows. If $\operatorname{dom} \mathit{freech} = \varnothing$, then $p? \notin \operatorname{dom} \mathit{freech}$, trivially.
The *DelPD*1 operation can be defined as an equivalence:

$$\mathit{DelPD1} \mathrel{\widehat=} \mathit{FreePID1}$$

The operations to access and set state components must be defined for *PTAB*1, just as they were for *PTAB*. The definitions are quite obvious, so we just give one as an example. As with the corresponding operations over *PTAB*, there is the tacit assumption that $p?$ is in *used*. The operations are not used as independent operations but as components of larger operations that require that $p? \in \mathit{used}$ or some equivalent condition.

$$\begin{array}{|l}
\hline
\mathit{SetProcState1} \\
\hline
\Delta PTAB1 \\
p? : PID \\
st? : PSTATE \\
\hline
\mathit{state1}' = \mathit{state1} \oplus \{p? \mapsto st?\} \\
\hline
\end{array}$$

The relationship between *PTAB* and *PTAB*1 is expressed by the predicate of the *AbsPTAB*1 schema. This schema is referred to below as the "abstraction relation".

$$
\begin{array}{|l}
\hline
AbsPTAB1 \\
PTAB \\
PTAB1 \\
\hline
\mathrm{dom}\, freech = PID \setminus used \\
\mathrm{dom}\, freech \cap used = \varnothing \\
\forall p : PID \bullet \\
\quad p \in used \Rightarrow prio(p) = prio1(p) \\
\forall p : PID \bullet \\
\quad p \in used \Rightarrow state(p) = state1(p) \\
\forall p : PID \bullet \\
\quad p \in used \Rightarrow wakingtime(p) = wakingtime1(p) \\
\forall p : PID \bullet \\
\quad p \in used \Rightarrow smsg(p) = smsg1(p) \\
\forall p : PID \bullet \\
\quad p \in used \Rightarrow stacktop(p) = stacktop1(p) \\
\hline
\end{array}
$$

It is clear that the predicate of the *AbsPTAB*1 schema is a function; indeed, it is an identity. Abstraction relations of this kind are extremely common. It is possible to calculate the various operations of the refinement from a functional abstraction relation and this we resist. Moreover, the fact that the abstraction relation is an identity implies that the refinement proofs are quite simple (perhaps even trivial); we include the proofs as a demonstration.

With the abstraction relation defined, it is possible to prove the initialisation theorem.

Theorem 1. $\forall PTAB'; PTAB1' \bullet PTAB1Init \wedge AbsPTAB1 \Rightarrow PTABInit.$

Proof. By the predicate of *AbsPTAB*1, $\mathrm{dom}\, freech' = PID \setminus used'$. The universally quantified formula in *PTAB*1*Init*'s predicate implies that $maxpid \in \mathrm{dom}\, freech'$ and for all $p < maxpid$, $p \in \mathrm{dom}\, freech'$. This implies that $PID = \mathrm{dom}\, freech'$, so, by the abstraction relation, $used' = \varnothing$. □

Until the end of this section, refinement proofs are presented, two for each operation that is refined. The proofs are the standard ones (cf. [12] or [13]).

Theorem 2. $\forall PTAB; PTAB1 \bullet \mathrm{pre}\, AddPD \wedge AbsPTAB1 \Rightarrow \mathrm{pre}\, AddPD1$

Proof. We have the following preconditions:

$\mathrm{pre}\, AddPD \mathrel{\widehat{=}} PID \setminus used \neq \varnothing$

and

$AddPD1 \mathrel{\widehat{=}} hdfree \neq nullpid$

By the abstraction relation, $\mathrm{dom}\, freech = PID \setminus used$. If $PID \setminus used \neq \varnothing$, it follows that $\mathrm{dom}\, freech \neq \varnothing$. By the invariant of *PTAB*1, $\mathrm{dom}\, freech \neq \varnothing$ implies that $hdfree \neq nullpid$. □

Theorem 3.

$$\begin{array}{l}\forall PTAB;\ PTAB';\ PTAB1;\ PTAB1';\\ \qquad pr? : PRIO;\ st? : PSTATE;\ p! : PID;\ serr! : SYSERR \bullet\\ \quad pre\ AddPD\\ \qquad \land AbsPTAB1 \land AbsPTAB1'\\ \qquad \land AddPD1\\ \quad \Rightarrow AddPD\end{array}$$

PROOF. By the invariant of $PTAB1$, it is clear that $hdfree \neq nullpid$ implies that $\mathrm{dom}\, freech \neq \varnothing$. By the abstraction relation, this implies that $PID \setminus used \neq \varnothing$, and so $used \subset PID$. If $used = \varnothing$, $used \subset PID$ since $\varnothing \subset S$, for all S; if, on the other hand, $used \neq \varnothing$, $used \subset PID$ by definition.

If $p! = hdfree$ then $p! \notin used$.

Now, $freech \lhd \{p!\}$ implies $used \cup \{p!\}$ and by the abstraction relation, $\mathrm{dom}\, freech' = PID \setminus used'$, so $\mathrm{dom}\, freech \lhd \{p!\} = (PID \setminus used) \cup \{p!\}$, which is equivalent to $PID \setminus (used \cup \{p!\})$ since $free \cup used = PID$, and this is equivalent to $PID \setminus used$ by the predicate of $AbsPTAB1'$. From this, we can infer that $used \cup \{p!\} = used'$.

By the abstraction relation, $AbsPTAB1$

$$\begin{array}{l}\forall p : PID \bullet\\ \qquad p \in used \Rightarrow prio(p) = prio1(p)\end{array}$$

and

$$\begin{array}{l}\forall p : PID \bullet\\ \qquad p \in used \Rightarrow state(p) = state1(p)\end{array}$$

Now, we need to observe that $AddPD$ is defined in terms of a sequential composition, so the start state of the second component is the after state of the first. Writing the after state for $used$ as $used''$, it can be seen that $used' = used''$. Therefore, $p! \notin \mathrm{dom}\, freech'$ is equivalent to $p! \notin \mathrm{dom}\, freech''$ and implies $p! \notin used'$ or $p! \notin used''$. From this, it can be inferred that $prio1 \oplus \{p! \mapsto pr?\} = prio \oplus \{p! \mapsto pr?\}$. Since $p! \notin used'$, $prio \oplus \{p? \mapsto pr?\} = prio \cup \{p? \mapsto pr?\}$ and $prio \cup \{p? \mapsto pr?\} = prio'$ since $prio1' = prio1 \oplus \{p! \mapsto pr?\}$ and $prio1'(p) = prio'(p)$ for all $p \in used'$ by $AbsPTAB1'$. $\square$

Theorem 4. $\forall PTAB;\ PTAB1;\ p? : PID \bullet pre\ DelPD \land AbsPTAB1 \Rightarrow pre\ DelPD1$

PROOF. The precondition of $DelPD$ is $p? \in used$ and that of $DelPD1$ is $p? \notin \mathrm{dom}\, freech$. By the abstraction relation, $\mathrm{dom}\, freech = PID \setminus used$, so $p? \in used$ implies that $p? \notin PID \setminus used$. From this, it may be inferred that $p? \notin \mathrm{dom}\, freech$. $\square$

Theorem 5.

$$\forall PTAB;\ PTAB';\ PTAB1;\ PTAB1';\ p? : PID;\ serr! : SYSERR \bullet$$
$$\quad pre\ DelPD \land$$
$$\qquad AbsPTAB1 \land AbsPTAB1' \land$$
$$\qquad DelPD1$$
$$\quad \Rightarrow DelPD$$

PROOF. First, we note that the precondition of *DelPD* is $p? \in used$. We have a proof composed of two cases.
Case 1. $\mathrm{dom}\, freech = \varnothing$ implies that $used = PID$ and $freech \cup \{p?\}$ implies that $\mathrm{dom}\, freech \cup \{p?\}$. By the identity in *AbsPTAB*1, $\mathrm{dom}\, freech = PID \setminus used$, this clearly implies $used \setminus \{p?\}$ iff $\mathrm{dom}\, freech \cup \{p?\}$. More formally, we can write this as follows. We start with $\mathrm{dom}\, freech = PID \setminus used$, so if $\mathrm{dom}\, freech = \varnothing$, we have:

$$\mathrm{dom}\, freech = PID \setminus used$$
$$= \mathrm{dom}\, freech \cup \{p?\} = PID \setminus (used \setminus \{p?\})$$
$$= \varnothing \cup \{p?\} = used \setminus \{p?\} \qquad = \{p?\} = used \setminus \{p?\}$$

By the predicate of *FreePID*1, $\mathrm{dom}\, freech' = \mathrm{dom}\, freech \cup \{p?\}$, and, by the predicate of *AbsPTAB*1′, $\mathrm{dom}\, freech' = PID \setminus used'$. Then, $\mathrm{dom}\, freech \cup \{p?\} = \mathrm{dom}\, freech' = PID \setminus used'$, so, by the above reasoning, $used' = used \setminus \{p?\}$.
Case 2. $\mathrm{dom}\, freech \neq \varnothing$. In a similar fashion, $\mathrm{dom}\, freech = PID \setminus used$, so

$$\mathrm{dom}\, freech \cup \{p?\} = PID \setminus (used \setminus \{p?\})$$
$$= \mathrm{dom}\, freech' = PID \setminus (used \setminus \{p?\}$$

Since $\mathrm{dom}\, freech' = PID \setminus used'$ by the predicate of *AbsPTAB*1′ and by the above reasoning, $\mathrm{dom}\, freech' = PID \setminus (used \cup \{p?\}) = used'$. □

At this point, it is necessary to point out that, throughout the specification and refinement of this kernel, there are many operations on the state-describing components of *PTAB* and its derivatives. For example, the operation to update the value of the *state* component of *PTAB* is

SetProcState
$\Delta PTAB$
$p? : PID$
$st? : PSTATE$
$state' = state \oplus \{p? \mapsto st?\}$

In each case, it would be possible to write such an operation as

$$(p? \in used \land Op \land SysOk) \lor Error$$

In the case of *SetProcState*, it would be

$$(p? \in used \land SetProcState \land SysOk) \lor UnusedPD$$

However, the operations are only defined in terms of their testing or of their effect on $PTAB$ components (and their refinements). The reason for this is that the operation or predicate is used within a context that ensures that $p? \in used$ is always the case. We argue that this condition does not have to be ensured by the operation because some other component will do it anyway. If the operations were defined as disjunctions, it would be necessary to use $(p \lor q) \land r \Leftrightarrow (p \land r) \lor (q \land r)$ to move and combine $SysOk$ (and possibly move the error schema).

As far as the precondition of these operations is concerned, they typically occur as conjuncts and therefore must be recalculated wherever they occur. There appears to be very little to be gained by explicitly calculating the precondition when defining the operation.

It might be argued that the refinement process is not complete until these two steps have been completed. We argue that the refinement of these operations is a rather trivial matter, a matter that can be done in one's head, by inspection, so the requirement that the proofs be recorded should not detain us—they are obvious given the abstraction relation. We can assure the reader that the necessary checking (making the assumption that $p? \in used$ and $p? \notin \mathrm{dom}\, freechain$) has been done by us in order to verify the refinement.

Should the above prove too offensive to the reader, they can always assume that the operation has been defined in the "export" (disjunctive) form and that the precondition has been calculated. The reader can, in any case, always supply the proofs for themselves; each should take no more than a couple of seconds.

3.3.3 Refinement Two

In this refinement, the function *freech* is replaced by the *next* function. The intention is that *next* allows us to represent a *list* of process descriptors (actually a list of process identifiers).

The *next* function will be used in other modules. In particular, it will be used by refinement of the $PROCESSQUEUE$ type to implement FIFO queues.

$PTAB2$

$freehd, freelst : GPID$
$prio2 : PID \rightarrow PPRIO$
$state2 : PID \rightarrow PSTATE$
$smsg2 : PID \rightarrow MSG$
$stacktop2 : PID \rightarrow ADDR$
$wakingtime2 : PID \rightarrow TIME$
$next : PID \rightarrowtail GPID$

$freehd = nullpid \Leftrightarrow freelst = nullpid$
$freehd = nullpid \Rightarrow next^*(\!| \{freehd\} |\!) = \varnothing$

$$
\begin{array}{l}
freehd \neq nullpid \Leftrightarrow \\
\quad \forall p : PID \bullet \\
\quad\quad p = freehd \Rightarrow nullpid \in next^{+}(\!| \{freehd\} |\!) \\
freehd \neq nullpid \Leftrightarrow \\
\quad \forall p : PID \bullet \\
\quad\quad p = freelst \Rightarrow next(freelst) = nullpid \\
freehd \neq nullpid \Rightarrow \exists_1 k : \mathbb{N} \bullet next^{k}(freehd) = nullpid
\end{array}
$$

The new function, *next*, replaces *freech* (as will be seen in the next paragraph, it actually does a little more). In this refinement, *next* is an injection, so it is 1-1. Furthermore, it is a total function for the reason that other operations (e.g., queues of various kinds) are implemented using *next*, thus accounting for the majority of process identifiers. When an identifier is not present in a structure, it is mapped to *nullpid* (this is the justification for the codomain type).

The fact that *next* will be used by other modules implies that we are not permitted to assume that all of its domain is relevant to the free list. This in turn implies that the *reflexive* transitive closure of the *next*, $next^*$, must be used to determine membership of the free list.

PTAB2Init

$$
\begin{array}{l}
PTAB2' \\
\hline
freehd' = minpid \\
freelst' = maxpid \\
\forall p : PID \bullet \\
\quad p = maxpid \Rightarrow next'(p) = nullpid \land \\
\quad p < maxpid \Rightarrow next'(p) = p + 1
\end{array}
$$

Note that the invariant on $PTAB2$ does not mention the state-denoting functions *prio*2, *state*2, *stacktop*2 and *wakingtime*2. In the present case, they are all total functions, so their domains are pre-defined. The question as to their initialisation also arises. It is considered that the operations defined below are sufficient to guarantee that a valid value is not supplied to a non-existant process.

Since the $PTAB$ refinement has already progressed some way, the abstraction relation is presented immediately.

AbsPTAB2

$$
\begin{array}{l}
PTAB1 \\
PTAB2 \\
\hline
freehd = hdfree \\
freelst = endfree
\end{array}
$$

$$freehd \neq nullpid \Leftrightarrow next^* (\! | \{freehd\} |\!) \setminus \{nullpid\} = \operatorname{dom} freech$$
$$\operatorname{dom} freech = \varnothing \Leftrightarrow freehd = freelst \land freehd = nullpid$$
$$freehd \neq nullpid \Leftrightarrow \forall p : PID \bullet p \in \operatorname{dom} freech \Rightarrow next(p) = freech(p)$$
$$\operatorname{dom} freech \subseteq \operatorname{dom} next$$
$$\operatorname{ran} freech \subseteq \operatorname{ran} next$$
$$\forall p : PID \bullet p \in \operatorname{dom} freech \Leftrightarrow next(p) = freech(p)$$
$$\forall p : PID \bullet \\ \quad p \notin next^* (\! | \{freehd\} |\!) \setminus \{nullpid\} \Rightarrow state1(p) = state2(p)$$
$$\forall p : PID \bullet \\ \quad p \notin next^* (\! | \{freehd\} |\!) \setminus \{nullpid\} \Rightarrow \\ \qquad prio1(p) = prio2(p)$$
$$\forall p : PID \bullet \\ \quad p \notin next^* (\! | \{freehd\} |\!) \setminus \{nullpid\} \Rightarrow \\ \qquad smsg1(p) = smsg2(p)$$
$$\forall p : PID \bullet \\ \quad p \notin next^* (\! | \{freehd\} |\!) \setminus \{nullpid\} \Rightarrow \\ \qquad stacktop1(p) = stacktop2(p)$$
$$\forall p : PID \bullet \\ \quad p \notin next^* (\! | \{freehd\} |\!) \setminus \{nullpid\} \Rightarrow \\ \qquad wakingtime1(p) = wakingtime2(p)$$

One of the interesting features of this schema is the implication

$$freehd \neq nullpid \Rightarrow \\ \quad next^* (\! | \{freehd\} |\!) \setminus \{nullpid\} = \operatorname{dom} freech$$

In what follows, relational images will be used quite extensively. In this case, the relational image is that of the transitive closure of the head of the *next* chain; the set that results includes the *nullpid* that terminates the *next* chain and this has to be removed to yield a set of type $\mathbb{F}\, PID$.

A second interesting feature is the use of the *next* function together with the *freehd* and *freelst* variables. The *next* function has a domain that includes the domain of *freech* and its codomain includes *freech*'s domain. The *freehd* and *freelst* variables record the head and last elements of the chain, so it is easy to remove elements from the head and add them at the end.

The initialisation theorem can now be proved. Over the years, we have found it useful to attempt the initialisation theorem as soon as the abstraction relation has been defined, for it is a good way of determining whether the abstraction relation is adequate.

Theorem 6. $\forall PTAB1'; PTAB2' \bullet PTAB1Init \land AbsPTAB2 \Rightarrow PTAB2Init$

PROOF. By the abstraction relation, $freehd' = hdfree'$ and $freelst' = endfree'$, so $freehd' = minpid \Rightarrow hdfree' = minpid$ and $freelst' = maxpid \Rightarrow$

$endfree' = maxpid$. By the invariants of $PTAB1$ and $PTAB2$, $next'(freelst') = nullpid = freech'(endfree')$. Finally, the quantified formulae are equivalent by the abstraction relation. The two conjuncts have the same antecedents and $p = maxpid$ and $p < maxpid$ imply that p ranges over all of PID. By the consequents, $p \in \mathrm{dom}\, next'$ for all $p \in PID$, which implies, by $\mathrm{dom}\, freech' \subseteq \mathrm{dom}\, next'$, that $\mathrm{dom}\, freech' = \mathrm{dom}\, next'$ for the reason that $\mathrm{dom}\, next' = PID$ by this quantified formula. This also implies that $\mathrm{dom}\, freech \neq \varnothing$, so $freehd' = nullpid$ is justified. □

The operations that are now defined should be familiar to the reader by now. In any case, they are defined in the obvious fashion, given the definition of $PTAB2$. The one exception is that the transitive closure of a relational image is frequently used for $PTAB2$ operations where a simple set operation is used by the corresponding operation over $PTAB1$.

GotFreePIDs2

$\Xi PTAB2$

$freehd \neq nullpid$

AllocPID2

$\Delta PTAB2$
$p! : PID$

$p! = freehd$
$freehd' = next(freehd)$

UsedPID2

$\Xi PTAB2$
$p? : PID$

$p? \notin next^{*}(\!|\ \{freehd\}\ |\!) \setminus \{nullpid\}$

AddPDESC2

$\Delta PTAB2$
$p? : PID$
$pr? : PPRIO$
$st? : PSTATE$

$prio2' = prio2 \oplus \{p? \mapsto pr?\}$
$state2' = state2 \oplus \{p? \mapsto st?\}$
$wakingtime2' = wakingtime2 \oplus \{p? \mapsto 0\}$
$stacktop2' = stacktop2 \oplus \{p? \mapsto nulladdr\}$

The next few operations deal with addition to the free chain. The definitions are directly analogous to those employed for $PTAB1$ and the overall structure of the composite operations is similar. For these reasons, we believe there is little to be said about these schemata.

$$
\begin{array}{|l}
\hline
\textit{SetFCLast2} \\
\Delta PTAB2 \\
p? : PID \\
\hline
freelst' = p? \\
\hline
\end{array}
$$

$$
\begin{array}{|l}
\hline
\textit{SetFCHead2} \\
\Delta PTAB2 \\
p? : PID \\
\hline
freehd' = p? \\
\hline
\end{array}
$$

$$
\begin{array}{|l}
\hline
\textit{AddFreechainLast2} \\
\Delta PTAB2 \\
p? : PID \\
\hline
next' = next \oplus \{p? \mapsto nullpid\} \\
\hline
\end{array}
$$

$$
\begin{array}{|l}
\hline
\textit{AddNewLastFreechain2} \\
\Delta PTAB2 \\
p? : PID \\
\hline
next' = next \oplus \{freelst \mapsto p?\} \\
\hline
\end{array}
$$

$$
\begin{array}{l}
AddPD2 \mathrel{\widehat=} \\
\quad ((GotFreePIDS2 \land AllocPID2) \\
\qquad \mathbin{;} ((UsedPID2[p!/p?] \land AddPDESC2[p!/p?] \land SysOk) \\
\qquad\quad \lor PDInUse)) \\
\quad \lor PTABFull
\end{array}
$$

This expands to:

AddPD2

$$
\begin{array}{l}
\Delta PTAB2 \\
p! : PID \\
serr! : SYSERR \\
pr? : PPRIO \\
st? : PSTATE \\
\hline
((freehd \neq nullpid \land \\
\qquad\qquad p! = freehd \land \\
\qquad\qquad freehd' = next(freehd)) \\
\qquad \fatsemi (p! \notin next^{*} (\!| \{next(freehd)\} |\!) \setminus \{nullpid\} \land \\
\qquad\qquad prio2' = prio2 \oplus \{p! \mapsto pr?\} \land \\
\qquad\qquad state2' = state2 \oplus \{p! \mapsto st?\} \land \\
\qquad\qquad serr! = sysok) \\
\qquad \lor\ serr! = pdinuse) \\
\lor\ serr! = ptabful
\end{array}
$$

Note that the form of this operation causes a little confusion, especially when transcribed to code.

Expanding the sequential composition, $\fatsemi$, we obtain the following schema:

AddPD2

$$
\begin{array}{l}
\Delta PTAB2 \\
p! : PID \\
serr! : SYSERR \\
pr? : PPRIO \\
st? : PSTATE \\
\hline
(\exists\, next'' : PID \rightarrowtail GPID \bullet \\
\qquad freehd \neq nullpid \land \\
\qquad p! = freehd \land \\
\qquad freehd'' = next(freehd) \land \\
\qquad p! \notin next^{*} (\!| \{freehd''\} |\!) \setminus \{nullpid\} \land \\
\qquad prio2' = prio2 \oplus \{p! \mapsto pr?\} \land \\
\qquad state2' = state2 \oplus \{p! \mapsto pr?\} \land \\
\qquad serr! = sysok) \\
\qquad \lor\ serr! = pdinuse \\
\lor\ serr! = ptabfull
\end{array}
$$

This can be simplified in a number of steps. First, $next'' = next$ and, what is more, $next' = next$ for the reason that it is never updated (all that is done is to move *freehd* down the chain). It is also the case that $freehd'' = freehd'$. The output $p!$ is retained. This entitles us to rewrite *AddPD2* as:

$$
\begin{array}{|l}
\hline
AddPD2 \\
\Delta PTAB2 \\
p! : PID \\
serr! : SYSERR \\
pr? : PPRIO \\
st? : PSTATE \\
\hline
(freehd \neq nullpid \land \\
\quad p! = freehd \land \\
\quad freehd' = next(freehd) \land \\
\quad p! \notin next^{*} (\!| \{next(freehd)\} |\!) \setminus \{nullpid\} \land \\
\quad prio2' = prio2 \oplus \{p! \mapsto pr?\} \land \\
\quad state2' = state2 \oplus \{p! \mapsto pr?\} \land \\
\quad serr! = sysok) \\
\quad \lor serr! = pdinuse \\
\lor serr! = ptabfull \\
\hline
\end{array}
$$

For reasons that will later become clear, it should be noted that $prio2 = prio2''$ and $state2 = state2''$.

Omitting the assignments to $serr!$ (since they contribute nothing to the precondition), we have

$$
\begin{array}{l}
\text{pre } AddPD2 \mathrel{\widehat{=}} \\
\quad \exists PTAB2'; \; p! : PID \bullet \\
\qquad freehd \neq nullpid \land \\
\qquad\quad p! = freehd \land \\
\qquad\quad freehd' = next(freehd) \land \\
\qquad\quad p! \notin next^{*} (\!| \{next(freehd)\} |\!) \setminus \{nullpid\} \land \\
\qquad\quad prio2' = prio2 \oplus \{p! \mapsto pr?\} \land \\
\qquad\quad state2' = state2 \oplus \{p! \mapsto pr?\}
\end{array}
$$

This simplifies to

$$
\begin{array}{l}
\text{pre } AddPD2 \mathrel{\widehat{=}} \\
\quad freehd \neq nullpid \land \\
\quad freehd \notin next^{*} (\!| \{next(freehd)\} |\!) \setminus \{nullpid\}
\end{array}
$$

This can be simplified to

$$freehd \neq nullpid$$

If $freehd \neq nullpid$, $next^{*} (\!| \{next(freehd)\} |\!) \setminus \{nullpid\} = next^{+} (\!| \{freehd\} \setminus \{nullpid\}$ and $freehd$ is not an element of this set by definition. If $freehd = nullpid$, then $next^{*} (\!| \{next(freehd)\} |\!) \setminus \{nullpid\} = \varnothing$, so $freehd$ cannot be an element.

Because we are dealing with modified relational images so frequently, it is essential to prove the following theorem.

Theorem 7. *The following are equivalent.*

$$p \in next^* (\!| \{next(freehd)\} |\!) \setminus \{nullpid\}$$

and

$$\begin{array}{l} p = freehd \\ \lor \exists k : \mathbb{N} \bullet \\ \quad 0 < k \land k \leq \# \operatorname{dom} next^* (\!| \{next(freehd)\} |\!) \setminus \{nullpid\} \bullet \\ \quad p = next^k(freehd) \end{array}$$

PROOF. By the definition of *,

$$\begin{array}{l} next^* (\!| \{next(freehd)\} |\!) \setminus \{nullpid\} \\ \quad = \{freehd\} \cup next^+ (\!| \{next(freehd)\} |\!) \setminus \{nullpid\} \end{array}$$

for the reason that $R^* = \bigcup\{k : \mathbb{N} \bullet R^k\}$ and $R^+ = \bigcup\{k : \mathbb{N}_1 \bullet R^k\}$. As usual, for $k > 0$, $R^k = R \,⨾\, R^{k-1}$, here, expressed as a function, so $next^k = next(next^{k-1}(x))$. We also note that the above expressions in *next* are well-typed ($\mathbb{F}\, PID$) owing to the elimination of *nullpid*.

For convenience, let $N = next^* (\!| \{next(freehd)\} |\!) \setminus \{nullpid\}$. If $p = freehd$, $p \in N$ by the identity at the start of this proof. Otherwise, assume that there is some $n - 1 < \# \operatorname{dom} N$ such that $\forall i : 1 \,..\, n - 1 \bullet p \neq next^i(freehd)$. Then, for n, either $p = next^n(freehd)$ or $p \neq next^n(freehd)$. If $p = next^n(freehd)$, it follows that $p \in N$ and we are done. Otherwise, we continue. If $n = \#N$ and $p \neq next^n(freehd)$, then $p \notin N$; otherwise, $p \in N$. □

This result permits us to re-write $p \in next^* (\!| \{next(freehd)\} |\!) \setminus \{nullpid\}$ as

$$\begin{array}{l} p = freehd \\ \lor \exists k : \mathbb{N} \bullet \\ \quad 0 < k \land k \leq \# \operatorname{dom} next^* (\!| \{next(freehd)\} |\!) \setminus \{nullpid\} \bullet \\ \quad p = next^k(hd) \end{array}$$

and $p \notin next^* (\!| \{next(freehd)\} |\!) \setminus \{nullpid\}$ as

$$\begin{array}{l} p \neq freehd \\ \lor \neg \exists k : \mathbb{N} \bullet \\ \quad 0 < k \land k \leq \# \operatorname{dom} next^* (\!| \{next(freehd)\} |\!) \setminus \{nullpid\} \bullet \\ \quad p = next^k(hd) \end{array}$$

The reason for this is that the quantified form of set membership is, we believe, much closer to a computationally realisable form than the somewhat more cryptic relational image.

There are other cases in which this equivalence can be used to re-write schemata. They will be indicated and the re-written schema will be given. Therefore, given the equivalence, *AddPD2* becomes

$$
\begin{array}{|l}
\multicolumn{1}{l}{\underline{\quad AddPD2 \quad}} \\
\Delta PTAB2 \\
p! : PID \\
serr! : SYSERR \\
pr? : PPRIO \\
st? : PSTATE \\
\hline
(freehd \neq nullpid \land \\
\qquad p! = freehd \land \\
\qquad freehd' = next(freehd) \land \\
\qquad p! \notin next^* (\!| \{next(freehd)\} |\!) \setminus \{nullpid\} \land \\
\qquad (p \neq freehd \\
\qquad\qquad \lor (\neg \exists k : \mathbb{N} \bullet \\
\qquad\qquad\qquad 0 < k \leq \#next^* (\!| \{next(freehd)\} |\!) \setminus \{nullpid\} \land \\
\qquad\qquad\qquad next^k(freehd) = p) \land \\
\qquad prio2' = prio2 \oplus \{p! \mapsto pr?\} \land \\
\qquad state2' = state2 \oplus \{p! \mapsto pr?\} \land \\
\qquad serr! = sysok) \\
\qquad \lor\ serr! = pdinuse \\
\lor\ serr! = ptabfull \\
\hline
\end{array}
$$

For *FreePID*2, we need to define *EmptyFreeChain*2. It is the negation of *GotFreePIDs*2:

$$
\begin{array}{|l}
\multicolumn{1}{l}{\underline{\quad EmptyFreeChain2 \quad}} \\
\Xi PTAB2 \\
\hline
freehd = nullpid \\
\hline
\end{array}
$$

(This schema is exactly as we would expect.)

The operation to deallocate a process identifier is similar to *FreePID*2. The reader can compare the two to see that this is the case (in fact, *FreePID*2 was defined by rewriting *FreePID*1, substituting the operations directly).

$$
\begin{array}{l}
FreePID2 \mathrel{\widehat=} \\
\quad ((EmptyFreeChain2 \land \\
\qquad AddFreechainLast2 \land SetFCLast2 \land SetFCHead2 \land \\
\qquad SysOk) \\
\qquad \lor (UsedPID2 \land \\
\qquad\quad (AddNewLastFreechain2 \mathbin{\circ\!\!\!\!\!;} AddFreechainLast2) \land \\
\qquad\quad SetFCLast2 \land \\
\qquad\quad SysOk) \\
\qquad\quad \lor\ UnusedPID
\end{array}
$$

The definition of *FreePID*2 expands into the following schema:

$$
\begin{array}{|l}
\textit{FreePID2} \\
\hline
\Delta PTAB2 \\
p? : PID \\
serr! : SYSERR \\
\hline
(freehd = nullpid \land \\
\quad next' = next \oplus \{p? \mapsto nullpid\} \land \\
\quad freelst' = p? \land \\
\quad freehd' = p? \land \\
\quad serr! = sysok) \\
\lor ((p? \notin next^{*} (\!|\ \{freehd\}\ |\!) \setminus \{nullpid\} \land \\
\quad (\exists next'' : PID \rightarrowtail GPID \bullet \\
\qquad next'' = next \oplus \{freelst \mapsto p?\} \land \\
\qquad next' = next'' \oplus \{p? \mapsto nullpid\}) \land \\
\quad freelst' = p? \land \\
\quad serr! = sysok) \\
\quad \lor serr! = unusedpd)
\end{array}
$$

The schema can be simplified, so we obtain the following:

$$
\begin{array}{|l}
\hline
\Delta PTAB2 \\
p? : PID \\
serr! : SYSERR \\
\hline
(freehd = nullpid \land \\
\quad next' = next \oplus \{p? \mapsto nullpid\} \land \\
\quad freelst' = p? \land \\
\quad freehd' = p? \land \\
\quad serr! = sysok) \\
\lor ((p? \neq freehd \lor \\
\quad \neg (\exists k : \mathbb{N} \bullet \\
\qquad 0 < k \land k \leq \#next^{*} (\!|\ \{freehd\}\ |\!) \setminus \{nullpid\} \land \\
\qquad next^{k}(freehd) = p) \\
\quad next' = (next \oplus \{freelst \mapsto p?\}) \oplus \{p? \mapsto nullpid\} \land \\
\quad freelst' = p? \land \\
\quad serr! = sysok) \\
\quad \lor serr! = unusedpd)
\end{array}
$$

The precondition of *FreePID*2 is required by the refinement proofs. It is calculated as follows.

$$
\begin{array}{l}
\text{pre } \textit{FreePID2} \mathrel{\widehat{=}} \\
\quad freehd = nullpid \\
\quad \lor p? \notin next^{*} (\!|\ \{freehd\}\ |\!) \setminus \{nullpid\}
\end{array}
$$

This simplifies to

$p? \notin next^*(\!|\ \{freehd\}\ |\!) \setminus \{nullpid\}$ pre $FreePID2 \mathrel{\widehat=}$
$\quad freehd = nullpid$
$\quad \lor\ p? \notin next^*(\!|\ \{freehd\}\ |\!) \setminus \{nullpid\}$

This simplifies to

$$p? \notin next^*(\!|\ \{freehd\}\ |\!) \setminus \{nullpid\}$$

If $freehd = nullpid$, then $next^*(\!|\ \{freehd\}\ |\!) \setminus \{nullpid\} = \varnothing$, so $p?$ cannot be an element.

We continue with the statement and proof of the theorems required by the refinement process.

Theorem 8.

$\forall\, PTAB1;\ PTAB2;\ pr? : PPRIO;\ st? : PSTATE\ \bullet$
$\quad pre\ AddPD1 \land AbsPTAB2 \Rightarrow AddPD2$

PROOF. If $freehd = nullpid$, then $next^*(\!|\ \{freehd\}\ |\!) \setminus \{nullpid\} = \varnothing$, so $p?$ cannot be an element. □

Theorem 9.

$\forall\, PTAB1;\ PTAB2;\ pr? : PPRIO;\ st? : PSTATE\ \bullet$
$\quad pre\ AddPD1 \land AbsPTAB2 \Rightarrow AddPD2$

PROOF. The precondition of $AddPD1$ is $hdfree \neq nullpid$, while that of $AddPD2$ is $freehd \neq nullpid$. By the predicate of $AbsPTAB2$, $freehd = hdfree$.
□

Theorem 10.

$\forall\, PTAB1;\ PTAB1';\ PTAB2;\ PTAB2';\ pr? : PPRIO;\ st? : PSTATE$
$\qquad p! : PID;\ serr! : SYSERR\ \bullet$
$\quad pre\ AddPD1\ \land$
$\qquad AbsPTAB2\ \land$
$\qquad AbsPTAB2'\ \land$
$\qquad AddPD2$
$\quad \Rightarrow AddPD1$

PROOF. By the predicate of $AbsPTAB2$, $freehd \neq nullpid$ implies $hdfree \neq nullpid$, so $freehd = hdfree$. We note that $freehd \neq nullpid$ is pre $AddPD1$. The same identity, this time in the after state, as required by $AbsPTAB2'$, permits us to reason that $freehd' = hdfree' = p!$.

It is given that $next' = next(freehd)$. This implies that

dom $next' =$
$\quad (next^*(\!|\ \{freehd\}\ |\!) \setminus \{nullpid\}) \setminus \{freehd\}$
$\quad = next^+(\!|\ \{freehd\}\ |\!) \setminus \{nullpid\})$
$\quad = next^*(\!|\ \{next(freehd)\}\ |\!) \setminus \{nullpid\}$

and by the predicate of $AbsPTAB2$

$$(next^* (\! | \{freehd\} |\!) \setminus \{nullpid\}) \setminus \{freehd\} \\ = (\mathrm{dom}\, freech) \setminus \{freehd\}$$

By the definition of $\lhd$, $\mathrm{dom}\, freech \setminus \{freehd\}$ implies $freech \lhd \{freehd\}$. We may infer that $\mathrm{dom}\, next' = \mathrm{dom}\, freech \setminus \{freehd\} = freech \lhd \{freehd\}$ and, for the reason that $freehd = p!$, we have $freech \lhd \{p!\}$. The predicate of $AbsPTAB2'$ permits us to infer that, since $next' = freech \lhd \{p!\}$, $freech' = freech \lhd \{p!\}$.

For the remainder, we need to remember that the operation is defined in terms of sequential composition. The variables updated by the first component are unaffected by the second, so $next' = next''$. We can express the condition on $prio1$ and $prio2$ and on $state1$ and $state2$ as:

$$\forall p : PID \bullet \\ p! \notin next^* (\! | \{next(freehd)\} |\!) \setminus \{nullpid\} \Rightarrow \\ prio1(p) = prio2(p)$$

and

$$\forall p : PID \bullet \\ p! \notin next^* (\! | \{next(freehd)\} |\!) \setminus \{nullpid\} \Rightarrow \\ state1(p) = state2(p)$$

The antecedent in both cases has already been established, so $prio1(p) = prio2(p)$ and $state1(p) = state2(p)$ for all p not in the $next$ chain, so $prio1 \oplus \{p! \mapsto pr?\} = prio2 \oplus \{p! \mapsto pr?\}$ and $state1 \oplus \{p! \mapsto st?\} = state2 \oplus \{p! \mapsto st?\}$. In the first case, $prio2 \oplus \{p! \mapsto st?\} = prio2'$ by the predicate of $AddPD2$ and, by the predicate of $AbsPTAB2'$, $prio2'(p) = prio1'(p)$ for all p not in the modified $next$ chain. The case for $state1$ is similar. □

Theorem 11. $\forall PTAB1; PTAB2; p? : PID \bullet \mathrm{pre}\, FreePID1 \land AbsPTAB2 \Rightarrow \mathrm{pre}\, FreePID2$

PROOF. The precondition of $FreePID1$ is $p? \notin \mathrm{dom}\, freech$ and that of $FreePID2$ is $p? \notin next^* (\! | \{freehd\} |\!) \{nullpid\}$. By the predicate of $AbsPTAB2$, $\mathrm{dom}\, freech = next^* (\! | \{freehd\} |\!) \setminus \{nullpid\}$. The result is immediate. □

Theorem 12.

$$\forall PTAB1; PTAB1'; PTAB2; PTAB2'; p? : PID; serr! : SYSERR \bullet \\ \mathrm{pre}\, FreePID1 \land \\ AbsPTAB2 \land \\ AbsPTAB2' \land \\ FreePID2 \\ \Rightarrow FreePID1$$

PROOF. The result immediately follows from the identities in $AbsPTAB1$ and $AbsPTAB2$. □

The schemata from this last refinement have now been shown to be correct. They can be converted directly into executable code.

3.4 Process Queue

Process queues are used in a variety of places, most notably in semaphores. The queue type defined in this section is not the one used by the scheduler. The scheduler employs a priority queue that is, ultimately, implemented as a vector (one-dimensional array). The queue defined here will be implemented as a list of process descriptor references. comprising th The plan is to refine the top-level representation to a chain in *next*. This will require two steps of refinement.

As usual, we begin with the statement of the error schemata. In the case of *PROCESSQUEUE*, there is only one such schema. It reports the condition that the process queue is empty (presumably this condition is reported when an attempt to dequeue an element has been attempted).

$$\begin{array}{|l}
\hline
\textit{ProcessQueueEmpty} \\
\hline
serr! : SYSERR \\
\hline
serr! = emptyqueue \\
\hline
\end{array}$$

3.4.1 Top Level

This is a relatively straightforward specification of a FIFO queue. It uses a sequence as its basic container structure.

The queue state space is defined as follows. The queue itself is *procs*.

$$\begin{array}{|l}
\hline
\textit{PROCESSQUEUE} \\
\hline
PTAB \\
procs : \mathrm{iseq}\, PID \\
\hline
\mathrm{ran}\, procs \subset used \\
\hline
\end{array}$$

Note that the invariant is being used to enforce a global condition upon the queue, namely that *all* elements of the queue must also be elements of *used*—in other words, every process identifier in the queue must be that of a process that exists in the system.

$$\begin{array}{|l}
\hline
\textit{PROCESSQUEUEInit} \\
\hline
PROCESSQUEUE' \\
\hline
procs' = \langle\, \rangle \\
\hline
\end{array}$$

The initialisation is as one would expect. The queue is set to empty (to the empty sequence, that is). This initialisation trivially preserves the invariant.

The next operation is a predicate that evaluates to *true* when the queue, *procs*, is not empty.

IsNotEmptyPROCESSQUEUE
$\Xi PROCESSQUEUE$

$procs \neq \langle \rangle$

The operation to enqueue a process identifier on the queue is defined next. It is defined in the obvious fashion.

EnqueuePROCESSQUEUE
$\Delta PROCESSQUEUE$
$p? : PID$

$procs' = procs \frown \langle p? \rangle$

By substitution of identicals, the precondition of the enqueue operation is obtained.

$$\text{pre } EnqueuePROCESSQUEUE \mathrel{\widehat{=}} procs \frown \langle p? \rangle = procs \frown \langle p? \rangle$$

This version of the precondition is clearly equivalent to the following:

$$\text{pre } EnqueuePROCESSQUEUE \mathrel{\widehat{=}} true$$

The next few operations are concerned with dequeueing elements. In the present case, the operation is decomposed into a number of smaller operations, the first of which merely returns the head of the queue.

TheHeadOfPROCESSQUEUE
$\Xi PROCESSQUEUE$
$p! : PID$

$p! = head\ procs$

Note that this operation leaves the queue, *procs*, invariant.

The previous operation cannot be used in isolation because it does not include checks that the queue is empty (if $procs = \langle \rangle$, $head\ procs$ is undefined). Therefore, the following is defined.

$$\begin{aligned}
&HeadOfPROCESSQUEUE \mathrel{\widehat{=}}\\
&\quad (IsNonEmptyPROCESSQUEUE \land\\
&\qquad TheHeadOfPROCESSQUEUE \land\\
&\qquad SysOk)\\
&\quad \lor ProcessQueueEmpty
\end{aligned}$$

This composite operation expands into:

HeadOfPROCESSQUEUE

$$
\begin{array}{l}
\Xi PROCESSQUEUE \\
p! : PID \\
serr! : SYSERR \\
\hline
(procs \neq \langle\rangle \land \\
\quad p! = head\ procs \land \\
\quad serr! = sysok) \\
\lor\ serr! = emptyqueue
\end{array}
$$

We calculate the precondition, should it be required by refinement proofs.

$$
\begin{array}{l}
\mathrm{pre}\ HeadOfPROCESSQUEUE \mathrel{\widehat=} \\
\quad procs \neq \langle\rangle
\end{array}
$$

The dequeue operation is defined in terms of the removal of the first element of the queue. Removal is performed by the following schema.

DelHeadOfPROCESSQUEUE

$$
\begin{array}{l}
\Delta PROCESSQUEUE \\
\hline
procs' = tail\ procs
\end{array}
$$

This is another partial operation (partial in the sense that when $procs = \langle\rangle$, $tail\ procs$ is undefined). In order to make the operation useful, it is necessary to test whether the queue, *procs*, is empty. Therfore, the following is required:

$$
\begin{array}{l}
DequeuePROCESSQUEUE \mathrel{\widehat=} \\
\quad (IsNotEmptyPROCESSQUEUE \land \\
\qquad HeadOfPROCESSQUEUEU \land \\
\qquad DelHeadOfPROCESSQUEUE \land \\
\qquad SysOk) \\
\quad \lor\ ProcessQueueEmpty
\end{array}
$$

This composite operation expands into:

DequeuePROCESSQUEUE

$$
\begin{array}{l}
\Delta PROCESSQUEUE \\
p! : PID \\
serr! : SYSERR \\
\hline
(procs \neq \langle\rangle \land \\
\quad p! = head\ procs \land \\
\quad procs' = tail\ procs \land \\
\quad serr! = sysok) \\
\lor\ serr! = emptyqueue
\end{array}
$$

The precondition is easily calculated:

$$\text{pre}\,\mathit{DequeuePROCESSQUEUE} \mathrel{\widehat=} \\ \quad \mathit{procs} \neq \langle\,\rangle$$

3.4.2 Refinement One

In this subsection, we will refer to *PROCESSQUEUE*'s refinement as *PQ*1; this is just so that typing is reduced.

$$\begin{array}{|l}
\multicolumn{1}{l}{__\mathit{PQ1}____} \\
\mathit{hdproc}, \mathit{lstproc} : \mathit{GPID} \\
\mathit{procseq} : \mathit{PID} \rightarrowtail\!\!\!\!\!+ \mathit{GPID} \\
\hline
\mathit{hdproc} = \mathit{nullpid} \Leftrightarrow \mathit{lstproc} = \mathit{nullpid} \\
(\mathit{hdproc} = \mathit{nullpid} \land \\
\quad \mathit{lstproc} = \mathit{nullpid} \Leftrightarrow \\
\quad \text{dom}\,\mathit{procseq} = \langle\,\rangle) \\
(\mathit{hdproc} \neq \mathit{nullpid} \Leftrightarrow \\
\quad \mathit{hdproc} \in \text{dom}\,\mathit{procseq} \land \\
\quad \mathit{lstproc} \in \text{dom}\,\mathit{procseq} \land \\
\quad \text{dom}\,\mathit{procseq} \neq \varnothing) \\
\hline
\end{array}$$

The sequence *procs* is represented by *procseq* a partial injection between *PID* and *GPID*. It will be remembered that $GPID = PID \cup \{nullpid\}$. The function *procseq* is 1-1, so each element maps to *exactly one* element of *PID*, thus permitting each domain element exactly one successor; *procseq* is *partial* because not all process identifiers are in the queue at any one time (and because they enter and leave the queue). The function *procseq* models the ordered part of the sequence *procs*, as well as *procs*' rôle as a container. The value *nullpid* is the value that is always assigned to the last element of *procseq*. The two variables *hdproc* and *lstproc* represent the first and last elements of the sequence, so when $hdproc = lstproc$ and $hdproc = nullpid$, the queue is empty.

We will now give the abstraction relation. It is very much as one would expect and it is, once more, an identity.

$$\begin{array}{|l}
\multicolumn{1}{l}{__\mathit{AbsPQ1}____} \\
\mathit{PROCESSQUEUE} \\
\mathit{PQ1} \\
\hline
\text{dom}\,\mathit{procseq} = \text{ran}\,\mathit{procs} \\
\mathit{hdproc} = \mathit{nullpid} \Leftrightarrow \mathit{procs} = \langle\,\rangle \\
(\mathit{hdproc} \neq \mathit{nullpid} \land \mathit{hdproc} = \mathit{lstproc} \Leftrightarrow \mathit{head}\,\mathit{procs} = \mathit{last}\,\mathit{procs}) \\
\mathit{hdproc} \neq \mathit{nullpid} \Leftrightarrow \\
\quad \mathit{hdproc} = \mathit{head}\,\mathit{procs}
\end{array}$$

$$hdproc \neq nullpid \Leftrightarrow$$
$$\quad lstproc = last\ procs$$
$$hdproc \neq nullpid \Leftrightarrow$$
$$\quad procseq(lstproc) = nullpid$$
$$hdproc \neq nullpid \Leftrightarrow$$
$$\quad \forall i : 1 \mathrel{..} \#procs - 1 \bullet$$
$$\qquad procseq(procs(i)) = procs(i + 1))$$

The initialisation operation is as one would expect:

PQ1Init

$$PQ1'$$

$$hdproc' = nullpid$$
$$lstproc' = nullpid$$

It merely sets the queue to empty.

The emptiness of $PQ1$ is determined by the following operation:

IsNonEmptyPQ1

$$\Xi PQ1$$

$$hdproc \neq nullpid$$

The invariant of $PQ1$ states that $hdproc \neq nullpid$ implies $hdproc \neq lstproc$, which, in turn, implies that *procseq* is not empty.

The operation to enqueue a process identifier is slightly more complex than for the top-level state space. It is necessary to divide enqueueing into two cases: where the queue is empty (so the newly added element will be both first and last), and where the queue is not empty (and so the newly added element is the last).

EnqueuePQ1

$$\Delta PQ1$$
$$p? : PID$$

$$(hdproc = nullpid \land$$
$$\quad procseq' = \{p? \mapsto nullpid\} \land$$
$$\quad hdproc' = p? \land$$
$$\quad lstproc' = p?)$$
$$\lor ((\exists procseq'' : PID \rightarrowtail\!\!\!\!\!\!\twoheadrightarrow GPID \bullet$$
$$\quad procseq'' = procseq \oplus \{lstproc \mapsto p?\} \land$$
$$\quad procseq' = procseq'' \cup \{p? \mapsto nullpid\} \land$$
$$\quad lstproc' = p?)$$

The existential quantifier can be removed using the one-point rule and the schema becomes

$$
\begin{array}{|l}
\multicolumn{1}{l}{\_\_ \mathit{EnqueuePQ1} \_\_\_\_} \\
\Delta PQ1 \\
p? : PID \\
\hline
(hdproc = nullpid \land \\
\quad procseq' = \{p? \mapsto nullpid\} \land \\
\quad hdproc' = p? \land \\
\quad lstproc' = p?) \\
\lor (procseq' = (procseq \oplus \{lstproc \mapsto p?\}) \cup \{p? \mapsto nullpid\} \land \\
\quad lstproc' = p?) \\
\hline
\end{array}
$$

Rewriting the identities, the schema now becomes

$$
\begin{array}{|l}
\multicolumn{1}{l}{\_\_ \mathit{EnqueuePQ1} \_\_\_\_} \\
\Delta PQ1 \\
p? : PID \\
\hline
(hdproc = nullpid \land \\
\quad \{p? \mapsto nullpid\} = \{p? \mapsto nullpid\} \land \\
\quad p? = p? \land \\
\quad p? = p?) \\
\lor (procseq \oplus \{lstproc \mapsto p?\}) \cup \{p? \mapsto nullpid\} \\
\quad = (procseq \oplus \{lstproc \mapsto p?\}) \cup \{p? \mapsto nullpid\} \land \\
\quad p? = p?) \\
\hline
\end{array}
$$

To calculate the precondition, the fact that $lstproc \in \operatorname{dom} procseq$ allows us to infer that $\operatorname{dom} procseq \neq \varnothing$, so we have

$$
\begin{array}{l}
(hdproc = nullpid) \lor (hdproc \neq nullpid) \\
\quad \Leftrightarrow true
\end{array}
$$

More formally,

$$\operatorname{pre} EnqueuePQ1 \mathrel{\widehat=} true$$

The next few operations constitute the sub-operations needed to define the dequeue operation. These operations are directly analogous to those required by *PROCESSQUEUE* and are presented in the same order. First, the operation to return the head of the queue is defined.

$$
\begin{array}{|l}
\multicolumn{1}{l}{\_\_ \mathit{TheHeadOfPQ1} \_\_\_\_} \\
\Xi PQ1 \\
p! : PID \\
\hline
p! = hdproc \\
\hline
\end{array}
$$

In the present case, returning the head of the queue is as easy as it was at top level. The head is always *hdproc*, so $p! = hdproc$ returns the head element.

The above operation does not guard for the empty queue, so the following is required:

$$
\begin{aligned}
&\mathit{HeadOfPQ1} \mathrel{\widehat=} \\
&\quad (\mathit{IsNonEmptyPQ1} \land \mathit{TheHeadOfPQ1} \land \mathit{SysOk}) \\
&\quad \lor \mathit{ProcessQueueEmpty}
\end{aligned}
$$

It expands into:

$$
\begin{array}{|l}
\hline
\textit{HeadOfPQ1} \\
\Xi \mathit{PQ1} \\
p! : \mathit{PID} \\
\mathit{serr}! : \mathit{SYSERR} \\
\hline
(\mathit{hdproc} \neq \mathit{nullpid} \land \\
\qquad p! = \mathit{hdproc} \land \\
\qquad \mathit{serr}! = \mathit{sysok}) \\
\lor\ \mathit{serr}! = \mathit{emptyqueue} \\
\hline
\end{array}
$$

A simple and easy calculation yields the precondition.

$$\text{pre}\ \mathit{HeadOfPQ1} \mathrel{\widehat=} \mathit{hdproc} \neq \mathit{nullpid}$$

The operation to remove the head of the queue is a little more complex than in the top-level case.

$$
\begin{array}{|l}
\hline
\textit{DelHeadOfPQ1} \\
\Delta \mathit{PQ1} \\
\hline
\mathit{procseq}' = \mathit{procseq} \ntriangleleft \{\mathit{hdproc}\} \\
\mathit{hdproc}' = \mathit{procseq}(\mathit{hdproc}) \\
\hline
\end{array}
$$

The head element must be removed and the head pointer must be updated. In this case, if the queue becomes empty by the deletion of the head element, the last element must be updated to *nullpid*. Note that when hdproc' is bound to *nullpid*, the invariant requires that $\mathit{lstproc}'$ is also assigned to that value.

To make the operation safer, the following is defined. Schema $\mathit{DequeuePQ1}$ is similar to the corresponding operation defined for *PROCESSQUEUE*.

$$
\begin{aligned}
&\mathit{DequeuePQ1} \mathrel{\widehat=} \\
&\quad (\mathit{IsNonEmptyPQ1} \land \mathit{HeadOfPQ1} \land \mathit{DelHeadOfPQ1} \land \mathit{SysOk}) \\
&\quad \lor \mathit{ProcessQueueEmpty}
\end{aligned}
$$

The definition expands into:

$$
\begin{array}{|l}
\multicolumn{1}{l}{\textit{DequeuePQ1}} \\
\hline
\Delta PQ1 \\
p! : PID \\
serr! : SYSERR \\
\hline
(hdproc \neq nullpid \land \\
\qquad p! = hdproc \land \\
\qquad procseq' = procseq \lhd \{hdproc\} \land \\
\qquad hdproc' = procseq(hdproc) \land \\
\qquad serr! = sysok) \\
\lor\ serr! = emptyqueue \\
\hline
\end{array}
$$

(Again, it is worth noting that, by the invariant, the assignment of *nullpid* to *hdproc'* implies that *lstproc'* is also bound to *nullpid*.)

Substitution of identicals yields the following as the precondition:

$$hdproc \neq nullpid$$

by the invariant of $PQ1$, this is equivalent to

$$\mathrm{dom}\, procseq \neq \varnothing$$

To see the first version, it should be noted that $hdproc = lstproc \land lstproc' = nullpid$ has the implication that $hdproc \neq lstproc \land lstproc' = lstproc$. In any case, $hdproc = lstproc$ and $hdproc \neq nullpid$ conjointly imply that $lstproc \neq nullpid$, so $\mathrm{dom}\, procseq \neq \varnothing$, so the precondition is quite adequate.

Theorem 13. $\forall\, PROCESSQUEUE';\ PQ1' \bullet PQ1Init \land AbsPTAB1' \Rightarrow PQInit$

PROOF. By the invaraiant of $PQ1$, $hdproc' = nullpid \Leftrightarrow lstproc' = nullpid$. Since $hdproc' = nullpid$, it follows that $procs' = \langle\,\rangle$. The initialisation schema of PQ is precisely $procs' = \langle\,\rangle$. □

Theorem 14. $\forall\, PROCESSQUEUE;\ PQ1;\ p? : PID \bullet \mathrm{pre}\, Enqueue \land AbsPQ1 \Rightarrow \mathrm{pre}\, Enqueue1$

PROOF. Trivial ($true \Rightarrow true$). □

Theorem 15.

$$
\begin{array}{l}
\forall\, PROCESSQUEUE;\ PROCESSQUEUE';\ PQ1;\ PQ1';\ p? : PID \bullet \\
\quad \mathrm{pre}\, Enqueue \land \\
\qquad AbsPQ1 \land AbsPQ1' \land \\
\qquad EnqueuePQ1 \\
\quad \Rightarrow Enqueue
\end{array}
$$

PROOF. By the invariant of $PQ1$, $hdproc = nullpid$, which, by the predicate of $AbsPQ1$, implies that $\mathrm{dom}\, procseq = \varnothing$. The abstraction relation states that $\mathrm{dom}\, procseq = \mathrm{ran}\, procs$, so $procs = \langle\rangle$.

By the predicate of $AbsPQ1'$, $hdproc' = head\, procs'$ and $lstproc' = last\, procs'$. We have $hdproc' = p? \land lstproc' = p?$, so $head\, procs' = last\, procs' = p?$, so $procs' = \langle p? \rangle = \langle\rangle \frown \langle p? \rangle = procs \frown \langle p? \rangle$.

Otherwise, $\mathrm{dom}\, procseq \neq \langle\rangle$. We have $(procseq \oplus \{lstproc \mapsto p?\} \cup \{p? \mapsto nullpid\})(p?) = nullpid$ and this implies that $lstproc' = p?$ (since the invariant requires that $procseq(lstproc) = nullpid$). This, by the predicate of $AbsPQ1'$, implies that $last\, procs' = p?$. Since $hdproc \neq nullpid$, the last conjunct of the abstraction schema,

$$\forall i : 1 \mathrel{..} \#procs;\ p : PID \bullet \\ \quad procseq(procs(i)) = procs(i+1)$$

allows us to infer that $procs \frown \langle p? \rangle$ is equivalent to $procseq'$ and, therefore, $procs \frown \langle p? \rangle = procs'$ as required. □

Theorem 16.

$$\forall PROCESSQUEUE;\ PQ1 \bullet \\ \quad pre\, DequeuePROCESSQUEUE \land AbsPQ1 \Rightarrow pre\, DequeuePQ1$$

PROOF. The precondition of $DequeuePROCESSQUEUE$ is $procs \neq \langle\rangle$ and that of $DequeuePQ1$ is $\mathrm{dom}\, procseq \neq \varnothing$. The predicate of the $AbsPQ1$ states that $\mathrm{dom}\, procseq = \mathrm{ran}\, procs$, so $procs \neq \langle\rangle$ implies that $\mathrm{ran}\, procs \neq \varnothing$. Therefore, we have $\mathrm{ran}\, procs \neq \varnothing$ and $\mathrm{ran}\, procs = \mathrm{dom}\, procseq$, so $\mathrm{dom}\, procseq = \varnothing$. □

Theorem 17.

$$\forall PROCESSQUEUE;\ PROCESSQUEUE';\ PQ1;\ PQ1'; \\ \qquad p! : PID;\ serr! : SYSERR \bullet \\ \quad pre\, DequeuePROCESSQUEUE \land \\ \qquad AbsPQ1 \land AbsPQ1' \land \\ \qquad DequeuePQ1 \\ \quad \Rightarrow DequeuePROCESSQUEUE$$

PROOF. First of all, we have $hdproc \neq nullpid$. By the invariant, this implies that $\mathrm{dom}\, procseq \neq \varnothing$ which, in turn, by the abstraction relation, $AbsPQ1$, implies that $\mathrm{ran}\, procs \neq \varnothing$ or $procs \neq \langle\rangle$.

Now, by the predicate of $AbsPQ1$, $hdproc = head\, procs$, so $head\, procs = p?$.

We have $procseq \lhd \{hdproc\}$ implies $(\mathrm{dom}\, procseq) \setminus \{hdproc\}$. By the abstraction schema, $AbsPQ1$, $hdproc = head\, procs$, so we are entitled to infer that $\mathrm{ran}\, procs \setminus \{head\, procs\} = (\mathrm{dom}\, procseq) \setminus \{hdproc\}$, so $head\, procs$ is removed from $procs$ when $hdproc$ is. By the identity, $hdproc' = procseq(hdproc)$,

$head\,procs' = procseq(head\,procs) = procseq(procs(1)) = procs(1+1) = procs(2)$. This implies that $procs' = tail\,procs$.

We can check that the result has sufficient elements by observing that $\#(procseq \lhd \{hdproc\}) = (\#\operatorname{dom} procseq) - 1 = \#\, tail\,procs = \#procs - 1$. □

3.4.3 Refinement Two

In this refinement, the process queue is reduced to a queue in the process table. This refimenent uses the *next* attribute of the process descriptor. The refinement process is achieved by reducing the function *procseq* to the *next* sequence in a manner that should be relatively clear and familiar.

This refinement saves space in the kernel by reducing every FIFO queue of processes to a head and end pointer and a chain using the *next* process attribute.

Comparison of the following schema and *PQ*1 will reveal that the differences are more apparent than real. In the present case, the *next* function in *PTAB*2 takes over from *procseq*, thus permitting the abbreviation of the *PQ*2 schema.

$$
\begin{array}{l}
\textit{PQ2} \\
\hline
\textit{PTAB2} \\
hdq, endq : GPID \\
\hline
hdq = nullpid \Leftrightarrow endq = nullpid \\
hdq \neq nullpid \Leftrightarrow \\
\qquad next(endq) = nullpid \\
hdq \neq nullpid \Rightarrow \\
\qquad endq \in next^{*}(\!|\ \{hdq\}\ |\!) \\
\hline
\end{array}
$$

Here, again, the transitive closure of a relational image is employed to denote a subset.

The initialisation schema is as one would expect:

$$
\begin{array}{l}
\textit{PQ2Init} \\
\hline
PQ2' \\
\hline
hdq' = nullpid \\
endq' = nullpid \\
\hline
\end{array}
$$

The operation to enqueue a process identifier on *PQ*2 is defined. Just as was the case with *PQ*1, the predicate is divided into two cases: the case in which the queue is empty and that in which the queue is non-empty.

In the first case, the head and last variables must be assigned to $p?$, the identifier of the process being enqueued, and $p?$ must be added to *next*. Since $p?$ is now the last element of the chain, the image of $p?$ under *next* must be *nullpid*, so $\{p? \mapsto nullpid\}$ must be added to *next*. In the second case, the queue is not empty, so $p?$ must be added to the end of the queue. To satisfy the invariant, $next'(p?) = nullpid$ so $nullpid$ must be added to $next$, as well as $p?$; for the reason that there are two additions, not one, what amounts to a sequential composition is hidden within this schema.

$$
\begin{array}{l}
\textit{EnqueuePQ2} \\
\hline
\Delta PQ2 \\
p? : PID \\
\hline
(hdq = nullpid \land \\
\qquad hdq' = p? \land \\
\qquad endq' = p? \land \\
\qquad next' = next \oplus \{p? \mapsto nullpid\}) \\
\lor\ (endq' = p? \land \\
\qquad (\exists\, next'' : PID \to GPID \bullet \\
\qquad\qquad next'' = next \oplus \{endq \mapsto p?\} \land \\
\qquad\qquad next' = next'' \oplus \{p? \mapsto nullpid\}) \\
\hline
\end{array}
$$

The schema simplifies to

$$
\begin{array}{l}
\textit{EnqueuePQ2} \\
\hline
\Delta PQ2 \\
p? : PID \\
\hline
(hdq = nullpid \land \\
\qquad hdq' = p? \land \\
\qquad endq' = p? \land \\
\qquad next' = next \oplus \{p? \mapsto nullpid\}) \\
\lor\ (endq' = p? \land \\
\qquad next' = (next \oplus \{endq \mapsto p?\}) \oplus \{p? \mapsto nullpid\} \\
\hline
\end{array}
$$

Immediately, the precondition can be calculated and can be questioned:

$$
\text{pre}\ \textit{EnqueuePQ2} \mathrel{\widehat{=}} \\
\qquad hdq = nullpid \lor endq = p?
$$

It is clear that $endq = p?$ implies that $hdq \neq nullpid$, so the precondition can be further simplified to

$$\text{pre}\ \textit{EnqueuePQ2} \mathrel{\widehat{=}} true$$

The remaining operations are defined in the same order as for $PQ1$. The definitions are all straightforward and should be immediately obvious, given the definition of $PQ1$ and $PQ2$.

$$
\begin{array}{l}
\textit{IsNonEmptyPQ2} \\
\hline
\Xi PQ2 \\
\hline
hdq \neq nullpid \\
\hline
\end{array}
$$

The invariant of $PQ2$ states that $hdq = nullpid$ exactly when $endq = nullpid$ and in this case, the image of hdq through $next$ is the emtpy set, so the queue must be empty.

The operation to remove the head of the queue is defined as follows. As should now be familiar, this definition will have to be strengthened to account for the empty queue.

TheHeadOfPQ2

$$\Xi PQ2$$
$$p! : PID$$

$$p! = hdq$$

The strengthened definition now follows.

$$HeadOfPQ2 \mathrel{\widehat=} (IsNonEmptyPQ2 \land TheHeadOfPQ2) \lor ProcessQueueEmpty$$

DelHeadOfPQ2

$$\Delta PQ2$$

$$hdq' = next(hdq)$$
$$next' = next \oplus \{hdq \mapsto nullpid\}$$
$$hdq = endq \land endq' = nullpid$$

The operation to dequeue an element from the queue is now defined.

$$DequeuePQ2 \mathrel{\widehat=} (HeadOfPQ2 \land DelHeadOfPQ2 \land SysOk) \lor ProcessQueueEmpty$$

It expands into

DequeuePQ2

$$\Delta PQ2$$
$$p! : PID$$
$$serr! : SYSERR$$

$$\begin{array}{l} (hdq \neq nullpid \land \\ \quad p! = hdq \land \\ \quad hdq' = next(hdq) \land \\ \quad next' = next \oplus \{hdq \mapsto nullpid\} \land \\ \quad serr! = sysok) \\ \lor\ serr! = emptyqueue \end{array}$$

The precondition can now be calculated.

$$\begin{array}{l} \mathrm{pre}\ DequeuePQ2 \mathrel{\widehat=} \\ \quad \exists\, PQ2';\ p! : PID \bullet \\ \qquad hdq \neq nullpid \land \\ \qquad p! = hdq \land \\ \qquad hdq' = next(hdq) \land \\ \qquad next' = next \oplus \{hdq \mapsto nullpid\} \end{array}$$

This version simplifies to

$$
\begin{array}{l}
\text{pre}\, DequeuePQ2 \mathrel{\widehat{=}} \\
\quad hdq \neq nullpid \land \\
\quad hdq = hdq \land \\
\quad next(hdq) = next(hdq) \land \\
\quad next \oplus \{hdq \mapsto nullpid\} = next \oplus \{hdq \mapsto nullpid\}
\end{array}
$$

and then to

$$hdq \neq nullpid$$

A more general statement of the above is

$$next^{*}(\!|\ \{hdq\}\ |\!) \setminus \{nullpid\} \neq \varnothing$$

Therefore, we have

$$\text{pre}\, DequeuePQ2 \mathrel{\widehat{=}} next^{*}(\!|\ \{hdq\}\ |\!) \setminus \{nullpid\} \neq \varnothing$$

The abstraction relation is now defined. It should be obvious.

$$
\begin{array}{|l}
\hline
\textit{AbsPQ2} \\
PQ1 \\
PQ2 \\
\hline
hdq = hdprocs \\
endq = lastprocs \\
\text{dom}\, procseq \subseteq \text{dom}\, next \\
\text{ran}\, procseq \subseteq \text{ran}\, next \\
\text{dom}\, procq = next^{*}(\!|\ \{hdq\}\ |\!) \setminus \{nullpid\} \\
\forall p : PID \bullet \\
\quad p \in \text{dom}\, procseq \Rightarrow procseq(p) = next(p) \\
\hline
\end{array}
$$

Once again, this abstraction relation is mostly the identity. The two $\subseteq$ relations do not cause much of a problem and should not deter us from considering the above a function, for they are not the most important conjuncts.

Theorem 18. $\forall PQ1'; PQ2' \bullet PQ2Init \land AbsPQ2' \Rightarrow PQ1Init$

PROOF. By the abstraction relation, $hdq' = hdproc'$ and $endq' = lstproc'$, so $hdq' = nullpid = hdproc'$ and $endq' = nullpid = lstproc'$. □

Theorem 19. $\forall PQ1;\ PQ2;\ p? : PID \bullet \text{pre}\, EnqueuePQ1 \land AbsPQ2 \Rightarrow \text{pre}\, EnqueuePQ2$

PROOF. Both preconditions are *true* and *true* ⇒ *true* is, clearly, *true*. □

Theorem 20.

$\forall PQ1;\ PQ1';\ PQ2;\ PQ2';\ p? : PID \bullet$
$\quad pre\ EnqueuePQ1 \land$
$\quad\quad AbsPTAB2 \land$
$\quad\quad AbsPTAB2' \land$
$\quad\quad EnqueuePQ2$
$\quad \Rightarrow EnqueuePQ1$

PROOF. Immediate from the abstraction relations. □

Theorem 21.

$\forall PQ1;\ PQ2 \bullet$
$\quad pre\ DequeuePQ1 \land AbsPQ2 \Rightarrow pre\ DequeuePQ2$

PROOF. The precondition of pre $DequeuePQ1$ is $\mathrm{dom}\ procseq \neq \varnothing$ and that of pre $DequeuePQ2$ is $next^*(\!|\ \{hdq\}\ |\!)\{nullpid\} \neq \varnothing$. By the abstraction relation, $AbsPQ2$, we have $\mathrm{dom}\ procseq = next^*(\!|\ \{hdq\}\ |\!)\{nullpid\}$. □

Theorem 22.

$\forall PQ1;\ PQ1';\ PQ2;\ PQ2';\ p! : PID;\ serr! : SYSERR \bullet$
$\quad pre\ DequeuePQ1 \land$
$\quad\quad AbsPQ2 \land$
$\quad\quad AbsPQ2' \land$
$\quad\quad DequeuePQ2$
$\quad \Rightarrow DequeuePQ1$

PROOF. The precondition of $DequeuePQ1$ is $hdproc \neq nullpid$.

The interesting part of the proof is as follows. $hdq' = next(hdq) = next' = next \oplus \{hd \mapsto nullpid\}$. By the predicate of $AbsPQ2'$, $hdq' = hdproc'$, so

$hdproc'$
$\quad = next(hdq)$
$\quad = procseq(hdq)$
$\quad = procseq(hdproc).$

We have $next' = next \oplus \{hdq \mapsto nullpid\}$, which implies that $procseq \lhd \{hdproc\} = procseq'$.

To see this, consider

$\mathrm{dom}\ procseq$
$\quad = next^*(\!|\ \{hdq\}\ |\!) \setminus \{nullpid\}$
$\quad = next^*(\!|\ \{next(hdq)\}\ |\!) \setminus \{nullpid\}$
$\quad = next^+(\!|\ \{hdq\}\ |\!) \setminus \{nullpid\}$
$\quad = (next^*(\!|\ \{hdq\}\ |\!) \setminus \{nullpid\}) \setminus \{hdq\}$
$\quad = (\mathrm{dom}\ procseq) \setminus \{hdq\}$
$\quad = (\mathrm{dom}\ procseq) \setminus \{hdproc\}$ By definition of $\lhd$
$\quad = procseq \lhd \{hdproc\}$

□

The schemata from this last refinement have now been shown to be correct. They can be converted directly into executable code.

3.5 Priority Queue

In this kernel, the data structure used by the scheduler is a priority queue. This is to be interpreted as a sequence of process identifiers, ordered by priority. The operations are the usual ones (enqueue, dequeue). The enqueue operation requires either that the sequence is sorted or that the appropriate place to insert the new element is found.

In this section, the priority queue is specified in terms of a sequence. The aim is eventually to refine it to a chain running through the *next* function in $PTAB2$.

As usual, the error schemata are defined first. There are two cases: the case in which the queue is full and that in which it is empty.

PRIOQFull

$serr! : SYSERR$

$serr! = schedqfull$

PRIOQEmpty

$serr! : SYSERR$

$serr! = schedqempty$

3.5.1 Top Level

PRIOQ

$PTAB$
$pq : \text{seq}\, PID$
$maxs : \mathbb{N}_1$

$\# pq \leq maxs$
$\text{ran}\, pq \subset used$
$\forall i : 1 \mathinner{..} \# pq - 1 \bullet$
$\quad prio(pq(i)) \leq prio(pq(i+1))$

The queue container is *pq* and its maximum size is represented by *maxs*. The elements of *pq* are held in ascending order so that the highest priority corresponds to the lowest index. The invariant requires that all elements of *pq must* be elements of *used* and that *nullpid* is never an element of the queue. It is also required that the identifier of the idle process should never be an element of *pq* but this is harder to do.

The initialisation operation merely sets the maximum length of the queue and the queue to empty.

$$
\begin{array}{|l}
\hline
\textit{PRIOQInit} \\
\hline
\textit{PRIOQ}' \\
\textit{mps}? : \mathbb{N}_1 \\
\hline
\textit{maxs}' = \textit{mps}? \\
\textit{pq}' = \langle\, \rangle \\
\hline
\end{array}
$$

The following schema determines whether the priority queue is empty.

$$
\begin{array}{|l}
\hline
\textit{IsEmptyPRIOQ} \\
\hline
\Xi \textit{PRIOQ} \\
\hline
\textit{pq} = \langle\, \rangle \\
\hline
\end{array}
$$

The current head of the priority queue is returned as $p!$ by the next schema. The priority queue is a sequence, so the *head* operation is applicable.

$$
\begin{array}{|l}
\hline
\textit{PRIOQHd} \\
\hline
\Xi \textit{PRIOQ} \\
p! : \textit{PID} \\
\hline
p! = \textit{head}\ \textit{pq} \\
\hline
\end{array}
$$

When enqueueing an element, it is necessary to be able to obtain the last element of the queue. The following schema represents an operation that does just that.

$$
\begin{array}{|l}
\hline
\textit{PRIOQLast} \\
\hline
\Xi \textit{PRIOQ} \\
p! : \textit{PID} \\
\hline
p! = \textit{last}\ \textit{pq} \\
\hline
\end{array}
$$

The operation of enqueueing an element is quite involved. This is because the queue is sorted by priority. The first part of the operation enqueues a new element on the head of the queue. This operation is performed whenever the priority of the new element, $p?$, is higher (lower in value, note) than the current head of *pq*.

$$
\begin{array}{|l}
\hline
\textit{PRIOQEnqueueHd} \\
\hline
\Delta \textit{PRIOQ} \\
p? : \textit{PID} \\
\hline
\langle p? \rangle \frown \textit{pq} = \textit{pq}' \\
\hline
\end{array}
$$

Next, the operation to enqueue an element at the end of the queue is defined. This operation is performed whenever the priority of the new element $p?$ is lower (higher in value, note) than the current last element of pq.

PRIOQEnqueueLast

$$\Delta PRIOQ$$
$$p? : PID$$

$$pq' = pq \frown \rangle p? \rangle$$

If the queue is empty and a new element is to be added, the following schema defines the operation to enqueue on an empty queue.

PRIOQAddSingleton

$$\Delta PRIOQ$$
$$p? : PID$$

$$pq' = \langle p? \rangle$$

Finally, there is the operation that inserts a new element, $p?$, into a queue. When this operation is used, it is known that the priority of $p?$ is less than that of the head of pq and greater than its last element.

PRIOQInsert

$$\Delta PRIOQ$$
$$p? : PID$$

$$\exists\, s_1, s_2 : \mathrm{seq}\, PID \mid s_1 \neq \langle\rangle \wedge s_2 \neq \langle\rangle \wedge s_1 \frown s_2 = pq \bullet$$
$$prio(last\, s_1) < prio(p?) \wedge$$
$$prio(p?) \leq prio(head\, s_2) \wedge$$
$$pq' = s_1 \frown \langle p? \rangle \frown s_2$$

This operation divides the queue, pq, into two parts, s_1 and s_2, where the last element of s_1 has a priority higher than that of $p?$ and the first element of s_2 has a priority that is at least that of $p?$.

The next schema defines one of the priority tests required by the enqueue operation. It is satisfied when the priority of $p?$, the element to be enqueued, is higher (i.e., of lower value) than that of the head of pq. In this case, $p?$ should be added to the head of the queue using *PRIOQEnqueueHd*.

ShouldAddPRIOQHd

$$\Xi PRIOQ$$
$$p? : PID$$

$$prio(p?) \leq prio(head\, pq)$$

The following schema defines a predicate that is satisfied when the priority of the last element of pq is lower than that of $p?$. When this is the case, $p?$ is added to pq at the end using *PRIOQEnqueueLast*.

$$\begin{array}{|l}
\multicolumn{1}{l}{\textit{ShouldAddPRIOQLast}}\\
\Xi PRIOQ\\
p? : PID\\
\hline
prio(last\ pq) < prio(p?)
\end{array}$$

The specification of the enqueue operation is given by the *PRIOQEnqueue* schema.

$$\begin{array}{l}
PRIOQEnqueue \mathrel{\widehat=}\\
\quad (CanEnqueuePRIOQ \land\\
\qquad ((IsEmptyPRIOQ \land PRIOQAddSingleton) \lor\\
\qquad\quad (ShouldAddPRIOQHd \land PRIOQEnqueueHd) \lor\\
\qquad\quad (ShouldAddPRIOQLast \land PRIOQEnqueueLast) \lor\\
\qquad\quad PRIOQInsert) \land\\
\qquad SysOk)\\
\quad \lor PRIOQFull
\end{array}$$

This schema expands as follows:

$$\begin{array}{|l}
\multicolumn{1}{l}{\textit{PRIOQEnqueue}}\\
\Delta PRIOQ\\
p? : PID\\
serr! : SYSERR\\
\hline
(\#pq < maxs \land\\
\quad ((pq = \langle\rangle \land pq' = \langle p?\rangle) \lor\\
\qquad (prio(p?) \leq prio(head\ pq) \land pq' = \langle p?\rangle \frown pq) \lor\\
\qquad (prio(last\ pq) < prio(p?) \land pq' = pq \frown \langle p?\rangle) \lor\\
\qquad (\exists s_1, s_2 : \mathrm{seq}\ PID \mid s_1 \neq \langle\rangle \land s_2 \neq \langle\rangle \land s_1 \frown s_2 = pq \bullet\\
\qquad\quad prio(last\ s_1) < prio(p?) \land\\
\qquad\quad prio(p?) \leq prio(head\ s_2) \land\\
\qquad\quad pq' = s_1 \frown (\langle p?\rangle \frown s_2)) \land\\
\qquad serr! = sysok)\\
\lor\ serr! = schedqfull
\end{array}$$

Before moving on, it is necessary to prove a small result. This will help us at a later stage. The result is similar to the "implicit" precondition.

Lemma 1. $\forall p : PID \bullet p \in ran\ pq' \Rightarrow p \in used$

PROOF. By the invariant of *PRIOQ*, $\mathrm{ran}\ pq \subset used$. Since there is no modification of *used* in the schema of *PRIOQEnqueue*, so the addition of $p?$ to pq does not affect *used*. Therefore, for the invariant to hold, it is necessary for $p? \in used$, so $\mathrm{ran}(pq \frown \langle p?\rangle) \subset used$.

Moreover, the invariant of $PTAB$ states that $\mathrm{dom}\, prio = used$. For this operation to be well-defined, $prio(p)?)$ must also be well-defined. For this to be the case, $p? \in used$, as required. □

The enqueue operation will be refined in the next subsection, so its precondition must be calculated.

$$
\begin{array}{l}
\mathrm{pre}\, PRIOQEnqueue \mathrel{\widehat=} \\
\quad \exists\, PRIOQ';\ serr! : SYSERR \bullet \\
\qquad (\#pq < maxs \land \\
\qquad\quad ((pq = \langle\rangle \land pq' = \langle p? \rangle) \lor \\
\qquad\qquad (prio(p?) \leq prio(head\, pq) \land pq' = \langle p? \rangle \frown pq) \lor \\
\qquad\qquad (prio(last\, pq) < prio(p?) \land pq' = pq \frown \langle p? \rangle) \lor \\
\qquad\qquad (\exists\, s_1, s_2 : \mathrm{seq}\, PID \mid s_1 \neq \langle\rangle \land s_2 \neq \langle\rangle \land s_1 \frown s_2 = pq \bullet \\
\qquad\qquad\quad prio(last\, s_1) < prio(p?) \land \\
\qquad\qquad\quad prio(p?) \leq prio(head\, s_2) \land \\
\qquad\qquad\quad pq' = s_1 \frown (\langle p? \rangle \frown s_2)) \land \\
\qquad\qquad serr! = sysok) \\
\qquad\quad \lor\ serr! = schedqfull
\end{array}
$$

Since $serr!$ does not contribute to the precondition and for the reason that $\mathrm{pre}(A \lor B) \Leftrightarrow \mathrm{pre}\, A \lor \mathrm{pre}\, B$, we can omit all occurrences of this variable immediately. This gives

$$
\begin{array}{l}
\mathrm{pre}\, PRIOQEnqueue \mathrel{\widehat=} \\
\quad \exists\, PRIOQ';\ serr! : SYSERR \bullet \\
\qquad (\#pq < maxs \land \\
\qquad\quad ((pq = \langle\rangle \land pq' = \langle p? \rangle) \lor \\
\qquad\qquad (prio(p?) \leq prio(head\, pq) \land pq' = \langle p? \rangle \frown pq) \lor \\
\qquad\qquad (prio(last\, pq) < prio(p?) \land pq' = pq \frown \langle p? \rangle) \lor \\
\qquad\qquad (\exists\, s_1, s_2 : \mathrm{seq}\, PID \mid s_1 \neq \langle\rangle \land s_2 \neq \langle\rangle \land s_1 \frown s_2 = pq \bullet \\
\qquad\qquad\quad prio(last\, s_1) < prio(p?) \land \\
\qquad\qquad\quad prio(p?) \leq prio(head\, s_2) \land \\
\qquad\qquad\quad pq' = s_1 \frown (\langle p? \rangle \frown s_2)))
\end{array}
$$

We can now simplify the precondition schema to

$$
\begin{array}{l}
\mathrm{pre}\, PRIOQEnqueue \mathrel{\widehat=} \\
\quad (\#pq < maxs \land \\
\qquad (pq = \langle\rangle \\
\qquad \lor\ (prio(p?) \leq prio(head\, pq)) \\
\qquad \lor\ (prio(last\, pq) < prio(p?)) \\
\qquad \lor\ (\exists\, s_1, s_2 : \mathrm{seq}\, PID \mid s_1 \neq \langle\rangle \land s_2 \neq \langle\rangle \land s_1 \frown s_2 = pq \bullet \\
\qquad\qquad prio(last\, s_1) < prio(p?) \land \\
\qquad\qquad prio(p?) \leq prio(head\, s_2))))
\end{array}
$$

It is clear that

$$
\begin{array}{l}
(prio(p?) \leq prio(head\ pq)) \\
\lor\ (prio(last\ pq) < prio(p?)) \\
\lor\ (\exists s_1, s_2 : \mathrm{seq}\ PID \mid s_1 \neq \langle\rangle \land s_2 \neq \langle\rangle \land s_1 \frown s_2 = pq \bullet \\
\qquad prio(last\ s_1) < prio(p?) \land \\
\qquad prio(p?) \leq prio(head\ s_2))
\end{array}
$$

implies that $prio(p?) \in PPRIO$ and that $pq \neq \langle\rangle$. It is also clear that $prio(p?) \in PPRIO \Leftrightarrow true$, so this part reduces to $pq \neq \langle\rangle$. Plugging this back into the rest of the precondition, we obtain

$$\#pq < maxs \land (pq = \langle\rangle \lor pq \neq \langle\rangle)$$

or

$$
\begin{array}{l}
\#pq < maxs \land true \Leftrightarrow \\
\qquad \#pq < maxs
\end{array}
$$

So, we may conclude that

$$\mathrm{pre}\ PRIOQEnqueue \mathrel{\widehat{=}} \#pq < maxs$$

The operation to remove an element of *pq* is defined by the following schema:

PRIOQRemove

$$
\begin{array}{l}
\Delta PRIOQ \\
p? : PID \\
\hline
\exists s_1, s_2 : \mathrm{seq}\ PID \bullet \\
\qquad s_1 \frown \langle p? \rangle \frown s_2 = pq \land \\
\qquad s_1 \frown s_2 = pq'
\end{array}
$$

Unfortunately, it is not possible to remove an element from an empty queue. Indeed, it is necessary to define an operation that first tests whether *pq* is empty. The reason for this is that when the scheduler's queue is empty, the idle process must be scheduled.

$$
\begin{array}{l}
DelPRIOQElem \mathrel{\widehat{=}} \\
\qquad \neg\ IsEmptyPRIOQ \land PRIOQRemove
\end{array}
$$

This operation expands into the following schema:

DelPRIOQElem

$$
\begin{array}{l}
\Delta PRIOQ \\
p? : PID \\
\hline
pq \neq \langle\rangle \\
\exists s_1, s_2 : \mathrm{seq}\ PID \bullet \\
\qquad s_1 \frown \langle p? \rangle \frown s_2 = pq \land \\
\qquad s_1 \frown s_2 = pq'
\end{array}
$$

This is an operation that will be used by the scheduler, so will be refined. For this reason, its precondition must be calculated.

$$\begin{array}{l}
\text{pre } \mathit{DelPRIOQElem} \mathrel{\widehat{=}} \\
\quad \exists\, \mathit{PRIOQ}' \bullet \\
\qquad pq \neq \langle\,\rangle \land \\
\qquad (\exists\, s_1, s_2 : \text{seq}\, \mathit{PID} \bullet \\
\qquad\quad s_1 \frown \langle p? \rangle \frown s_2 = pq \land \\
\qquad\quad s_1 \frown s_2 = pq')
\end{array}$$

This simplifies to:

$$\begin{array}{l}
\text{pre } \mathit{DelPRIOQElem} \mathrel{\widehat{=}} \\
\quad pq \neq \langle\,\rangle \land p? \in \text{ran}\, pq
\end{array}$$

The second conjunct is justified as follows.I It is clear that $\text{ran}\, pq = \text{ran}(s_1 \frown \langle p? \rangle \frown s_2)$ by the definition of $\frown$ and of sequence. Therefore, let $\text{ran}\, s_1 = R_1$ and $\text{ran}\, s_2 = R_2$. It follows that, since $p? \in \text{ran}\, pq$, $p? \notin R_1 \cup R_2$, so $\text{ran}\, pq = R_1 \cup R_2 \cup \{p?\}$.

Finally, we observe that $p? \in \text{ran}\, pq$ implies $pq \neq \langle\,\rangle$, so

$$\text{pre } \mathit{DelPRIOQElem} \mathrel{\widehat{=}} p? \in \text{ran}\, pq$$

The scheduler requires that it must be possible to inspect the head of *pq* and also to remove *pq*'s head as a separate operation. Dequeueing is, therefore, composed of these two operations. The following schema defines an operation to remove the head of *pq*. Since *pq* is just a sequence, the *tail* operation is perfect for our needs.

$$\begin{array}{|l}
\hline
\mathit{PRIOQDelHd} \\
\hline
\Delta \mathit{PRIOQ} \\
\hline
pq' = \mathit{tail}\; pq \\
\hline
\end{array}$$

For the precondition, calculation yields

$$\begin{array}{l}
\mathit{tail}\; pq = \mathit{tail}\; pq \\
\quad \Leftrightarrow \mathit{true}
\end{array}$$

However, this is not of much use. The stronger precondition, namely $pq \neq \langle\,\rangle$ is preferred.

The dequeue operation is composed of returning the head and then removing it. This is the core of the following definition.

$$\begin{array}{l}
\mathit{PRIOQDequeue} \mathrel{\widehat{=}} \\
\quad (\neg\, \mathit{IsEmptyPRIOQ} \land \mathit{PRIOQHd} \land \mathit{PRIOQDelHd} \land \mathit{SysOk}) \\
\quad \lor\, \mathit{PRIOQEmpty}
\end{array}$$

The interesting part is the second conjunct:

$$
\begin{array}{|l}
\hline
\textit{PRIOQHd} \wedge \textit{PRIOQDelHd} \\
\Delta \textit{PRIOQ} \\
p! : \textit{PID} \\
\hline
p! = \textit{head}\ pq \\
pq' = \textit{tail}\ pq \\
\hline
\end{array}
$$

Again, calculation yields the weak precondition, *true*. A moment's thought shows that the precondition $pq \neq \langle\rangle$ also implies the operation.

The entire schema expands into

$$
\begin{array}{|l}
\hline
\textit{PRIOQDequeue} \\
\Delta \textit{PRIOQ} \\
p! : \textit{PID} \\
\textit{serr}! : \textit{SYSERR} \\
\hline
(pq \neq \langle\rangle \wedge \\
\qquad p! = \textit{head}\ pq \wedge \\
\qquad pq' = \textit{tail}\ pq \wedge \\
\qquad \textit{serr}! = \textit{sysok}) \\
\vee\ \textit{serr}! = \textit{schedqempty} \\
\hline
\end{array}
$$

Schema *PRIOQDequeue*'s precondition can now be calculated. We first have

$$
\begin{array}{l}
\text{pre}\ \textit{PRIOQDequeue} \mathrel{\widehat{=}} \\
\quad \exists\, \textit{PRIOQ}'; p! : \textit{PID}; \textit{serr}! : \textit{SYSERR} \bullet \\
\qquad (pq \neq \langle\rangle \wedge \\
\qquad\qquad p! = \textit{head}\ pq \wedge \\
\qquad\qquad pq' = \textit{tail}\ pq \wedge \\
\qquad\qquad \textit{serr}! = \textit{sysok}) \\
\qquad \vee\ \textit{serr}! = \textit{schedqempty}
\end{array}
$$

This simplifies to:

$$
\begin{array}{l}
\text{pre}\ \textit{PRIOQDequeue} \mathrel{\widehat{=}} \\
\quad (pq \neq \langle\rangle \wedge \\
\qquad \textit{head}\ pq = \textit{head}\ pq \wedge \\
\qquad \textit{tail}\ pq = \textit{tail}\ pq \wedge \\
\qquad \textit{sysok} = \textit{sysok}) \\
\quad \vee\ \textit{schedqempty} = \textit{schedqempty}
\end{array}
$$

This is clearly equivalent to

$$
\begin{array}{l}
\text{pre}\ \textit{PRIOQDequeue} \mathrel{\widehat{=}} \\
\quad pq \neq \langle\rangle
\end{array}
$$

3.5.2 Refinement One

The first refinement consists of replacing the sequence by a function. The domain of the function is a numeric type, $1 \mathrel{..} maxs1$, where $maxs1 = maxs$ or the maximum length of the sequence, pq, in the top-level specification (the maximum number of elements in this queue, too). The range is PID, as was the case in the specification. Therefore, the domain permits the function to represent as many values as the original sequence. The variable $maxs1$ records the maximum size of the queue at this level, $pq1$. The final variable is $nxtp$, the index of the next element to be added to $pq1$ (which can be thought of as a one-dimensional array or vector).

PRIOQ1

$pq1 : 1 \mathrel{..} maxs1 \rightarrow PID$
$maxs1 : \mathbb{N}_1$
$nxtp : 1 \mathrel{..} maxs + 1$

$\forall i : 1 \mathrel{..} nxtp - 2 \bullet$
$\quad prio1(pq1(i)) \leq prio(pq1(i + 1))$

Note that $pq1$ is ordered by priority. The condition that every element of $pq1$ is in *used* (or, equivalently, at this level, not in the free chain) is not repeated. The reason for this is that it can be inferred from the equivalent schema in the specification.

The initialisation operation is defined next.

PRIOQInit1

$PRIOQ1'$
$mps? : \mathbb{N}_1$

$maxs1' = mps?$
$nxtp' = 1$

The initialisation consists only of setting the maximum length of the queue and setting the initial value of $nxtp$ to 1 (i.e., the beginning of the vector).

The next schema defines a predicate that is true when $pq1$ is empty.

IsEmptyPRIOQ1

$\Xi PRIOQ1$

$nxtp = 1$

This operation's predicate should be compared with the initialisation schema. In both cases $nxtp$ takes the value 1. The scheme adopted here is that the element is assigned to the element indexed by $nxtp$ which is then incremented.

The following few operations are concerned with accessing the first and last elements of the queue, with determining whether the element to be added to the queue has an appropriate priority and with inserting a new element into the queue. The operations correspond directly to those in the specification as presented in the last section.

$$
\begin{array}{|l}
\textit{PRIOQHd1} \\
\hline
\Xi \mathit{PRIOQ1} \\
p! : \mathit{PID} \\
\hline
p! = pq1(1) \\
\hline
\end{array}
$$

$$
\begin{array}{|l}
\textit{PRIOQLast1} \\
\hline
\Xi \mathit{PRIOQ1} \\
p! : \mathit{PID} \\
\hline
p! = pq1(nxtp - 1) \\
\hline
\end{array}
$$

The next schema defines an operation that is satisfied when the length of the queue is less than the maximum.

$$
\begin{array}{|l}
\textit{CanEnqueuePRIOQ1} \\
\hline
\Xi \mathit{PRIOQ1} \\
\hline
nxtp < maxs + 1 \\
\hline
\end{array}
$$

As in the specification, this operation enqueues an element at the head of the queue (because it has a priority higher than any queue element).

$$
\begin{array}{|l}
\textit{PRIOQEnqueueHd1} \\
\hline
\Delta \mathit{PRIOQ1} \\
p? : \mathit{PID} \\
\hline
pq1' = pq1 \oplus \{1 \mapsto p?\} \\
\hline
\end{array}
$$

The following operation enqueues an element at the end of the queue (because it has a priority lower than any in the queue).

$$
\begin{array}{|l}
\textit{PRIOQEnqueueLast1} \\
\hline
\Delta \mathit{PRIOQ1} \\
p? : \mathit{PID} \\
\hline
pq1' = pq1 \oplus \{nxtp \mapsto p?\} \\
nxtp' = nxtp + 1 \\
\hline
\end{array}
$$

The next schema defines an operation that moves the elements of a vector up by one place. Note that this is an example of how arrays (vectors) and functions are considered equivalent.

$$
\begin{array}{|l}
\hline
\textit{MovePRIOQUp1} \\
\Delta PRIOQ1 \\
\hline
\forall i : 1 \mathrel{..} nxtp - 1 \bullet \\
\qquad pq1' = pq1 \oplus \{i + 1 \mapsto pq1(i)\} \\
nxtp' = nxtp + 1 \\
\hline
\end{array}
$$

Finally, we are able to define the enqueue operation. As with the specification, the operation is defined in small parts that are composed to form the final operation. First, the operation to enqueue on the head is defined.

$$
\begin{array}{l}
PRIOQEnqueueHd1 \mathrel{\widehat{=}} \\
\qquad MovePRIOQUp1 \mathbin{\raise.4ex\hbox{$\scriptscriptstyle\circ$}\kern-.1em\raise-.1ex\hbox{$\scriptscriptstyle 9$}} PRIOQEnqueueHd1
\end{array}
$$

This expands into:

$$
\begin{array}{|l}
\hline
\textit{PRIOQEnqueueHd1} \\
\Delta PRIOQ1 \\
p? : PID \\
\hline
\exists pq1'' : 1 \mathrel{..} maxs1 \rightarrow PID \bullet \\
\qquad (\forall i : 1 \mathrel{..} nxtp - 1 \bullet \\
\qquad\qquad pq1'' = pq1 \oplus \{i + 1 \mapsto pq1(i)\}) \land \\
\qquad nxtp' = nxtp + 1 \land \\
pq1' = pq1'' \oplus \{1 \mapsto p?\} \\
\hline
\end{array}
$$

If the queue is empty, the following is used to enqueue the new element.

$$
\begin{array}{|l}
\hline
\textit{PRIOQAddSingleton1} \\
\Delta PRIOQ1 \\
p? : PID \\
\hline
pq1' = \{nxtp \mapsto p?\} \\
nxtp' = nxtp + 1 \\
\hline
\end{array}
$$

This schema defines the inverse of the *MovePRIOQUp1* schema. In this case, the elements of the vector are moved down one place and the first element is over-written.

$$
\begin{array}{|l}
\hline
\textit{PRIOQMoveUpFrom} \\
\Delta PRIOQ1 \\
where? : 1 \mathrel{..} maxs1 \\
\hline
\forall j : where? + 1 \mathrel{..} nxtp - 1 \bullet \\
\qquad pq1' = pq1 \oplus \{j + 1 \mapsto pq1(j)\} \\
\hline
\end{array}
$$

The next operation sets the $i + 1$st element to $p?$. This is used when inserting a new element into the queue.

$$\begin{array}{|l}
\textit{PRIOQSetIthSucc} \\
\hline
\Delta PRIOQ1 \\
p? : PID \\
i? : 1 \mathrel{..} maxs1 \\
\hline
pq1' = pq1 \oplus \{i + 1 \mapsto p?\} \\
\hline
\end{array}$$

This schema defines a predicate that is true when the new element should be enqueued on the head of $pq1$ (i.e, when it has a higher priority than the current head—recall that higher priority is equivalent to *lower* value for the priority).

$$\begin{array}{|l}
\textit{ShouldAddPRIOQHd1} \\
\hline
\Xi PRIOQ1 \\
p? : PID \\
\hline
prio1(p?) \leq prio1(pq1(1)) \\
\hline
\end{array}$$

The test for adding at the end is defined next.

$$\begin{array}{|l}
\textit{ShouldAddPRIOQLast1} \\
\hline
\Xi PRIOQ1 \\
p? : PID \\
\hline
prio1(pq1(nxtp - 1)) < prio1(p?) \\
\hline
\end{array}$$

Next comes a predicate that is true when the priority of the element to be added to the queue is somewhere between those of the head and the last elements.

$$\begin{array}{|l}
\textit{PRIOQInsertMidPoss1} \\
\hline
\Xi PRIOQ1 \\
p? : PID \\
i? : 1 \mathrel{..} maxs1 \\
\hline
prio1(pq1(i)) < prio1(p?) \\
prio1(p?) \leq prio1(pq1(i + 1)) \\
\hline
\end{array}$$

Associated with this predicate is the *PRIOQInsert1* operation. This operation inserts a new element somewhere between the head and the last elements, based upon its priority.

$$\begin{array}{l}
PRIOQInsert1 \mathrel{\widehat{=}} \\
\quad \exists\, i : 1 \mathrel{..} nxtp - 2 \bullet \\
\qquad PRIOQInsertMidPoss1[i/i?] \land \\
\qquad (PRIOQMoveUpFrom[i/where?] \mathbin{;} PRIOQSetIthSucc[i/i?]) \land \\
\qquad nxtp' = nxtp + 1
\end{array}$$

This expands into:

$$
\begin{array}{l}
\Delta PRIOQ1 \\
p? : PID \\
\hline
\exists\, i : 1 \mathrel{..} nxtp - 2 \bullet \\
\quad prio1(pq1(i)) < prio1(p?) \wedge \\
\quad prio1(p?) \leq prio1(pq1(i+1)) \wedge \\
\quad (\exists\, pq1'' : 1 \mathrel{..} maxs1 \rightarrow PID \bullet \\
\qquad (\forall\, j : i+1 \mathrel{..} nxtp - 1 \bullet \\
\qquad\quad pq1'' = pq1 \oplus \{j+1 \mapsto pq1(j)\}) \wedge \\
\qquad pq1' = pq1'' \oplus \{i+1 \mapsto p?\}) \wedge \\
\quad nxtp' = nxtp + 1
\end{array}
$$

Finally, the enqueue operation can be defined. It is given by the following formula:

$$
\begin{array}{l}
PRIOQEnqueue1 \mathrel{\widehat=} \\
\quad (CanEnqueuePRIOQ1 \wedge \\
\qquad ((IsEmptyPRIOQ1 \wedge PRIOQAddSingleton1) \vee \\
\qquad\quad (ShouldAddPRIOQHd1 \wedge PRIOQEnqueueHd1) \vee \\
\qquad\quad (ShouldAddPRIOQLast1 \wedge PRIOQEnqueueLast1) \vee \\
\qquad\quad PRIOQInsert1) \wedge \\
\qquad SysOk) \\
\quad \vee\ PRIOQFull
\end{array}
$$

This complex definition expands into the following schema

$$
\begin{array}{l}
\underline{\quad PRIOQEnqueue1 \quad} \\
\Delta PRIOQ1 \\
p? : PID \\
serr! : SYSERR \\
\hline
(nxtp < maxs1 + 1 \wedge \\
\quad ((nxtp = 1 \wedge pq1' = \{1 \mapsto p?\} \wedge nxtp' = 2) \vee \\
\qquad (prio1(p?) \leq prio1(pq1(1)) \wedge \\
\qquad\quad (\exists\, pq1'' : 1 \mathrel{..} maxs1 \rightarrow PID \bullet \\
\qquad\qquad (\forall\, i : 1 \mathrel{..} nxtp - 1 \bullet \\
\qquad\qquad\quad pq1'' = pq1 \oplus \{i+1 \mapsto pq1(i)\}) \wedge \\
\qquad\qquad nxtp' = nxtp + 1 \wedge pq1' = pq1'' \oplus \{1 \mapsto p?\})) \\
\qquad \vee\ (prio1(pq1(nxtp - 1)) < prio1(p?) \wedge \\
\qquad\quad pq1' = pq1 \oplus \{nxtp \mapsto p?\} \wedge nxtp' = nxtp + 1) \\
\qquad \vee\ (\exists\, i : 1 \mathrel{..} nxtp - 2 \bullet \\
\qquad\quad prio1(pq1(i)) < prio(p?) \wedge prio1(p?) \leq prio1(pq1(i+1)) \wedge \\
\qquad\quad (\exists\, pq1'' : 1 \mathrel{..} maxs1 \rightarrow PID \bullet
\end{array}
$$

$$
\begin{array}{l}
\quad\quad(\forall j : i+1 \mathinner{..} nxtp - 1 \bullet \\
\quad\quad\quad pq1'' = pq1 \oplus \{j+1 \mapsto pq1(j)\}) \wedge \\
\quad\quad pq1' = pq1'' \oplus \{i+1 \mapsto p?\}) \wedge nxtp' = nxtp + 1)) \wedge \\
serr! = sysok) \vee serr! = schedqfull
\end{array}
$$

The schema's predicate can be simplified in a fairly obvious way. After simplification, the schema becomes

PRIOQEnqueue1

$$
\begin{array}{l}
\Delta PRIOQ1 \\
p? : PID \\
serr! : SYSERR \\
\hline
(nxtp \leq maxs1 \wedge \\
\quad ((nxtp = 1 \wedge pq1' = \{1 \mapsto p?\} \wedge nxtp' = 2) \vee \\
\quad\quad (prio1(p?) \leq prio1(pq1(1)) \wedge \\
\quad\quad\quad (\forall i : 1 \mathinner{..} nxtp - 1 \bullet \\
\quad\quad\quad\quad pq1' = (pq1 \oplus \{i+1 \mapsto pq1(i)\}) \oplus \{1 \mapsto p?\}) \wedge \\
\quad\quad\quad\quad nxtp' = nxtp + 1) \vee \\
\quad\quad (prio1(pq1(nxtp - 1)) < prio1(p?) \wedge \\
\quad\quad\quad pq1' = pq1 \oplus \{nxtp \mapsto p?\} \wedge \\
\quad\quad\quad nxtp' = nxtp + 1) \vee \\
\quad\quad (\exists i : 1 \mathinner{..} nxtp - 2 \bullet \\
\quad\quad\quad prio1(pq1(i)) < prio1(p?) \wedge prio1(p?) \leq prio1(pq1(i+1)) \wedge \\
\quad\quad\quad (\forall j : i+1 \mathinner{..} nxtp - 1 \bullet \\
\quad\quad\quad\quad pq1' = (pq1 \oplus \{j+1 \mapsto pq1(j)\}) \oplus \{i+1 \mapsto p?\} \wedge \\
\quad\quad\quad nxtp' = nxtp + 1)) \wedge \\
\quad\quad serr! = sysok) \\
\vee\ serr! = schedqfull
\end{array}
$$

The enqueue operation is a refinement, so we need to calculate its precondition. It is given by the following predicate:

$$
\begin{array}{l}
\mathrm{pre}\, PRIOQEnqueue1 \mathrel{\widehat=} \\
\quad \exists PRIOQ1'; serr! : SYSERR \bullet \\
\quad\quad (nxtp \leq maxs1 \wedge \\
\quad\quad\quad ((nxtp = 1 \wedge pq1' = \{1 \mapsto p?\} \wedge nxtp' = 2) \vee \\
\quad\quad\quad (prio1(p?) \leq prio1(pq1(1)) \wedge \\
\quad\quad\quad\quad (\exists pq1'' : 1 \mathinner{..} maxs1 \rightarrow PID \bullet \\
\quad\quad\quad\quad\quad (\forall i : 1 \mathinner{..} nxtp - 1 \bullet \\
\quad\quad\quad\quad\quad\quad pq1'' = pq1 \oplus \{i+1 \mapsto pq1(i)\}) \wedge \\
\quad\quad\quad\quad\quad\quad nxtp' = nxtp + 1 \wedge \\
\quad\quad\quad\quad\quad\quad pq1' = pq1'' \oplus \{1 \mapsto p?\})) \vee
\end{array}
$$

$$
\begin{array}{l}
\quad (prio1(pq1(nxtp - 1)) < prio1(p?) \land \\
\qquad pq1' = pq1 \oplus \{nxtp \mapsto p?\} \land \\
\qquad nxtp' = nxtp + 1) \lor \\
\quad (\exists\, i : 1 \mathrel{..} nxtp - 2 \bullet \\
\qquad prio1(pq1(i)) < prio1(p?) \land prio1(p?) \leq prio1(pq1(i + 1)) \land \\
\qquad (\exists\, pq1'' : 1 \mathrel{..} maxs1 \rightarrow PID \bullet \\
\qquad\quad (\forall\, j : i + 1 \mathrel{..} nxtp - 1 \bullet \\
\qquad\qquad pq1'' = pq1 \oplus \{j + 1 \mapsto pq1(j)\}) \land \\
\qquad\qquad pq1' = pq1'' \oplus \{i + 1 \mapsto p?\} \land \\
\qquad\qquad nxtp' = nxtp + 1)) \land \\
\quad serr! = sysok) \\
\lor\, serr! = schedqfull
\end{array}
$$

Since $serr!$ makes no contribution to the precondition, we can omit it. The second outermost disjunct can be immediately deleted by this fact. The inner occurrence can be removed by noting that $\mathrm{pre}(A \lor B) \Leftrightarrow \mathrm{pre}\,A \lor \mathrm{pre}\,B$ and $serr! = sysok$, by the one-point rule, is $sysok = sysok$ (a tautology). So, simplifying the existential quantifier involving $pq1''$ using the one-point rule

$$
\begin{array}{l}
\mathrm{pre}\, PRIOQEnqueue1 \mathrel{\widehat=} \\
\quad \exists\, PRIOQ1';\ serr! : SYSERR \bullet \\
\qquad (nxtp \leq maxs1 \land \\
\qquad\quad ((nxtp = 1 \land pq1' = \{1 \mapsto p?\} \land nxtp' = 2) \lor \\
\qquad\quad (prio1(p?) \leq prio1(pq1(1)) \land \\
\qquad\qquad (\forall\, i : 1 \mathrel{..} nxtp - 1 \bullet \\
\qquad\qquad\quad pq1' = (pq1 \oplus \{i + 1 \mapsto pq1(i)\}) \oplus \{1 \mapsto p?\}) \land \\
\qquad\qquad\quad nxtp' = nxtp + 1 \land \\
\qquad\quad (prio1(pq1(nxtp - 1)) < prio1(p?) \land \\
\qquad\qquad pq1' = pq1 \oplus \{nxtp \mapsto p?\} \land \\
\qquad\qquad nxtp' = nxtp + 1) \lor \\
\qquad\quad (\exists\, i : 1 \mathrel{..} nxtp - 2 \bullet \\
\qquad\qquad prio1(pq1(i)) < prio1(p?) \land prio1(p?) \leq prio1(pq1(i + 1)) \land \\
\qquad\qquad (\forall\, j : i + 1 \mathrel{..} nxtp - 1 \bullet \\
\qquad\qquad\quad pq1' = (pq1 \oplus \{j + 1 \mapsto pq1(j)\}) \oplus \{i + 1 \mapsto p?\} \land \\
\qquad\qquad\qquad nxtp' = nxtp + 1))))
\end{array}
$$

Next, the one-point rule is applied repeatedly to give

$$
\begin{array}{l}
\mathrm{pre}\, PRIOQEnqueue1 \mathrel{\widehat=} \\
\quad nxtp \leq maxs1 \land \\
\quad (nxtp = 1 \land \\
\quad \lor\, (prio1(p?) \leq prio1(pq1(1))) \\
\quad \lor\, (prio1(pq1(nxtp - 1)) < prio1(p?)) \\
\quad \lor\, (\exists\, i : 1 \mathrel{..} nxtp - 2 \bullet \\
\qquad prio1(pq1(i)) < prio1(p?) \land prio1(p?) \leq prio1(pq1(i + 1))))
\end{array}
$$

Again, the 3 disjuncts

$$
\begin{array}{l}
(prio1(p?) \leq prio1(pq1(1))) \\
\vee\ (prio1(pq1(nxtp - 1)) < prio1(p?)) \\
\vee\ (\exists\, i : 1 \,..\, nxtp - 2 \bullet \\
\qquad prio1(pq1(i)) < prio1(p?) \wedge prio1(p?) \leq prio1(pq1(i + 1)))
\end{array}
$$

jointly imply that $prio1(p) \in PPRIO$. This permits us to reduce these disjuncts to *true*. In addition, they also imply that $nxtp > 1$ for the reason that there must be at least one element in $pq1$ for any of these comparisons to succeed.

We therefore have at this stage $nxtp < maxs1 + 1 \wedge (nxtp = 1 \wedge nxtp > 1)$. The second conjunct implies that $nxtp \geq 1$ and we can infer that $1 \leq nxtp < maxs1 + 1$ or $1 \leq nxtp \leq maxs1$. This is equivalent to $nxtp \in 1 \,..\, maxs1$, which is the definition of $nxtp$'s type, so reduces to *true*.

The precondition, therefore, reduces to

$$\text{pre}\, PRIOQEnqueue1 \mathrel{\widehat{=}} nxtp \leq maxs1$$

We must now handle the operations that remove elements from the priority queue. The first operation to be defined removes a specified element, $p?$, from the queue. If $p?$ is not present in the queue, the operation just terminates, otherwise it removes $p?$ and adjusts the insertion point ($nxtp$).

PRIOQRemove1

$$
\begin{array}{l}
\Delta PRIOQ1 \\
p? : PID \\
\hline
\exists\, i : 1 \,..\, nxtp - 1 \bullet \\
\qquad pq1(i) = p? \wedge \\
\qquad (\forall\, j : i + 1 \,..\, nxtp - 1 \bullet \\
\qquad\qquad pq1' = pq1 \oplus \{j - 1 \mapsto pq1(j)\}) \wedge \\
\qquad nxtp' = nxtp - 1
\end{array}
$$

The operation to remove the head of the priority queue is defined next and is

PRIOQDelHd1

$$
\begin{array}{l}
\Delta PRIOQ1 \\
\hline
nxtp' = nxtp - 1 \\
\forall\, i : 1 \,..\, nxtp - 2 \bullet \\
\qquad pq1' = pq1 \oplus \{i \mapsto pq1(i + 1)\}
\end{array}
$$

The precondition of this operation is as now given.

$$\text{pre}\, PRIOQDelHd1 \mathrel{\widehat{=}} nxtp > 1$$

This can be seen from the following. If $nxtp = 1$, there are no elements in $pq1$, so the operation must fail.

The operation performing the dequeue operation is the following

$$
\begin{array}{l}
PRIOQDequeue1 \mathrel{\widehat=} \\
\quad (\neg\ IsEmptyPRIOQ1 \land PRIOQHd1 \land PRIOQDelHd1 \land SysOk) \\
\quad \lor\ PRIOQEmpty
\end{array}
$$

The entire schema, after expansion, is

$$
\begin{array}{|l}
\hline
\textit{PRIOQDequeue1} \\
\Delta PRIOQ1 \\
p! : PID \\
serr! : SYSERR \\
\hline
(nxtp > 1 \land \\
\quad p! = pq1(1) \land \\
\quad (\forall i : 1 \mathinner{..} nxtp - 2 \bullet \\
\qquad pq1' = pq1 \oplus \{i \mapsto pq1(i+1)\}) \land \\
\quad nxtp' = nxtp - 1 \land \\
\quad serr! = sysok) \\
\lor\ serr! = schedqempty \\
\hline
\end{array}
$$

The precondition is

$$
\begin{array}{l}
\mathrm{pre}\ PRIOQDequeue1 \mathrel{\widehat=} \\
\quad \exists\ PRIOQ1';\ p! : PID;\ serr! : SYSERR \bullet \\
\qquad (nxtp > 1 \land \\
\qquad p! = pq1(1) \land \\
\qquad (\forall i : 1 \mathinner{..} nxtp - 2 \bullet \\
\qquad\quad pq1' = pq1 \oplus \{i \mapsto pq1(i+1)\}) \land \\
\qquad nxtp' = nxtp - 1 \land \\
\qquad serr! = sysok) \\
\quad \lor\ serr! = schedqempty
\end{array}
$$

For well-advertised reasons, this immediately reduces to

$$
\begin{array}{l}
\mathrm{pre}\ PRIOQDequeue1 \mathrel{\widehat=} \\
\quad \exists\ PRIOQ1';\ p! : PID;\ serr! : SYSERR \bullet \\
\qquad (nxtp > 1 \land \\
\qquad p! = pq1(1) \land \\
\qquad (\forall i : 1 \mathinner{..} nxtp - 2 \bullet \\
\qquad\quad pq1' = pq1 \oplus \{i \mapsto pq1(i+1)\}) \land \\
\qquad nxtp' = nxtp - 1)
\end{array}
$$

This now reduces to

$$
\begin{array}{l}
\text{pre}\, PRIOQDequeue1 \mathrel{\widehat=} \\
\quad \exists\, PRIOQ1';\ p! : PID;\ serr! : SYSERR \bullet \\
\quad\quad (nxtp > 1 \land \\
\quad\quad pq1(1) = pq1(1) \land \\
\quad\quad (\forall\, i : 1 \mathinner{\ldotp\ldotp} nxtp - 2 \bullet \\
\quad\quad\quad pq1 \oplus \{i \mapsto pq1(i+1)\} = pq1 \oplus \{i \mapsto pq1(i+1)\}) \land \\
\quad\quad nxtp - 1 = nxtp - 1)
\end{array}
$$

or

$$\text{pre}\, PRIOQDequeue1 \mathrel{\widehat=} nxtp > 1$$

This can be expressed as the proposition that the queue is not empty.

The abstraction relation is now presented.

$$
\begin{array}{|l}
\hline
AbsPRIOQ1 \\
PRIOQ \\
PRIOQ1 \\
\hline
maxs1 = maxs \\
nxtp = \#pq + 1 \\
\forall\, i : 1 \mathinner{\ldotp\ldotp} nxtp - 1 \bullet \\
\quad pq(i) = pq1(i) \\
\hline
\end{array}
$$

The important parts are the second and third conjuncts. The second conjunct, $nxtp = \#pq + 1$ states that $nxtp - 1$ is always the current length of the queue; $nxtp$ always points to the next free element in the queue vector or has the value of the maximum length of the queue plus one. The third conjunct states that all the elements in $pq1$ are also in pq and all elements appear in the same order. The abstraction relation inherits the constraint that all elements in pq and $pq1$ must be elements of $used$ (or, equally, not on the free chain).

Theorem 23.

$$
\begin{array}{l}
\forall\, PRIOQ';\ PRIOQ1 \bullet \\
\quad PRIOQInit1 \land AbsPRIOQ1' \Rightarrow PRIOQInit
\end{array}
$$

PROOF. By the abstraction relation, $maxs' = maxs1'$, and by the predicate of $PRIOQInit1$, $maxs1' = mps?$, so $maxs' = mps?$. Also by the abstraction relation, $nxtp' = \#pq' + 1$; by the predicate of $PRIOQInit1$, $nxtp' = 1 = \#pq' + 1$, so $\#pq' = 0$. $\square$

Theorem 24.

$$
\begin{array}{l}
\forall\, PRIOQ;\ PRIOQ1;\ p? : PID \bullet \\
\quad \text{pre}\, PRIOQEnqueue \land AbsPRIOQ \Rightarrow \text{pre}\, PRIOQEnqueue1
\end{array}
$$

PROOF. We have

$$\text{pre}\, PRIOQEnqueue \mathrel{\widehat=} \#pq < maxs$$

and

$$\text{pre}\, PRIOQEnqueue1 \mathrel{\widehat=} nxtp < maxs1 + 1$$

.

By the predicate of $AbsPRIOQ$, $maxs = maxs1$ and $nxtp = \#pq + 1$. Since $\#pq = nxtp - 1$, and $\#pq < maxs$, then $nxtp - 1 < maxs1$ and $nxtp < maxs1 + 1$, as required. □

Theorem 25.

$$\begin{array}{l} \forall\, PRIOQ;\ PRIOQ';\ PRIOQ1;\ PRIOQ1';\ p? : PID;\ serr! : SYSERR \bullet \\ \quad pre\, PRIOQEnqueue \land \\ \qquad AbsPRIOQ1 \land AbsPRIOQ1' \land \\ \qquad PRIOQEnqueue1 \\ \quad \Rightarrow PRIOQEnqueue \end{array}$$

PROOF. The precondition of $PRIOQEnqueue$ is $\#pq < maxs$.

Now, $nxtp < maxs + 1$, by $AbsPRIOQ1$, $maxs1 = maxs$ and $nxtp = \#pq + 1$, substituting, we obtain $\#pq + 1 < maxs + 1 \Leftrightarrow \#pq < maxs$.

Given $nxtp = 1$, by $absPRIOQ1$, $pq = \langle\,\rangle$, for $nxtp = 1$ implies $\#pq = 0$. It is clear that $\{1 \mapsto p?\} = pq1'(1) = p?$, and we note that $\{1 \mapsto p?\} = \langle p?\rangle$, If $\{1 \mapsto p?\} = pq1'(1) = p?$ and, by $AbsPRIOQ1'$, $pq1'(i) = pq'(i)$, for all $i \in 1 \mathinner{..} \#pq'$, so $pq1'(1) = pq'(1) = head\, pq'$ by the definition of $head$. Now, $nxtp' = 2$, which implies that $\#pq' = 1$ since $nxtp' = \#pq' + 1$ by the predicate of $AbsPRIOQ1'$ and we have $2 = nxtp' = \#pq' + 1$, so $nxtp' - 1 = \#pq' = 1$. Therefore, $pq' = \langle p?\rangle$.

By $AbsPTAB1$, $prio1(p) = prio(p)$, provided that $p \in used$. By the predicate of $AbsPRIOQ1$, $pq1(1) = pq(1) = head\, pq$. From this, we have $prio1(p?) \leq prio(pq1(1)) \Leftrightarrow prio(p?) \leq prio(head\, pq)$. It should be noted that $last\, pq$ can be handled in a similar fashion, noting that $nxtp = \#pq + 1$, so $nxtp - 1 = \#pq$ and $pq(\#pq) = last\, pq$. This allows us to infer that $prio1(pq1(nxtp - 1)) < prio1(p?) \Leftrightarrow prio(last\, pq) < prio(p?)$. Now, returning to $prio(p?) \leq prio(head\, pq)$, we have, by $AbsPRIOQ1$,

$$\begin{array}{l} \forall\, i : 1 \mathinner{..} nxtp - 1 \bullet \\ \quad pq1' = (pq1 \oplus \{i + 1 \mapsto pq1(i)\})) \oplus \{1 \mapsto p?\} \\ \qquad = (pq \oplus \{i + 1 \mapsto pq(i)\}) \oplus \{1 \mapsto p?\} \end{array}$$

and

$$\begin{array}{l} (pq \oplus \{i + 1 \mapsto pq(i)\}) \oplus \{1 \mapsto p?\} \\ \quad = \{1 \mapsto p?\} \oplus (pq \oplus \{i + 1 \mapsto pq(i)\}) \\ \quad = \langle p?\rangle \frown pq \end{array}$$

The second line is justified by the fact that the domains of the two maplets are disjoint. More specifically, $\{i + 1 \mapsto pq(i)\}$ is undefined at 1.

In the next case, we have $pq1' = pq1 \oplus \{nxtp \mapsto p?\}$. By *AbsPRIOQ*1, $nxtp = \#pq + 1$, so, by *AbsPRIOQ*1′, $pq1'(nxtp) = pq'(nxtp) = pq'(\#pq + 1)$ and $p? = pq1'(nxtp) = pq'(nxtp) = pq'(\#pq + 1)$ which implies that $pq' = pq \frown \langle p? \rangle$.

By the arguments given above, it can be inferred that the condition (the guard) is correct. We may then concentrate on the quantified formulæ. Note that the existential has range $1 \mathrel{..} nxtp - 2$, so $pq1(1)$ and $pq1(nxtp - 1)$ are not to be altered.

The predicate $prio1(pq1(i)) < prio(p?) \wedge prio1(p?) \leq prio1(pq1(i + 1))$ divides $pq1$ into two segments, one with priority $< prio(p?)$ and one with priority $> prio(p?)$. Neither segment can, then, be empty. We can, therefore, consider two segments, s_1 and s_2 of pq, s.t. $s_1 \neq \langle\rangle$ and $s_2 \neq \langle\rangle$ and s.t. $s_1 \frown s_2 = pq$. This is valid according to the conjunct of *AbsPRIOQ*1 which states $\forall i : 1 \mathrel{..} \#pq \bullet pq1(i) = pq(i)$.

Now, let $\#s_1 = i$, so $pq(i) = s_1(i) = last\ s_1$ and $pq1(i + 1) = (s_1 \frown s_2)(i + 1) = pq(i + 1) = head\ s_2$. Let $j = i + 1$, then the quantified formula implies that $pq1'(j) = pq1(j)$ and, in particular, that $pq1'(i+1) = pq1(i)$ and $pq1'(nxtp) = pq1(nxtp - 1)$ and we now have three segments:

$$pq1'(k) = pq1(k), 1 \leq k \leq i$$
$$pq1'(i + 1) = pq1(i + 1)$$
$$pq1'(l) = pq1(i + 1 + n), i + 1 \leq n \leq nxtp - 1$$

For the central segment, it can be seen from the universal that $pq1'(i+1) = p?$ (i.e., $\{i + 1 \mapsto p?\}$), so by *AbsPRIOQ*1′, $pq'(i + 1) = p?$. We can identify the first component, $pq1'(k) = pq1(k)$, with s_1 since $k < nxtp - 1$ and $pq1(k) = pq(k)$ by *AbsPRIOQ*1. The third segment is s_2 by *AbsPRIOQ*1. Since *AbsPRIOQ*1′ requires that $pq1'(i) = pq'(i)$, $i \in 1 \mathrel{..} \#pq'$, we have $pq1' = s_1 \frown \langle p? \rangle \frown s_2 = pq'$.

Finally, $nxtp' = nxtp + 1$ in each case. By *AbsPRIOQ*1, $nxtp = \#pq + 1$, $nxtp + 1 = \#pq + 2$ which implies that $\#pq' = \#pq + 1$.

□

Theorem 26. $\forall\ PRIOQ;\ PRIOQ1 \bullet \text{pre}\ PRIOQDequeue \wedge AbsPRIOQ1 \Rightarrow \text{pre}\ PRIOQDequeue1$

Proof. The preconditions are as follows:

$$\text{pre}\ PRIOQDequeue \mathrel{\widehat{=}} pq \neq \langle\rangle$$
$$\text{pre}\ PRIOQDequeue1 \mathrel{\widehat{=}} nxtp > 1$$

By the abstraction relation, the predicate of *AbsPRIOQ*1, $nxtp = \#pq + 1$, so $pq \neq \langle\rangle$ implies that $\#pq > 0$. If $\#pq = 0$, then $nxtp = 1$. Therefore, $pq \neq \langle\rangle$ implies that $nxtp > 1$. □

Theorem 27.

$\forall PRIOQ; PRIOQ'; PRIOQ1; PRIOQ1'; p! : PID; serr! : SYSERR \bullet$
$\quad pre\ PRIOQDequeue \land$
$\qquad AbsPRIOQ1 \land$
$\qquad AbsPRIOQ1' \land$
$\qquad PRIOQDequeue1$
$\quad \Rightarrow PRIOQDequeue$

PROOF. The preconditon of $PRIOQDequeue$ is $pq \neq \langle\rangle$.

Now, $nxtp > 1$, impiles that $pq \neq \langle\rangle$. By $AbsPRIOQ1$, $nxtp = \#pq + 1$, so if $\#pq = 0$, $nxtp = 1$ and $\#pq = 0$ implies that $pq = \langle\rangle$. Therefore, it follows that $nxtp > 1$ implies $pq \neq \langle\rangle$.

The assignment, $p! = pq1(1)$ is equivalent to $p! = pq(1) = head\ pq$. The predicate of $AbsPRIOQ1$ states that $\forall i : 1..\#pq \bullet pq1(i) = pq(i)$, so $pq1(1) = pq(1)$ and, using the definition of $head$, it is immediate that $pq(1) = head\ pq$.

Now, the quantified formala can be handled, $\forall i : 1..\#pq \bullet pq1(i) = pq(i)$, as follows.

$$\begin{aligned}
&\forall i : 1 \mathrel{..} nxtp - 2 \bullet \\
&\quad pq1' = pq \oplus \{i \mapsto pq1(i+1)\} \\
&\qquad = pq \oplus \{i \mapsto pq1(i+1)\} \\
&\qquad = pq \oplus \{i \mapsto pq(i+1)\} \\
&\qquad = tail\ pq
\end{aligned}$$

To see this, consider that

$$\begin{aligned}
&(tail\ pq)(1) = pq(2) \\
&\ldots (tail\ pq)(\#\ tail\ pq) = pq(\#tailpq + 1) \\
&\qquad = pq(\#pq)
\end{aligned}$$

since $\#pq = \#\ tail\ pq + 1$. By the predicate of $AbsPRIOQ1'$, $pq1' = pq'$ for all $i \in 1 \mathrel{..} \#pq'$, so $pq1' = tail\ pq = pq'$. □

Theorem 28. $\forall PRIOQ; PRIOQ1 \bullet pre\ PRIOQDelHD \land AbsPRIOQ1 \Rightarrow pre\ PRIOQDelHd1$

PROOF. The two preconditions are

$\text{pre}\ PRIOQDelHd \mathrel{\widehat{=}} pq \neq \langle\rangle$

$\text{pre}\ PRIOQDelHd1 \mathrel{\widehat{=}} nxtp > 1$

The proof is concluded in a manner similar to the proof of Theorem 26 □

Theorem 29.

$\forall PRIOQ; PRIOQ'; PRIOQ1; PRIOQ1' \bullet$
$\quad pre\ PRIOQDelHd \land$
$\qquad AbsPRIOQ1 \land$
$\qquad AbsPRIOQ1' \land$
$\qquad PRIOQDelHd1$
$\quad \Rightarrow PRIOQDelHd$

PROOF. The definition of *PRIOQDelHd* is

$$\begin{array}{|l}\Delta PRIOQ \\ \hline pq' = tail\ pq\end{array}$$

and it precondition is $pq \neq \langle\rangle$.

The definition of *PRIOQDelHd*1 is

$$\begin{array}{|l}\Delta PRIOQ1 \\ \hline nxtp' = nxtp - 1 \\ \forall i : 1 \mathinner{..} nxtp - 2 \bullet \\ \quad pq1' = pq1 \oplus \{i \mapsto pq1(i+1)\}\end{array}$$

and its precondition is $nxtp > 1$.

It should be clear that

$$\forall i : 1 \mathinner{..} nxtp - 2 \bullet \\ \quad (tail\ pq)(i) = pq1 \oplus \{i \mapsto pq1(i+1)\}$$

so $pq1' = tail\ pq = pq'$. To see this consider the following:

$$(tail\ pq)(1) = pq(2) = pq1(2)$$

$$\vdots$$

$$last(tail\ pq) = tail\ pq(\#\ tail\ pq) = pq1(nxtp - 1)$$

□

The result of this refinement is a collection of schemata that can be translated to executable code. This produces a priority queue implemented in terms of a vector, a perfectly adequate implementation. However, we continue with a second refinement which will refine the vector to a list threaded through the *next* function (i.e., a list of process identifiers or, equivalently, a list of process descriptors).

3.5.3 Refinement Two

In this refinement, the queue elements are now stored in *next*, a component of *PTAB*2. In many real-time kernels, the ready queue (which is really the priority queue) is implemented as a small vector of process identifiers or references. The vector implementation saves a few operations and is justified by the fact that only a few processes are usually in the ready queue at any time. The advantages of the current approach are that any number of processes can be in the ready queue and that it occupies no extra space whatsoever;

access and update of the two structures take very roughly the same number of instructions on most contemporary processors.

The state space for this refinement is the following.

$$
\begin{array}{|l}
\textit{PRIOQ2} \\
\hline
\textit{PTAB2} \\
\textit{qhd}, \textit{qlst} : \textit{GPID} \\
\textit{qlen} : \mathbb{N} \\
\textit{maxs2} : \mathbb{N}_1 \\
\hline
\textit{qlen} \leq \textit{maxs2} \land \textit{qhd} = \textit{nullpid} \Leftrightarrow \textit{qlst} = \textit{nullpid} \\
\textit{qhd} = \textit{nullpid} \Leftrightarrow \textit{qlen} = 0 \land \textit{qhd} \neq \textit{nullpid} \Leftrightarrow \textit{next}(\textit{qlst}) = \textit{nullpid} \\
\textit{qhd} \neq \textit{nullpid} \Leftrightarrow \textit{qlst} \in \textit{next}^* (\!| \{\textit{qhd}\} |\!) \setminus \{\textit{nullpid}\}
\end{array}
$$

The variables *qhd* and *qlst* represent the head and last elements of the ready queue; the length of the queue is represented by *qlen*. The maximum length to which the ready queue can grow is determined by *maxs2*. The invariant states that the length of the queue must always be less than $maxs2 + 1$ and that when the queue is empty, $qhd = qlst = nullpid$. There is more that could be included in the invariant but the above is quite adequate for our current needs.

The initialisation schema is defined next. Given the last paragraph, the predicate of *PRIOQInit2* should be clear.

$$
\begin{array}{|l}
\textit{PRIOQInit2} \\
\hline
\textit{PRIOQ2}' \\
\textit{mps?} : \mathbb{N}_1 \\
\hline
\textit{qhd}' = \textit{qlst}' = \textit{nullpid} \\
\textit{maxs2}' = \textit{mps?} \\
\textit{qlen}' = 0
\end{array}
$$

The operations now follow in the same order as they were presented for *PRIOQ1*, so nothing will be said about them unless there is a point of interest.

$$
\begin{array}{|l}
\textit{IsEmptyPRIOQ2} \\
\hline
\Xi \textit{PRIOQ2} \\
\hline
\textit{qlen} = 0
\end{array}
$$

The approach adopted to the definition of the enqueue operation is the same as in the last subsection.

$$
\begin{array}{|l}
\textit{PRIOQHd2} \\
\hline
\Xi \textit{PRIOQ2} \\
\textit{p!} : \textit{PID} \\
\hline
\textit{p!} = \textit{qhd}
\end{array}
$$

$$
\begin{array}{|l}
\hline
\textit{PRIOQLast2} \\
\Xi PRIOQ2 \\
p! : PID \\
\hline
p! = qlst \\
\hline
\end{array}
$$

$$
\begin{array}{|l}
\hline
\textit{CanEnqueuePRIOQ2} \\
\Xi PRIOQ2 \\
\hline
qlen < maxs2 \\
\hline
\end{array}
$$

$$
\begin{array}{|l}
\hline
\textit{PRIOQEnqueueHd2} \\
\Delta PRIOQ2 \\
p? : PID \\
\hline
qhd' = p? \\
next' = next \oplus \{p? \mapsto qhd\} \\
qlen' = qlen + 1 \\
\hline
\end{array}
$$

$$
\begin{array}{|l}
\hline
\textit{PRIOQAddSingleton2} \\
\Delta PRIOQ2 \\
p? : PID \\
\hline
qhd' = p? \\
qlst' = p? \\
next' = next \oplus \{p? \mapsto nullpid\} \\
qlen' = 1 \\
\hline
\end{array}
$$

$$
\begin{array}{|l}
\hline
\textit{ShouldAddPRIOQHd2} \\
\Xi PRIOQ2 \\
p? : PID \\
\hline
prio2(p?) \leq prio2(qhd) \\
\hline
\end{array}
$$

$$
\begin{array}{|l}
\hline
\textit{ShouldAddPRIOQLast2} \\
\Xi PRIOQ2 \\
p? : PID \\
\hline
prio2(qlst) < prio2(p?) \\
\hline
\end{array}
$$

The following is the insertion operation:

$$
\begin{array}{l}
\textit{PRIOQInsert2} \\
\hline
\Delta PRIOQ2 \\
p? : PID \\
\hline
\exists p_1, p_2 : PID \bullet \\
\quad p_1 \in next^*(\!|\ \{qhd\}\ |\!) \setminus \{nullpid\} \land \\
\quad p_2 \in next^*(\!|\ \{qhd\}\ |\!) \setminus \{nullpid\} \land \\
\quad prio2(p_1) \leq prio2(p?) \land \\
\quad prio2(p?) < prio2(p_2) \land \\
\quad next(p_1) = p_2 \land \\
\quad next' = next \oplus \{p_1 \mapsto p?, p? \mapsto p_2\} \land \\
\quad qlen' = qlen + 1
\end{array}
$$

Note how *next* is updated by the addition of $p?$. Also, the update of *next* is really a sequential composition since two elements are added to it. The two elements have been reduced to one as a notational nicety.

Finally, the enqueue operation proper is defined.

$$
\begin{array}{l}
PRIOQEnqueue2 \mathrel{\widehat=} \\
\quad (CanEnqueuePRIOQ2 \land \\
\qquad ((IsEmptyPRIOQ2 \land PRIOQAddSingleton2) \\
\qquad \lor (ShouldAddPRIOQHd2 \land PRIOQEnqueueHd2) \\
\qquad \lor (ShouldAddPRIOQLast2 \land PRIOQEnqueueLast2) \\
\qquad \lor PRIOQInsert2) \land \\
\qquad SysOk) \\
\quad \lor PRIOQFull
\end{array}
$$

It expands into

$$
\begin{array}{l}
\textit{PRIOQEnqueue2} \\
\hline
\Delta PRIOQ2 \\
p? : PID \\
serr! : SYSERR \\
\hline
qlen < maxs2 \\
(qlen = 0 \land \\
\quad qhd' = p? \land qlst' = p? \land \\
\quad next' = next \oplus \{p? \mapsto nullpid\} \land \\
\quad qlen' = 1) \\
\lor (prio2(p?) \leq prio2(qhd) \land \\
\quad qhd' = p? \land \\
\quad next' = next \oplus \{p? \mapsto qhd\} \land \\
\quad qlen' = qlen + 1) \\
\lor (prio2(qlst) < prio2(p?) \land \\
\quad qlst' = p? \land \\
\quad next' = next \oplus \{qlst \mapsto p?, p? \mapsto nullpid\} \land \\
\quad qlen' = qlen + 1)
\end{array}
$$

$$
\begin{array}{l}
\lor (\exists p_1, p_2 : PID \bullet \\
\quad p_1 \in next^*(\!| \{qhd\} |\!) \setminus \{nullpid\} \land \\
\quad p_2 \in next^*(\!| \{qhd\} |\!) \setminus \{nullpid\} \land \\
\quad prio2(p_1) \leq prio2(p?) \land \\
\quad prio2(p?) < prio2(p_2) \land \\
\quad next(p_1) = p_2 \land \\
\quad next' = next \oplus \{p_1 \mapsto p?, p? \mapsto p_2\} \land \\
\quad qlen' = qlen + 1) \land \\
\quad \lor\ serr! = sysok) \\
\lor\ serr! = schedqfull
\end{array}
$$

The predicate of this schema can be simplified to

$$
\begin{array}{l}
qlen < maxs2 \land \\
\quad [((qlen = 0 \land \\
\qquad qhd' = p? \land qlst' = p? \land \\
\qquad next' = next \oplus \{p? \mapsto nullpid\}) \\
\quad \lor (prio2(p?) \leq prio2(qhd) \land \\
\qquad qhd' = p? \land \\
\qquad next' = next \oplus \{p? \mapsto qhd\}) \\
\quad \lor (prio2(qlst) < prio2(p?) \land \\
\qquad qlst' = p? \land \\
\qquad next' = next \oplus \{qlst \mapsto p?, p? \mapsto nullpid\}) \\
\quad \lor (\exists p_1, p_2 : PID \bullet \\
\qquad p_1 \in next^*(\!| \{qhd\} |\!) \setminus \{nullpid\} \land \\
\qquad p_2 \in next^*(\!| \{qhd\} |\!) \setminus \{nullpid\} \land \\
\qquad prio2(p_1) \leq prio2(p?) \land \\
\qquad prio2(p?) < prio2(p_2) \land \\
\qquad next(p_1) = p_2 \land \\
\qquad next' = next \oplus \{p_1 \mapsto p?, p? \mapsto p_2\})) \\
\quad \land\ qlen' = qlen + 1 \\
\quad \land\ serr! = sysok] \\
\lor\ serr! = schedqfull
\end{array}
$$

It is also clear that the calculation of $prio2(p?)$ can be turned into a local variable using existential quantification

$$
\begin{array}{l}
\exists pr : PPRIO \mid pr = prio2(p?) \bullet \\
\quad qlen < maxs2 \land \\
\qquad [((qlen = 0 \land \\
\qquad\quad qhd' = p? \land qlst' = p? \land \\
\qquad\quad next' = next \oplus \{p? \mapsto nullpid\}) \\
\qquad \lor (pr \leq prio2(qhd) \land \\
\qquad\quad qhd' = p? \land \\
\qquad\quad next' = next \oplus \{p? \mapsto qhd\})
\end{array}
$$

$$
\begin{array}{l}
\quad\quad \lor\ (prio2(qlst) < pr \land \\
\quad\quad\quad\quad qlst' = p? \land \\
\quad\quad\quad\quad next' = next \oplus \{qlst \mapsto p?, p? \mapsto nullpid\}) \\
\quad\quad \lor\ (\exists p_1, p_2 : PID \bullet \\
\quad\quad\quad\quad p_1 \in next^*(\!|\ \{qhd\}\ |\!) \setminus \{nullpid\} \land \\
\quad\quad\quad\quad p_2 \in next^*(\!|\ \{qhd\}\ |\!) \setminus \{nullpid\} \land \\
\quad\quad\quad\quad prio2(p_1) \leq prio2(p?) \land \\
\quad\quad\quad\quad prio2(p?) < prio2(p_2) \land \\
\quad\quad\quad\quad next(p_1) = p_2 \land \\
\quad\quad\quad\quad next' = next \oplus \{p_1 \mapsto p?, p? \mapsto p_2\})) \\
\quad\quad \land\ qlen' = qlen + 1 \\
\quad\quad \land\ serr! = sysok] \\
\quad \lor\ serr! = schedqfull
\end{array}
$$

This is one case in which the re-introduction of quantifiers can lead to better code.

The precondition of *PRIOQEnqueue2* is

$$\text{pre}\ PRIOQEnqueue2 \mathrel{\widehat=} qlen < maxs2$$

As above, the deletion and dequeueing operations are defined next.

$$
\begin{array}{|l}
\hline
\textit{PRIOQDelHd2} \\
\Delta PRIOQ2 \\
\hline
qlen' = qlen - 1 \\
qhd' = next(qhd) \\
\hline
\end{array}
$$

By calculation, we obtain

$$\text{pre}\ PRIOQDelHd2 \mathrel{\widehat=} true$$

but this is not particularly useful. Instead, the following weaker form is employed:

$$\text{pre}\ PRIOQDelHd2 \mathrel{\widehat=} qlen > 0$$

This formula is also employed by the predicate of *PRIOQDelHd2*.

$$
\begin{array}{l}
PRIOQDequeue2 \mathrel{\widehat=} \\
\quad (\neg\ IsEmptyPRIOQ2 \land \\
\quad\quad PRIOQHd2 \land \\
\quad\quad PRIOQDelHd2 \land \\
\quad\quad SysOk) \\
\quad \lor\ PRIOQEmpty
\end{array}
$$

This complex definition expands into

$$
\begin{array}{|l}
\hline
\textit{PRIOQDequeue2} \\
\Delta PRIOQ2 \\
p! : PID \\
serr! : SYSERR \\
\hline
(qlen \neq 0 \land \\
\quad p! = qhd \land \\
\quad qlen' = qlen - 1 \land \\
\quad qhd' = next(qhd) \land \\
\quad serr! = sysok) \\
\lor\ serr! = schedqempty \\
\hline
\end{array}
$$

This operation's precondition is immediately calculated

$\text{pre}\, PRIOQDequeue2 \mathrel{\widehat{=}} qlen \neq 0$

However, since $qlen \in \mathbb{N}$, this can be re-written as

$\text{pre}\, PRIOQDequeue2 \mathrel{\widehat{=}} qlen > 0$

To end the sequence of definitions, the abstraction relation is now defined.

$$
\begin{array}{|l}
\hline
\textit{AbsPRIOQ2} \\
PRIOQ1 \\
PRIOQ2 \\
\hline
maxs2 = maxs2 \\
nxtp > 1 \Leftrightarrow qhd = pq1(1) \\
nxtp > 1 \Leftrightarrow qlst = pq1(nxtp - 1) \\
qlen = nxtp - 1 \\
next(pq1(nxtp - 1)) = nullpid \\
\forall i : 1 \mathinner{\ldotp\ldotp} nxtp - 2 \bullet \\
\quad i = j - 1 \Rightarrow \\
\quad next(pq1(i)) = pq1(i + 1) \\
\hline
\end{array}
$$

This is yet another identity, so the proofs of refinement are straightforward.

Theorem 30. $\forall PRIOQ1;\ PRIOQ2 \bullet PRIOQInit2 \land AbsPRIOQ2' \Rightarrow PRIOQInit1$

PROOF. By the abstraction relation, $qlen' = nxtp' - 1$, so we have $1 - 1 = 0 = qlen'$. In addition, the same realtion states that $maxs2 = maxs1$. □

Theorem 31. $\forall PRIOQ1;\ PRIOQ2;\ p? : PID \bullet \text{pre}\, PRIOQEnqueue1 \land AbsPRIOQ2 \Rightarrow \text{pre}\, PRIOQEnqueue2$

PROOF. The two preconditions are

$\text{pre}\, PRIOQEnqueue1 \mathrel{\widehat=} nxtp \leq maxs1$
and
$\text{pre}\, PRIOQEnqueue2 \mathrel{\widehat=} qlen < maxs2$

Since $maxs1 = maxs2$, we have

$nxtp \leq maxs2$
and
$qlen < maxs2$

The abstraction relation, states that $qlen = nxtp - 1$, so $qlen + 1 \leq maxs2$, which imples that $qlen < maxs2$ as required. □

Theorem 32.

$$\begin{aligned}
&\forall PRIOQ1;\ PRIOQ1';\ PRIOQ2;\ PRIOQ2';\ p? : PID;\ serr! : SYSERR \bullet\\
&\quad pre\, PRIOQEnqueue1\\
&\qquad \wedge AbsPRIOQ2\\
&\qquad \wedge AbsPRIOQ2'\\
&\qquad \wedge PRIOQEnqueue2\\
&\quad \Rightarrow PRIOQEnqueue1
\end{aligned}$$

PROOF. There are four cases.
Case 1. $qlen < maxs2$. By the abstraction relation, $qlen = nxtp - 1$ and $maxs2 = maxs1$, so $nxtp - 1 < maxs2$ implies $nxtp - 1 < maxs1$, which implies $nxtp \leq maxs1$. Ad $qlen = 0$, again using $qlen = nxtp - 1$, $0 = nxtp - 1$ implies $nxtp = 1$. By the predicate of $AbsPRIOQ2'$ $qhd' = pq1'(1)$ and $qlst' = pq1'(nxtp' - 1)$, so $qhd' = p?$ implies $pq1 \oplus \{1 \mapsto p?\} = pq1'$ and $qlst' = p?$ implies $pq1 \oplus \{1 \mapsto p?\} = pq1'$ since $nxtp = 1$. The identity $qlen' = qlen + 1$, implies that $nxtp' = nxtp + 1 = nxtp' = 2$.
Case 2. $prio2(p?)$ implies $prio1(p?)$ by $AbsPTAB1$; this is justified by the invariant condition that $\operatorname{ran} pq \subset used$. We also have $prio2(qhd) = prio2(pq1(1))$ $= prio1(pq1(1))$ by the abstraction relation and therefore $pq1' = pq1 \oplus \{1 \mapsto p?\}$. By the universal formula in the abstraction relation, $next' = next \oplus \{p? \mapsto qhd\}$ implies $next' = next \oplus \{p? \mapsto pq1(1)\}$; this now implies that $pq1'(1) = p?$, $pq1'(2) = pq1(1)$ and by induction, we have $pq1' = (pq1 \oplus \{i + 1 \mapsto pq1(i)\}) \oplus \{1 \mapsto p?\}$. The increase in $qlen$ is as in Case 1 above.
Case 3. The abstraction relation permits us to infer that $prio2(qlst) = prio2(pq1(nxtp - 1)) = prio1(pq1(nxtp - 1))$ since $pq1(nxtp - 1)$ is a known process. For $p?$ to be an element of the queue, $p?$ must be a defined process, so $prio2(p?) = prio1(p?)$ by $AbsPTAB2$. We note that $qlst = pq1(nxtp - 1)$, so that we may continue. Next, we deal with $next' = next \oplus \{qlst \mapsto p?, p? \mapsto nullpid\}$. First, we note that the map $\{p? \mapsto nullpid\}$ is required by the invariant of $PRIOQ2$, thus permitting us to concentrate on the map $\{qlst \mapsto p?\}$, which implies that $next'(qlst) = p?$, so $next'(nxtp - 1) = p?$ so $next'(nxtp) = p?$. The increment of $nxtp$ and $qlen$ is as in Case 1 above.

Case 4. Since $p_1, p_2 \in next^* (\| \{qhd\} \|) \setminus \{nullpid\}$, it follows, by the invariant, that $\{p_1, p_2\} \subset used$, so $prio2(p_1) = prio1(p_1)$ and $prio2(p_2) = prio1(p_1)$. For $p?$ to be a valid element of the queue, it must also be a defined process identifier ($p? \in used$ or equivalent). If $next(p_1) = p_2$, it must be true that $\exists i : 1 \mathinner{..} nxtp - 2 \bullet p_1 = pq1(i) \land pq1(i+1) = p_2$ (this follows from the abstraction relation). The remainder can be proved by induction. □

Theorem 33.

$$\forall PRIOQ1;\ PRIOQ2 \bullet \\ \quad pre\ PRIOQDequeue1 \land AbsPRIOQ2 \Rightarrow pre\ PRIOQDequeue2$$

PROOF. The two preconditions are:

pre $PRIOQDequeue1 \mathrel{\widehat=} nxtp > 1$
and
pre $PRIOQDequeue2 \mathrel{\widehat=} qlen \neq 0$

The abstraction relation states that $qlen = nxtp - 1$, so $nxtp > 1$ iff $qlen + 1 > 1$, which implies that $qlen > 0$ and it follows that $qlen \neq 0$. □

Theorem 34.

$$\begin{array}{l} \forall PRIOQ1;\ PRIOQ1';\ PRIOQ2;\ PRIOQ2';\ p! : PID;\ serr! : SYSERR \bullet \\ \quad pre\ PRIOQDequeue1 \\ \qquad \land AbsPRIOQ2 \\ \qquad \land AbsPRIOQ2' \\ \qquad \land PRIOQDequeue2 \\ \quad \Rightarrow PRIOQDequeue1 \end{array}$$

PROOF. We start with $qlen \neq 0$, because of the definition of $qlen$'s type, this implies that $qlen > 0$. By the abstraction relation, $qlen = nxtp - 1$, so $qlen \neq 0$ implies $nxtp - 1 \neq 0$ and $qlen > 0$ implies $nxtp - 1 > 0$, so $nxtp > 1$, as required.

By the abstraction relation, $pq1(1) = qhd$ if the queue is not empty; it cannot be empty by the definition of the operation, so this equation holds. It follows that $p! = qhd$ implies $p! = pq1(1)$.

The queue-length reduction, $qlen' = qlen - 1$ requires us to take the predicate of $AbsPRIOQ2'$ into account. By $AbsPRIOQ2$, we have $qlen = nxtp - 1$ and, by $AbsPRIOQ2'$, we have $qlen' = nxtp' - 1$. From this, $qlen - 1 = nxtp - 2$, so $qlen' = nxtp - 2$ or $nxtp' - 1 = nxtp - 2$, so $nxtp' = nxtp - 1$.

Finally, since $pq1(1) = qhd$, and $qhd' = next(qhd)$, then $qhd' = next(qhd) = pq1(2)$. Using the quantified formula in the abstraction relation, it can be inferred that $\forall i : 1 \mathinner{..} nxtp - 2 \bullet pq1' = pq1 \oplus \{i \mapsto pq1(i+1)\}$; this can be verified by a simple induction. □

Theorem 35. $\forall PRIOQ1;\ PRIOQ2 \bullet pre\ PRIOQDelHd1 \land AbsPRIOQ2 \Rightarrow pre\ PRIOQDelHd2$

PROOF. The precondition of *PRIOQDelHd1* is $nxtp > 1$ and that of *PRIOQDelHd2* is $qlen > 0$. The abstraction relation states that $qlen = nxtp - 1$. From the abstraction relation, we have $qlen + 1 = nxtp$, and so $qlen + 1 > 1$, from which it follows that $qlen > 0$. □

Theorem 36.

$$
\begin{array}{l}
\forall PRIOQ1;\ PRIOQ1';\ PRIOQ2;\ PRIOQ2' \bullet \\
\quad pre\ PRIOQDelHd1 \\
\qquad \land\ AbsPRIOQ2 \\
\qquad \land\ AbsPRIOQ2' \\
\qquad \land\ PRIOQDelHd2 \\
\quad \Rightarrow PRIOQDelHd1
\end{array}
$$

PROOF. By the predicate of $AbsPRIOQ2$, $nxtp = qlen - 1$ and, by that of $AbsPRIOQ2'$, we have $nxtp' = qlen' - 1$, so $qlen' = nxtp' + 1$. In the predicate of $PRIOQDelHd2$, $qlen' = qlen - 1$, so $qlen - 1 = nxtp - 2$, so $qlen' = nxtp - 2$, from which it follows that $nxtp' - 1 = nxtp - 2$, or $nxtp' = nxtp - 1$.

Now, assuming $qlen > 1$, by the predicate of *AbsPRIOQ2*, $qhd = pq1(1)$ and $next(qhd) = next(pq1(1)) = pq1(2)$. Using the quantified formula, the index of each element of $pq1$ decreases by 1.

On the other hand, if $qlen = 1$, the $next(qhd) = nullpid$, so $qhd' = qlst$ which, by the invariant, implies that $qhd' = nullpid$ and $qlen = 0$, so $nxtp = 1$ and the queue is empty. □

The schemata from this last refinement have now been shown to be correct. They can be converted directly into executable code.

3.6 The Scheduler

The scheduler is comprised of the priority queue whose refinement has just been undertaken, together with a variable to identify the currently executing process, a variable to identify the process that was executing immediately before the current one; there is also a varible to identify the idle process.

The scheduler undergoes 3 refinements to reach the level at which code can be extracted. Without further ado, we press on, therefore.

3.6.1 Top Level

This section contains the specification of the scheduler.

Before presenting the specification, let us prove the following little theorem. The variable *curr* denotes the current process; *SchedNext* is the name of the scheduler routine.

The idle process (sometimes called the “null” process) is just a process that does little or nothing. It can be implemented as a simple loop, such as:

```
while true do
   skip
od
```

The idle process is executed when there is nothing else to do.

As far as this part of the specification is concerned, support for the idle process is required.

It is assumed that the idle process is an element of *used*. This has the implication that the identifier of the idle process cannot be *nullpid*.

Here, then, is the definition of the scheduler's state space. The variable *curr* denotes the currently executing process, *prev* denotes the previously executed process, *iprc* is the identifier of the idle process (it is a write-once variable that is set at initialisation time). Finally, *sq* is the scheduler's queue, an instance of *PRIOQ*. It will be remembered that *PRIOQ* is a schema, so we have a *promotion* in this case. This is good for it reduces the amount of work required of us.

SCHED

$curr, prev : PID$
$iprc : PID$
$sq : PRIOQ$

$iprc \neq nullpid$

Theorem 37. *If* $pq \neq \langle\rangle$, $\forall p : PID \bullet p \in ran\, pq \Rightarrow p \in used$.

Proof. By the invariant of *PRIOQ*, $\operatorname{ran} pq \subset used$. This clearly implies that $\forall p : PID \bullet p \in \operatorname{ran} pq \Rightarrow p \in used$. □ It has two corollaries.

Corollary 1. $curr \in used \vee state(curr) = psterm$.

Proof. There is only one operation that sets $state(curr)$ to *psterm*. That is *TerminateSelf*. As part of its operation, it deletes *curr* from the process table and causes a reschedule via a call to *SchedNext*. Before the call to *SchedNext*, *TerminateSelf* sets the state of the current process as $state' = state \oplus \{curr \mapsto psterm\}$, so $state(curr) = psterm$.

The other operations updating *curr* are *SchedNext* (as noted in the last paragraph) and *SuspendMe*.

The *SuspendMe* operation removes the head from the ready queue, *pq*, if there is one and requeues *curr*. If the ready queue is empty, *iprc* (the idle process) is selected instead. The old queue head (or *iprc*) is made *curr* for execution. The setting of *curr* is performed by $SetNewCurrentProcess[head\ pq/p?]$. If the ready queue, *pq*, is empty, *curr* is updated by *MakeIdleProcessCurrent*.

Inspection of *SchedNext* shows that the same two operations are used to set the state of *curr* and *prev*. Their definitions are repeated.

$$\begin{array}{|l}
\hline
\textit{SetNewCurrentProcess} \\
\Delta SCHED \\
p? : PID \\
\hline
curr' = p? \\
prev' = curr \\
\hline
\end{array}$$

$$\begin{array}{|l}
\hline
\textit{MakeIdleProcessCurrent} \\
\Delta SCHED \\
\hline
curr' = iprc \\
prev' = curr \\
\hline
\end{array}$$

It can be seen that neither operator affects *used* in any way (indeed, *used* is not mentioned by either schema). It is therefore necessary to determine where $p?$ and *iprc* originate.

In *SuspendMe* and in *SchedNext*, there is a substitution instance of *SetNewCurrentProcess*, *SetNewCurrentProcess*$[head\ pq/p?]$. This expands to

$$curr' = head\ pq$$
$$prev' = curr$$

By Theorem 37, $head\ pq \in used$.

The null or idle process is created by *CreateNullProcess* which is defined in terms of *AddPD*. The output, $p!$, of *AddPD* is then assigned to *iprc* via *SCHEDInit*. The initialisation *SCHEDInit* in the system initialisation has an instance of

$$\begin{array}{|l}
\hline
\textit{SCHEDInit} \\
SCHED' \\
p? : PID \\
\hline
curr' = minpid \land prev' = minpid \land iprc' = p? \\
sq' = \theta PRIQOInit \\
\hline
\end{array}$$

in a substitution instance $[ipid/p?]$. Inspection of the definition of *CreateNull-Process* shows that there are no operations that rebind *ipid*. Now, *AddPD* implies that $ipid \in used$, so $iprc = ipid$.

It should be noted that it will usually be the case that *iprc* is bound to *minpid*. This permits the inference that $curr \in used$ at initialisation time, also. □

Corollary 2. $prev \in used \lor state(prev) = psterm$

PROOF. As noted in Corollary 1, only *TerminateSelf* can set the process state to *psterm*. The *TerminateSelf* operation is defined in terms of *SchedNext* which, at various points, updates *prev* ($prev' = curr$). The variable *prev* is *always* a copy of *curr*. The critical operation is *SetNewCurrentProcess*, whose definition is

$$\begin{array}{|l}
\Delta SCHED \\
p? : PID \\
\hline
curr' = p? \\
prev' = curr
\end{array}$$

So, the value bound $prev'$ is identical to that bound to *curr*, so must have the same properties. In particular, if $curr \in used$, $prev' \in used$ and if $state(curr) = psterm$, $state(prev') = psterm$.

It should be clear that the assignment $prev' = curr$ establishes the binding of *prev* from that point until it is next updated. This permits us to reach the conclusion that $prev \in used \lor state(prev) = psterm$.

Finally, as noted above, *iprc* is usually bound to *minpid*, so the statement of this corollary also applies at initialisation time. □

Here is the framing or promotion schema.

$$\begin{array}{|l}
\multicolumn{1}{l}{\Phi SCHED} \\
\Delta SCHED \\
\Delta PRIOQ \\
\hline
sq = \theta PRIOQ \\
sq' = \theta PRIOQ'
\end{array}$$

The definition of the initialisation schema is repeated. The definition is comparatively straightforward, as can be seen. The only thing to notice is that $sq' = \theta PRIOQInit$, since *sq* is of a schema type.

$$\begin{array}{|l}
\multicolumn{1}{l}{SCHEDInit} \\
SCHED' \\
p? : PID \\
\hline
curr' = minpid \land prev' = minpid \land iprc' = p? \\
sq' = \theta PRIOQInit
\end{array}$$

Recall that *PRIOQ* includes *PTAB* in its state.

The next operation returns the identifier of the idle process.

$$\begin{array}{|l}
\multicolumn{1}{l}{IDLEPROCESSIdent} \\
\Xi SCHED \\
p! : PID \\
\hline
p! = iprc
\end{array}$$

When the identifier of the currently executing process is required to be set, this schema defines the operation that performs it.

$$\begin{array}{l}
\textit{SetCurrentProcessId} \\
\hline
\Delta SCHED \\
p? : PID \\
\hline
curr' = p?
\end{array}$$

The names of the next few schemata should be all that is required to interpret them.

$$\begin{array}{l}
\textit{MakeCurrentPrevious} \\
\hline
\Delta SCHED \\
\hline
prev' = curr
\end{array}$$

$$\begin{array}{l}
\textit{IsCurrentProcess} \\
\hline
\Xi SCHED \\
p? : PID \\
\hline
p? = curr
\end{array}$$

$$\begin{array}{l}
\textit{CurrentProcessId} \\
\hline
\Xi SCHED \\
p! : PID \\
\hline
p! = curr
\end{array}$$

$$\begin{array}{l}
SetStateToRunning \mathrel{\widehat=} \\
\quad \exists\, st : PSTATE \mid st = psrunning \bullet \\
\qquad SetProcState[st/st?]
\end{array}$$

or

$$\begin{array}{l}
\textit{SetStateToRunning} \\
\hline
\Delta PTAB \\
p? : PID \\
\hline
state' = state \oplus \{p? \mapsto psrunning\}
\end{array}$$

$$\begin{array}{l}
SetNewCurrentProcess \mathrel{\widehat=} \\
\quad (MakeCurrentPrevious \land SetCurrentProcessId) \\
\quad \fatsemi (CurrentProcessId[c/p!] \land SetStateToRunning[c/p?]) \setminus \{c\}
\end{array}$$

After simplification, this expands into

$$\begin{array}{|l}
\Delta SCHED \\
p? : PID \\
\hline
curr' = p? \\
prev' = curr \\
state' = state \oplus \{curr' \mapsto psrunning\}
\end{array}$$

$$\begin{array}{|l}
\textit{IsPreviousProcess} \\
\hline
\Xi SCHED \\
p? : PID \\
\hline
p? = prev
\end{array}$$

$$\begin{array}{|l}
\textit{IsCurrentProcessIdle} \\
\hline
\Xi SCHED \\
\hline
curr = iprc
\end{array}$$

This predicate is true iff the previously active process was the idle process.

$$\begin{array}{|l}
\textit{IsPrevProcessIdle} \\
\hline
\Xi SCHED \\
\hline
prev = iprc
\end{array}$$

$$\begin{array}{l}
SetProcessStateToReady \mathrel{\widehat=} \\
\quad \exists\, st : PSTATE \mid st = psready \bullet \\
\qquad SetProcState[st/st?]
\end{array}$$

This expands and simplifies to

$$\begin{array}{|l}
\textit{SetProcessStateToReady} \\
\hline
\Delta PTAB \\
p? : PID \\
\hline
state' = state \oplus \{p? \mapsto psready\}
\end{array}$$

The operation that places a process identifier in the scheduler's ready queue is called *MakeReady*. The main part of *MakeReady* is defined by the following

$$
\begin{array}{l}
\mathit{MakeReady}_a \mathrel{\widehat=} \\
\quad \exists \Delta PRIOQ \bullet \\
\qquad \Phi SCHED \land PRIOQEnqueue
\end{array}
$$

To make life a little easier and to avoid errors, the following operation is defined. It sets the state of the process being added to the ready queue as well as performing the queue-insertion operation. This operation is used in a lot of places and it is easy to forget to set the state; this is the reason for defining this operation.

$$
\begin{array}{l}
\mathit{MakeReady} \mathrel{\widehat=} \\
\quad (\mathit{SetProcessStateToReady} \land \mathit{MakeReady}_a)
\end{array}
$$

It expands into the following. It should be noted that the strict expansion of the promoted action should yield a queue whose name is *sq.pq*.

$$
\begin{array}{|l}
\textit{MakeReady} \\
\hline
\Delta PRIOQ \\
p? : PID \\
serr! : SYSERR \\
\hline
state' = state \oplus \{p? \mapsto psready\} \land \\
(\# sq.pq < maxs \land \\
\quad ((sq.pq = \langle\rangle \land sq.pq' = \langle p? \rangle) \lor \\
\qquad (prio(p?) \leq prio(head\ sq.pq) \land sq.pq' = \langle p? \rangle \frown sq.pq) \lor \\
\qquad (prio(last\ sq.pq) < prio(p?) \land sq.pq' = sq.pq \frown \langle p? \rangle) \lor \\
\qquad (\exists s_1, s_2 : \mathrm{seq}\, PID \mid s_1 \neq \langle\rangle \land s_2 \neq \langle\rangle \land s_1 \frown s_2 = sq.pq \bullet \\
\qquad\quad prio(last\ s_1) < prio(p?) \land \\
\qquad\quad prio(p?) \leq prio(head\ s_2) \land \\
\qquad\quad sq.pq' = s_1 \frown (\langle p? \rangle \frown s_2)) \land \\
\qquad serr! = sysok) \\
\lor\ serr! = schedqfull
\end{array}
$$

This schema can be simplified to the following:

$$
\begin{array}{|l}
\hline
\Delta PRIOQ \\
p? : PID \\
serr! : SYSERR \\
\hline
(\# sq.pq < maxs \land \\
\quad ((sq.pq = \langle\rangle \land sq.pq' = \langle p? \rangle) \lor \\
\qquad (prio(p?) \leq prio(head\ sq.pq) \land sq.pq' = \langle p? \rangle \frown sq.pq) \lor \\
\qquad (prio(last\ sq.pq) < prio(p?) \land sq.pq' = sq.pq \frown \langle p? \rangle) \lor \\
\qquad (\exists s_1, s_2 : \mathrm{seq}\, PID \mid s_1 \neq \langle\rangle \land s_2 \neq \langle\rangle \land s_1 \frown s_2 = sq.pq \bullet \\
\qquad\quad prio(last\ s_1) < prio(p?) \land \\
\qquad\quad prio(p?) \leq prio(head\ s_2) \land
\end{array}
$$

$$
\begin{array}{l}
\qquad\qquad sq.pq' = s_1 \frown \langle p? \rangle \frown s_2)) \wedge \\
\qquad state' = state \oplus \{p? \mapsto psready\} \wedge \\
\qquad serr! = sysok) \\
\vee\ serr! = schedqfull
\end{array}
$$

The precondition is

$$\mathrm{pre}\ MakeReady \mathrel{\widehat{=}} \#sq < maxs$$

Note that this precondition can rely upon the lemma proved above (Lemma 1) to ensure that $p? \in used$, so that the update of *state* is well defined.

Next, we define a number of operations in terms of promotion. Each definition is accompanied by its simplification; in some cases, a complete step-by-step simplification is given so that the reader can be sure of the derivation, as well as the logical form of these operations.

The test for an empty ready queue in the scheduler is defined by the following

$$
\begin{array}{l}
IsEmptySCHEDQ \mathrel{\widehat{=}} \\
\quad \exists\, \Delta PRIOQ \bullet \\
\qquad \Phi SCHED \wedge IsEmptyPRIOQ
\end{array}
$$

Its predicate expands into (using the same abuse of notation mentioned above)

$$
\begin{array}{l}
\exists\, pq, pq' : \mathrm{seq}\, PID;\ maxs, maxs' : \mathbb{N} \bullet \\
\quad sq = \theta PRIOQ \wedge \\
\quad sq' = \theta PRIOQ' \wedge \\
\quad pq = \langle\, \rangle
\end{array}
$$

or

$$
\begin{array}{l}
sq = \langle\!|\ pq \mapsto pq, maxs \mapsto maxs\ |\!\rangle \wedge \\
\quad sq' = \langle\!|\ pq \leadsto pq', maxs \leadsto maxs'\ |\!\rangle \wedge \\
\quad pq = \langle\, \rangle
\end{array}
$$

which is

$$
\begin{array}{l}
\exists\, pq, pq' : \mathrm{seq}\, PID;\ maxs, maxs' : \mathbb{N} \bullet \\
\quad sq = \langle\!|\ pq \mapsto pq, maxs \mapsto maxs\ |\!\rangle \wedge \\
\quad sq' = \langle\!|\ pq \leadsto pq', maxs \mapsto maxs'\ |\!\rangle \wedge \\
\quad pq = \langle\, \rangle
\end{array}
$$

or

$$
\begin{array}{l}
sq = sq' \wedge \\
sq.maxs = sq.maxs' \wedge \\
sq.pq = \langle\, \rangle
\end{array}
$$

The scheduler's dequeue operation is defined as the following promotion

$$SCHEDQDequeue \mathrel{\widehat=} \exists \Delta PRIOQ \bullet \Phi SCHED \land PRIOQDequeue$$

It simplifies to

$$\begin{array}{l} sq.pq = pq \\ sq.maxs = maxs \\ ((sq.pq \neq \langle\rangle \\ \quad p! = head\ sq.pq \\ \quad sq'.pq = tail\ sq.pq \\ \quad serr! = sysok) \\ \lor\ serr! = schedqempty) \end{array}$$

An operation that returns the head element of the ready queue is as follows

$$SCHEDQHd \mathrel{\widehat=} \exists \Delta PRIOQ \bullet \Phi SCHED \land PRIOQHd$$

It expands and simplifies to

$$\begin{array}{l} sq = sq' \\ sq.maxs = sq'.maxs \\ p! = head\ sq.pq \end{array}$$

The operation to remove the head of the scheduler's queue is another promotion

$$SCHEDQDelHd \mathrel{\widehat=} \exists \Delta PRIOQ \bullet \Phi SCHED \land PRIOQDelHd$$

The predicate expands and simplifies to

$$\begin{array}{l} sq.pq = pq \\ sq'.maxs = sq.maxs \\ sq'.pq = tail\ sq.pq \end{array}$$

The arbitrary element deletion operation is another promotion.

$$DelSCHEDQElem \mathrel{\widehat=} \exists \Delta PRIOQ \bullet \Phi SCHED \land DelPRIOQElem$$

This expands into

$$\begin{array}{l}\exists\, pq, pq' : \mathrm{seq}\, PID;\; maxs, maxs' : \mathbb{N} \bullet \\ \quad sq = \theta PRIOQ \land \\ \quad sq' = \theta PRIOQ' \land \\ \quad pq \neq \langle\rangle \land \\ \quad (\exists\, s_1, s_2 : \mathrm{seq}\, PID \bullet \\ \qquad s_1 \frown \langle p? \rangle \frown s_2 = pq \land \\ \qquad pq' = s_1 \frown s_2)\end{array}$$

Ignoring the intermediate steps, we have

$$\begin{array}{l} sq.maxs = sq'.maxs \\ sq.pq \neq \langle\rangle \\ (\exists\, s_1, s_2 : \mathrm{seq}\, PID \bullet \\ \quad s_1 \frown \langle p? \rangle \frown s_2 = sq.pq \land \\ \qquad sq'.pq = s_1 \frown s_2)\end{array}$$

The precondition is not much of a surprise, as the following calculation shows.

$$\begin{array}{l}\mathrm{pre}\, DelSCHEDQElem \mathrel{\widehat=} \\ \quad \mathrm{pre}\, \Phi SCHED \land \mathrm{pre}\, DelPRIOQElem \\ \quad \Leftrightarrow \mathrm{pre}\, DelPRIOQElem\end{array}$$

This is equivalent to

$$p? \in \mathrm{ran}\, pq$$

or

$$\mathrm{ran}\, pq \neq \varnothing$$

When there is nothing else to do, the idle process is executed. The following schema defines the operation that sets the schedulers' local variables ready to switch to the idle process' context.

MakeIdleProcessCurrent

$$\begin{array}{l} \Delta SCHED \\ \hline curr' = iprc \\ prev' = curr \end{array}$$

Under the right conditions, the current process is continued:

ContinueCurrent

$$\begin{array}{l} \Xi SCHED \\ \hline curr' = curr \\ prev' = prev \end{array}$$

This is just an identity (which is what is required).

If the current process' state is not *psready* or *psrunning*, it can no longer be considered for execution by the scheduler. The next definition is of a predicate that performs this test.

$$
\begin{array}{l}
CurrentProcessStateIsReadyOrRunning \mathrel{\widehat=} \\
\quad (CurrentProcessId[c/p!] \land \\
\quad (\exists st : PSTATE \mid st = psready \bullet \\
\qquad ProcState[c/p?, st/st!]) \land \\
\quad (\exists st : PSTATE \mid st = psrunning \bullet \\
\qquad ProcState[c/p?, st/st!])) \setminus \{c\}
\end{array}
$$

The definition expands into:

$$
\begin{array}{|l}
\hline
CurrentProcessStateIsReadyOrRunning \\
\Xi SCHED \\
\Xi PTAB \\
\hline
\exists c : PID \bullet \\
\quad curr = c \land \\
\quad (\exists st : PSTATE \mid st = psready \bullet \\
\qquad state(c) = st) \\
\quad \lor (\exists st : PSTATE \mid st = psrunning \bullet \\
\qquad state(c) = st) \\
\hline
\end{array}
$$

It simplifies to:

$$
\begin{array}{|l}
\hline
\Xi SCHED \\
\Xi PTAB \\
\hline
(state(curr) = psready) \lor (state(curr) = psrunning) \\
\hline
\end{array}
$$

Note that $\neg$ *CurrentProcessStateIsReadyOrRunning* is

$$
\begin{array}{|l}
\hline
\neg\ CurrentProcessStateIsReadyOrRunning \\
\Xi SCHED \\
\Xi PTAB \\
\hline
state(curr) \neq psready \land state(curr) \neq psrunning \\
\hline
\end{array}
$$

It is easy, when not paying sufficient attention, to forget to change $\lor$ to $\land$ when negating.

Before defining *SchedNext*, we need

$$
\begin{array}{l}
QueueHdHasHigherPriority \mathrel{\widehat=} \\
\quad (CurrentPriority[cp/pr!] \land \\
\qquad SCHEDQHd[h/p!] \land \\
\qquad ProcPrio[h/p?, hpr/pr!] \land \\
\qquad hpr < cp) \setminus \{h, hpr, cp\}
\end{array}
$$

This expands to

$$
\begin{array}{|l}
\multicolumn{1}{l}{\textit{QueueHdHasHigherPriority}} \\
\Xi PTAB \\
\Xi SCHED \\
\hline
\exists\, h, cp : PID;\ hpr : PPRIO \bullet \\
\quad prio(curr) = cp \land \\
\quad head\ sq.pq = h \land \\
\quad prio(h) = hpr \land \\
\quad hpr < cp \\
\hline
\end{array}
$$

The predicate of this schema simplifies to

$prio(head\ sq.pq) < prio(curr)$

The schema is

$$
\begin{array}{|l}
\multicolumn{1}{l}{\textit{QueueHdHasHigherPriority}} \\
\Xi PTAB \\
\Xi SCHED \\
\hline
prio(head\ sq.pq) < prio(curr) \\
\hline
\end{array}
$$

Finally, we reach the scheduling function itself. It is a complex operation but should not prove difficult to understand.

$$
\begin{array}{l}
SchedNext \mathrel{\widehat=} \\
\quad (IsCurrentProcessIdle \land \\
\qquad ((IsEmptySCHEDQ \land ContinueCurrent) \\
\qquad\quad \lor (SCHEDQDequeue[p/p!] \land \\
\qquad\qquad SetNewCurrentProcess[p/p?] \\
\qquad\qquad \fatsemi CTXTSW) \setminus \{p\})) \\
\quad \lor (IsEmptySCHEDQ \land MakeIdleProcessCurrent \fatsemi CTXTSW) \\
\quad \lor ((\lnot\ CurrentProcessStateIsReadyOrRunning \\
\qquad\quad \lor QueueHdHasHigherPriority) \land \\
\qquad (SCHEDQHd[hpid/p!] \land \\
\qquad\quad SCHEDQDelHd \land \\
\qquad\quad SetNewCurrentProcess[hpid/p?] \\
\qquad\quad \fatsemi CTXTSW) \setminus \{hpid\}) \\
\quad \lor ContinueCurrent
\end{array}
$$

Since *CTXTSW* does not have any variables that interact with any others in *SchedNext*, it is possible to reduce the strength of $\fatsemi$ to $\land$.

The definition expands into the following schema. The context-switching operation, *CTXTSW*, is left unexpanded (its predicate consists solely of $intno' = context\_swictch$).

$$
\begin{array}{l}
\Delta SCHED \\
\hline
(curr = iprc \land \\
\quad ((sq.pq = \langle\rangle \land curr' = curr \land prev' = prev) \\
\qquad \lor (\exists p : PID \bullet \\
\qquad\quad p = head\ pq \land curr' = p \land prev' = curr \land \\
\qquad\quad state' = state \oplus \{head\ sq.pq \mapsto psrunning\} \land CTXTSW))) \\
\lor (sq.pq = \langle\rangle \land prev' = curr \land curr' = iprc \land CTXTSW) \\
\lor ((state(curr) \neq psready \land state(curr) \neq psrunning \\
\qquad \lor prio(head\ sq.pq) < prio(curr)) \land \\
\quad (\exists hpid : PID \bullet \\
\qquad head\ sq.pq = hpid \land \\
\qquad sq'.pq = tail\ sq.pq \land \\
\qquad curr' = hpid \land \\
\qquad state' = state \oplus \{hpid \mapsto psrunning\} \land \\
\qquad prev' = curr \land CTXTSW)) \\
\lor (curr' = curr \land prev' = prev)
\end{array}
$$

This simplifies to

$$
\begin{array}{l}
\Delta SCHED \\
\hline
(curr = iprc \land \\
\quad ((sq.pq = \langle\rangle \land curr' = curr \land prev' = prev) \\
\qquad \lor (curr' = head\ sq.pq \land prev' = curr \land \\
\qquad\quad state' = state \oplus \{head\ sq.pq \mapsto psrunning\} \land CTXTSW))) \\
\lor (sq.pq = \langle\rangle \land prev' = curr \land curr' = iprc \land CTXTSW) \\
\lor ((state(curr) \neq psready \land state(curr) \neq psrunning \\
\qquad \lor prio(head\ sq.pq) < prio(curr)) \land \\
\quad sq'.pq = tail\ sq.pq \land \\
\quad curr' = head\ sq.pq \land \\
\quad state' = state \oplus \{head\ sq.pq \mapsto psrunning\} \land \\
\quad prev' = curr \land CTXTSW) \\
\lor (curr' = curr \land prev' = prev)
\end{array}
$$

To calculate the precondition of *SchedNext*, it is first noted that *SchedNext* takes the form of a disjunction, so it is permitted to decompose the precondition into disjuncts since $\text{pre}(P \lor Q) \Leftrightarrow \text{pre}\, P \lor \text{pre}\, Q)$. Therefore, we decompose the *SchedNext* schema into its components and handle them separately; then we combine the result to form the precondition.

$$
\begin{array}{l}
\text{pre } \mathit{SchedNext} \mathrel{\widehat=} \\
\quad \text{pre}[(\mathit{IsCurrentProcessIdle} \wedge \\
\qquad ((\mathit{IsEmptySCHEDQ} \wedge \mathit{ContinueCurrent}) \\
\qquad\quad \vee (\mathit{SCHEDQDequeue}[p/p!] \wedge \mathit{SetNewCurrentProcess}[p/p?] \\
\qquad\qquad \mathbin{;} \mathit{CTXTSW}) \setminus \{p\})) \\
\quad \vee (\mathit{IsEmptySCHEDQ} \wedge \mathit{MakeIdleProcessCurrent} \mathbin{;} \mathit{CTXTSW}) \\
\quad \vee ((\neg\ \mathit{CurrentProcessStateIsReadyOrRunning} \\
\qquad\quad \vee \mathit{QueueHdHasHigherPriority}) \wedge \\
\qquad (\mathit{SCHEDQHd}[hpid/p!] \wedge \\
\qquad\quad \mathit{SCHEDQDelHd} \wedge \\
\qquad\quad \mathit{SetNewCurrentProcess}[hpid/p?] \\
\qquad\quad \mathbin{;} \mathit{CTXTSW}) \setminus \{hpid\}) \\
\quad \vee \mathit{ContinueCurrent}]
\end{array}
$$

The *SchedNext* operation is composed of disjunctions. Each disjunct can be treated independently, so we have:

$$
\begin{array}{l}
\text{pre } \mathit{SchedNext} \mathrel{\widehat=} \\
\quad \text{pre}(\mathit{IsCurrentProcessIdle} \wedge \\
\qquad ((\mathit{IsEmptySCHEDQ} \wedge \mathit{ContinueCurrent}) \\
\qquad\quad \vee (\mathit{SCHEDQDequeue}[p/p!] \wedge \\
\qquad\qquad \mathit{SetNewCurrentProcess}[p/p?] \\
\qquad\qquad \mathbin{;} \mathit{CTXTSW}) \setminus \{p\})) \\
\quad \vee \text{pre}(\mathit{IsEmptySCHEDQ} \wedge \mathit{MakeIdleProcessCurrent} \mathbin{;} \mathit{CTXTSW}) \\
\quad \vee \text{pre}((\neg\ \mathit{CurrentProcessStateIsReadyOrRunning} \\
\qquad\quad \vee \mathit{QueueHdHasHigherPriority}) \wedge \\
\qquad (\mathit{SCHEDQHd}[hpid/p!] \wedge \\
\qquad\quad \mathit{SCHEDQDelHd} \wedge \\
\qquad\quad \mathit{SetNewCurrentProcess}[hpid/p?] \\
\qquad\quad \mathbin{;} \mathit{CTXTSW}) \setminus \{hpid\}) \\
\quad \vee \text{pre } \mathit{ContinueCurrent}
\end{array}
$$

Taking each disjunct in turn, we obtain, after simplification:

$$
\begin{array}{l}
\text{pre } \mathit{SchedNext} \mathrel{\widehat=} \\
\quad curr = iprc \\
\quad \vee\ sq.pq = \langle\rangle \\
\quad \vee\ (state(curr) \neq psready \vee state(curr) \neq psrunning \\
\qquad \vee\ prio(head\ sq.pq) < prio(curr))
\end{array}
$$

and we note that the precondition of the fourth disjunct simplifies to *true*.

There are two

Theorem 38. $curr \in used \vee curr = minpid$.

PROOF. By inspection, it can be seen that *curr* is assigned a value that is $head\ sq.pq$. Since $\operatorname{ran} sq.pq \subset used$, $curr \in used$. The idle process, *iprc*, as will be seen, is allocated a normal *PID*, like any other process, so $iprc \in used$. After the initialisation of the scheduler, $curr' = minpid$. □

Corollary 3. $prev \in used \lor prev = minpid$.

PROOF. In all cases, *prev* obtains is value by assignments $prev' = curr$. Given that $curr \in used$, it follows immediately $prev \in used$. The other case holds immediately after the initialisation operation has been applied. □

In this kernel, processes can request that they be suspended, This is the operation as far as the scheduler is concerned.

$$
\begin{array}{l}
SuspendMe \mathrel{\widehat=} \\
\quad ((IsEmptySCHEDQ \land MakeIdleProcessCurrent) \\
\qquad \lor ((SCHEDQDequeue[p/p!] \mathbin{;} \\
\qquad\qquad (CurrentProcessId[c/p!] \land MakeReady[c/p?]) \setminus \{c\}) \\
\qquad \mathbin{;} SetNewCurrentProcess[p/p?]) \setminus \{p\}) \\
\quad \mathbin{;} CTXTSW
\end{array}
$$

(Note, again, that $\mathbin{;} CTXTSW$ can be reduced in strength to $\land\ CTXTSW$.)

The definition of *SuspendMe* expands and simplifies to the following schema:

$$
\begin{array}{|l}
\hline
SuspendMe \\
\Delta SCHED \\
\Delta PRIOQ \\
\hline
state' = state \oplus \{curr \mapsto psready\} \\
((pq = \langle\rangle \land curr' = prev \land prev' = curr) \\
\lor (curr' = head\ pq \land \\
\qquad (\#(tail\ pq) < maxs \land \\
\qquad\quad prev' = curr \land \\
\qquad\quad ((tail\ pq = \langle\rangle \land pq' = \langle curr\rangle) \\
\qquad\qquad \lor (prio(curr) \leq prio(head\ tail\ pq) \land pq' = \langle curr\rangle \frown tail\ pq) \\
\qquad\qquad \lor (prio(last\ tail\ pq) < prio(curr) \land pq' = (tail\ pq) \frown \langle curr\rangle) \\
\qquad\qquad \lor (\exists s_1, s_2 : \mathrm{seq}\ PID \mid s_1 \neq \langle\rangle \land s_2 \neq \langle\rangle \land s_1 \frown s_2 = tail\ pq \bullet \\
\qquad\qquad\quad prio(last\ s_1) < prio(curr) \land \\
\qquad\qquad\quad prio(curr) \leq prio(head\ s_2) \land \\
\qquad\qquad\quad pq' = s_1 \frown \langle curr\rangle \frown s_2) \land \\
\qquad\quad serr! = sysok)) \\
\qquad \lor serr! = schedqfull) \land \\
CTXTSW \\
\hline
\end{array}
$$

The movement of $prev' = curr$ is justified by the combination of *Distrib*$\lor$ and $p \land q \Rightarrow p$; the conjunction of *CTXTSW* is also a simplification of the orginal statement (the simplification is justified above).

The precondition is

$$\mathrm{pre}\ SuspendMe \mathrel{\widehat=} pq = \langle\rangle \lor \#\ tail\ pq < maxs$$

There is an argument that *SuspendMe* should be defined as follows

$$
\begin{array}{l}
SuspendMe \mathrel{\widehat=} \\
\quad ((IsEmptySCHEDQ \land MakeIdleProcessCurrent \land \\
\qquad (CurrentProcessId[c/p!] \land \\
\qquad MakeReady[c/p?]) \setminus c) \\
\qquad \lor ((SCHEDQDequeue[p/p!] \mathbin{;} \\
\qquad\quad (CurrentProcessId[c/p!] \land MakeReady[c/p?]) \setminus \{c\}) \\
\qquad \mathbin{;} SetNewCurrentProcess[p/p?]) \setminus \{p\}) \\
\quad \mathbin{;} CTXTSW
\end{array}
$$

After expansion and simplification (note that $CTXTSW$ is moved inwards using the Distrib rule for $\land$ over $\lor$), we have

$$
\begin{array}{|l}
\hline
SuspendMe \\
\Delta SCHED \\
\Delta PRIOQ \\
\hline
state' = state \oplus \{curr \mapsto psready\} \\
((sq.pq = \langle\rangle \land curr' = iprc \land prev' = curr \land sq.pq' = \langle curr \rangle \land CTXTSW) \\
\lor (curr' = head\ sq.pq \land \\
\quad (\#(tail\ sq.pq) < maxs \land \\
\qquad prev' = curr \land \\
\qquad ((tail\ sq.pq = \langle\rangle \land sq.pq' = \langle curr \rangle) \\
\qquad\quad \lor (prio(curr) \leq prio(head\ tail\ sq.pq) \land \\
\qquad\qquad sq.pq' = \langle curr \rangle \frown tail\ sq.pq) \\
\qquad\quad \lor (prio(last\ tail\ sq.pq) < prio(curr) \land \\
\qquad\qquad sq.pq' = (tail\ sq.pq) \frown \langle curr \rangle) \\
\qquad\quad \lor (\exists s_1, s_2 : \mathrm{seq}\ PID \mid s_1 \neq \langle\rangle \land s_2 \neq \langle\rangle \land s_1 \frown s_2 = tail\ sq.pq \bullet \\
\qquad\qquad prio(last\ s_1) < prio(curr) \land \\
\qquad\qquad prio(curr) \leq prio(head\ s_2) \land \\
\qquad\qquad sq.pq' = s_1 \frown \langle curr \rangle \frown s_2) \land \\
\qquad CTXTSW \land \\
\qquad serr! = sysok)) \\
\quad \lor serr! = schedqfull) \\
\hline
\end{array}
$$

The precondition is the same as in the other version.

3.6.2 Refinement One

There is a number of things that should be said about the refinement of the scheduler. The first thing is that, since the scheduler consists of three simple variables and a promoted schema, the refinement of the three variables will consist of the identity, leaving the refinement of the promoted schema. However, the refinement of a promotion is equivalent to the promotion of a refinement, so there is nothing to do for the reason that the refinement of *PRIOQ* has already been completed in the last section. For these reasons, all we need do in this and the next subsection is to write out the definitions of the various schemata using the operations of the current level of refinement. In this subsection, the current level of refinement is 1; in the next, it is 2.

We have little or nothing to say about these refinements. We have not said all there is to say about them already but believe that what we have not said is inessential[1].

$$
\begin{array}{l}
MakeReady1 \mathrel{\widehat=} \\
\quad SetProcessStateToReady1 \land \\
\quad \exists \Delta PRIOQ1 \bullet \\
\qquad \Phi SCHED \land PRIOQEnqueue1
\end{array}
$$

$$
\begin{array}{l}
CurrentProcessStateIsReadyOrRunning1 \mathrel{\widehat=} \\
\quad (CurrentProcessId[c/p!] \land \\
\qquad (\exists st_1, st_2 : PSTATE \mid st_1 = psready \land st_2 = psrunning \bullet \\
\qquad\quad ProcState1[c/p?, st_1/st!] \lor ProcState1[c/p?, st_2/st!])) \setminus \{c\}
\end{array}
$$

This expands to

$$
\begin{array}{|l}
\hline
\textit{CurrentProcessStateIsReadyOrRunning1} \\
\Xi PTAB1 \\
\Xi SCHED \\
\hline
\exists c : PID \bullet \\
\quad c = curr \land \\
\quad (\exists st_1, st_2 : PSTATE \mid st_1 = psready \land st_2 = psrunning \bullet \\
\qquad st_1 = state1(c) \lor st_2 = state1(c)) \\
\hline
\end{array}
$$

It can be simplified to

$$
\begin{array}{|l}
\hline
\textit{CurrentProcessStateIsReadyOrRunning1} \\
\Xi PTAB1 \\
\Xi SCHED \\
\hline
psready = state1(curr) \lor psrunning = state1(curr) \\
\hline
\end{array}
$$

$$
\begin{array}{l}
QueueHdHasHigherPriority1 \mathrel{\widehat=} \\
\quad (CurrentPriority[cp/pr!] \land \\
\qquad SCHEDQHd1[h/p!] \land \\
\qquad ProcPrio1[h/p?, hpr/pr!] \land \\
\qquad hpr < cp) \setminus \{h, hpr, cp\}
\end{array}
$$

This expands into

[1] We hope!

$$
\begin{array}{|l}
\hline
\textit{QueueHdHasHigherPriority1} \\
\Xi SCHED \\
\Xi PTAB1 \\
\hline
\exists h : PID;\ hpr, cp : PPRIO \bullet \\
\quad prio1(curr) = cp \land \\
\quad h = pq1(1) \land \\
\quad prio1(h) = hpr \land \\
\quad hpr < cp \\
\hline
\end{array}
$$

and then to

$$
\begin{array}{|l}
\hline
\textit{QueueHdHasHigherPriority1} \\
\Xi SCHED \\
\Xi PTAB1 \\
\hline
\exists hpr, cp : PPRIO \bullet \\
\quad h = pq1(1) \land \\
\quad prio1(h) = hpr \land \\
\quad hpr < prio1(curr) \\
\hline
\end{array}
$$

and finally to

$$
\begin{array}{|l}
\hline
\textit{QueueHdHasHigherPriority1} \\
\Xi SCHED \\
\Xi PTAB1 \\
\hline
prio1(pq1(1)) < prio1(curr) \\
\hline
\end{array}
$$

$$
\begin{array}{l}
SchedNext1 \mathrel{\widehat{=}} \\
\quad (IsCurrentProcessIdle \land \\
\qquad ((IsEmptySCHEDQ1 \land ContinueCurrent) \\
\qquad\quad \lor (SCHEDQDequeue1[p/p!] \land SetNewCurrentProcess[p/p?] \\
\qquad\qquad ⨾ CTXTSW) \setminus \{p\})) \\
\quad \lor (IsEmptySCHEDQ1 \land MakeIdleProcessCurrent ⨾ CTXTSW) \\
\quad \lor ((\neg\ CurrentProcessStateIsReadyOrRunning1 \\
\qquad\quad \lor QueueHdHasHigherPriority1) \land \\
\qquad (SCHEDQHd1[hpid/p!] \land \\
\qquad\quad SCHEDQDelHd1 \land \\
\qquad\quad SetNewCurrentProcess[hpid/p?] ⨾ CTXTSW) \setminus \{hpid\}) \\
\quad \lor ContinueCurrent
\end{array}
$$

The precondition, when simplified, is

$$\begin{array}{l}
\mathrm{pre}\ \mathit{SchedNext1} \mathrel{\widehat=} \\
\quad \mathit{curr} = \mathit{iprc} \\
\quad \vee\ \mathit{nxtp} = 1 \\
\quad \vee\ (\mathit{prio1}(\mathit{pq1}(1)) < \mathit{prio1}(\mathit{curr}) \\
\qquad \vee\ \mathit{psready} \neq \mathit{state1}(\mathit{curr}) \vee \mathit{psrunning} \neq \mathit{state1}(\mathit{curr}))
\end{array}$$

The reader should not be surprised at the similarity between this precondition and that of *SchedNext1*. This is clearly because the abstraction relation is an identity.

The first refinement of *SuspendMe1* is

$$\begin{array}{l}
\mathit{SuspendMe1} \mathrel{\widehat=} \\
\quad ((\mathit{IsEmptySCHEDQ1} \wedge \mathit{MakeIdleProcessCurrent} \wedge \\
\qquad (\mathit{CurrentProcessId}[c/p!] \wedge \\
\qquad \mathit{MakeReady1}[c/p?]) \setminus c) \\
\qquad \vee\ ((\mathit{SCHEDQDequeue1}[p/p!] \mathbin{;} \\
\qquad\quad (\mathit{CurrentProcessId}[c/p!] \wedge \mathit{MakeReady1}[c/p?]) \setminus \{c\}) \\
\qquad \mathbin{;} \mathit{SetNewCurrentProcess}[p/p?]) \setminus \{p\}) \\
\quad \mathbin{;} \mathit{SwitchContext}
\end{array}$$

3.6.3 Refinement Two

These refinements are mostly concerned with the *PTAB2* component of scheduler operations. We have already refined the priority queue as far as we require, so all components included from the priority queue are the same as in the previous refinement. The priority queue component is a promoted component, so there are no refinement proofs required. The other immediate components of the scheduler are scalar variables and they cannot be refined for the very reason that they have reached their final level of refinement already. This leaves components of *PTAB* as candidates for refinement proofs. In each case, there is the requirement that $p? \in \mathit{used}$ (or equivalent under refinement) and this condition is met by the implicit precondition to *PRIOQ* that $\mathrm{ran}\, pq \subset \mathit{used}$. We believe, therefore, that no refinement proofs are required in this subsection. We will, though, include the refinements of the primary schemata plus some auxilliary operations.

$$\begin{array}{l}
\mathit{CurrentProcessStateIsReadyOrRunning2} \mathrel{\widehat=} \\
\quad (\mathit{CurrentProcessId}[c/p!] \wedge \\
\qquad (\exists\, st_1, st_2 : \mathit{PSTATE} \mid st_1 = \mathit{psready} \wedge st_2 = \mathit{psrunning} \bullet \\
\qquad\quad \mathit{ProcState2}[c/p?, st_1/st!] \vee \mathit{ProcState2}[c/p?, st_2/st!])) \setminus \{c\}
\end{array}$$

As in the previous cases, this operation refines to

CurrentProcessStateIsReadyOrRunning2

$\Xi PTAB1$
$\Xi SCHED$

$\mathit{psready} = \mathit{state2}(\mathit{curr}) \vee \mathit{psrunning} = \mathit{state2}(\mathit{curr})$

$$
\begin{array}{l}
QueueHdHasHigherPriority2 \mathrel{\widehat=} \\
\quad (CurrentPriority[cp/pr!] \land \\
\qquad SCHEDQHd1[h/p!] \land \\
\qquad ProcPrio2[h/p?, hpr/pr!] \land \\
\qquad hpr < cp) \setminus \{h, hpr, cp\}
\end{array}
$$

As in the previous cases, this expands and simplifies to

$$
\begin{array}{|l}
\hline
QueueHdHasHigherPriority1 \\
\Xi SCHED \\
\Xi PTAB1 \\
\hline
prio2(pq1(1)) < prio2(curr) \\
\hline
\end{array}
$$

$$
\begin{array}{l}
SchedNext2 \mathrel{\widehat=} \\
\quad (IsCurrentProcessIdle \land \\
\qquad ((IsEmptySCHEDQ1 \land ContinueCurrent) \\
\qquad\quad \lor (SCHEDQDequeue1[p/p!] \land SetNewCurrentProcess[p/p?] \\
\qquad\qquad \fatsemi CTXTSW) \setminus \{p\})) \\
\quad \lor (IsEmptySCHEDQ1 \land MakeIdleProcessCurrent \fatsemi CTXTSW) \\
\quad \lor ((\neg\ CurrentProcessStateIsReadyOrRunning2 \\
\qquad\quad \lor QueueHdHasHigherPriority2) \land \\
\qquad (SCHEDQHd1[hpid/p!] \land \\
\qquad\quad SCHEDQDelHd1 \land \\
\qquad\quad SetNewCurrentProcess[hpid/p?] \fatsemi CTXTSW) \setminus \{hpid\}) \\
\quad \lor ContinueCurrent
\end{array}
$$

The second refinement of *SuspendMe* is

$$
\begin{array}{l}
SuspendMe2 \mathrel{\widehat=} \\
\quad ((IsEmptySCHEDQ2 \land MakeIdleProcessCurrent \land \\
\qquad (CurrentProcessId[c/p!] \land \\
\qquad MakeReady2[c/p?]) \setminus c) \\
\qquad \lor ((SCHEDQDequeue2[p/p!] \fatsemi \\
\qquad\quad (CurrentProcessId[c/p!] \land MakeReady2[c/p?]) \setminus \{c\}) \\
\qquad \fatsemi SetNewCurrentProcess[p/p?]) \setminus \{p\}) \\
\quad \fatsemi CTXTSW
\end{array}
$$

The schemata from this last refinement have now been shown to be correct. They can be converted directly into executable code.

3.7 Semaphores

The kernel allows processes to synchronise using semaphores. This section contains the definition of the semaphore type.

The kernel only uses semphores. It would be very easy to extend it so that it included, say, condition variables. We refrain from such extensions because of their effect on the length of this book.

Semaphores are defined as a counter and a queue. The queue is the FIFO queue type defined for processes. This is done using promotion. This enables the separate refinement of the queue of waiting processes, *waiters* (of type *PROCESSQUEUE*). Since the *PROCESSQUEUE* type has already been specified and refined, there is no work to do with respect to its use in the current context. The only thing we really have to do is to rename the components of the *PROCESSQUEUE* and its operations so that they are more appropriate to semaphores.

The definition of the semaphore state space schema is

$$\begin{array}{|l}
\hline
\textit{SEMAPHORE} \\
\hline
scnt : \mathbb{Z} \\
waiters : PROCESSQUEUE \\
\hline
\end{array}$$

where *scnt* is the semaphore's counter and *waiters* is the queue of waiting processes.

3.7.1 Top Level

We will need to prove the following result:

Theorem 39. *If* $waiters \neq \langle\rangle$, $\forall p : PID \bullet p \in \operatorname{ran} waiters \Rightarrow p \in used$

It should be noted that the schema for semaphore has an often ignored interaction with the scheduler. If there is more than one waiter and the current process waits on the same semaphore, if the scheduler's queue is now empty, the semaphore will hang indefinitely because the idle process will run. Consideration of this leads to the inevitable conclusion that this is correct behaviour for the semaphore. If all runnable processes are waiting on the semaphore, there is no process to signal on it, so they must wait indefinitely.

A promotion schema is clearly required so that the relevant operations on *PROCESSQUEUE* can be promoted to semaphore operations.

$$\begin{array}{|l}
\hline
\Phi SEMAPHORE \\
\hline
\Delta SEMAPHORE \\
\Delta PROCESSQUEUE \\
\hline
waiters = \theta PROCESSQUEUE \\
waiters' = \theta PROCESSQUEUE' \\
\hline
\end{array}$$

The operations to add and remove a waiting process (a "waiter") are defined by promotion as follows:

$AddWaiter \mathrel{\widehat=}$
$\quad \exists \Delta SEMAWAITERS \bullet$
$\qquad \Phi SEMAPHORE \land EnqueuePROCESSQUEUE$

$RemoveWaiter \mathrel{\widehat=}$
$\quad \exists \Delta SEMAWAITERS \bullet$
$\qquad \Phi SEMAPHORE \land DequeuePROCESSQUEUE$

Semaphores are initialised by clearing their queue of waiters and by setting the counter to some value (here *ival?*). Appropriate setting of the semaphore gives a binary semaphore and a larger value for *ival?* will give a general semaphore.

SEMAPHOREInit

$SEMAPHORE'$
$ival? : \mathbb{Z}$

$scnt' = ival?$
$waiters' = \theta PROCESSQUEUEInit$

The wait and signal operations require the counter to be incremented and decremented, so the following operations are required. Note that they do not depend upon promotion but act on the variables of the *SEMAPHORE* type.

IncSEMACNT

$\Delta SEMAPHORE$

$scnt' = scnt + 1$

DecSEMACNT

$\Delta SEMAPHORE$

$scnt' = scnt - 1$

The following schema defines a predicate which is true iff *scnt* is negative.

NegativeSemaCount

$\Xi SEMAPHORE$

$scnt < 0$

The next schema defines a predicate which is true iff *scnt* is not positive—i.e., is either 0 or negative.

NonpositiveSemaCount

$\Xi SEMAPHORE$

$scnt \leq 0$

A process that is waiting on a semaphore has a state value *pswaitsema* (reasonably enough!). The following schema on *PTAB* defines the appropriate action:

$$
\begin{array}{l}
SetStateToWaitSema \mathrel{\widehat=} \\
\quad \exists\, st : PSTATE \mid st = pswaitsema \bullet \\
\qquad SetProcState[st/st?]
\end{array}
$$

This expands and simplifies to

$$
\begin{array}{l}
\textit{SetStateToWaitSema} \\
\hline
\Delta PTAB \\
p? : PID \\
\hline
state' = state \oplus \{p? \mapsto pswaitsema\}
\end{array}
$$

The operation that waits on a semaphore is defined as:

$$
\begin{array}{l}
WaitSema \mathrel{\widehat=} \\
\quad DecSEMACNT \mathbin{⨟} \\
\qquad ((NegativeSemaCount \land \\
\qquad\quad SetStateToWaitSema \land \\
\qquad\quad AddWaiter[caller?/p?] \mathbin{⨟} \\
\qquad\quad SchedNext) \\
\qquad \lor ContinueCurrent)
\end{array}
$$

The caller, *caller?*, is always the currently executing process, so $caller? = curr$, so the *WaitSema* operation is, more correctly

$$
\begin{array}{l}
WaitSema \mathrel{\widehat=} \\
\quad DecSEMACNT \mathbin{⨟} \\
\qquad ((NegativeSemaCount \land \\
\qquad\quad (CurrentProcessId[c/p!] \land \\
\qquad\qquad SetStateToWaitSema[c/p?] \land \\
\qquad\qquad AddWaiter[c/p?]) \setminus \{c\} \\
\qquad\quad \mathbin{⨟} SchedNext) \\
\qquad \lor ContinueCurrent)
\end{array}
$$

Notice that *WaitSema* can be equivalently expressed as follows

$$
\begin{array}{l}
WaitSema \mathrel{\widehat=} \\
\quad DecSEMACNT \mathbin{⨟} \\
\qquad ((NegativeSemaCount \land \\
\qquad\quad (CurrentProcessId[c/p!] \land \\
\qquad\qquad SetStateToWaitSema[c/p?] \land \\
\qquad\qquad (\exists\, \Delta PROCESSQUEUE \bullet \\
\qquad\qquad\quad \Phi SEMAPHORE \land \\
\qquad\qquad\qquad EnqueuePROCESSQUEUE[c/p?])) \setminus \{c\} \land \\
\qquad\quad \mathbin{⨟} SchedNext) \\
\qquad \lor ContinueCurrent)
\end{array}
$$

The full expansion is as follows. The *WaitSema* schema expands first (after elimination of the existential quantifier by the one-point rule) into

$$
\begin{array}{l}
\textit{WaitSema}_a \\
\hline
\Delta PTAB \\
\Delta SEMAPHORE \\
\Delta PROCESSQUEUE \\
\Delta SCHED \\
serr! : SYSERR \\
\hline
(scnt' = scnt - 1 \land \\
\quad (scnt' < 0 \land \\
\quad\quad state' = state \oplus \{curr \mapsto pswaitsema\} \land \\
\quad\quad waiters.procs = waiters.procs \frown \langle curr \rangle \fatsemi \\
\quad\quad SchedNext) \\
\quad \lor (curr' = curr \land prev' = prev)) \\
\hline
\end{array}
$$

Its second expansion is

$$
\begin{array}{l}
\textit{WaitSema} \\
\hline
\Delta SCHED \\
\Delta PTAB \\
\Delta SEMAPHORE \\
\Delta PROCESSQUEUE \\
serr! : SYSERR \\
\hline
\exists\, state'' : PID \nrightarrow PSTATE \bullet \\
\quad (scnt' = scnt - 1 \land \\
\quad\quad ((scnt' < 0 \land \\
\quad\quad\quad waiters.procs' = waiters.procs \frown \langle curr \rangle \land \\
\quad\quad\quad state'' = state \oplus \{curr \mapsto pswaitsema\} \land \\
\quad (curr = iprc \land \\
\quad\quad ((pq = \langle\rangle \land curr' = curr \land prev' = prev) \\
\quad\quad\quad \lor (curr' = head\, pq \land prev' = curr \land \\
\quad\quad\quad\quad state' = state \oplus \{head\, pq \mapsto psrunning\} \\
\quad\quad\quad\quad \land CTXTSW))) \\
\quad \lor (pq = \langle\rangle \land prev' = curr \land curr' = iprc \land CTXTSW) \\
\quad \lor ((state''(curr) \neq psready \land state''(curr) \neq psrunning \\
\quad\quad\quad \lor prio(head\, pq) < prio(curr)) \land \\
\quad\quad pq' = tail\, pq \land \\
\quad\quad curr' = head\, pq \land \\
\quad\quad state' = state \oplus \{head\, pq \mapsto psrunning\} \land \\
\quad\quad prev' = curr \land \\
\quad\quad CTXTSW) \\
\quad \lor (curr' = curr \land prev' = prev) \\
\quad \lor (curr' = curr \land prev' = prev)) \\
\hline
\end{array}
$$

In the call to *SchedNext*, the state of *curr* is clearly *pswaitsema*, this can be used as an additional fact in simplifying the predicate.

$$
\begin{array}{|l}
\hline
\textit{WaitSema} \\
\Delta SCHED \\
\Delta PTAB \\
\Delta SEMAPHORE \\
\Delta PROCESSQUEUE \\
serr! : SYSERR \\
\hline
((scnt \leq 0 \land \\
\qquad waiters.procs' = waiters.procs \frown \langle curr \rangle \land \\
\qquad state' = state \oplus \{curr \mapsto pswaitsema\} \land \\
((pq = \langle\rangle \land prev' = curr \land curr' = iprc) \\
\lor (pq = tail\ pq \land \\
\qquad curr' = head\ pq \land \\
\qquad state' = state \oplus \{head\ pq \mapsto psrunning\} \land \\
\qquad prev' = curr))) \\
\qquad \lor (curr' = curr \land prev' = prev)) \\
\hline
\end{array}
$$

and its precondition is

$$\text{pre } WaitSema \mathrel{\widehat=} scnt \leq 0$$

Note that the *SignalSema* operation can be performed by *any* piece of code, not just the current process. This implies that it can be called by, for example, a device interface.

Finally, it should be noted that $curr' = curr \land prev' = prev$ is just skip when implemented. Next we have the signal operation (the V operation in the original):

$$
\begin{array}{l}
SignalSema \mathrel{\widehat=} \\
\quad IncSEMACNT \mathbin{;} \\
\qquad (NonPositiveSemaCount \land \\
\qquad\quad (\exists p : PID \bullet \\
\qquad\qquad RemoveWaiter[p/p!] \land \\
\qquad\qquad MakeReady[p/p?])) \land \\
\qquad\quad ContinueCurrent)
\end{array}
$$

Schema *SignalSema* expands into:

$$
\begin{array}{|l}
\hline
\textit{SignalSema} \\
\Delta SEMAPHORE \\
\Delta PROCESSQUEUE \\
serr! : SYSERR \\
\hline
scnt' = scnt + 1 \land \\
\qquad (scnt' \leq 0 \land \\
\qquad\qquad waiters.procs' = tail\ waiters.procs \land
\end{array}
$$

$$
\begin{array}{l}
\quad MakeReady[head\ waiters.procs/p?]) \land \\
(curr' = curr \land prev' = prev)
\end{array}
$$

Note how this specification is much simpler than in [4]. This is because we are interested only in the refinement not in a (relatively) complete micro model of the operation of the semaphore.

The *SignalSema* operation expands next into the following schema:

SignalSema

$$
\begin{array}{l}
\Delta PRIOQ \\
\Delta SEMAPHORE \\
\Delta PROCESSQUEUE \\
serr! : SYSERR
\end{array}
$$

$$
\begin{array}{l}
(scnt < 0 \land \\
\quad waiters.procs' = tail\ waiters.procs \land \\
\quad\quad ((\#sq.pq < maxs \land \\
\quad\quad\quad ((sq.pq = \langle\rangle \land sq.pq' = \langle head\ waiters.procs\rangle) \\
\quad\quad\quad\quad \lor (prio(head\ waiters.procs) \leq prio(head\ sq.pq) \land \\
\quad\quad\quad\quad\quad sq.pq' = \langle head\ waiters.procs\rangle \frown sq.pq) \\
\quad\quad\quad\quad \lor (prio(last\ sq.pq) < prio(head\ waiters.procs) \land \\
\quad\quad\quad\quad\quad sq.pq' = sq.pq \frown \langle head\ waiters.procs\rangle) \\
\quad\quad\quad\quad \lor (\exists s_1, s_2 : \mathrm{seq}\ PID \mid \\
\quad\quad\quad\quad\quad\quad\quad s_1 \neq \langle\rangle \land s_2 \neq \langle\rangle \land s_1 \frown s_2 = sq.pq \bullet \\
\quad\quad\quad\quad\quad prio(last\ s_1) < prio(head\ waiters.procs) \land \\
\quad\quad\quad\quad\quad prio(head\ waiters.procs) \leq prio(head\ s_2) \land \\
\quad\quad\quad\quad\quad sq' = s_1 \frown \langle head\ waiters\rangle \frown s_2)) \land \\
\quad\quad\quad\quad state' = state \oplus \{head\ waiters \mapsto psready\} \land \\
\quad\quad\quad\quad serr! = sysok) \\
\quad\quad \lor serr! = schedqfull)) \\
\quad\quad \land (curr' = curr \land prev' = prev)
\end{array}
$$

The final conjunct $(curr' = curr \land prev' = prev)$ reduces to skip because it is just the identity applied to the scheduler's state. It could, therefore, be omitted; it will be left as a reminder when translating the schema.

There is not a great deal that can be done with this schema! Let us, instead, calculate the precondition.

$$
\begin{array}{l}
\mathrm{pre}\ SignalSema \mathrel{\widehat{=}} \\
\quad scnt + 1 \leq 0 \land \#sq.pq < maxs \land waiters.procs \neq \langle\rangle
\end{array}
$$

or:

$$
scnt < 0 \land \#sq.pq < maxs \land waiters.procs \neq \langle\rangle
$$

3.7.2 Refinement

Because of the use of promotion in the definition of *SEMAPHORE*, there is very little to do as far as refinement is concerned. The refinement of *scnt* is just *scnt* itself (it is just a scalar variable), while the refinement of the queue type has already been completed. The only slight complication is the alteration of the *state* variable in *PTAB*; two refinements of *PTAB* should be taken into account.

The production of refinement schemata consists only of substituting new names into those presented above. There is no need to engage in any correctness proofs because they have already been done.

The substitution of the apporpriate promoted schemata into the schemata defining *WaitSema* and *SignalSema* produces schemata that are suitable for translation into code.

The schemata derived in this section can be implemented directly as executable code. In the current case, the semaphore construct is composed of already refined constructs, its implementation is less obvious in the schemata.

3.8 Semaphore Table

Now that we have semaphores, a table to hold them can be defined. This table will be maintained by the kernel, so a measure of control can be exerted on the number of semaphores in the system.

The table has the usual operations.

Following our convention, the error schemata are defined first. There are two error schemata: *NotAllocSema* for when an attempt has been made to perform an operation on a semaphore that has not been allocated and *NoFreeSemas* which reports that the semaphore table is full.

NotAllocSema

$serr! : SYSERR$

$serr! = notallocsema$

NoFreeSemas

$serr! : SYSERR$

$serr! = nofreesemas$

3.8.1 Top Level

This subsection contains the specification of the semaphore table. The table supports the following operations:

- Initialisation.
- Allocate a new semaphore.
- Free a semaphore.

Since semaphores were specified and refined to near code in the last section, the semaphore table can be specified using promotion.

An indentifier type for semaphores must first be defined. This is an atomic type. Its elements are semaphore identifiers.

$[SID]$

This type will be refined.

The semaphore table is defined as follows:

$$
\begin{array}{l}
\textit{SEMATBL} \\
\hline
semas : SID \pfun SEMAPHORE \\
semasinuse : \mathbb{F}\, SID \\
\hline
semasinused = \operatorname{dom} semas
\end{array}
$$

The variable *semas* is the table, a partial mapping from semaphore identifiers to semaphores; *semasinuse* contains the identifiers of those semaphores that are currently in use. The *semasinuse* variable is used to determine whether it is possible to allocate another semaphore, whether a semaphore is in use, and so on.

The initialisation schema is defined as:

$$
\begin{array}{l}
\textit{SEMATBLInit} \\
\hline
SEMATBL' \\
\hline
semasinuse' = \varnothing
\end{array}
$$

This is very much as would be expected. By making $semasinuse' = \varnothing$, the domain of *semas* is also made empty.

The promotion schema is a textbook case:

$$
\begin{array}{l}
\Phi SEMATBL \\
\hline
\Delta SEMATBL \\
\Delta SEMAPHORE \\
s? : SID \\
\hline
s? \in semasinuse \\
semas(s?) = \theta SEMAPHORE \\
semas' = semas \oplus \{s? \mapsto \theta SEMAPHORE'\}
\end{array}
$$

The following schema defines the operation to free a semaphore. Freeing a semaphore consists of removing the semaphore's identifier from *semasinuse*.

$$
\begin{array}{|l}
\hline
\textit{FreeSema} \\
\Delta SEMATBL \\
s? : SID \\
\hline
semasinuse' = semasinuse \setminus \{s?\} \\
\hline
\end{array}
$$

The following schema defines the allocation operation for semaphore identifiers. A semaphore can be allocated only when an identifier has been allocated, so this schema amounts to the first stage in allocating a semaphore.

$$
\begin{array}{|l}
\hline
\textit{AllocSID} \\
\Delta SEMATBL \\
s! : SID \\
\hline
s! \notin semasinuse \\
semasinuse' = semasinuse \cup \{p!\} \\
\hline
\end{array}
$$

The operation is nondeterministic. The identifier to be returned, $s!$, is chosen nondeterministically so that it does not occur in *semasinuse* (the operation *must* be used only when it is known that $semasinuse \neq \varnothing$). The newly allocated identifier is added to *semasinuse* in the last conjunct.

The next schema defines a predicate which is satisfied when there are some elements of *SID* that are not elements of *semasinuse*.

$$
\begin{array}{|l}
\hline
\textit{FreeSIDs} \\
\Xi SEMATBL \\
\hline
semasinuse \subset SID \\
\hline
\end{array}
$$

The following defines the initialisation of a semaphore, once allocated. Given a semaphore identifier, $s?$, the associated semaphore is initialised using $\theta SEMAPHOREInit$. There is no magic here; the value used to initialise the semaphore is merely implicitly declared in the signature of the *InitSema* schema).

$$
\begin{array}{|l}
\hline
\textit{InitSema} \\
\Delta SEMATBL \\
s? : SID \\
\hline
semas' = semas \cup \{s? \mapsto \theta SEMAPHOREInit\} \\
\hline
\end{array}
$$

The operation to allocate semaphores is

$$
\begin{array}{l}
AllocSema \mathrel{\widehat=} \\
\qquad (AllocSID \land InitSema \land SysOk) \\
\qquad \lor NoFreeSemas
\end{array}
$$

It expands into:

$$
\begin{array}{|l}
\hline
\textit{AllocSema} \\
\Delta SEMATBL \\
s! : SID \\
serr! : SYSERR \\
\hline
(s? \notin semasinuse \land \\
\quad semasinuse' = semasinuse \cup \{s!\} \land \\
\quad semas' = semas \cup \{s? \mapsto \theta SEMAPHOREInit\} \land \\
\quad serr! = sysok) \\
\lor\ serr! = nofreesemas \\
\hline
\end{array}
$$

The precondition is

$$\text{pre}\ AllocSema \mathrel{\widehat{=}} \exists\, s : SID \bullet s \in semasinuse$$

To free a semaphore, the *ReleaseSema* operation is used. This operation is defined as follows.

$$
\begin{array}{l}
ReleaseSema \mathrel{\widehat{=}} \\
\quad (SemaInUse \land FreeSema \land SysOk) \\
\quad \lor\ NotAllocSema
\end{array}
$$

This definition expands into the following schema:

$$
\begin{array}{|l}
\hline
\textit{ReleaseSema} \\
\Delta SEMATBL \\
s? : SID \\
serr! : SYSERR \\
\hline
(s? \in semasinuse \land \\
\quad semasinuse' = semasinuse \setminus \{s?\} \land \\
\quad serr! = sysok) \\
\lor\ serr! = notallocsema \\
\hline
\end{array}
$$

The *ReleaseSema* schema's precondition is given by the following schema.

$$\text{pre}\ ReleaseSema \mathrel{\widehat{=}} s? \in semasinuse$$

The semaphore operations can be promoted to operations on the table. The definitions are quite standard and are as follows:

$$
\begin{array}{l}
STWaitSema \mathrel{\widehat{=}} \\
\quad \exists\, \Delta SEMAPHORE \bullet \\
\quad\quad \Phi SEMATBL \land WaitSema
\end{array}
$$

and

$STSignalSema \mathrel{\widehat{=}}$
　　　$\exists\, \Delta SEMAPHORE \bullet$
　　　　　$\Phi SEMATBL \wedge SignalSema$

There is no refinement necessary for these operations.

3.8.2 Refinement One

The first object of concern is the type SID. This was an atomic type when initially defined. For this refinement, it is itself refined to:

$SID == minsid \mathrel{..} maxsid$

In addition, it is necessary to define:

$$
\begin{array}{|l}
minsid, maxsid : \mathbb{N}_1 \\
\hline
minsid < maxsid
\end{array}
$$

Good values for $minsid$ are zero or one.

The semaphore table type can now be defined as the following schema

$$
\begin{array}{|l}
\underline{ST1} \\
semas1 : SID \rightarrow SEMAPHORE \\
sinuse : SID \rightarrow \{0,1\}
\end{array}
$$

Here, the set, $semasinuse$, is replaced by a function. The evaluation of the function for an arbitrary value of s is $sinuse(s) = 1$ iff $s \in semasinuse$, $sinuse(s) = 0$ otherwise. In other words, $sinuse$ is the characteristic function of $semasinuse$. The other component, $semas1$, is now a total function but its domain and codomain are identical. Moreover, it is intended that the value of $semas1(s)$ is defined at s iff $sinuse(s) = 1$.

The initialisation schema is very much as one might expect:

$$
\begin{array}{|l}
\underline{ST1Init} \\
ST1' \\
\hline
\forall\, s : SID \bullet \\
\quad sinuse'(s) = 0
\end{array}
$$

The operation to allocate a semaphore is, again, nondeterministic.

$$
\begin{array}{|l}
\underline{AllocST1} \\
\Delta ST1 \\
s! : SID \\
\hline
\exists\, s : SID \bullet \\
\quad sinuse(s) = 0 \wedge \\
\quad sinuse' = sinuse \oplus \{s \mapsto 1\} \wedge \\
\quad s! = s
\end{array}
$$

Here, the nondeterminism is located in the choice of s, not $s!$, as was the case in the last subsection. The predicate of this schema is equivalent to

$$
\begin{array}{l}
sinuse(s!) = 0 \\
sinuse' = sinuse \oplus \{s! \mapsto 1\}
\end{array}
$$

which, we believe, makes the nondeterminism harder to detect. Nonetheless, the two definitions of the operation are perfectly adequate for our needs; we do not care which particular identifier is chosen, as long as one is. The identifier should not be in current use; once chosen, it should be marked as being in use. This is what the operation states, so it is adequate.

$$
\begin{array}{|l}
\hline
\textit{FreeSID1} \\
\hline
\Delta ST1 \\
s? : SID \\
\hline
sinuse' = sinuse \oplus \{s? \mapsto 0\} \\
\hline
\end{array}
$$

The operation to free a semaphore identifier is just an update of the *sinuse* function. This is obvious given the relationship between *semasinuse* and *sinuse*.

The semaphore initialisation operation is next.

$$
\begin{array}{|l}
\hline
\textit{InitSema1} \\
\hline
\Delta ST1 \\
s? : SID \\
\hline
semas1' = semas1 \oplus \{s? \mapsto \theta SEMAPHOREInit\} \\
\hline
\end{array}
$$

The next schema defines a predicate that is satisfied when $s?$ is in use.

$$
\begin{array}{|l}
\hline
\textit{SemaInUse1} \\
\hline
\Xi ST1 \\
s? : SID \\
\hline
sinuse(s?) = 1 \\
\hline
\end{array}
$$

The allocation operation should cause no problems. It is defined as

$$
\begin{array}{l}
AllocSema1 \mathrel{\widehat=} \\
\qquad (AllocSID1 \land InitSema![s!/s?] \land SysOk) \\
\qquad \lor\ NoFreeSema
\end{array}
$$

and expands into:

$$
\begin{array}{|l}
\hline
\textit{AllocSema1} \\
\Delta ST1 \\
s! : SID \\
serr! : SYSERR \\
\hline
((\exists s : SID \bullet \\
\quad sinuse(s) = 0 \land \\
\quad sinuse' = sinuse \oplus \{s \mapsto 1\} \land \\
\quad s! = s) \land \\
\quad semas1' = semas1 \oplus \{s! \mapsto \theta SEMAPHOREInit\} \land \\
\quad serr! = sysok) \\
\lor serr! = nofreesema \\
\hline
\end{array}
$$

The precondition of *AllocSema1* is easily calculated. It is

$$
\begin{array}{l}
\text{pre } AllocSema1 \mathrel{\widehat=} \\
\quad \exists s : SID \bullet \\
\qquad sinuse(s) = 0
\end{array}
$$

The operation to free a semaphore is the following:

$$
\begin{array}{l}
ReleaseSema1 \mathrel{\widehat=} \\
\quad (SemaInUse1 \land FreeSID1 \land SysOk) \\
\quad \lor NotAllocSema
\end{array}
$$

It expands into the next schema:

$$
\begin{array}{|l}
\hline
\textit{ReleaseSema} \\
\Delta ST1 \\
s? : SID \\
\hline
(sinuse(s?) = 1 \land \\
\quad sinuse' = sinuse \oplus \{s? \mapsto 0\} \land \\
\quad serr! = sysok) \\
\lor serr! = notallocsema \\
\hline
\end{array}
$$

An abstraction relation is needed so that this level of representation can be related to the top-level specification. The abstraction relation is the obvious one.

$$
\begin{array}{|l}
\hline
\textit{AbsST1} \\
ST \\
ST1 \\
\hline
\forall s : SID \bullet \\
\quad sinuse(s) \Leftrightarrow s \in semasinuse \\
\forall s : SID \bullet \\
\quad s \in semasinuse \Rightarrow semas1(s) = semas(s) \\
\hline
\end{array}
$$

3.8.3 Refinement One–Again

The first refinement of *SEMATBL* refines the partial function to what amounts to an array indexed by *SID*. The other component of $ST1$, *sinuse*, is a mapping between semaphore identifiers and the set $\{0, 1\}$, which is used to represent *semasinuse*. The object of this refinement is to find a more compact representation for *semasinuse* or *sinuse*. The aim is to refine *sinuse* to a bitmap.

First, the number of bits per machine word must be defined.

$$bpw : \mathbb{N}_1$$

Next, it is necessary to define how many words are required to represent the elements of *SID*, one element per bit.

$$msize : \mathbb{N}_1$$

$$msize = \lceil \frac{maxsid - minsid}{bpw} \rceil$$

Clearly, if $minsid = 0$, this simplifies to

$$\lceil \frac{maxsid}{bpw} \rceil$$

One machine word can represent values in the range $0 \mathrel{..} 2^{bpw} - 1$. This can also be written as $\{0 \mathrel{..} bpw - 1\}$ if $\log_2 s$, $s \in SID$ is used. Therefore, the type

$$MWORD == \{0 \mathrel{..} bpw - 1\}$$

is defined.

The first definition of the bitmap is:

$$BMASK == 0 \mathrel{..} msize - 1 \rightarrow MWORD$$

This can be interpreted as a vector of *msize* elements each of which is a set of bits. It can be verified that the union of the domain elements of *BMASK* covers all elements of *SID*.

An encoding is required for elements of *SID*. It is fairly obvious and that integer division and mod are appropriate. Integer division will be written $\div$.

Let $bm : BMASK$, so

$$s \in semasinuse \Leftrightarrow (s \bmod bpw) \in bm(s \div bpw)$$
$$\quad \Rightarrow \{(s \bmod bpw)\} \subseteq bm(s \div bpw)$$
$$semasinuse \cup \{s\} \Leftrightarrow \{(s \bmod bpw)\} \cup bm(s \div bpw)$$
$$semasinuse \setminus \{s\} \Leftrightarrow bm(s \div bpw) \setminus \{(s \bmod bpw)\}$$

These equivalents are straightforward to verify. For example, the implication on line two can be proved from the biconditional on line one using the fact that $x \in X \subseteq Y \Rightarrow x \in Y$.

We have defined $MWORD$ as $\{0 \mathinner{..} bpw - 1\}$. This can be improved upon with relative ease. First, consider the effect of redefining $MWORD$ as $0 \mathinner{..} bpw - 1$ and define a new type, BM, as:

$BM : 0 \mathinner{..} bpw - 1 \to \{0,1\}$

This is the characteristic function of the membership function defined for SID. In particular, if $f \in BM$ $(f : BM)$, define $x \in \operatorname{dom} f \Leftrightarrow f(x) = 1$ and $x \notin \operatorname{dom} f \Leftrightarrow f(x) = 0$.

The following operations can be defined. Note that BM has a fixed finite domain, so it is possible to iterate over it.

$$
\begin{array}{l}
\& : BM \times BM \to BM \\
\hline
\forall f_1, f_2 : BM \bullet \\
\quad \exists_1 f_r : BM \mid f_r = f_1 \& f_2 \bullet \\
\quad\quad \forall i : 0 \mathinner{..} bpw - 1 \bullet \\
\quad\quad\quad f_1(i) = 1 \land f_2(i) = 1 \Rightarrow f_r(i) = 1 \land \\
\quad\quad\quad f_1(i) \neq 1 \lor f_2(i) \neq 1 \Rightarrow f_r(i) = 0
\end{array}
$$

$$
\begin{array}{l}
\mid : BM \times BM \to BM \\
\hline
\forall f_1, f_2 : BM \mid f_r = f_1 | f_2 \bullet \\
\quad \exists_1 f_r : BM \bullet \\
\quad\quad \forall i : 0 \mathinner{..} bpw - 1 \bullet \\
\quad\quad\quad f_1(i) = 1 \lor f_2(i) = 1 \Rightarrow f_r(i) = 1 \land \\
\quad\quad\quad f_1(i) = 0 \land f_2(i) = 0 \Rightarrow f_r(i) = 0
\end{array}
$$

$$
\begin{array}{l}
\sim : BM \to BM \\
\hline
\forall f_1 : BM \bullet \\
\quad \exists_1 f_r : BM \mid f_r = \sim f_1 \bullet \\
\quad\quad \forall i : 0 \mathinner{..} bpw - 1 \bullet \\
\quad\quad\quad f_1(i) = 1 \Rightarrow f_r(i) = 0 \land \\
\quad\quad\quad f_1(i) = 0 \Rightarrow f_r(i) = 1
\end{array}
$$

$$
\begin{array}{l}
\uparrow : BM \times BM \to BM \\
\hline
\forall f_1, f_2 : BM \bullet \\
\quad \exists_1 f_r : BM \mid f_r = f_1 \uparrow f_2 \bullet \\
\quad\quad \forall i : 0 \mathinner{..} bpw - 1 \bullet \\
\quad\quad\quad f_1(i) = f_2(i) \Rightarrow f_r(i) = 0 \land \\
\quad\quad\quad f_1(i) \neq f_2(i) \Rightarrow f_r(i) = 1
\end{array}
$$

In particular, it should be noted that $x \in X$ can be written as $(\{x\} \cap X) \neq \varnothing$. This is the memebership test for bit maps, as a moment's thought reveals.

Lemma 2. & *represents set intersection. It is bitwise "and."*

Proof. Actually, quite easy given the definitions. If f_1 and f_2 are interpreted as the characteristic function of $\in$, the definition of $\cap$ is readily retrieved. Given two sets, X and Y, $x \in X \cap Y \Leftrightarrow x \in X \wedge x \in Y$. $\square$

Lemma 3. | *represents set union. It is bitwise "or."*

Proof. Again, taking f_1 and f_2 to be the characteristic function of $\in$, the function is immediately seen to define $\cup$: given two sets, X and Y, $x \in X \cup Y \Leftrightarrow (x \in X) \vee (x \in Y)$; if $x \notin X \wedge x \notin Y$, it is not in $X \cup Y$. This is equivalent to an expansion of the definition of $|$. $\square$

Lemma 4. $\sim$ *rerpesents set complementation. It is bitwise complement.*

Proof. This is, again, easy to deduce. If $x \in X$, $x \notin\sim X$; if $x \notin\sim X$, $x \in X$. $\square$

Lemma 5. $\uparrow$ *represents a form of set difference, specifically symmetric set difference.*

Proof. The easiest way to view this is with a Venn diagram from which it can be deduced that $X \uparrow Y = (X \cup Y) \setminus (X \cap Y)$, or $X \uparrow Y = (X \setminus Y) \cup (Y \setminus X)$. This is the symmetric set difference operator; it is also an exclusive-or operation. $\square$

These operations correspond to bit operations provided by languages like C, C++ and Ada.

Note that the above construction can easily be generalised. The domain *SID* upon which this construction is based can be replaced by any arbitrary set, X, subject to the restrictions that (a) X is discrete, (b) X is bounded above and below.

With these operations in place, a bit map type can be defined for the semaphore table type.

Now let us define a new type:

$$BITMAP \mathrel{\widehat{=}} 0 \mathinner{..} msize - 1 \rightarrow BM$$

or, in expanded form:

$$BITMAP \mathrel{\widehat{=}} 0 \mathinner{..} msize = 1 \rightarrow (0 \mathinner{..} bpw - 1 \rightarrow \{0, 1\})$$

Let s be an arbitrary element of *SID* and let

$$w = s \div bpw$$
$$b = \{s \bmod bpw \mapsto 1\} \oplus (\lambda\, i : 0 \mathinner{..} bpw - 1 \bullet 0)$$

In the identity expression defining b, the λ expression defines a function whose domain is $0 \mathinner{..} bpw - 1$ and whose value is uniformly zero (i.e., if f is the function, $\forall x : 0 \mathinner{..} bpw - 1 \bullet ((\lambda\, i : 0 \mathinner{..} bpw - 1 \bullet 0)x) = 0$). The maplet $\{s \bmod bpw \mapsto 1\}$ clearly has the value at $s \bmod bpw$: viz., $\{s \bmod bpw \mapsto 1\}(s \bmod bpw) = 1$.

Therefore, the composition of these two functions has the following behaviour. Let the function $\{s \bmod bpw \mapsto 1\} \oplus (\lambda\, i : 0 \mathinner{..} bpw - 1 \bullet 0)$ be called f, then:

$$f(x) = \begin{cases} 1, & x = s \bmod bpw \\ 0, & \text{otherwise} \end{cases}$$

Now assume:

$sinuse : BITMAP$

We can write the following identities. Each identity is justified by one or more of the lemmata above.

$$s \in semasinuse \Leftrightarrow sinuse(w) \mid b$$

$$semasinuse \cup \{s\} \Leftrightarrow sinuse(w) \mid b$$

$$semasinuse \setminus \{s\} \Leftrightarrow (\sim sinuse(w) \uparrow b$$

The appropriate updates are as follows:

$$\begin{aligned} & semasinuse' = semasinuse \cup \{s\} \Leftrightarrow \\ & \qquad sinuse = sinuse \oplus \{w \mapsto sinuse(w) \mathbin{\&} b\} \\ & semasinuse' = semasinuse \setminus \{s\} \Leftrightarrow \\ & \qquad sinuse = sinuse \oplus \{w \mapsto (\sim sinuse(w)) \uparrow b\} \end{aligned}$$

Using this new structure, it is possible to define new schemata for the semaphore table. These schemata will be given a $_a$ subscript for now (and the state schema will be similarly annotated).

$SemaInUse_a$

$$\Xi ST1_a$$
$$s? : SID$$

$$\begin{aligned} & sinuse(s? \div bpw) \mathbin{\&} ((\lambda\, i : 0 \mathinner{..} bpw - 1 \bullet 0) \oplus \{s? \bmod bpw \mapsto 1\}) \\ & \qquad \neq ((\lambda\, i : 0 \mathinner{..} bpw - 1 \bullet 0) \oplus \{s? \bmod bpw \mapsto 1\}) \end{aligned}$$

$FreeSID_a$

$$\Delta ST1_a$$
$$s? : SID$$

$$\begin{aligned} & \exists\, w : 0 \mathinner{..} bpw - 1;\ b : 0 \mathinner{..} bpw - 1 \to \{0, 1\} \bullet \\ & \qquad w = s? \div bpw \land \\ & \qquad b = (\lambda\, i : 0 \mathinner{..} bpw - 1 \bullet 0) \oplus \{s? \bmod bpw \mapsto 1\} \land \\ & \qquad sinuse' = sinuse \oplus \{w \mapsto ((\sim sinuse(w)) \uparrow b)\} \end{aligned}$$

Using the one-point rule twice, the predicate becomes

$$
\begin{aligned}
&sinuse' = \\
&\quad sinuse \oplus \{(s? \div bpw) \mapsto \\
&\qquad\qquad ((\sim sinuse(s? \div bpw)) \\
&\qquad\qquad\quad \uparrow (\lambda\, i : 0 \mathinner{\ldotp\ldotp} bpw - 1 \bullet 0) \oplus \{s? \bmod bpw \mapsto 1\})\}
\end{aligned}
$$

$$
\begin{array}{|l}
\hline
\textit{AllocST1}_a \\
\Delta ST1_a \\
s! : SID \\
\hline
\exists\, s : SID \bullet \\
\quad (\exists\, w : 0 \mathinner{\ldotp\ldotp} bpw - 1;\ b : 0 \mathinner{\ldotp\ldotp} bpw - 1 \rightarrow \{0,1\} \bullet \\
\qquad w = s \div bpw \land \\
\qquad b = (\lambda\, i : 0 \mathinner{\ldotp\ldotp} bpw - 1 \bullet 0) \oplus \{s \bmod bpw \mapsto 1\} \land \\
\qquad (sinuse(w)\ \&\ b) \neq b \land \\
\qquad sinuse' = sinuse \oplus \{w \mapsto (sinuse(w) \mid b)\} \land \\
\qquad s! = s) \\
\hline
\end{array}
$$

$$
\begin{aligned}
&\exists\, w : 0 \mathinner{\ldotp\ldotp} bpw - 1;\ b, b_v : 0 \mathinner{\ldotp\ldotp} bpw - 1 \rightarrow \{0,1\} \bullet \\
&\quad w = s! \div bpw \land \\
&\quad b_v = \{s! \bmod bpw \mapsto 1\} \land \\
&\quad b = (\lambda\, i : 0 \mathinner{\ldotp\ldotp} bpw - 1 \bullet 0) \oplus b_v \land \\
&\quad (sinuse(w)\ \&\ b) \neq b \land \\
&\quad sinuse' = sinuse \oplus \{w \mapsto (sinuse(w) \mid b)\} \land \\
&\quad s! = w + b_v
\end{aligned}
$$

where + is integer addition. The last line is jutified by the observation that if $b = s \bmod bpw$ and $w = s \div bpw$ then $w \times b = s$. This predicate can be further simplified:

$$
\begin{aligned}
&sinuse(s? \div bpw)\ \&\ (\lambda\, i : 0 \mathinner{\ldotp\ldotp} bpw - 1 \bullet 0) \oplus \{s? \bmod bpw \mapsto 1\} \\
&\qquad \neq (\lambda\, i : 0 \mathinner{\ldotp\ldotp} bpw - 1 \bullet 0) \oplus \{s? \bmod bpw \mapsto 1\} \\
&sinuse' = \\
&\qquad sinuse \oplus \{(s? \div bpw) \mapsto sinuse(s? \div bpw) \mid \\
&\qquad\qquad (\lambda\, i : 0 \mathinner{\ldotp\ldotp} bpw - 1 \bullet 0) \oplus \{s? \bmod bpw \mapsto 1\} \\
&s! = (s? \div bpw) \times (s? \bmod bpw)
\end{aligned}
$$

The argument preceding the definition of these schemata amounts to their refinement proof.

The specification at this level can therefore be completed as follows.

$$SID == minsid \mathinner{\ldotp\ldotp} maxsid$$

$$
\begin{array}{|l}
minsid, maxsid : \mathbb{N}_1 \\
\hline
minsid < maxsid
\end{array}
$$

$$msize : \mathbb{N}_1$$

$$bpw : \mathbb{N}_1$$

The semaphore table is now defined by the following schema:

$$\begin{array}{l}
\textit{ST1} \\
\hline
semas1 : SID \rightarrow SEMAPHORE \\
sinuse : BITMAP \\
\hline
\end{array}$$

The initialisation operation is given by the next schema.

$$\begin{array}{l}
\textit{ST1Init} \\
\hline
ST1' \\
\hline
\forall w : 0 \mathrel{..} msize - 1 \bullet \\
\quad \forall b : 0 \mathrel{..} bpw - 1 \rightarrow \{0, 1\} \bullet \\
\quad\quad sinuse'(w)(b) = 0 \\
\hline
\end{array}$$

The next schema defines the operation to initialise a semaphore once its identifier, $s?$, has been allocated.

$$\begin{array}{l}
\textit{InitSema1} \\
\hline
\Delta ST1 \\
s? : SID \\
\hline
semas1' = semas1 \oplus \{s? \mapsto \theta SEMAPHOREInit\} \\
\hline
\end{array}$$

The deallocation operation is given by

$$FreeSID1 \mathrel{\widehat{=}} FreeSID_a$$

and the allocation operation by

$$AllocSID1 \mathrel{\widehat{=}} AllocST1_a$$

The operation to allocate a new semaphore identifier and to initialise the semaphore is defined as

$$\begin{array}{l}
AllocSema1 \mathrel{\widehat{=}} \\
\quad (AllocSID1 \land InitSema[s!/s?] \land SysOk) \\
\quad \lor NoFreeSema
\end{array}$$

The operation that performs the required checks when freeing a semaphore is the following

$$\begin{array}{l}
ReleaseSema1 \mathrel{\widehat{=}} \\
\quad (SemaInUse1 \land FreeSID1 \land SysOk) \lor NotAllocSema
\end{array}$$

We now define the abstraction relation

$$
\begin{array}{|l}
\hline
AbsST1 \\
SEMATBL \\
ST1 \\
\hline
\forall s : SID \bullet \\
\quad s \in semasinuse \Leftrightarrow semas(s) = semas1(s) \\
\forall s : SID \bullet \\
\quad s \in semasinuse \Leftrightarrow \\
\qquad (\exists w : 0 \mathrel{..} msize - 1;\ b : 0 \mathrel{..} bpw - 1 \rightarrow \{0,1\} \bullet \\
\qquad\quad sinuse(w)(b) = 1) \\
\hline
\end{array}
$$

Theorem 40. $\forall SEMATBL';\ ST1' \bullet SEMATBLInit \wedge AbsST1 \Rightarrow ST1Init$

PROOF. The predicate of *SEMATBLInit* is $semasinuse' = \varnothing$. By the abstraction relation,

$$
\begin{array}{l}
\forall s : SID \bullet \\
\quad s \notin semasinuse \Leftrightarrow \\
\qquad \not(\exists w : 0 \mathrel{..} msize - 1;\ b : 0 \mathrel{..} bpw - 1 \rightarrow \{0,1\} \bullet \\
\qquad\quad sinuse(w)(b) = 1)
\end{array}
$$

The predicate of $ST1Init$ is

$$
\begin{array}{l}
\forall w : 0 \mathrel{..} msize - 1;\ b : 0 \mathrel{..} bpw - 1 \rightarrow \{0,1\} \bullet \\
\quad sinuse(w)(b) = 0
\end{array}
$$

By predicate calculus ($\neg \exists x \bullet P(x) \Leftrightarrow \neg\neg \forall x \bullet \neg P(x) \Leftrightarrow \forall x \bullet \neg P(x)$) the two are equivalent. □

Theorem 41.

$$
\begin{array}{l}
\forall SEMATBL;\ ST1 \bullet \\
\quad \text{pre}\ AllocSema \wedge AbsST1 \Rightarrow \text{pre}\ AllocSema1
\end{array}
$$

PROOF. The two preconditions are

$$\text{pre}\ AllocSema \mathrel{\widehat=} s \notin semasinuse$$

and

$$\text{pre}\ AllocSema1 \mathrel{\widehat=} sinuse(s \div bpw)(s \bmod bpw) = 0$$

First note that

$$((\lambda i : 0 \mathrel{..} bpw - 1 \bullet 0) \oplus \{s \bmod bpw \mapsto 1\})(x) = \begin{cases} 1, & x = s \\ 0, & \text{otherwise} \end{cases}$$

By the definition of &, it is evident that

$$\begin{aligned}&sinuse(s \div bpw)\&(\lambda\, i : 0 \mathrel{..} bpw - 1 \bullet 0) \oplus \{s \bmod bpw \mapsto 1\}\\ &\quad \neq (\lambda\, i : 0 \mathrel{..} bpw - 1 \bullet 0) \oplus \{s \bmod bpw \mapsto 1\}\end{aligned}$$

when $sinuse(s \div bpw)(b \bmod bpw) = 0$. By the above defintiions, this is equivalent to $s \notin semasinuse$. □

Theorem 42.

$$\begin{aligned}&\forall\, SEMATBL;\ SEMATBL';\ ST1;\ ST1';\ s! : SID \bullet\\ &\quad pre\, AllocSema \land\\ &\qquad AbsST1 \land\\ &\qquad AbsST1' \land\\ &\qquad AllocSema1\\ &\quad \Rightarrow AllocSema\end{aligned}$$

PROOF. The important part of predicate of $AllocSema1$ is

$$sinuse' = sinuse \oplus \{w \mapsto (sinuse(w) \mid b)\}$$

where $w = s \div bpw$ and $b = s \bmod bpw$. Expanding the right-hand side, the following is obtained

$$\begin{aligned}&sinuse'\\ &\quad = sinuse \oplus\\ &\qquad \{w \mapsto (sinuse(s \div bpw)\\ &\qquad\quad \mid (\lambda\, i : 0 \mathrel{..} bpw - 1 \bullet 0) \oplus \{s \bmod bpw \mapsto 1\})\end{aligned}$$

It should be noted that $((\lambda\, i : 0 \mathrel{..} bpw - 1 \bullet 0) \oplus \{s \bmod bpw \mapsto 1\}))(x) = 1$ if $x = s \bmod bpw$, so $sinuse(w)(b) = 1$ iff $s = w + b$. From this, it can be inferred that $sinuse'(w)(b) = 1$, i.e., $s? \in semasinuse'$ by the abstraction relation. □

Theorem 43. $\forall\, SEMATBL;\ ST1;\ s? : SID \bullet pre\, ReleaseSema \land AbsST1 \Rightarrow pre\, ReleaseSema1$.

PROOF. In this case, we have

$$\begin{aligned}&sinuse(s? \div bpw)\&(\lambda\, i : 0 \mathrel{..} bpw - 1 \bullet 0) \oplus \{s? \bmod bpw \mapsto 1\}\\ &\quad = (\lambda\, i : 0 \mathrel{..} bpw - 1 \bullet 0) \oplus \{s? \bmod bpw \mapsto 1\}\end{aligned}$$

For this to be true, $sinuse(s? \div bpw)(s? \bmod bpw) = 1$, so $s \in semasinuse$ by the abstraction relation. □

Theorem 44.

$$\begin{aligned}&\forall\, SEMATBL;\ SEMATBL';\ ST1;\ ST1';\ s? : SID;\ serr! : SYSERR \bullet\\ &\quad pre\, ReleaseSema \land\\ &\qquad AbsST1 \land\\ &\qquad AbsST1' \land\\ &\qquad ReleaseSema1\\ &\quad \Rightarrow ReleaseSema\end{aligned}$$

PROOF. This is the dual of *AllocSema*.

Let $w = s? \div bpw$ and $v = s? \bmod bpw$.

The interesting part is $w \mapsto (\sim sinusew(w)) \uparrow b$. By the definition of $\sim$, and thinking pointwise,

$$\sim sinuse(w)(v) = \begin{cases} 0, & sinuse(w)(v) = 1, \\ 1, & \text{otherwise} \end{cases}$$

That is, $\sim$ complements $sinuse(w)$'s elements.

Now, let $b = (\lambda\, i : 0\,..\,bpw - 1 \bullet 0) \oplus \{s \bmod bpw \mapsto 1\}$, noting that $((\lambda\, i : 0\,..\,bpw - 1 \bullet 0) \oplus \{s \bmod bpw \mapsto 1\})(s \bmod bpw) = 1)$, it should be clear that

$$\begin{aligned} &\sim sinuse(w) \uparrow (\lambda\, i : 0\,..\,bpw - 1 \bullet 0) \oplus \{s \bmod bpw \mapsto 1\} \\ &\quad = \begin{cases} 0, \text{ if } \sim sinuse(w)(s \bmod bpw) = 1 \\ 1, \text{otherwise} \end{cases} \end{aligned}$$

Therefore, if $sinuse(w)(v) = 1$, $sinuse'(w)(v) = 0$ for the important part of the predicate of *ReleaseSema*1 is

$$sinuse' = sinuse \oplus \{w \mapsto ((\sim sinuse(w) \uparrow b)\}$$

Writing out the interesting part, we have

$$\begin{aligned} &\sim sinuse(w) \uparrow (\lambda\, i : 0\,..\,bpw - 1 \bullet 0) \oplus \{s \bmod bpw \mapsto 1\} \\ &\quad = \begin{cases} 0, \text{ if } \sim sinuse(w)(s \bmod bpw) = 1 \\ 1, \text{otherwise} \end{cases} \end{aligned}$$

By *AbsST*1′,

$$\begin{aligned} &\forall\, s : SID \bullet \\ &\quad s \in semasinuse' \Leftrightarrow \\ &\qquad (\exists\, w : 0\,..\,msize - 1;\ b : 0\,..\,bpw - 1 \to \{0,1\} \bullet \\ &\qquad\quad sinuse'(w)(b) = 1) \end{aligned}$$

it can be seen that the above expression is equivalent to $semasinuse \setminus \{s?\}$ which is equivalent, by $FreeSID_a$'s predicate, to $semasinuse'$. □

The schemata derived in this subsection can now be translated into executable code. The code will employ a bitmask to represent those slots in the table that are in use.

3.9 Synchronous Messages

This section is concerned with the specification and refinement of the synchronous message-passing subsystem in the kernel. Message passing is used as the primary means for processes to exchange information while using semaphores as a synchronisation mechanism.

3.9.1 Preliminaries

First, a few definitions are required. In particular, it is necessary to define a type to represent the data held by messages. The type representing messages, *MSG*, was defined at the start of this chapter, as was the constant *nullmsg*.

$[MDATA]$

Using this new type, the type of messages, *MSG*, can be defined.

$$MSG \mathrel{\widehat=} PID \times PID \times MDATA$$

In addition, a constructor function is useful, so one is defined

$$
\begin{array}{|l}
mkmsg : PID \times PID \times MDATA \\
\hline
\forall s, t : PID;\ d : MDATA \bullet \\
\qquad mkmsg(s, t, d) = (s, (t, d))
\end{array}
$$

Furthermore, some functions to access the components of a message are needed. In particular, functions to access the sender's and destination's identifiers is required; a function to return the data held in a message is required.

$$
\begin{array}{|l}
msgsrc, msgdest : MSG \rightarrow PID \\
msgdata : MSG \rightarrow MDATA \\
\hline
\forall m : MSG \bullet \\
\qquad msgsrc(m) = fst\ m \\
\qquad msgdest(m) = fst(snd\ m) \\
\qquad msgdata(m) = snd^2\ m
\end{array}
$$

Just to make schema definition and manipulation a little easier, the following schema is defined. It just creates a new message and returns it as m.

$$
\begin{array}{|l}
\hline
\textit{MakeMessage} \\
\hline
sndr?, dest? : PID \\
payload? : MDATA \\
m : MSG \\
\hline
m = mkmsg(sndr?, dest?, payload?) \\
\hline
\end{array}
$$

The error schemata now follow. The names for these schemata are intended to be suggestive as to their functions.

$$
\begin{array}{|l}
\hline
\textit{AlreadyHasMsg} \\
\hline
serr! : SYSERR \\
\hline
serr! = procalreadyhasmsg \\
\hline
\end{array}
$$

DestinationNotReceiving

$$
\begin{array}{|l}
serr! : SYSERR \\
\hline
serr! = destinationnotrcving
\end{array}
$$

BadDestination

$$
\begin{array}{|l}
serr! : SYSERR \\
\hline
serr! = badmsgdestination
\end{array}
$$

NullMsgValue

$$
\begin{array}{|l}
serr! : SYSERR \\
\hline
serr! = nomsg
\end{array}
$$

The two following operations are added to $PTAB$:

SourceExists

$$
\begin{array}{|l}
\Xi PTAB \\
src? : PID \\
\hline
src? \in used
\end{array}
$$

and

DestinationExists

$$
\begin{array}{|l}
\Xi PTAB \\
dest? : PID \\
\hline
dest? \in used
\end{array}
$$

3.9.2 Top Level

The top-level specification can now be started.

The process table, $PTAB$, is also extended by the addition of a new state variable:

$$
\begin{array}{|l}
\hline
\textit{PTAB} \\
\quad \vdots \\
smsg : PID \twoheadrightarrow MSG \\
\quad \vdots \\
\hline
\vdots \\
\mathrm{dom}\ smsg = \mathrm{dom}\ prio \vdots \\
\hline
\end{array}
$$

The mapping, *smsg*, maps process identifiers to messages, including, of course, the *nullmsg*. Each process maps to exactly one message. The idea is that each process should have at most one message available to it at any one time.

The initialisation schema is implicit and can be inferred from that of *PTAB*.

$$
\begin{array}{|l}
\hline
\textit{GotSynchMsg} \\
\Xi PTAB \\
p? : PID \\
\hline
smsg(p?) \neq nullmsg \\
\hline
\end{array}
$$

A sending process can send a message (attach it to the *smsg* slot) only when the destination has no message in *smsg*. In other words, if d is the destination, then a sender, s, can tell that d can be passed a message when $smsg(d) = nullmsg$. This justifies the definition

$$CanSendSynchMsg \mathrel{\widehat=} \neg\ GotSynchMsg$$

which expands into:

$$
\begin{array}{|l}
\hline
\Xi PTAB \\
p? : PID \\
\hline
smsg(p?) = nullmsg \\
\hline
\end{array}
$$

The actual operation of sending a synchronous message is considered to be assigning the destination's *smsg* to the message. In symbols:

$$
\begin{array}{|l}
\hline
\textit{SendSynchMsg} \\
\Delta PTAB \\
dest? : PID \\
m? : MSG \\
\hline
smsg' = smsg \oplus \{dest? \mapsto m?\} \\
\hline
\end{array}
$$

When a process receives a message, it should copy the contents of the message to some place and to set *smsg* to *nullmsg*.

$$\begin{array}{|l}
\multicolumn{1}{l}{\textit{ClrSynchMsgSlot}} \\
\hline
\Delta PTAB \\
p? : PID \\
\hline
smsg' = smsg \oplus \{p? \mapsto nullmsg\} \\
\hline
\end{array}$$

Receiving proper is considered to be the act of removing the latest message from *smsg*. The next schema puts this into symbols.

$$\begin{array}{|l}
\multicolumn{1}{l}{\textit{ReceiveSMsg}} \\
\hline
\Xi PTAB \\
p? : PID \\
m! : MSG \\
\hline
m! = smsg(p?) \\
\hline
\end{array}$$

Ideally, when one process is to send a message to another, it should check the state that the destination is in. If the destination is in the *psreceiving* state, the message can be sent. This is captured by the following definition.

$$\begin{array}{l}
IsDestinationReceiving \mathrel{\widehat=} \\
\quad \exists\, st : PSTATE \mid st = psreceiving \bullet \\
\qquad ProcState[st/st!]
\end{array}$$

This definition expands into:

$$\begin{array}{|l}
\multicolumn{1}{l}{\textit{IsDestinationReceiving}} \\
\hline
\Xi PTAB_S \\
p? : PID \\
\hline
state(p?) = psreceiving \\
\hline
\end{array}$$

Conversely, when a process wants to receive a message, it should enter the *psreceiving* state. The following defines this operation.

$$\begin{array}{l}
MakeReceiver \mathrel{\widehat=} \\
\quad \exists\, st : PSTATE \mid st = psreceiving \bullet \\
\qquad SetProcState[st/st?]
\end{array}$$

The schema that results by expansion is the following.

$$\begin{array}{|l}
\multicolumn{1}{l}{\textit{MakeReceiver}} \\
\hline
\Delta PTAB_S \\
p? : PID \\
\hline
state' = state \oplus \{p? \mapsto psreceiving\} \\
\hline
\end{array}$$

Similarly, if a process wants to send a message, it should enter the *pssending* state. It might have to wait in this state before it can actually send the message.

$$\begin{array}{l} MakeSender \mathrel{\widehat=} \\ \quad \exists\, st : PSTATE \mid st = pssending \bullet \\ \qquad SetProcState[st/st?] \end{array}$$

This definition expands to form the following schema:

$$\begin{array}{|l} \hline MakeSender \\ \Delta PTAB \\ p? : PID \\ \hline state' = state \oplus \{p? \mapsto pssending\} \\ \hline \end{array}$$

The complete operation to send a synchronous message is defined thus:

$$\begin{array}{l} SendASynchMsg \mathrel{\widehat=} \\ \quad (DestinationExists \land \\ \qquad ((IsDestinationReceiver[dest?/p?] \land \\ \qquad\quad ((\neg\ GotSynchMsg[dest?/p?] \land \\ \qquad\qquad SendSynchMsg \land \\ \qquad\qquad MakeSender \\ \qquad\qquad \fatsemi (MakeReady[dest?/p?] \fatsemi SchedNext) \land \\ \qquad\qquad SysOk) \\ \qquad\quad \lor AlreadyHasMsg)) \\ \qquad \lor DestinationNotReceiving)) \\ \quad \lor BadDestination \end{array}$$

The basic idea is that the destination must be a process that is currently in the system and must be in the receiving state but not have a message assigned to it by *smsg*. If this is the case, the sender places the message in *smsg* and sets its state to *pssending*. It then places the destination on the scheduler's ready queue and calls *SchedNext* so that a reschedule is performed. The remainder of the operations just set *serr*! appropriately, depending upon the condition being reported.

This operation contains a reschedule at is core. This will lead to an interesting argument when simplifying this definition.

We now need to expand and simplify this definition. This will be done in pieces.

The composition $(MakeReady[dest?/p?] \fatsemi SchedNext)$ must be calculated and simplified.

$$
\begin{array}{l}
SchedNext \mathrel{\widehat=} \\
\quad (IsCurrentProcessIdle \land \\
\qquad ((IsEmptySCHEDQ \land ContinueCurrent) \\
\qquad\quad \lor (SCHEDQDequeue[p/p!] \land SetNewCurrentProcess[p/p?] \\
\qquad\qquad \fatsemi CTXTSW) \setminus \{p\})) \\
\quad \lor (IsEmptySCHEDQ \land MakeIdleProcessCurrent \fatsemi CTXTSW) \\
\quad \lor ((\neg\ CurrentProcessStateIsReadyOrRunning \\
\qquad\quad \lor QueueHdHasHigherPriority) \land \\
\qquad (SCHEDQHd[hpid/p!] \land \\
\qquad\quad SCHEDQDelHd \land \\
\qquad\quad SetNewCurrentProcess[hpid/p?] \fatsemi CTXTSW) \setminus \{hpid\}) \\
\quad \lor ContinueCurrent
\end{array}
$$

We know *a priori* that the current process is not idle (for otherwise, how could this call have been made?), the first disjunct can be omitted. Equally, we know that the ready queue (*pq*) cannot be empty if the first component of the composition $MakeReady[dest?/p?] \fatsemi SchedNext$ succeeds. This permits us to remove the disjunct $IsEmptySCHEDQ \land MakeIdleProcessCurrent$. We are left, therefore, with

$$
\begin{array}{l}
\quad \lor ((\neg\ CurrentProcessStateIsReadyOrRunning \\
\qquad\quad \lor QueueHdHasHigherPriority) \land \\
\qquad (SCHEDQHd[hpid/p!] \land \\
\qquad\quad SCHEDQDelHd \land \\
\qquad\quad SetNewCurrentProcess[hpid/p?] \fatsemi CTXTSW) \setminus \{hpid\}) \\
\quad \lor ContinueCurrent
\end{array}
$$

The state of *curr* is *pssending* when *SchedNext* is executed, so it is obvious that $\neg\ CurrentProcessStateIsReadyOrRunning$ is satisfied. To see this, consider

$$
\begin{array}{l}
\neg\ CurrentProcessStateIsReadyOrRunning \\
\Leftrightarrow state(curr) \neq psready \land state(curr) \neq psrunning
\end{array}
$$

We have $state(curr) = pssending$, so, given the last equivalence, we have

$$state(curr) \neq psready \land state(curr) \neq psrunning \land state(curr) = pssending$$

which is true, so the disjunction

$$\neg\ CurrentProcessStateIsReadyOrRunning \lor QueueHdHasHigherPriority)$$

is satisfied; this permits $MakeReady[dest?/p?] \fatsemi SchedNext$ to be simplified to

$$
\begin{array}{l}
MakeReady[dest?/p?] \\
\quad \fatsemi (SCHEDQHd[hpid/p!] \land \\
\qquad SCHEDQDelHd \land SetNewCurrentProcess[hpid/p?] \fatsemi CTXTSW) \setminus \{hpid\}
\end{array}
$$

Noting that $\fatsemi CTXTSW$ can be simplified to $\land\ CTXTSW$ because it does not affect any variables that occur in the rest of the schema, this composition now expands into

$$
\begin{array}{l}
MakeReady \\
\fatsemi \\
\quad (\exists hpid : PID \bullet \\
\qquad hpid = head\ sq.pq'' \land \\
\qquad sq.pq' = tail\ sq.pq'' \land \\
\qquad curr' = hpid \land prev' = curr \land \\
\qquad CTXTSW)
\end{array}
$$

and the existential simplifies to

$$
\begin{array}{l}
MakeReady \\
\fatsemi \\
\quad (curr' = head\ sq.pq'' \land prev' = curr \land sq.pq' = tail\ sq.pq'' \land CTXTSW)
\end{array}
$$

This composition simplifies to the following predicate:

$$
\begin{array}{l}
(\#sq.pq < maxs \land \\
\quad ((sq.pq = \langle\rangle \land \\
\qquad \land\ curr' = dest? \land prev' = curr'' \land sq.pq' = \langle\rangle \land CTXTSW) \lor \\
\qquad (prio(dest?) \leq prio(head\ sq.pq) \land \\
\qquad\quad curr' = dest? \land prev' = curr \land CTXTSW) \lor \\
\qquad (prio(last\ sq.pq) < prio(dest?) \\
\qquad\quad \land\ curr' = head\ sq.pq'' \land prev' = curr \land \\
\qquad\quad sq.pq' = (tail\ sq.pq) \frown \langle dest? \rangle \land CTXTSW) \lor \\
\qquad (\exists s_1, s_2 : \mathrm{seq}\ PID \mid s_1 \neq \langle\rangle \land s_2 \neq \langle\rangle \land s_1 \frown s_2 = sq.pq \bullet \\
\qquad\quad prio(last\ s_1) < prio(dest?) \land \\
\qquad\quad prio(dest?) \leq prio(head\ s_2) \land \\
\qquad\quad sq.pq' = (tail\ s_1) \frown (\langle dest? \rangle \frown s_2)) \land \\
\qquad state' = state \oplus \{dest? \mapsto psready\} \land \\
\qquad curr' = head\ s1 \land prev' = curr \land \\
\qquad CTXTSW \land \\
\qquad serr! = sysok) \\
\lor\ serr! = schedqfull
\end{array}
$$

The complete expansion of *SendASynchMsg* is

$$
\begin{array}{|l}
\hline
SendASynchMsg \\
\Delta PTAB \\
\Delta SCHED \\
dest? : PID \\
m? : MSG \\
serr! : SYSERR \\
\hline
\exists state'' : PID \pfun PSTATE \bullet \\
(dest? \in used \land \\
\quad ((state(dest?) = psreceiving \land \\
\qquad ((smsg(dest?) = nullmsg \land \\
\qquad\quad smsg' = smsg \oplus \{dest? \mapsto m?\} \land
\end{array}
$$

$$
\begin{array}{l}
\qquad\qquad state'' = state \oplus \{p? \mapsto pssending\} \land \\
\qquad\qquad (\#sq.pq < maxs \land \\
\qquad\qquad\quad ((sq.pq = \langle\rangle \land \\
\qquad\qquad\qquad \land\ curr' = dest? \land prev' = curr'' \land sq.pq' = \langle\rangle \\
\qquad\qquad\qquad\quad \land\ CTXTSW) \lor \\
\qquad\qquad\qquad (prio(dest?) \leq prio(head\ sq.pq) \land \\
\qquad\qquad\qquad\quad curr' = dest? \land prev' = curr \land CTXTSW) \lor \\
\qquad\qquad\qquad (prio(last\ sq.pq) < prio(dest?) \\
\qquad\qquad\qquad\quad \land\ curr' = head\ sq.pq'' \land prev' = curr \land \\
\qquad\qquad\qquad\quad sq.pq' = (tail\ sq.pq) \frown \langle dest? \rangle \land CTXTSW) \\
\qquad\qquad\qquad \lor\ (\exists s_1, s_2 : \operatorname{seq} PID \mid \\
\qquad\qquad\qquad\qquad\qquad s_1 \neq \langle\rangle \land s_2 \neq \langle\rangle \land s_1 \frown s_2 = sq.pq \bullet \\
\qquad\qquad\qquad\quad prio(last\ s_1) < prio(dest?) \land \\
\qquad\qquad\qquad\quad prio(dest?) \leq prio(head\ s_2) \land \\
\qquad\qquad\qquad\quad sq.pq' = (tail\ s_1) \frown \langle dest? \rangle \frown s_2)) \land \\
\qquad\qquad\qquad state' = state \oplus \{dest? \mapsto psready\} \land \\
\qquad\qquad\qquad curr' = head\ s1 \land prev' = curr \land \\
\qquad\qquad\qquad CTXTSW \land \\
\qquad\qquad\qquad serr! = sysok) \\
\qquad\qquad \lor\ serr! = schedqfull \\
\qquad\qquad serr! = sysok) \\
\qquad serr! = procalreadyhasmsg)) \\
\quad serr! = destinationnotrcving)) \\
\lor\ serr! = badmsgdestination
\end{array}
$$

It is easy to see how this can be re-arranged as follows

SendASynchMsg

$$
\begin{array}{l}
\Delta PTAB \\
\Delta SCHED \\
dest? : PID \\
m? : MSG \\
serr! : SYSERR \\
\hline
(dest? \in used \land \\
\quad ((state(dest?) = psreceiving \land \\
\qquad ((smsg(dest?) = nullmsg \land \\
\qquad\quad ((sq.pq = \langle\rangle \land curr' = dest? \land \\
\qquad\qquad state' = state \oplus \{p? \mapsto pssending, dest? \mapsto psrunning\}) \\
\qquad\quad \lor\ ((\#sq.pq < maxs \land \\
\qquad\qquad \lor\ (prio(dest?) \leq prio(head\ sq.pq) \land curr' = dest? \land \\
\qquad\qquad\quad state' = state \oplus \{p? \mapsto pssending, dest? \mapsto psrunning\})
\end{array}
$$

$$
\begin{array}{l}
\qquad\qquad\qquad\qquad \lor\ (prio(last\ sq.pq) < prio(dest?) \land \\
\qquad\qquad\qquad\qquad\qquad curr' = head\ sq.pq \land \\
\qquad\qquad\qquad\qquad\qquad sq.pq' = (tail\ sq.pq) \frown \langle dest? \rangle \land \\
\qquad\qquad\qquad\qquad\qquad state' = state \oplus \{p? \mapsto pssending, dest? \mapsto psready\}) \\
\qquad\qquad\qquad\qquad \lor\ (\exists\, s_1, s_2 : \mathrm{seq}\, PID \mid s_1 \neq \langle\rangle \land s_2 \neq \langle\rangle \land s_1 \frown s_2 = sq.pq \bullet \\
\qquad\qquad\qquad\qquad\qquad prio(last\ s_1) < prio(dest?) \land \\
\qquad\qquad\qquad\qquad\qquad prio(dest?) \leq prio(head\ s_2) \land \\
\qquad\qquad\qquad\qquad\qquad sq.pq' = (tail\ s_1) \frown \langle dest? \rangle \frown s_2 \land \\
\qquad\qquad\qquad\qquad\qquad curr' = head\ s_1) \land \\
\qquad\qquad\qquad\qquad prev' = curr \land \\
\qquad\qquad\qquad\qquad CTXTSW \land \\
\qquad\qquad\qquad\qquad serr! = sysok) \\
\qquad\qquad\qquad \lor\ serr! = schedqfull)) \\
\qquad\qquad \lor\ serr! = procalreadyhasmsg)) \\
\qquad \lor\ serr! = destinationnotrcving)) \\
\lor\ ser! = badmsgdestination)
\end{array}
$$

The precondition can now be seen to be

$$
\begin{array}{l}
\mathrm{pre}\ SendASynchMsg \mathrel{\widehat{=}} \\
\qquad dest? \in used \land \\
\qquad state(dest?) = psreceiving
\end{array}
$$

However, $dest? \in used$ is an implicit precondition provided by $PTAB$'s invariant. It can, if required, be omitted.

We now turn our attention to the top-level message reception operation. First, we define a simple operation that actually receives a message.

$$
\begin{array}{l}
RcvSynchMsg \mathrel{\widehat{=}} \\
\qquad (GotSynchMsg \land ReceiveMsg \land ClrSynchMsgSlot \land SysOk) \\
\qquad \lor\ NullMsgValue
\end{array}
$$

The definition expands into

$$
\begin{array}{l}
\underline{\quad RcvSynchMsg \qquad\qquad\qquad\qquad\qquad\qquad} \\
\Delta PTAB \\
p? : PID \\
m! : MSG \\
\hline
(smsg(p?) \neq nullmsg \land \\
\qquad m! = smsg(p?) \land \\
\qquad smsg' = smsg \oplus \{p? \mapsto nullmsg\} \land \\
\qquad serr! = sysok) \\
\lor\ m! = nullmsg
\end{array}
$$

Next, the full top-level operation is defined. This operation, like the send-message operation, includes a reschedule. The presence of the reschedule (i.e., the *SchedNext* schema) complicates the expansion of the operation, just as it did for the send-message operation.

$$
\begin{array}{l}
\mathit{ReceiveSynchMsg} \mathrel{\widehat{=}} \\
\quad \mathit{MakeReceiver} \\
\quad\quad \fatsemi \mathit{SchedNext} \\
\quad\quad \fatsemi (\mathit{RcvSynchMsg} \land \\
\quad\quad\quad ((\mathit{IsSysOk} \land \\
\quad\quad\quad\quad (\exists\, s : \mathit{PID} \mid s = \mathit{msgsrc}(m!) \bullet \\
\quad\quad\quad\quad\quad \mathit{MakeReady}[s/p?]) \land \\
\quad\quad\quad\quad \mathit{SysOk}) \\
\quad\quad\quad \lor \mathit{NullMsgValue})
\end{array}
$$

The definition expands into

$$
\begin{array}{l}
\textit{ReceiveSynchMsg} \\
\hline
\Delta \mathit{SCHED} \\
\Delta \mathit{PTAB} \\
m! : \mathit{MSG} \\
\mathit{serr}! : \mathit{SYSERR} \\
\hline
\exists\, \mathit{state}'' : \mathit{PID} \pfun \mathit{PSTATE};\ \mathit{sq.pq}'' : \mathrm{seq}\, \mathit{PID} \bullet \\
\mathit{state}'' = \mathit{state} \oplus \{p? \mapsto \mathit{psreceiving}\} \\
\fatsemi \\
(\mathit{curr} = \mathit{iprc} \land \\
\quad ((\mathit{sq.pq}'' = \langle\rangle \land \mathit{curr}' = \mathit{curr} \land \mathit{prev}' = \mathit{prev}) \\
\quad\quad \lor (\mathit{curr}' = \mathit{head}\ \mathit{sq.pq} \land \mathit{prev}' = \mathit{curr} \fatsemi \mathit{CTXTSW}))) \\
\lor (\mathit{sq.pq} = \langle\rangle \land \mathit{prev}' = \mathit{curr} \land \mathit{curr}' = \mathit{iprc} \fatsemi \mathit{CTXTSW}) \\
\lor ((\mathit{state}(\mathit{curr}) \neq \mathit{psready} \land \mathit{state}(\mathit{curr}) \neq \mathit{psrunning} \\
\quad\quad \lor \mathit{prio}(\mathit{head}\ \mathit{sq.pq}) < \mathit{prio}(\mathit{curr})) \land \\
\quad \mathit{sq.pq}'' = \mathit{tail}\ \mathit{sq.pq} \land \\
\quad \mathit{curr}' = \mathit{head}\ \mathit{sq.pq} \land \\
\quad \mathit{prev}' = \mathit{curr} \\
\quad \fatsemi \mathit{CTXTSW}) \\
\lor (\mathit{curr}' = \mathit{curr} \land \mathit{prev}' = \mathit{prev}) \fatsemi \\
((\mathit{smsg}(p?) \neq \mathit{nullmsg} \land \\
\quad m! = \mathit{smsg}(p?) \land \\
\quad \mathit{smsg}' = \mathit{smsg} \oplus \{p? \mapsto \mathit{nullmsg}\} \land \\
\quad \mathit{serr}! = \mathit{sysok}) \\
\lor (m! = \mathit{nullmsg} \land \mathit{serr}! = \mathit{nomsg}))
\end{array}
$$

$$
\begin{array}{l}
\land\ serr! = sysok \\
\land\ \exists\, s : PID \mid s = msgsrc(m!) \bullet \\
\qquad state' = state'' \oplus \{s \mapsto psready\} \land \\
\qquad (\#sq.pq < maxs \land \\
\qquad\qquad ((sq.pq'' = \langle\rangle \land sq.pq' = \langle s \rangle) \lor \\
\qquad\qquad\quad (prio(s) \leq prio(head\ sq.pq'') \land sq.pq' = \langle s \rangle \frown sq.pq'') \lor \\
\qquad\qquad\quad (prio(last\ sq.pq'') < prio(s) \land sq.pq' = sq.pq'' \frown \langle s \rangle) \lor \\
\qquad\qquad\quad (\exists\, s_1, s_2 : \operatorname{seq} PID \mid s_1 \neq \langle\rangle \land s_2 \neq \langle\rangle \land s_1 \frown s_2 = sq.pq'' \bullet \\
\qquad\qquad\qquad prio(last\ s_1) < prio(s) \land \\
\qquad\qquad\qquad prio(s) \leq prio(head\ s_2) \land \\
\qquad\qquad\qquad sq.pq' = s_1 \frown \langle s \rangle \frown s_2)) \land \\
\qquad\qquad\quad serr! = sysok) \\
\qquad\qquad \lor\ serr! = schedqfull \\
\land\ serr! = sysok \lor serr! = nomsg
\end{array}
$$

We now turn to the simplification of this schema.

It should be clear that the caller, $p?$, is always the current process, $curr$, so $curr = p?$. It is also clear that $state(curr) = psrunning$. However, it is not known *a priori* whether the scheduler's ready queue is empty or not. Given that the predicate can be written as

$$
\begin{array}{l}
state'' = state \oplus \{p? \mapsto psreceiving\} \\
\fatsemi SchedNext \\
\fatsemi (((smsg(p?) \neq nullmsg \land \\
\qquad\quad m! = smsg(p?) \land \\
\qquad\quad smsg' = smsg \oplus \{p? \mapsto nullmsg\} \land \\
\qquad\quad serr! = sysok) \\
\quad \lor\ serr! = nomsg \land m! = nullmsg) \\
\quad \land\ ((serr! = sysok \land \\
\qquad\qquad (\exists\, s : PID \mid s = msgsrc(p?) \bullet MakeReady[s/p?]) \land \\
\qquad\qquad serr! = sysok) \\
\qquad \lor\ serr! = nomsg)
\end{array}
$$

Since it is known that the current process is not the idle process, the first disjunct of *SchedNext* can be omitted, leaving

$$
\begin{array}{l}
(IsEmptySCHEDQ \land MakeIdleProcessCurrent \fatsemi CTXTSW) \\
\lor\ ((\neg\ CurrentProcessStateIsReadyOrRunning \\
\qquad\quad \lor\ QueueHdHasHigherPriority) \land \\
\quad (SCHEDQHd[hpid/p!] \land \\
\qquad\quad SCHEDQDelHd \land \\
\qquad\quad SetNewCurrentProcess[hpid/p?] \\
\qquad\quad \fatsemi CTXTSW) \setminus \{hpid\}) \\
\lor\ ContinueCurrent
\end{array}
$$

When the message-receiving operation is called, the state of *curr* must be *psrunning* and *CurrentProcessStateIsReadyOrRunning* is defined as

$$state(curr) = psready \lor state(curr) = psrunning$$

so $\neg$ *CurrentProcessStateIsReadyOrRunning* is

$$state(curr) \neq psready \land state(curr) \neq psrunning$$

so the current process' state satisfies this condition, so the remaining guard need not be attempted.

The predicate of *SchedNext* can now be simplified to

$$\begin{array}{l}(IsEmptySCHEDQ \land MakeIdleProcessCurrent \mathbin{⨟} CTXTSW)\\ \lor\ (SCHEDQHd[hpid/p!] \land\\ \qquad\qquad SCHEDQDelHd \land\\ \qquad\qquad SetNewCurrentProcess[hpid/p?] \mathbin{⨟} CTXTSW) \setminus \{hpid\}\end{array}$$

It can be further simplified: the update of *prev* can be factored out using $(p \land q) \lor (r \land q) \Rightarrow (p \lor r) \land q$ to yield

$$\begin{array}{l}(((sq.pq = \langle\rangle \land curr' = iprc)\\ \quad \lor (sq.pq'' = tail\ sq.pq \land\\ \qquad\quad curr'' = head\ pq)) \land\\ \quad prev'' = curr \land\\ \quad CTXTSW)\end{array}$$

The sequential composition of *CTXTSW* can be reduced to conjunction, as noted many times above, and can also be moved to the end. The movement can be justified by the same theorem as above. Note that this predicate is part of a sequential composition, so its after-state must be doubly primed.

The existential $\exists\, s : PID \mid s = msgsrc(m!) \bullet MakeReady[s/p?]$ simplifies as follows. First, the existential formula expands into the following. (It must be remembered that the before state of this schema is the intermediate state of a sequential composition.)

MakeReady[*s*/*p*?]

$$\begin{array}{l}\Delta PRIOQ\\ p? : PID\\ serr! : SYSERR\\ \hline state' = state \oplus \{s \mapsto psready\}\\ (\#sq.pq'' < maxs \land\\ \quad ((sq.pq'' = \langle\rangle \land sq.pq' = \langle s\rangle) \lor\\ \qquad (prio(s) \leq prio(head\ sq.pq'') \land sq.pq' = \langle s\rangle \frown sq.pq'') \lor\\ \qquad (prio(last\ sq.pq'') < prio(s) \land sq.pq' = sq.pq'' \frown \langle s\rangle) \lor\\ \qquad (\exists\, s_1, s_2 : \mathrm{seq}\, PID \mid s_1 \neq \langle\rangle \land s_2 \neq \langle\rangle \land s_1 \frown s_2 = sq.pq'' \bullet\\ \qquad\quad prio(last\ s_1) < prio(s) \land\\ \qquad\quad prio(s) \leq prio(head\ s_2) \land\end{array}$$

$$
\begin{array}{l}
\qquad\qquad sq.pq' = s_1 \frown \langle s \rangle \frown s_2)) \land \\
\qquad serr! = sysok) \\
\lor\ serr! = schedqfull
\end{array}
$$

Using the one-point rule to substitute $msgsrc(m!)$ for s, the predicate becomes

$$
\begin{array}{l}
state' = state \oplus \{msgsrc(m!) \mapsto psready\} \\
(\#sq.pq'' < maxs \land \\
\quad ((sq.pq'' = \langle\rangle \land sq.pq' = \langle msgsrc(m!)\rangle) \lor \\
\qquad (prio(msgsrc(m!)) \leq prio(head\ sq.pq'') \land \\
\qquad\quad sq.pq' = \langle msgsrc(m!)\rangle \frown sq.pq'') \lor \\
\qquad (prio(last\ sq.pq'') < prio(msgsrc(m!)) \land \\
\qquad\quad sq.pq' = sq.pq'' \frown \langle msgsrc(m!)\rangle) \\
\qquad \lor (\exists s_1, s_2 : \mathrm{seq}\ PID \mid s_1 \neq \langle\rangle \land s_2 \neq \langle\rangle \land s_1 \frown s_2 = sq.pq'' \bullet \\
\qquad\quad prio(last\ s_1) < prio(msgsrc(m!)) \land \\
\qquad\quad prio(msgsrc(m!)) \leq prio(head\ s_2) \land \\
\qquad\quad sq.pq' = s_1 \frown \langle msgsrc(m!)\rangle \frown s_2)) \land \\
\qquad serr! = sysok) \\
\lor\ serr! = schedqfull
\end{array}
$$

The *ReceiveSynchMsg* operation can now be considerably simplified. This yields the following schema:

ReceiveSynchMsg

$$
\begin{array}{l}
\Delta SCHED \\
\Delta PTAB \\
m! : MSG \\
serr! : SYSERR
\end{array}
$$

$$
\begin{array}{l}
((smsg(curr) \neq nullmsg \land \\
\quad m! = smsg(curr) \land \\
\quad smsg' = smsg \oplus \{curr \mapsto nullmsg\} \land \\
\quad state' = (state \oplus \{curr \mapsto psreceiving\}) \oplus \{msgsrc(m!) \mapsto psready\} \land \\
((sq.pq = \langle\rangle \land curr' = iprc \land sq.pq' = \langle msgsrc(m!)\rangle \land CTXTSW) \\
\lor\ [(\#sq.pq \leq maxs \land \\
\quad (curr' = head\ sq.pq \land \\
\qquad prev' = curr \land \\
\qquad ((prio(msgsrc(m!)) \leq prio(head\ tail\ sq.pq) \land \\
\qquad\quad sq.pq' = \langle msgsrc(m!)\rangle \frown tail\ sq.pq) \\
\qquad \lor (prio(last\ sq.pq) < prio(msgsrc(m!)) \land \\
\qquad\quad sq.pq' = tail\ sq.pq \frown \langle msgsrc(m!)\rangle) \\
\qquad \lor (\exists s_1, s_2 : \mathrm{seq}\ PID \mid s_1 \neq \langle\rangle \land s_2 \neq \langle\rangle \land s_1 \frown s_2 = sq.pq \bullet \\
\qquad\quad prio(last\ s_1) < prio(msgsrc(m!)) \land \\
\qquad\quad prio(msgsrc(m!)) \leq prio(head\ s_2) \land \\
\qquad\quad s_1 \frown \langle msgsrc(m!)\rangle \frown s_2 = sq.pq')) \land
\end{array}
$$

$$
\begin{array}{l}
\quad\quad CTXTSW \land \\
\quad\quad serr! = sysok)) \\
\quad \lor\ serr! = schedqfull])) \\
\quad \lor\ serr! = nomsg
\end{array}
$$

The precondition is immediately

$$
\begin{array}{l}
\text{pre } ReceiveSynchMsg \mathrel{\widehat{=}} \\
\quad smsg(p?) \neq nullmsg
\end{array}
$$

To justify this, it is noted that the first disjunct simplifies to $smsg(curr) \neq nullmsg$. Similarly, $sq.sq.pq = \langle\rangle \land curr' = iprc \land sq.pq' = \langle msgsrc(m!)\rangle \land CTXTSW$ simplifies to $sq.sq.pq = \langle\rangle \land true \land true \land intno' = context\_switch$, so it finally reduces to $sq.sq.pq = \langle\rangle$. Given this, the remainder of the simplification is as follows:

$$
\begin{array}{l}
smsg(p?) \neq nullmsg \land sq.pq = \langle\rangle \\
\lor\ (\#sq.pq \leq maxs \land \\
\quad\quad (prio(msgsrc(m!)) \leq prio(head\ tail\ sq.pq) \\
\quad\quad \lor\ prio(last\ sq.pq) < prio(msgsrc(m!)) \\
\quad\quad \lor\ (\exists s_1, s_2 : \operatorname{seq} PID \mid s_1 \neq \langle\rangle \land s_2 \neq \langle\rangle \land s_1 \frown s_2 = sq.pq \bullet \\
\quad\quad\quad prio(last\ s_1) < prio(msgsrc(m!)) \land \\
\quad\quad\quad\quad prio(msgsrc(m!)) \leq prio(head\ s_2))))
\end{array}
$$

Now, from

$$
\begin{array}{l}
(prio(msgsrc(m!)) \leq prio(head\ tail\ sq.pq) \\
\lor\ (prio(last\ sq.pq) < prio(msgsrc(m!))) \\
\lor\ (\exists s_1, s_2 : \operatorname{seq} PID \mid s_1 \neq \langle\rangle \land s_2 \neq \langle\rangle \land s_1 \frown s_2 = sq.pq \bullet \\
\quad prio(last\ s_1) < prio(msgsrc(m!)) \land \\
\quad\quad prio(msgsrc(m!)) \leq prio(head\ s_2)
\end{array}
$$

it can be inferred that $prio(msgsrc(m!)) \in PPRIO$. This is true, so all that remains is

$$
smsg(p?) \neq nullmsg \land sq.pq = \langle\rangle \lor \#sq.pq \leq maxs
$$

The disjunction $sq.pq = \langle\rangle \land \#sq.pq \leq maxs$ imply $sq.pq = \langle\rangle \lor sq.pq \neq \langle\rangle$, so we are left with $smsg(p?) \neq nullmsg$, which is our precondition.

3.9.3 Refinement One

This is the first of two refinments. It is concerned with the refinement of the scheduler's structures and the process table. The second refinement concerns the refinement of $PTAB1$ to $PTAB2$.

In a sense, all refinements are trivial because, once more, the abstration relation is a set of identities. Furthermore, the operations in this section are defined in terms of promotions that are embedded in operations over $PTAB$. However, we present the refinement (making use of promotion and of the existing refinements of $PTAB$) just to convince ourselves that the refinement really does work and in an attempt to convince the reader of the correctness of the development.

The contents of this subsection mirror that of the last. For this reason, we will not comment as much.

$$\begin{array}{|l}
\multicolumn{1}{l}{DestinationExists1} \\
\hline
\Xi PTAB1 \\
dest? : PID \\
\hline
dest? \notin \mathrm{dom}\, freech \\
\hline
\end{array}$$

$$\begin{array}{l}
MakeReceiver1 \mathrel{\widehat=} \\
\quad \exists\, st : PSTATE \mid st = psreceiving \bullet \\
\qquad SetProcState1[st/st?]
\end{array}$$

$$\begin{array}{l}
MakeSender1 \mathrel{\widehat=} \\
\quad \exists\, st : PSTATE \mid st = pssending \bullet \\
\qquad SetProcState1[st/st?]
\end{array}$$

$$\begin{array}{|l}
\multicolumn{1}{l}{IsDestinationReceiving1} \\
\hline
\Xi PTAB1 \\
p? : PID \\
\hline
state1(p?) = psreceiving \\
\hline
\end{array}$$

$$\begin{array}{|l}
\multicolumn{1}{l}{GotSynchMsg1} \\
\hline
\Xi PTAB1 \\
p? : PID \\
\hline
smsg1(p?) \neq nullmsg \\
\hline
\end{array}$$

$$\begin{array}{|l}
\multicolumn{1}{l}{ClrSynchMsgSlot1} \\
\hline
\Delta PTAB1 \\
p? : PID \\
\hline
smsg1' = smgs1 \oplus \{p? \mapsto nullmsg\} \\
\hline
\end{array}$$

Partly out of interest and partly to see whether any simplifications can be performed (which they can), the major operations are fully expanded (and simplified). However, as noted above, there is little that can usefully be done in the refinement process for reasons given above.

$$
\begin{array}{l}
SendASynchMsg1 \mathrel{\widehat=} \\
\quad (DestinationExists1 \wedge \\
\quad\quad ((IsDestinationReceiver1[dest?/p?] \wedge \\
\quad\quad\quad ((\neg\ GotSynchMsg1[dest?/p?] \wedge \\
\quad\quad\quad\quad SendSynchMsg1 \wedge \\
\quad\quad\quad\quad MakeSender1 \\
\quad\quad\quad\quad \mathbin{\fatsemi}(MakeReady[dest?/p?] \mathbin{\fatsemi} SchedNext) \wedge \\
\quad\quad\quad\quad SysOk) \\
\quad\quad\quad \vee\ AlreadyHasMsg)) \\
\quad\quad \vee\ DestinationNotReceiving)) \\
\quad \vee\ BadDestination
\end{array}
$$

Immediately, we are in a position to prove the following theorems. The proofs are quite straightforward but are omitted because of their length.

Theorem 45.

$$
\begin{array}{l}
\forall PTAB;\ PTAB1;\ SCHED;\ dest? : PID;\ m? : MSG \bullet \\
\quad \mathit{pre}\ SendASynchMsg \wedge AbsPTAB1 \Rightarrow \mathit{pre}\ SendASynchMsg1
\end{array}
$$

PROOF. Omitted. □

Theorem 46.

$$
\begin{array}{l}
\forall PTAB;\ PTAB';\ PTAB1;\ PTAB1';\ SCHED; \\
\quad\quad dest? : PID;\ m? : MSG;\ serr! : SYSERR \bullet \\
\quad \mathit{pre}\ SendASynchMsg \\
\quad\quad \wedge\ AbsPTAB1 \\
\quad\quad \wedge\ AbsPRIOQ1 \\
\quad\quad \wedge\ SendASynchMsg1 \\
\quad \Rightarrow SendASyncMsg1
\end{array}
$$

PROOF. Omitted. □

The first-level refinement of the receive operation is defined as:

$$
\begin{array}{l}
ReceiveSynchMsg \mathrel{\widehat=} \\
\quad MakeReceiver1 \\
\quad\quad \mathbin{\fatsemi} SchedNext \\
\quad\quad \mathbin{\fatsemi}(RcvSynchMsg1 \wedge \\
\quad\quad\quad ((IsSysOk \wedge \\
\quad\quad\quad\quad (\exists\, s : PID \mid s = msgsrc(m!) \bullet \\
\quad\quad\quad\quad\quad MakeReady[s/p?]) \wedge \\
\quad\quad\quad\quad SysOk) \\
\quad\quad\quad \vee\ NullMsgValue)
\end{array}
$$

3.9.4 Refinement Two

The second-level refinements can be derived with ease.

$$
\begin{array}{l}
SendASynchMsg2 \mathrel{\widehat=} \\
\quad (DestinationExists2 \land \\
\quad\quad ((IsDestinationReceiver2[dest?/p?] \land \\
\quad\quad\quad ((\lnot\ GotSynchMsg1[dest?/p?] \land \\
\quad\quad\quad\quad SendSynchMsg1 \land \\
\quad\quad\quad\quad MakeSender2 \\
\quad\quad\quad\quad \mathbin{;}(MakeReady[dest?/p?] \mathbin{;} SchedNext) \land \\
\quad\quad\quad\quad SysOk) \\
\quad\quad\quad \lor AlreadyHasMsg)) \\
\quad\quad \lor DestinationNotReceiving)) \\
\quad \lor BadDestination
\end{array}
$$

and

$$
\begin{array}{l}
ReceiveSynchMsg2 \mathrel{\widehat=} \\
\quad MakeReceiver2 \\
\quad\quad \mathbin{;}SchedNext \\
\quad\quad \mathbin{;}(RcvSynchMsg2 \land \\
\quad\quad\quad ((IsSysOk \land \\
\quad\quad\quad\quad (\exists s : PID \mid s = msgsrc(m!) \bullet \\
\quad\quad\quad\quad\quad MakeReady[s/p?]) \land \\
\quad\quad\quad\quad SysOk) \\
\quad\quad\quad \lor NullMsgValue)
\end{array}
$$

Although it is not entirely clear from the schemata in this section, the constructs derived here can now be translated directly into executable code. The reason that matters are not clear is that the operations are defined in terms of a mixture of existing schemata (e.g., the scheduler and the process table) and new ones. However, the claim that an implementation is the next step can be readily verified.

3.10 The Clock

This section contains the specification of the real-time clock. The clock is used by processes to determine the current time. It is also used to determine how long processes have slept and when to wake them.

The time between clock ticks is denoted by the following constant

$$
\mid\ ticklength : TIME
$$

On some machines, this will be 100ms, on others it will be another value.

The error schema is the following. It denotes the fact that a process is requesting a 0 sleep time.

SleepTooShort

$err! : SYSERR$

$err! = sleeptimetooshort$

This is the basic clock. It just contains the time since the system was booted in multiples of *ticklength* seconds.

TIMESINCEBOOT

$tnow : TIME$

Clearly, when the system starts, the time is 0.

TIMESINCEBOOTInit

$TIMESINCEBOOT'$

$tnow' = 0$

The clock is updated every time the hardware clock interrupts the processor. The hardware clock interrupts every *ticklength* seconds, so on every interrupt, the software clock is updated as follows.

UpdateTIMESINCEBOOT

$\Delta TIMESINCEBOOT$

$tnow' = tnow + ticklength$

To find out what the current time is, the following schema is used:

TimeNow

$\Xi TIMESINCEBOOT$

$tn! : TIME$

$tn! = tnow$

$ticksper sec : \mathbb{N}$

Unfortunately, people want the time in seconds, minutes and hours. The following schema defines the variables used to record the time in human-oriented units.

CLOCKTIME

$secs, mins, hrs : TIME$

$0 \leq secs < 60$

$0 \leq mins < 60$

Note that the invariant merely states the moduli for seconds and minutes. We consider it unnecessary to include days; they could be added, should the reader wish.

The clock time is initialised in the obvious manner.

$$
\begin{array}{|l}
\textit{CLOCKTIMEInit} \\
\hline
\textit{CLOCKTIME}' \\
\hline
secs' = 0 \\
mins' = 0 \\
hrs' = 0 \\
\hline
\end{array}
$$

On every hardware interrupt, the time since boot is incremented. At the same time, the human-readable time is also updated when there have been enough interrupts since the last one. This is the purpose of *tickspersec*—after *tickspersec* interrupts, the seconds counter is incremented by one, possibly causing the other counters to be updated.

$$
\begin{array}{|l}
\textit{UpdateClockTime} \\
\hline
\Delta \textit{CLOCKTIME} \\
t? : \textit{TIME} \\
\hline
((t? \bmod tickspersec = 0) \land \\
\quad ((secs + 1 \bmod 60 = 0 \land \\
\quad\quad secs' = 0 \land \\
\quad\quad ((mins + 1 \bmod 60 = 0 \land \\
\quad\quad\quad mins' = 0 \land \\
\quad\quad\quad hrs' = hrs + 1) \\
\quad\quad \lor\ mins' = mins + 1)) \\
\quad \lor\ secs' = secs + 1)) \\
\hline
\end{array}
$$

To find out what the human-readable time is since boot, use the following operation:

$$
\begin{array}{|l}
\textit{ClocktimeNow} \\
\hline
\Xi \textit{CLOCKTIME} \\
s!, m!, h! : \textit{TIME} \\
\hline
s! = secs \\
m! = mins \\
h! = hrs \\
\hline
\end{array}
$$

It is now necessary to consider the operations required by the sleep timer.

When a process requests a period of sleep, it also specifies the period through which it will sleep. The period is specified in seconds and is added to the current time to produce the time at which the process is to be awakened. This is what the following schema does. The variable *tn*? denotes the time now, *stm*? is the length to time the process wants to remain asleep and *cst*! is the computed sleep time—i.e., the time at which the process should be returned to the ready queue. The time is expressed in seconds since boot.

$$
\begin{array}{|l}
\hline
\textit{CorrectWakeTime} \\
tn? \, TIME \\
stm? : TIME \\
cst! : TIME \\
\hline
stm? + tn? = cst! \\
\hline
\end{array}
$$

The above operation requires the current time (in units since boot time) and the following composition defines the required operation:

$$
\begin{array}{l}
\textit{ComputeWakeTime} \mathrel{\widehat=} \\
\quad (\textit{TimeNow}[tn/tn!] \land \textit{CorrectWakeTime}[tn/tn?]) \setminus \{tn\}
\end{array}
$$

This expands and simplifies into:

$$
\begin{array}{|l}
\hline
\textit{ComputeWakeTime} \\
\Xi TIMESINCEBOOT \\
stm? : TIME \\
cst! : TIME \\
\hline
stm? + tnow = cst! \\
\hline
\end{array}
$$

The schemata defined in this section can be translated directly into executable code. In the present case, there is no refinement because the state schema contains only simple variables.

3.11 Sleepers

We need a conception of time. For the purposes of this specification, the following suffices:

$$TIME \mathrel{\widehat=} \mathbb{N}$$

(It was defined at the start of this chapter.)

We also need an extension of *PTAB*:

$$
\begin{array}{|l}
\hline
PTAB \\
PTAB \\
\vdots \\
wakingtime : PID \rightarrowtail\!\!\!\!\!\rightarrow TIME \\
\vdots
\end{array}
$$

$$
\begin{array}{|l}
\hline
\vdots \\
\mathrm{dom}\, wakingtime = \mathrm{dom}\, prio \\
\vdots \\
\hline
\end{array}
$$

The reader is reminded of the convention that a process without a waking time has a zero as the value of *wakingtime*. That is, if p is a process that is not sleeping, $waketime(p) = 0$.

The *wakingtime* function must be refined along with the remainder of *PTAB*, it should be noted. This refinement can be omitted for the reason that *wakingtime* has exactly the same form as *prio*.

The following *PTAB* schemata are also required.

$$
\begin{array}{|l}
\textit{SetWaitingTime} \\
\hline
\Delta PTAB \\
p? : PID \\
t? : TIME \\
\hline
wakingtime' = wakingtime \oplus \{p? \mapsto t?\} \\
\hline
\end{array}
$$

In order to arrive at a valid waiting time, the actual time, t_a, is added to the time t_r, requested by process, $p?$. When defining the ISR, this will be taken into account. Furthermore, a value of $t_r = 0$ will be considered invalid.

$$
\begin{array}{|l}
\textit{WaitingTime} \\
\hline
\Xi PTAB \\
p? : PID \\
t! : TIME \\
\hline
t! = wakingtime(p?) \\
\hline
\end{array}
$$

The waiting (waking) time must be cleared when a process is awakened (i.e., returned to the scheduler's ready queue). The following schema defines this operation:

$$
\begin{array}{|l}
\textit{ClearWaitingTime} \\
\hline
\Delta PTAB \\
p? : PID \\
\hline
\exists t : TIME \mid t = 0 \bullet wakingtime' = wakingtime \oplus \{p? \mapsto t\} \\
\hline
\end{array}
$$

The predicate of this schema simplifies to $wakingtime' = wakingtime \oplus \{p? \mapsto 0\}$.

We need a way to determine whether a process is sleeping. This will be used when determining whether a sleep request can be honoured.

IsProcessSleeping

$$
\begin{array}{|l}
\Xi PTAB \\
p? : PID \\
\hline
wakingtime(p?) > 0
\end{array}
$$

The relevant error schemata are as follows.

TooManySleepers

$$
\begin{array}{|l}
serr! : SYSERR \\
\hline
serr! = toomanysleepers
\end{array}
$$

There are too many processes in the system that are asleep.

AlreadyAsleep

$$
\begin{array}{|l}
serr! : SYSERR \\
\hline
serr! = alreadyasleep
\end{array}
$$

The process requesting a sleep period is already recorded as being asleep. (Has someone hacked in?)

3.11.1 Top Level

We can proceed to the top-level specification of the sleep module. The specification is contained in this subsection.

This is another case in which we require *PTAB* to be included in a the state schema.

SLEEPERS

$$
\begin{array}{|l}
PTAB \\
slps : \mathbb{F}\, PID \\
maxslps : \mathbb{N}_1 \\
\hline
slps \subset used \\
\forall p : PID \bullet \\
\qquad p \in slps \Rightarrow state(p) = pssleeping \\
\forall p : PID \bullet \\
\qquad p \in slps \Rightarrow wakingtime(p) > 0 \\
\forall p : PID \bullet \\
\qquad p \in slps \Rightarrow p \in used
\end{array}
$$

The correctness of the final universal can be seen when it is considered that not all processes in *used* are asleep at any given time but all processes that are asleep are in *used*. We will need to prove the following.

Theorem 47. *If $p \in slps$, then $p \in used$.*

The initialisation operation is the obvious one:

```
┌─ SLEEPERSInit ─────────────────────────
│ SLEEPERS'
│ smax? : ℕ₁
├──────────
│ slps' = ∅
│ maxslps' = smax?
└────────────────────────────────────────
```

$$\begin{array}{|l}\hline \textit{SLEEPERSInit} \\ \hline SLEEPERS' \\ smax? : \mathbb{N}_1 \\ \hline slps' = \varnothing \\ maxslps' = smax? \\ \hline \end{array}$$

The following is a predicate that is true iff there are currently processes that are asleep.

$$\begin{array}{|l}\hline \textit{GotSleepers} \\ \hline \Xi SLEEPERS \\ \hline slps \neq \varnothing \\ \hline \end{array}$$

The following is a predicate that is true iff the process $p?$ is currently asleep (i.e., an element of *slps*).

$$\begin{array}{|l}\hline \textit{IsAsleep} \\ \hline \Xi SLEEPERS \\ p? : PID \\ \hline p? \in slps \\ \hline \end{array}$$

The variable *maxslps* is the maximum number of process identifiers that can be in *slps*—i.e., it is the maximum cardinality for *slps*. A sleeper can be added if $\# slps$ is strictly less than the maximum size which it can attain.

$$\begin{array}{|l}\hline \textit{CanAddSleeper} \\ \hline \Xi SLEEPERS \\ \hline \# slps < maxslps \\ \hline \end{array}$$

The operation to add a sleeper, $p?$, to the sleepers set, *slps*, is specified by the following schema. It is the obvious operation, given the definitions.

$$\begin{array}{|l}\hline \textit{AddSleeperProc} \\ \hline \Delta SLEEPERS \\ p? : PID \\ \hline slps' = slps \cup \{p?\} \\ \hline \end{array}$$

To define the first main operation, it is necessary to define two new operations on *PTAB*.

SetWaitingTime

$$\Delta PTAB$$
$$p? : PID$$
$$t? : TIME$$

$$wakingtime' = wakingtime \oplus \{p? \mapsto t?\}$$

SetStateToSleeping

$$\Delta PTAB$$
$$p? : PID$$

$$state' = state \oplus \{p? \mapsto pssleeping\}$$

The operation to add a sleeper process is defined by

$$
\begin{aligned}
&AddSleeper \mathrel{\widehat=} \\
&\quad (IsAsleep \land AlreadyAsleep) \\
&\quad \lor (CanAddSleeper \land \\
&\quad\quad AddSleeperProc \land \\
&\quad\quad SetWaitingTime \land \\
&\quad\quad SysOk) \\
&\quad \lor TooManySleepers
\end{aligned}
$$

(Note that the operation represented by this schema requires a reschedule after use.) The definition expands into the following schema:

AddSleeper

$$\Delta SLEEPERS$$
$$\Delta SCHED$$
$$p? : PID$$
$$t? : TIME$$
$$serr! : SYSERR$$

$$
\begin{aligned}
&(p? \in slps \land serr! = alreadyasleep) \\
&\lor (\#slps < maxslps \land \\
&\quad slps' = slps \cup \{p?\} \land \\
&\quad wakingtime' = wakingtime \oplus \{p? \mapsto t?\} \land \\
&\quad serr! = sysok) \\
&\lor serr! = toomanysleepers
\end{aligned}
$$

Since *AddSleeper* is a major operation, we need to calculate its precondition. The calculation is simple and the precondition obvious.

$$
\begin{aligned}
&\text{pre } AddSleeper \mathrel{\widehat=} \\
&\quad p? \in slps \lor \#slps < maxslps
\end{aligned}
$$

When a process' sleep time expires, it must be removed from the set of sleeping processes. The following schema defines this operation—it is, again, obvious.

$$
\begin{array}{|l}
\hline
\textit{RemoveSleeper} \\
\Delta SLEEPERS \\
p? : PID \\
\hline
slps' = slps \setminus \{p?\} \\
\hline
\end{array}
$$

If the time a process, p, requires to wake is t, and $0 < t \leq now$, p should wake up now. This is expressed by the following schema:

$$
\begin{array}{|l}
\hline
\textit{ShouldWakeUp} \\
t? : TIME \\
now? : TIME \\
\hline
0 < t? \\
t? \leq now? \\
\hline
\end{array}
$$

A process should wake if the following condition is met:

$$
\begin{array}{l}
ShouldWake \mathrel{\widehat=} \\
\quad (WakingTime[t/t!] \land ShouldWakeUp[t/t?]) \setminus \{t\}
\end{array}
$$

This condition can be expanded into the following schema. It turns out to be an important operation in deciding which processes to wake when such a decision is required.

$$
\begin{array}{|l}
\hline
\textit{ShouldWake} \\
\Xi PTAB \\
p? : PID \\
now? : TIME \\
\hline
\exists t : TIME \bullet \\
\qquad t = waitingtime(p?) \land \\
\qquad 0 < t \land t \leq now? \\
\hline
\end{array}
$$

After simplification, it becomes:

$$
\begin{array}{|l}
\hline
\textit{ShouldWake} \\
\Xi PTAB \\
p? : PID \\
now? : TIME \\
\hline
0 < waitingtime(p?) \leq now? \\
\hline
\end{array}
$$

Next, we define the *FindAndWake* operation.

$$
\begin{array}{l}
FindAndWake \mathrel{\widehat=} \\
\quad GotSleepers \land \\
\quad (\forall p : PID \bullet \\
\qquad IsAsleep[p/p?] \land \\
\qquad ShouldWake[p/p?] \Rightarrow \\
\qquad RemoveSleeper[p/p?] \land \\
\qquad ClearWaitingTime[p/p?] \land \\
\qquad MakeReady[p/p?]
\end{array}
$$

It expands into

$$
\begin{array}{|l}
\hline
FindAndWake \\
\Delta SLEEPERS \\
\Xi PTAB \\
\Delta SCHED \\
now? : TIME \\
\hline
slps \neq \varnothing \\
\forall p : PID \bullet \\
\quad p \in slps \land \\
\quad 0 < waitingtime(p) \leq now? \Rightarrow \\
\quad waitingtime' = waitingtime \oplus \{p \mapsto 0\} \land \\
\quad slps' = slps \setminus \{p\} \land \\
\quad state' = state \oplus \{p \mapsto psready\} \land \\
\quad (\#sq.pq < maxs \land \\
\qquad ((sq.pq = \langle\rangle \land sq.pq' = \langle p \rangle) \lor \\
\qquad\quad (prio(p) \leq prio(head\ sq.pq) \land sq.pq' = \langle p \rangle \frown sq.pq) \lor \\
\qquad\quad (prio(last\ sq.pq) < prio(p) \land sq.pq' = sq.pq \frown \langle p \rangle) \lor \\
\qquad\quad (\exists s_1, s_2 : \mathrm{seq}\, PID \mid s_1 \neq \langle\rangle \land s_2 \neq \langle\rangle \land s_1 \frown s_2 = sq.pq \bullet \\
\qquad\qquad prio(last\ s_1) < prio(p) \land \\
\qquad\qquad prio(p) \leq prio(head\ s_2) \land \\
\qquad\qquad sq.pq' = s_1 \frown \langle p \rangle \frown s_2)) \land \\
\qquad\quad state' = state \oplus \{p \mapsto psready\} \land \\
\qquad\quad serr! = sysok) \\
\qquad \lor\ serr! = schedqfull \\
\hline
\end{array}
$$

Note that sequential composition is not required between *ClearWaitingTIme* and *MakeReady* because the components of *PTAB* they update are distinct.

The *FindAndWake* operation is important, so its precondition must be calculated. The precondition is

$$
\begin{array}{l}
\mathrm{pre}\ FindAndWake \mathrel{\widehat=} \\
\quad slps \neq \varnothing \land \forall p : PID \bullet p \in slps \land 0 < waitingtime(p) \leq now? \land \#sq < maxs
\end{array}
$$

or, after simplification, it becomes

$$
\begin{array}{l}
\text{pre } FindAndWake \mathrel{\widehat=} \\
\quad slps \neq \varnothing \land \\
\quad \{p : PID \mid p \in slps \land 0 < waitingtime(p) \leq now?\} \subseteq slps \land \\
\quad \#sq + \#\{p : PID \mid p \in slps \land 0 < waitingtime(p) \leq now?\} < maxs
\end{array}
$$

When a process is sleeping, its *state* value should be *pssleeping*. Setting *state* to *pssleeping* is performed by the following operation:

$$
\begin{array}{l}
SetStateToSleeping \mathrel{\widehat=} \\
\quad \exists\, st : PSTATE \mid st = pssleeping \bullet \\
\qquad SetProcState[st/st?]
\end{array}
$$

The operation expands and simplifies to:

$$
\begin{array}{|l}
\hline
\textit{SetStateToSleeping} \\
\Delta PTAB \\
p? : PID \\
\hline
state' = state \oplus \{p? \mapsto pssleeping\} \\
\hline
\end{array}
$$

The following is a predicate. It is used to determine when a process is trying to sleep for a period of 0 seconds—any longer period is valid.

$$
\begin{array}{|l}
\hline
\textit{BadSleepTime} \\
t? : TIME \\
\hline
t? = 0 \\
\hline
\end{array}
$$

An operation, called *SendMeToSleep* is required. It is defined by

$$
\begin{array}{l}
SendMeToSleep \mathrel{\widehat=} \\
\quad (BadSleepTime \land SleepTooShort) \\
\quad \lor (ComputeWakeTime[t?/stm?, cst/cst!] \land AddSleeper[cst/t?] \land \\
\qquad SetStateToSleeping) \setminus \{cst\}
\end{array}
$$

Again this operation requires a reschedule after use.

Expansion of this definition yields the following schema:

$$
\begin{array}{|l}
\hline
\textit{SendMeToSleep} \\
\Delta SLEEPERS \\
\Xi TIMESINCEBOOT \\
\Delta PTAB \\
p? : PID \\
t? : TIME \\
tnow? : TIME \\
serr! : SYSERR \\
\hline
(t? = 0 \land serr! = sleeptimetooshort) \\
\lor (\exists\, cst : TIME \mid cst = t? + tnow \bullet \\
\qquad (p? \in slps \land serr! = alreadyasleep)
\end{array}
$$

$$
\begin{array}{l}
\quad \lor (\#slps < maxslps \land \\
\qquad slps' = slps \cup \{p?\} \land \\
\qquad wakingtime' = wakingtime \oplus \{p? \mapsto t? + tnow?\} \land \\
\qquad serr! = sysok) \\
\quad \lor serr! = toomanysleepers \land \\
\qquad\quad serr! = sysok)) \\
\qquad \lor serr! = toomanysleepers) \\
\quad \land state' = state \oplus \{p? \mapsto pssleeping\}
\end{array}
$$

We can immediately simplify this schema to the following:

$$
\begin{array}{l}
\Xi TIMESINCEBOOT \\
\Delta SLEEPERS \\
\Delta PTAB \\
p? : PID \\
t? : TIME \\
tnow? : TIME \\
serr! : SYSERR \\
\hline
(t? = 0 \land serr! = sleeptimetooshort) \\
(p? \in slps \land serr! = alreadyasleep) \\
\lor (\#slps < maxslps \land \\
\qquad slps' = slps \cup \{p?\} \land \\
\qquad wakingtime' = wakingtime \oplus \{p? \mapsto t? + tnow?\} \land \\
\qquad serr! = sysok) \\
\lor serr! = toomanysleepers \land \\
serr! = sysok)) \\
\lor serr! = toomanysleepers) \\
\land state' = state \oplus \{p? \mapsto pssleeping\}
\end{array}
$$

By repeated application of *Distrib*-$\lor$ and $p \land q \vdash p$, the predicate can be transformed into

$$
\begin{array}{l}
(t? = 0 \land serr! = sleeptimetooshort) \\
\lor (p? \in slps \land serr! = alreadyasleep) \\
\lor (\#slps < maxslps \land \\
\qquad slps' = slps \cup \{p?\} \land \\
\qquad wakingtime' = wakingtime \oplus \{p? \mapsto t? + tnow?\} \land \\
\qquad state' = state \oplus \{p? \mapsto pssleeping\} \land \\
\qquad serr! = sysok) \\
\lor serr! = toomanysleepers \land \\
serr! = sysok)) \\
\lor serr! = toomanysleepers)
\end{array}
$$

The precondition of this important operation is easy to calculate.

$$\text{pre } SendMeToSleep \mathrel{\widehat=} t? = 0 \lor p? \in slps \lor \#slps < maxslps$$

3.11.2 Refinement One

Having defined the sleeper set and the operations required to maintain it, it is time to engage in the first refinement. The strategy is to refine the set to a singly linked list of process identifiers in the *next* mapping in *PTAB*. By implementing the sleeper set this way, space is saved; the list is, in any case, limited in length.

The first step of the refinement is to find a representation for the sleeper set. The identifier set *slps* is replaced by *slps*1 but now *slps*1 is a partial (finite) injection from process identifiers to *GPID*s (process identifiers plus *nullpid*). The idea is that *slps*1 contains the elements of *slps* in some order. The first element is denoted by *hds* and the last by *ends*—we can talk of "first" and "last" because of the temporal ordering on the insertion of identifiers into *slps*. The number of elements in *slps*1 is recorded in *slcnt*1, so $slcnt1 = \#slps$. The limit on the size of *slps*1 is *maxslps*1 (which is intended to be equal to *maxslps*). The refinement state space is given by the following schema:

SLEEPERS1

$$\begin{array}{l}
slps1 : PID \rightarrowtail\!\!\!\!\!\!\shortmid\;\; GPID \\
hds, ends : GPID \\
slcnt1 : \mathbb{N} \\
maxslps1 : \mathbb{N}_1 \\
\hline
hds = nullpid \Leftrightarrow ends = nullpid \\
hds = nullpid \Leftrightarrow \mathrm{dom}\ slps1 = \varnothing \\
hds = nullpid \Leftrightarrow maxslps1 = 0 \\
slcnt1 = \#\mathrm{dom}\ slps1 \\
hds \neq nullpid \Leftrightarrow \\
\quad slps1(ends) = nullpid \land \\
\quad hds \in \mathrm{dom}\ slps1 \land \\
\quad ends \in \mathrm{dom}\ slps1 \land \\
\quad \#\mathrm{dom}\ slps1 > 0
\end{array}$$

SLEEPERSInit1

$$\begin{array}{l}
SLEEPERS1' \\
smax? : \mathbb{N}_1 \\
\hline
maxslps1' = smax? \\
hds' = ends' = nullpid \\
slcnt1' = 0
\end{array}$$

IsAsleep1

$$\Xi SLEEPERS1$$
$$p? : PID$$

$$p? \in \mathrm{dom}\ slps1$$

(We can, and will, do better than this.)

CanAddSleeper1

$$\Xi SLEEPERS1$$

$$slcnt1 < maxslps1$$

AddSleeperProc1

$$\Delta SLEEPERS1$$
$$p? : PID$$

$$\begin{array}{l}
(hds = nullpid \land \\
\quad hds' = p? \land \\
\quad ends' = p? \land \\
\quad slps1' = slps1 \oplus \{p? \mapsto nullpid\}) \\
\lor (ends' = p? \land \\
\quad slps1' = slps1 \oplus \{ends \mapsto p?, p? \mapsto nullpid\}) \\
\land\ slcnt1' = slcnt1 + 1
\end{array}$$

$$\begin{array}{l}
AddSleeper1 \mathrel{\widehat=} \\
\quad (IsAsleep \land AlreadyAsleep) \\
\quad \lor (CanAddSleeper \land AddSleeperProc \land SetWaitingTime \land SysOk) \\
\quad \lor\ TooManySleepers
\end{array}$$

This expands to:

$$\Delta SLEEPERS1$$
$$\Delta PTAB1$$
$$p? : PID$$
$$t? : TIME$$
$$serr! : SYSERR$$

$$\begin{array}{l}
(p? \in \mathrm{dom}\ slps1 \land serr! = alreadyasleep) \\
\lor (p? \notin \mathrm{dom}\ slps1 \land \\
\quad (slcnt1 < maxslps1 \land \\
\quad\quad ((hds = nullpid \land \\
\quad\quad\quad hds' = ends' = p? \land
\end{array}$$

$$
\begin{array}{l}
\quad\quad slps1' = slps1 \oplus \{p? \mapsto nullpid\}) \\
\quad \lor (ends' = p? \land slps1' = slps1 \oplus \{ends \mapsto p?, p? \mapsto nullpid\})) \land \\
\quad slcnt1' = slcnt1 + 1 \land \\
\quad wakingtime' = wakingtime \oplus \{p? \mapsto t?\} \land \\
\quad serr! = sysok)) \\
\lor\ serr! = toomanysleepers
\end{array}
$$

$$
\begin{array}{|l}
\multicolumn{1}{l}{DelSleeperProc1} \\
\Delta SLEEPERS1 \\
p? : PID \\
\hline
(hds = p? \land \\
\quad slps1' = slps1 \lhd \{p?\} \land \\
\quad hds' = slps1(hds)) \\
\lor (\exists p_1 : PID \mid p? = slps1(p_1) \bullet \\
\quad (\exists slps1'' : PID \rightarrowtail\!\!\!\!\!\twoheadrightarrow GPID \bullet \\
\quad\quad slps1'' = slps1 \oplus \{p_1 \mapsto slps1(p?)\}) \land \\
\quad slps1' = slps1 \lhd \{p?\}) \\
slcnt1' = slcnt1 - 1
\end{array}
$$

This simplifies to:

$$
\begin{array}{|l}
\Delta SLEEPERS1 \\
p? : PID \\
\hline
(hds = p? \land slps1' = slps1 \lhd \{p?\} \land \\
\quad hds' = slps1(p?)) \\
\lor (\exists p_1 : PID \mid p? = slps1(p_1) \bullet \\
\quad\quad slps1' = (slps1 \lhd \{p?\}) \oplus \{p_1 \mapsto slps1(p?)\}) \\
slcnt1' = slcnt1 - 1
\end{array}
$$

The test whether there are any processes in the list of sleepers is now refined to a test of the counter, *slcnt*1. The counter is incremented by one when a process is added to the list and decremented by one when a process is removed.

$$
\begin{array}{|l}
\multicolumn{1}{l}{GotSleepers1} \\
\Xi SLEEPERS1 \\
\hline
slcnt1 \neq 0
\end{array}
$$

The removal of a process from the list of sleeping processes is refined to the following schema. If the process to be removed, $p?$, is the head of the list, the head, *hds*, is updated and $p?$ removed from *slps*1. Otherwise, $p?$ is just removed from $slps1$. In both cases, $slcnt1$ is decremented by one, as stated above.

$$
\begin{array}{|l}
\hline
\textit{RemoveSleeper1} \\
\Delta SLEEPERS1 \\
p? : PID \\
\hline
((p? = hds \land \\
\quad hds' = slps1(hds) \land \\
\quad slps1' = slps1 \lhd \{p?\}) \\
\lor\ slps1' = slps1 \lhd \{p?\}) \\
slcnt1' = slcnt1 - 1 \\
\hline
\end{array}
$$

The following is the refinement of the *ShouldWakeUp* predicate. The condition is the same as in the specification.

$$
\begin{array}{|l}
\hline
\textit{ShouldWakeUp1} \\
t?, now? : TIME \\
\hline
0 < t? \\
t? \leq now? \\
\hline
\end{array}
$$

The *ShouldWake* predicate is refined to the following:

$$
\begin{array}{l}
ShouldWake1 \mathrel{\widehat=} \\
\quad (WakingTime1[t/t!] \land ShouldWakeUp1[t/t?]) \setminus \{t\}
\end{array}
$$

The definition expands into the following schema:

$$
\begin{array}{|l}
\hline
\textit{ShouldWake1} \\
\Xi PTAB \\
p? : PID \\
now? : TIME \\
\hline
\exists t : TIME \bullet \\
\quad t = waitingtime1(p?) \land \\
\quad 0 < t \land t \leq now? \\
\hline
\end{array}
$$

which can be simplified using the one-point rule to

$$
\begin{array}{|l}
\hline
\textit{ShouldWake1} \\
\Xi PTAB \\
p? : PID \\
now? : TIME \\
\hline
0 < waitingtime1(p?) \leq now? \\
\hline
\end{array}
$$

The form of the refinement of *FindAndWake* is identical to the specification (only identifiers are altered).

$$
\begin{array}{l}
FindAndWake1 \mathrel{\widehat=} \\
\quad GotSleepers1 \land \\
\quad (\forall p : PID \bullet \\
\qquad IsAsleep1[p/p?] \land \\
\qquad ShouldWake1[p/p?] \Rightarrow \\
\qquad RemoveSleeper1[p/p?] \land \\
\qquad ClearWaitingTime1[p/p?] \land \\
\qquad MakeReady1[p/p?]
\end{array}
$$

In order to work with the definition, it must be expanded. The expansion is as follows:

$$
\begin{array}{l}
\textbf{FindAndWake1} \\
\hline
\Delta SLEEPERS1 \\
\Delta SCHED1 \\
now? : TIME \\
\hline
slcnt1 \neq 0 \\
\forall p : PID \bullet \\
\quad p \in \mathrm{dom}\, slps1 \land \\
\quad 0 < waitingtime1(p) \leq now? \Rightarrow \\
\quad slps1' = slps1 \lhd \{p\} \qquad ((p = hds \land \\
\qquad hds' = slps1(hds) \land \\
\qquad slps1' = slps1 \lhd \{p?\}) \\
\quad \lor\ slps1' = slps1 \lhd \{p?\}) \land \\
\quad slcnt1' = slcnt1 - 1 \land \\
\quad waitingtime1' = waitingtime1 \oplus \{p \mapsto 0\} \land \\
\quad state1' = state1 \oplus \{p \mapsto psready\} \land \\
\quad (nxtp \leq maxs1 \land \\
\qquad ((nxtp = 1 \land sq.pq1' = \{1 \mapsto p\} \land nxtp' = 2) \lor \\
\qquad\quad (prio1(p) \leq prio1(sq.pq1(1)) \land \\
\qquad\qquad (\forall i : 1 \mathinner{..} nxtp - 1 \bullet \\
\qquad\qquad\quad sq.pq1' = (sq.pq1 \oplus \{i + 1 \mapsto sq.pq1(i)\}) \oplus \{1 \mapsto p\}) \land \\
\qquad\qquad\quad nxtp' = nxtp + 1) \lor \\
\qquad\quad (prio1(sq.pq1(nxtp - 1)) < prio1(p) \land \\
\qquad\qquad sq.pq1' = sq.pq1 \oplus \{nxtp \mapsto p\} \land \\
\qquad\qquad nxtp' = nxtp + 1) \lor \\
\qquad\quad (\exists i : 1 \mathinner{..} nxtp - 2 \bullet \\
\qquad\qquad prio1(sq.pq1(i)) < prio1(p) \land \\
\qquad\qquad\quad prio1(p) \leq prio1(sq.pq1(i + 1)) \\
\qquad\qquad \lor (\forall j : i + 1 \mathinner{..} nxtp - 1 \bullet \\
\qquad\qquad\quad sq.pq1' = (sq.pq1 \oplus \{j + 1 \mapsto sq.pq1(j)\}) \oplus \{i + 1 \mapsto p\} \\
\qquad\qquad \land\ nxtp' = nxtp + 1)) \land
\end{array}
$$

$$
\begin{array}{l}
\quad\quad serr! = sysok) \\
\quad \lor\ serr! = schedqfull
\end{array}
$$

The precondition of *FindAndWake1* must be calculated. The calculation yields the following predicate:

$$
\begin{array}{l}
\mathrm{pre}\ FindAndWake1 \mathrel{\widehat=} \\
\quad slcnt1 \neq 0 \\
\quad nxtp + \#\{p : PID \mid p \in \mathrm{dom}\ slps1 \land 0 < waitingtime1(p) \leq now?\} < maxs1 \\
\quad \{p : PID \mid p \in \mathrm{dom}\ slps1 \land 0 < waitingtime1(p) \leq now?\} \subseteq \mathrm{dom}\ slps1
\end{array}
$$

The composite operation that places processes in a sleeping state refines to the following definition (it is similar to the specification):

$$
\begin{array}{l}
SendMeToSleep1 \mathrel{\widehat=} \\
\quad (BadSleepTime \land SleepTooShort) \\
\quad \lor\ (ComputeWakeTime[t?/stm?, cst/cst!] \land AddSleeper1[cst/t?] \land \\
\quad\quad\quad SetStateToSleeping1) \setminus \{cst\}
\end{array}
$$

Its expansion is the following schema:

$$
\begin{array}{|l}
\textbf{SendMeToSleep1} \\
\hline
\Delta PTAB1 \\
\Delta SLEEPERS1 \\
p? : PID \\
t?, now? : TIME \\
serr! : SYSERR \\
\hline
(t? = 0 \land serr! = sleeptimetooshort) \\
\lor\ (\exists\, cst : TIME \bullet \\
\quad (cst = t? + now? \land \\
\quad\quad (p? \in \mathrm{dom}\ slps1 \land serr! = alreadyasleep) \\
\quad\quad \lor\ (p? \notin \mathrm{dom}\ slps1 \land \\
\quad\quad\quad (slcnt1 < maxslps1 \land \\
\quad\quad\quad ((hds = nullpid \land \\
\quad\quad\quad\quad hds' = ends' = p? \land \\
\quad\quad\quad\quad slps1' = slps1 \oplus \{p? \mapsto nullpid\}) \\
\quad\quad\quad \lor\ (ends' = p? \land slps1' = slps1 \oplus \{ends \mapsto p?, p? \mapsto nullpid\})) \land \\
\quad\quad\quad slcnt1' = slcnt1 + 1 \land \\
\quad\quad\quad wakingtime' = wakingtime \oplus \{p? \mapsto t?\} \land \\
\quad\quad\quad serr! = sysok)) \\
\quad\quad\quad \lor\ serr! = toomanysleepers) \\
\quad \land\ state1' = state \oplus \{p? \mapsto pssleeping\})
\end{array}
$$

This schema can be simplified in a fairly obvious way. After simplification, the following is obtained:

$$
\begin{array}{l}
\Delta PTAB1 \\
\Delta SLEEPERS1 \\
p? : PID \\
t?, now? : TIME \\
serr! : SYSERR \\
\hline
(t? = 0 \land serr! = sleeptimetooshort) \\
\qquad \lor (p? \in \mathrm{dom}\, slps1 \land serr! = alreadyasleep) \\
\qquad \lor (p? \notin \mathrm{dom}\, slps1 \land \\
\qquad\qquad (slcnt1 < maxslps1 \land \\
\qquad\qquad ((hds = nullpid \land \\
\qquad\qquad\qquad hds' = ends' = p? \land \\
\qquad\qquad\qquad slps1' = slps1 \oplus \{p? \mapsto nullpid\}) \\
\qquad\qquad \lor (ends' = p? \land slps1' = slps1 \oplus \{ends \mapsto p?, p? \mapsto nullpid\})) \land \\
\qquad\qquad slcnt1' = slcnt1 + 1 \land \\
\qquad\qquad \land\, state1' = state \oplus \{p? \mapsto pssleeping\}) \\
\qquad\qquad wakingtime' = wakingtime \oplus \{p? \mapsto t? + now?\} \land \\
\qquad\qquad serr! = sysok)) \\
\qquad\qquad \lor\, serr! = toomanysleepers)
\end{array}
$$

Since this is an important operation, its precondition must be calculated. It is easy to see that the precondition is

$$
\begin{array}{l}
\mathrm{pre}\ SendMeToSleep1 \mathrel{\widehat=} \\
\qquad t? = 0 \lor p? \in \mathrm{dom}\, slps1 \lor slcnt1 < maxslps1
\end{array}
$$

Finally, we have the abstraction relation. It is an extremely simple relation and is given as the predicate of the following schema.

$$
\begin{array}{l}
\underline{\ AbsSLEEPERS1\ } \\
SLEEPERS \\
SLEEPERS1 \\
\hline
maxslps1 = maxslps \\
\mathrm{dom}\, slps1 = slps \\
slcnt1 = \#slps
\end{array}
$$

Theorem 48.

$$
\begin{array}{l}
\forall\, SLEEPERS'; SLEEPERS1' \bullet \\
\qquad SLEEPERSInit \land AbsSLEEPERS1' \Rightarrow SLEEPERSInit1
\end{array}
$$

PROOF. By the abstraction relation, $maxslps1' = maxslps' = smax?$. Also by the invariant of $SLEEPERRS1'$, $hds' = ends' = nullpid \Rightarrow \mathrm{dom}\, slps1' = \varnothing = slps'$ by the one-point rule. Finally, $\#slps' = slcnt1'$ and $slps' = \varnothing$, so $\#slps' = 0$, from which we are entitled to conclude that $slcnt1' = 0$. □

Theorem 49.

$$\forall\, SLEEPERS;\ SLEEPERS1;\ now? : TIME \bullet$$
$$\quad pre\, FindAndWake \wedge AbsSLEEPERS1 \Rightarrow pre\, FindAndWake1$$

PROOF. The preconditions are

$$\begin{aligned}
&\text{pre}\, FindAndWake \mathrel{\widehat{=}}\\
&\quad slps \neq \varnothing \wedge\\
&\quad \{p : PID \mid p \in slps \wedge 0 < waitingtime(p) \leq now?\} \subseteq slps \wedge\\
&\quad \#sq.pq + \#\{p : PID \mid p \in slps \wedge 0 < waitingtime(p) \leq now?\} < maxs \wedge
\end{aligned}$$

and

$$\begin{aligned}
&\text{pre}\, FindAndWake1 \mathrel{\widehat{=}}\\
&\quad slcnt1 \neq 0\\
&\quad nxtp + \#\{p : PID \mid p \in \operatorname{dom} slps1 \wedge 0 < waitingtime1(p) \leq now?\} < maxs1\\
&\quad \{p : PID \mid p \in \operatorname{dom} slps1 \wedge 0 < waitingtime1(p) \leq now?\} \subseteq \operatorname{dom} slps1
\end{aligned}$$

The abstraction relation, *AbsSLEEPERS*1 gives the relevant identities. The predicate of *AbsSLEEPERS*1 states that $p \in \operatorname{dom} slps1 \Leftrightarrow p \in slps$ and $slps \subset used$, so the refinement of *waitingtime* is correct. The remainder of the proof is immediate. □

Theorem 50.

$$\begin{aligned}
&\forall\, SLEEPERS;\ SLEEPERS';\ SLEEPERS1;\ SLEEPERS1';\\
&\qquad now? : TIME;\ serr! : SYSERR \bullet\\
&\quad pre\, FindAndWake \wedge\\
&\qquad AbsSLEEPERS1 \wedge\\
&\qquad AbsSLEEPERS1' \wedge\\
&\qquad FindAndWake1\\
&\quad \Rightarrow FindAndWake1
\end{aligned}$$

PROOF. The predicate of *AbsSLEEPERS*1 states that $slcnt1 = \#slps$, so $slcnt1 \neq 0$ implies $slps \neq \varnothing$. Next, $p \in \operatorname{dom} slps1$, by the predicate of *AbsSLEEPERS*1, implies $p \in slps$, since $\operatorname{dom} slps1 = slps$. The invariant of *SLEEPERS* states that $slps \subset used$ and this guarantees that $p \in \operatorname{dom} waitingtime$; from this, it may be inferred first that $waitingtime(p) = waitingtime1(p)$ and consequently that $0 < waitingtime1(p) \leq now?$ implies that $0 < waitingtime(p) \leq now?$.

As far as the update of *slps*1 is concerned, the important conjunct is $slps1' = slps1 \mathbin{⩤} \{p\}$. The predicate of *AbsSLEEPERS*1′ states that $slps' = \operatorname{dom} slps1$. This fact permits the following inference $slps1' = slps1 \mathbin{⩤} \{p\}$ implies that

$$\begin{aligned}
&\operatorname{dom} slps1'\\
&\quad = (\operatorname{dom} slps) \setminus \{p\}\\
&\quad = slps \setminus \{p\}\\
&\quad = slps'
\end{aligned}$$

as required.

By *AbsSLEEPERS*1, $slcnt1 = \#slps$ and by *AbsSLEEPERS*1′, $slcnt1 = \#slps'$, so $slcnt1' = slcnt - 1 = \#slps - 1 = slps'$.

The update of *waitingtime*1 is justified as follows. It is known, for reasons that have already been given, that $p \in used$, so $waitingtime1(p) = waitingtime(p)$ for all $p \in slps$. It also follows that $waitingtime1'(p) = waitingtime'(p)$ for all $p \in used$, so

$$
\begin{aligned}
& waitingtime1' \\
& \quad = waitingtime1 \oplus \{p \mapsto 0\} \\
& \quad = waitingtime \oplus \{p \mapsto 0\} \\
& \quad = waitingtime'
\end{aligned}
$$

The update of *state*1 and its equivalence to *state* also follows the same line of reasoning

$$
\begin{aligned}
& state1' \\
& \quad = state1 \oplus \{p \mapsto psready\} \\
& \quad = state \oplus \{p \mapsto psready\} \\
& \quad = state'
\end{aligned}
$$

The refinement of *MakeReady* has already been taken into account above. As noted there, *MakeReady* is defined in terms of promotion.

□

Theorem 51.

$$
\begin{aligned}
& \forall\, SLEEPERS;\ SLEEPERS1;\ p? : PID;\ t? : TIME;\ now? : TIME \bullet \\
& \quad \text{pre}\ SendMeToSleep \land AbsSLEEPERS1 \Rightarrow \text{pre}\ SendMeToSleep1
\end{aligned}
$$

PROOF. We have:

$$\text{pre}\ SendMeToSleep \mathrel{\widehat=} \#slps < maxslps \lor t? = 0 \lor p? \notin slps$$

$$\text{pre}\ SendMeToSleep1 \mathrel{\widehat=} t? = 0 \lor slcnt1 < maxslps1 \lor p? \notin \text{dom}\ slps1$$

Clearly $t? = 0$ is the same in both cases and the result can be deduced using $\lor$-introduction.

For the second case, the abstraction relation states that $slcnt1 = \#slps$ and $maxslps = maxslps1$, so substituting into $\#slps < maxslps$, $slcnt1 < maxslps1$ is obtained. Again, a step of $\lor$-introduction permits the conclusion to be reached, viz. $t? = 0 \lor slcnt1 < maxslps1$.

Finally, $p? \notin \text{dom}\ slps1$ and, by the abstraction relation, $\text{dom}\ slps1 = slps$, so $p? \notin slps$ is equivalent to $p? \notin \text{dom}\ slps1$. □

Theorem 52.

$$\begin{array}{l} \forall SLEEPERS;\ SLEEPERS';\ SLEEPERS1;\ SLEEPERS1'; \\ \qquad p? : PID;\ t?, now? : TIME;\ serr! : SYSERR \bullet \\ \quad pre\ SendMeToSleep \land \\ \qquad AbsSLEEPERS1 \land \\ \qquad AbsSLEEPERS1' \land \\ \qquad SendMeToSleep1 \\ \quad \Rightarrow SendMeToSleep \end{array}$$

PROOF. We can safely ignore the first disjunct,

$$t? = 0 \land serr! = sleeptimetooshort$$

It is the same in both cases and contributes only $t? = 0$ to the precondition.

Everything is relatively straightforward; the interesting part is the update of $slps1$. We start with $slps1 = slps1 \oplus \{p? \mapsto nullpid\}$. By $AbsSLEEPERS1$, $\mathrm{dom}\ slps1 = slps$, so taking domains, we have

$$\begin{array}{ll} \mathrm{dom}\ slps1' & \\ \quad = \mathrm{dom}(slps1 \oplus \{p? \mapsto nullpid\} & \\ \quad = \mathrm{dom}(slps1 \cup \{p? \mapsto nullpid\}), & p? \notin \mathrm{dom}\ slps1 \\ \quad = (\mathrm{dom}\ slps1) \cup (\mathrm{dom}\{p? \mapsto nullpid\}) & \\ \quad = (\mathrm{dom}\ slps1) \cup \{p?\} & \\ \quad = slps \cup \{p?\} & \\ \quad = slps' & \end{array}$$

where the last step is justified by $AbsSLEEPERS1'$ ($\mathrm{dom}\ slps1' = slps'$).

Similarly, for $slps1' = slps1 \oplus \{p? \mapsto hds\}$, for the same reason, we again take domains

$$\begin{array}{ll} \mathrm{dom}\ slps1' & \\ \quad = \mathrm{dom}(slps1 \oplus \{send \mapsto p?, p? \mapsto nullpid\}) & \\ \quad = \mathrm{dom}(slps1 \cup \{send \mapsto p?, p? \mapsto nullpid\}), & p? \notin \mathrm{dom}\ slps1 \\ \quad = \mathrm{dom}\ slps1 \cup (\mathrm{dom}\{p? \mapsto nullpid\}) & \\ \quad = \mathrm{dom}\ slps1 \cup \{p?\} & \\ \quad = slps \cup \{p?\} & \\ \quad = slps' & \end{array}$$

again, the final step is justified by $AbsSLEEPERS1'$ ($\mathrm{dom}\ slps1' = slps'$).

Finally, since $p? \in used$ and $slps \subset used$ and $\forall p : PID \bullet p \in used \Rightarrow wakingtime(p) = wakingtime1(p)$ in $AbsPTAB1$, and $\forall p : PID \bullet p \in used' \Rightarrow wakingtime'(p) = wakingtime1'(p)$, we can infer that

$$\begin{array}{l} wakingtime1' \\ \quad = wakingtime1 \oplus \{p? \mapsto t? + now?\} \\ \quad = wakingtime \oplus \{p? \mapsto t? + now?\} \\ \quad = wakingtime' \end{array}$$

The correspondence between $state$ and $state1$ is proved in a similar fashion.
□

3.11.3 Refiment Two

SLEEPERS2

$PTAB1$
$slcnt2 : \mathbb{N}$
$maxslprs2 : \mathbb{N}$
$shd, send : GPID$

$shd = nullpid \Leftrightarrow send = nullpid$
$shd \neq nullpid \Leftrightarrow slcnt2 > 0$
$shd \neq nullpid \Leftrightarrow$
$\quad next^{*}(\!|\ \{shd\}\ |\!) \setminus \{nullpid\} \neq \varnothing shd \neq nullpid \Leftrightarrow$
$\quad next(send) = nullpid$
$shd \neq nullpid \Leftrightarrow$
$\quad \forall p : PID \bullet$
$\quad\quad p \in next^{*}(\!|\ \{shd\}\ |\!) \setminus \{nullpid\} \Rightarrow$
$\quad\quad\quad \exists k : \mathbb{N} \bullet k \geq 0 \wedge k \leq maxslprs2 \wedge next^{k}(shd) = p$

SLEEPERSInit2

$SLEEPERS2$
$smax? : \mathbb{N}_1$

$maxslprs2' = smax?$
$shd' = nullpid$
$slcnt2' = 0$

IsAsleep2

$\Xi SLEEPERS2$
$p? : PID$

$shd = p? \vee$
$send = p? \vee$
$p? \in next^{+}(\!|\ \{shd\}\ |\!) \setminus \{nullpid\}$

CanAddSleeper2

$\Xi SLEEPERS2$

$slcnt2 < maxslprs2$

$$
\begin{array}{|l}
\hline
\textit{AddSleeperProc2} \\
\Delta SLEEPERS2 \\
p? : PID \\
\hline
slcnt2' = slcnt2 + 1 \\
(shd = nullpid \land \\
\quad shd' = p? \land \\
\quad send' = p? \land \\
\quad next' = next \oplus \{p? \mapsto nullpid\}) \\
\lor (send' = p? \land \\
\quad next' = next \oplus \{send \mapsto p?, p? \mapsto nullpid\}) \\
\hline
\end{array}
$$

$$
\begin{array}{|l}
\hline
\textit{DelSleeperProc2} \\
\Delta SLEEPERS2 \\
p? : PID \\
\hline
slcnt2' = slcnt2 - 1 \\
((shd = p? \land shd' = next(shd)) \\
\lor (\exists p_1 : PID \mid p? = next(p_1) \bullet \\
\quad next' = next \oplus \{p_1 \mapsto next(p?)\}) \\
\hline
\end{array}
$$

$$
\begin{array}{l}
AddSleeper2 \mathrel{\widehat=} \\
\quad (IsAsleep2 \land AlreadyAsleep) \\
\quad \lor (CanAddSleeper2 \land \\
\qquad (\neg\ IsAsleep2 \land \\
\qquad\quad AddSleeperProc2 \land \\
\qquad\quad SetWaitingTime2 \land \\
\qquad\quad SysOk)) \\
\quad \lor TooManySleepers
\end{array}
$$

$$
\begin{array}{|l}
\hline
\textit{AddSleeper2} \\
\Delta SLEEPERS2 \\
p? : PID \\
serr! : SYSERR \\
t? : TIME \\
\hline
(shd = p? \lor p? \in next^+ (\!|\ \{shd\}\ |\!) \setminus \{nullpid\} \land \\
\quad serr! = alreadyasleep) \\
\lor (shd \neq p? \land \\
\quad \lor (slcnt2 < maxslprs2 \land \\
\qquad p? \notin next^+ (\!|\ \{shd\}\ |\!) \setminus \{nullpid\} \land \\
\qquad wakingtime2' = wakingtime2 \oplus \{p? \mapsto t?\} \land \\
\qquad slcnt2' = slcnt2 + 1 \land
\end{array}
$$

$$
\begin{array}{l}
\quad ((shd = nullpid \land \\
\qquad shd' = p? \land \\
\qquad send' = p? \land \\
\qquad next' = next \oplus \{p? \mapsto nullpid\}) \\
\quad \lor (send' = p? \land \\
\qquad next' = next \oplus \{send \mapsto p?, p? \mapsto nullpid\}) \\
\quad \land serr! = sysok)) \\
\lor serr! = toomanysleepers
\end{array}
$$

Note that

$$
\begin{array}{l}
p? \neq shd \land \\
p? \notin next^{+}(\!|\ \{shd\}\ |\!) \setminus \{nullpid\}
\end{array}
$$

can be rewritten as

$$
\begin{array}{l}
p? \neq shd \land \\
\neg \exists k : \mathbb{N} \bullet \\
\quad 0 < k \land k \leq \#next^{*}(\!|\ \{shd\}\ |\!) \setminus \{nullpid\} \land \\
\quad next^{k}(shd) \neq p?
\end{array}
$$

GotSleepers2

$$
\begin{array}{l}
\Xi SLEEPERS1 \\
\hline
slcnt2 \neq 0
\end{array}
$$

RemoveSleeper2

$$
\begin{array}{l}
\Delta SLEEPERS2 \\
p? : PID \\
\hline
(p? = shd \land \\
\qquad shd' = next(hds)) \\
\lor next' = next \oplus \{p? \mapsto nullpid\} \\
slcnt2' = slcnt2 - 1
\end{array}
$$

ShouldWakeUp2

$$
\begin{array}{l}
p? : PID \\
t?, now? : TIME \\
\hline
0 < t? \\
t? \leq now?
\end{array}
$$

$ShouldWake2 \mathrel{\widehat=}$
$\quad (WakingTime2[t/t!] \land ShouldWakeUp2[t/t?]) \setminus \{t\}$

This expands into

$$
\begin{array}{|l}
\hline
\textit{ShouldWake2} \\
\Xi PTAB \\
p? : PID \\
now? : TIME \\
\hline
\exists t : TIME \bullet \\
\quad t = waitingtime2(p?) \land \\
\quad 0 < t \land t \leq now? \\
\hline
\end{array}
$$

or

$$
\begin{array}{|l}
\hline
\textit{ShouldWake2} \\
\Xi PTAB \\
p? : PID \\
now? : TIME \\
\hline
0 < waitingtime2(p?) \leq now? \\
\hline
\end{array}
$$

$FindAndWake2 \mathrel{\widehat=}$
$\quad GotSleepers2 \land$
$\quad (\forall p : PID \bullet$
$\quad\quad IsAsleep2[p/p?] \land ShouldWake2[p/p?] \Rightarrow$
$\quad\quad RemoveSleeper2[p/p?] \land ClearWaitingTime2[p/p?] \land MakeReady1[p/p?]$

This expands into

$$
\begin{array}{|l}
\hline
\textit{FindAndWake2} \\
\Delta SLEEPERS2 \\
\Delta SCHED \\
\Delta PTAB2 \\
now? : TIME \\
\hline
slcnt2 \neq 0 \\
\forall p : PID \bullet \\
\quad p \in next^*(\!|\ \{shd\}\ |\!) \setminus \{nullpid\} \land 0 < waitingtime2(p) \leq now? \Rightarrow \\
\quad\quad ((p = shd \land shd' = next(hds))
\end{array}
$$

$$
\begin{array}{l}
\quad \lor\ next' = next \oplus \{p \mapsto nullpid\}) \land \\
\quad slcnt2' = slcnt2 - 1 \land \\
\quad waitingtime2' = waitingtime2 \oplus \{p \mapsto 0\} \land \\
\quad MakeReady1[p/p?]
\end{array}
$$

$$
\begin{array}{l}
\text{pre } FindAndWake2 \mathrel{\widehat=} \\
\quad slcnt2 \neq 0 \land \\
\quad nextp + \#\{p : PID \mid 0 < waitingtime2(p) \leq now? \land \\
\qquad\qquad next^{*}(\!|\ \{shd\}\ |\!) \setminus \{nullpid\}\} - 1 < maxs1 \land \\
\quad \{p : PID \mid 0 < waitingtime2(p) \leq now? \land \\
\qquad\qquad p \in \mathrm{next}^{*}(\!|\ \{shd\}\ |\!) \setminus \{nullpid\}\} \\
\qquad\quad \subseteq next^{*}(\!|\ \{shd\}\ |\!) \setminus \{nullpid\}
\end{array}
$$

$$
\begin{array}{l}
SendMeToSleep2 \mathrel{\widehat=} \\
\quad (BadSleepTime \land SleepTooShort) \\
\quad \lor\ (ComputeWakeTime[t?/stm?, cst/cst!] \land \\
\qquad AddSleeper2[cst/t?] \land \\
\qquad SetStateToSleeping2) \setminus \{cst\}
\end{array}
$$

This expands into and simplifies to

$$
\begin{array}{l}
\textbf{schema } SendMeToSleep2 \\
\quad \Delta SLEEPERS2 \\
\quad \Delta PTAB2 \\
\quad t?, now? : TIME \\
\quad p? : PID \\
\quad serr! : SYSERR \\
\hline
\quad (t? = 0 \land serr! = sleeptimetooshort) \\
\qquad \lor\ (slcnt2 < maxslps2 \land \\
\qquad\quad (shd = p? \lor \\
\qquad\qquad (\exists k : \mathbb{N} \bullet \\
\qquad\qquad\quad 0 < k \land k \leq \#next^{+}(\!|\ \{shd\}\ |\!) \setminus \{nullpid\} \land \\
\qquad\qquad\quad next^{k}(shd) = p)) \land \\
\qquad\qquad serr! = alreadyasleep) \\
\qquad\quad \lor\ (shd \neq p? \land p? \notin next^{+}(\!|\ \{shd\}\ |\!) \setminus \{nullpid\} \land \\
\qquad\qquad wakingtime2' = wakingtime2 \oplus \{p? \mapsto t? + now?\} \land \\
\qquad\qquad slcnt2' = slcnt2 + 1 \land \\
\qquad\qquad ((shd = nullpid \land shd' = p? \land send' = p? \land \\
\qquad\qquad\quad next' = next \oplus \{p? \mapsto nullpid\}) \\
\qquad\qquad \lor\ (shd' = p? \land next' = next \oplus \{p? \mapsto shd\})) \\
\qquad\qquad \land\ state2' = state2 \oplus \{p? \mapsto pssleeping\} \\
\qquad\qquad \land\ serr! = sysok)) \\
\qquad \lor\ serr! = toomanysleepers)
\end{array}
$$

This is interesting because $shd = p? \vee p? \in next^{+}(\!|\ \{shd\}\ |\!) \setminus \{nullpid\}$ is equivalent to $p? \in next^{*}(\!|\ \{shd\}\ |\!) \setminus \{nullpid\}$.

$$
\begin{array}{l}
\text{pre}\ \mathit{SendMeToSleep2} \mathrel{\widehat=} \\
\quad t? = 0 \\
\quad \vee\ (shd = p? \vee \\
\qquad (\exists k : \mathbb{N} \bullet \\
\qquad\quad 0 < k \wedge k \leq \#next^{+}(\!|\ \{shd\}\ |\!) \setminus \{nullpid\} \wedge \\
\qquad\quad next^{k}(shd) = p)) \\
\quad \vee\ slcnt2 < maxslps2
\end{array}
$$

AbsSLEEPERS2

$$
\begin{array}{l}
\mathit{SLEEPERS1} \\
\mathit{SLEEPERS2} \\
\hline
maxslprs2 = maxslprs1 \\
\text{dom}\ slps1 \subseteq \text{dom}\ next \\
\text{ran}\ slps1 \subseteq \text{ran}\ next \\
slscnt2 = slscnt1 \\
\text{dom}\ slps1 = next^{*}(\!|\ \{shd\}\ |\!) \setminus \{nullpid\} \\
\forall p : PID \bullet \\
\quad p \in \text{dom}\ slps1 \Rightarrow \\
\qquad slps1(p) = next(p) \\
shd = hds \\
send = ends
\end{array}
$$

Theorem 53.

$$
\begin{array}{l}
\forall\ \mathit{SLEEPERS1}';\ \mathit{SLEEPERS2}' \bullet \\
\quad \mathit{SLEEPERSInit2} \wedge \mathit{AbsSLEEPERS2}' \Rightarrow \mathit{SLEEPERSInit1}
\end{array}
$$

PROOF. By the abstraction relation, $maxslprs2' = maxslps1'$, and since $maxslprs2' = smax?$, we may infer $maxslps1' = smax?$.

Again, by the abstraction relation, $slcnt2' = slcnt1'$, and since $slcnt2' = 0$, we are entitled to infer that $slcnt1' = 0$.

We deal with *hds* and *ends* as follows. The abstraction relation states that $hds' = shd$ and $shd' = nullpid$, so $hds' = nullpid$ by the transitivity of identity. Given that $shd' = nullpid \Rightarrow send' = nullpid$ and, by the abstraction relation, $send' = ends'$, Modus Ponens allows us to infer that $ends' = nullpid$. By transitivity of identity, we have the desired $shd' = ends' = nullpid$. □

Theorem 54.

$$
\begin{array}{l}
\forall\ \mathit{SLEEPERS1};\ \mathit{SLEEPERS2};\ now? : \mathit{TIME} \bullet \\
\quad \text{pre}\ \mathit{FindAndWake1} \wedge \mathit{AbsSLEEPERS2} \Rightarrow \text{pre}\ \mathit{FindAndWake2}
\end{array}
$$

PROOF.

$$\text{pre } FindAndWake1 \mathrel{\widehat=}$$
$$slcnt1 \neq 0$$
$$nxtp + \#\{p : PID \mid p \in \operatorname{dom} slps1 \wedge 0 < waitingtime1(p) \leq now?\} < maxs1$$
$$\{p : PID \mid p \in \operatorname{dom} slps1 \wedge 0 < waitingtime1(p) \leq now?\} \subseteq \operatorname{dom} slps1$$

$$\text{pre } FindAndWake2 \mathrel{\widehat=}$$
$$slcnt2 \neq 0 \wedge$$
$$nextp + \#\{p : PID \mid 0 < waitingtime2(p) \leq now? \wedge next^{*}(\!| \{shd\} |\!) \setminus \{nullpid\}\} - 1 < maxs1 \wedge$$
$$\{p : PID \mid 0 < waitingtime2(p) \leq now? \wedge p \in \text{next}^{*}(\!| \{shd\} |\!) \setminus \{nullpid\}\} \subseteq next^{*}(\!| \{shd\} |\!) \setminus \{nullpid\}$$

The abstraction relation, *AbsSLEEPERS*2 gives the relevant identities. By a previous result, we have it that $p \in \operatorname{dom} slps1 \Leftrightarrow p \in slps$ and $slps \subset used$ and $nxtp\#next^{*}(\!| \{shd\} |\!) \setminus \{nullpid\} = \operatorname{dom} slps1$, so the refinement of *waitingtime*1 is correct. The remainder of the proof is immediate. □

Theorem 55.

$$\forall SLEEPERS1;\ SLEEPERS1';\ SLEEPERS2;\ SLEEPERS2';\ now? : TIME;\ serr! : SYSERR \bullet$$
$$pre\ FindAndWake1 \wedge AbsSLEEPERS2 \wedge AbsSLEEPERS2' \wedge FindAndWake2$$
$$\Rightarrow FindAndWake1$$

PROOF. By the predicate of *AbsSLEEPER*2, $slcnt2 = slcnt1$, so $slcnt2 \neq 0$ implies $slcnt1 \neq 0$. By that same predicate, $next^{*}(\!| \{shd\} |\!) \setminus \{nullpid\} = \operatorname{dom} slps1$, so $p \in next^{*}(\!| \{shd\} |\!) \setminus \{nullpid\}$ implies that $p \in \operatorname{dom} slps1$.

Next, it is clear that $next^{*}(\!| \{freehd\} |\!) \setminus \{nullpid\} = \operatorname{dom} slps1$ by the predicate of the abstraction relation *AbsSLEEPERS*2 and that $\operatorname{dom} slps1 = slps$ by *AbsSLEEPERS*1 and $slps \subset used$, $p \in next^{*}(\!| \{freehd\} |\!) \setminus \{nullpid\}$ $(*)$ implies that $0 < waitingtime2(p) \leq now?$ implies $0 < waitingtime1(p) \leq now?$.

The removal of p from the list of sleepers is given, in *FindAndWake2*, as

$$(p = shd \wedge shd' = next(shd))$$
$$\vee (\exists p_1 : PID \bullet next(p_1) = p \wedge next' = next \oplus \{p_1 \mapsto next(p)\}$$

It is clear that each should be taken separately (and an appeal to $\vee$-I would be made if one wanted a fully formal proof).

By the predicate of the schema $AbsSLEEPERS2$, $hds = shd$ and by the predicates of both $AbsSLEEPERS2$ and $AbsSLEEPERS2'$, $shd' = next(shd) = slps1(hds) = hds'$. The identity $next(shd) = slps1(hds)$ is justified by the observation that

$$hds \in next^*(\!|\ \{hds\}\ |\!) \setminus \{nullpid\} = \mathrm{dom}\ slps1$$

Next, the existential contains $next' = next \oplus \{p_1 \mapsto next(p)\}$. This implies that $p \notin \mathrm{dom}\ next'$ and, by $AbsSLEEPERS2'$, $next'(p) = slps1'(p)$, for all $p \in \mathrm{dom}\ slps1'$ (or equivalently, $p \in next^*(\!|\ \{shd\}\ |\!) \setminus \{nullpid\})$. For $p \notin \mathrm{dom}\ slps1'$ and $p \in \mathrm{dom}\ slps1$ both to be true, it must be the case that $\mathrm{dom}\ slps1' = (\mathrm{dom}\ slps1) \setminus \{p\}$ which is equivalent to $slps1 \setminus \{p\}$ and $slps1 \setminus \{p\} = slps1'$.

By the abstraction relations, $slcnt2 = slcnt1$ and $slcnt2' = slcnt1'$, so $slcnt2' = slcnt2 - 1 = slcnt1 - 1 = slcnt1'$.

The update of $waitingtime2$ and $state2$ can be handled in a simple way. The chain of equivalences $*$ above is required.

Finally, $MakeReady1$, as observed elsewhere is defined in terms of promotion and its refinement has already been undertaken.

□

Theorem 56.

$$\forall\ SLEEPERS1;\ SLEEPERS2;\ p? : PID;\ t?, now? : TIME \bullet$$
$$pre\ SendMeToSleep1 \wedge AbsSLEEPERS1 \Rightarrow pre\ SendMeToSleep2$$

PROOF. We have

$$\begin{aligned} \mathrm{pre}\ SendMeToSleep1 \mathrel{\widehat=}\ & t? = 0 \\ & \vee\ slcnt1 < maxslps1 \\ & \vee\ p? \notin \mathrm{dom}\ slps1 \end{aligned}$$

$$\begin{aligned} \mathrm{pre}\ SendMeToSleep2 \mathrel{\widehat=}\ & \\ & t? = 0 \vee slcnt2 < maxslps2 \vee \\ & \quad p? \notin next^*(\!|\ \{shd\}\ |\!) \setminus \{nullpid\} \end{aligned}$$

The abstraction relation states that $slcnt1 = slcnt2$ and that $maxslps1 = maxslps2$. Furthermore, $next^*(\!|\ \{shd\}\ |\!) \setminus \{nullpid\} = \mathrm{dom}\ slps1$. □

Theorem 57.

$$\begin{aligned} \forall\ & SLEEPERS1;\ SLEEPERS1';\ SLEEPERS2;\ SLEEPERS2'; \\ & \quad p? : PID;\ t?, now? : TIME;\ serr! : SYSERR \bullet \\ & pre\ SendMeToSleep1 \wedge \\ & \quad AbsSLEEPERS2 \wedge \\ & \quad AbsSLEEPERS2' \wedge \\ & \quad SendMeToSleep2 \\ & \Rightarrow SendMeToSleep1 \end{aligned}$$

PROOF. We can ignore with impunity the first conjunct ($t? = 0 \wedge serr! = sleeptimetooshort$).

By the predicate of $AbsSLEEPERS2$, we have $slcnt2 = slcnt1$ and $maxslps1 = maxslps2$, so $slcnt2 < maxslps2 \Leftrightarrow slcnt1 < maxslps1$.

The guard

$$shd = p? \vee p? \in next^*(\!|\ \{shd\}\ |\!) \setminus nullpid\}$$

implies

$$p? \in next^*(\!|\ \{shd\}\ |\!) \setminus nullpid\}$$

which, in turn, by the predicate of $AbsSLEEPERS2$, implies that $p? \in \operatorname{dom} slps1$.

If $shd = nullpid$, $next^*(\!|\ \{shd\}\ |\!) \setminus nullpid\} = \varnothing$, which implies that $\operatorname{dom} slps1 = \varnothing$. We now reason as follows.

$$\begin{aligned} & next' \\ & \quad = next \oplus \{p? \mapsto nullpid\} \\ & \quad = slps1 \oplus \{p? \mapsto nullpid\}, \qquad \text{since } \operatorname{dom} slps1 = \varnothing \\ & \quad = slps1' \end{aligned}$$

The last step is justified by $AbsSLEEPERS2'$.

In addition, we have

$$\begin{aligned} & next' \\ & \quad = next \oplus \{send \mapsto p?, p? \mapsto nullpid\} \\ & \quad = slps1 \oplus \{endss \mapsto p?, p? \mapsto nullpid\}, \qquad \text{since } send = ends \\ & \quad = slps1' \end{aligned}$$

The last step is, once more, justified by $AbsSLEEPERS2'$.

Since $p?$ is not an element of the free chain, the proof of $wakingtime2' = wakingtime1'$ and $state2' = state1'$ is straightforward.

In the final section, it will become clear that we are justified in assuming that $p?$ is not on the free chain. □

The operations and data structures derived in this section can now be translated directly into execuable code.

3.12 User Interface

Here, the interface operations are defined. These are the operations that constitute the system as far as user processes are seen.

3.12.1 System Initialisation

This consists of

- Creation and initialisation of process table ($PTAB$);
- Creation of idle (null) process
- Initialisation of scheduler
- Initialisation of semaphore table
- Initialisation of sleeper list

This operation creates the idle process (variously called "null process" or "idle process").

$$
\begin{array}{l}
\mathit{CreateNullProcess} \mathrel{\widehat=} \\
\quad \exists\, st : PSTATE;\ pr : PPRIO \bullet \\
\qquad st = psready \land \\
\qquad pr = minprio \land \\
\qquad AddPD[st/st?, pr/pr?] \land \\
\qquad InitProcessStack
\end{array}
$$

It expands into

$$
\begin{array}{|l}
\textit{CreateNullProcess} \\
\hline
\Delta PTAB \\
p! : PID \\
serr! : SYSERR \\
\hline
((used \subset PID \land \\
\qquad p! \notin used \land \\
\qquad used' = used \cup \{p!\} \land \\
\qquad p! \in used' \land \\
\qquad prio' = prio \cup \{p! \mapsto pr\} \land \\
\qquad state' = state \cup \{p! \mapsto st\} \land \\
\qquad smsg' = smsg \cup \{p? \mapsto nullmsg\} \land \\
\qquad wakingtime' = wakingtime \cup \{p! \mapsto 0\} \land \\
\qquad InitProcessStack \land \\
\qquad serr! = sysok) \\
\lor\ serr! = pdinuse) \\
\lor\ serr! = ptabful \\
\hline
\end{array}
$$

The update of *state* by the addition of $p!$ satisfies the update condition for *prio* (etc.) as already noted. This is because the *AddPD* operation is a sequential composition and what would be the intermediate state, $used''$, is identical to the after state, $used'$, because it is not further updated.

The *InitProcessStack* operation is defined below when discussing the creation of new processes in general.

The definition of *CreateNullProcess* is just a substitution instance of *AddPD*. The refinement of this operation is just the refinement of *AddPD* suitably instantitated.

$$
\begin{array}{l}
SystemInit \mathrel{\widehat=} \\
\quad PTABInit \\
\quad \mathbin{;}(TIMESINCEBOOTInit \land CLOCKTIMEInit) \\
\quad \mathbin{;}(CreateNullProcess[ipid/p!, err/serr!] \land \\
\qquad ((IsSysOk \land SCHEDInit[ipid/p?] \land SEMATBLInit) \\
\quad \lor ReturnSysErr[err/terr?])) \setminus \{ipid, err\} \\
\quad \mathbin{;}ExitCritical
\end{array}
$$

After re-arrangement, the predicate simplifies to

$$
\begin{array}{l}
tnow' = 0 \\
secs' = 0 \\
mins' = 0 \\
hrs' = 0 \\
curr' = minpid \\
prev' = minpid \\
iprc' = ipid \\
sq'.pq = \langle\,\rangle \\
semasinuse' = \varnothing \\
used' = \{ipid\} \\
prio' = \{ipid \mapsto pr?\} \\
state' = \{ipid \mapsto st?\} \\
smsg' = \{ipid \mapsto nullmsg\} \\
wakingtime' = \{ipid \mapsto 0\}
\end{array}
$$

The assignment to $prio'$, $state'$, $smsg'$ and $wakingtime'$ are justified by the fact that $\mathrm{dom}\, prio' = \mathrm{dom}\, state' = \mathrm{dom}\, smsg' = \mathrm{dom}\, wakingtime' = used'$ and $used' = \{ipid\}$. The initialisation of the scheduler is obtained by expanding $\theta PRIOQInit$ to $sq'.pq = \langle\,\rangle$.

Some of the components of the definition of *SystemInit* do not refine. Removing them, the following is revealed

$$
\begin{array}{l}
PTABInit \\
\mathbin{;}CreateNullProcess \\
\mathbin{;}SEMATABInit
\end{array}
$$

This forms the core of the refinement. (For verification purposes, the invariant components can be added and checked that the result satisfies the refinement homomorphism)

The initial process is the one that is started first. More important, it is the root process and is responsible for the creation of all processes in the system.

$$
\begin{array}{l}
CreateInitialProcess \mathrel{\widehat=} \\
\quad NewProcess \\
\quad \mathbin{;}SchedNext
\end{array}
$$

Since *SchedNext* is defined in terms of a promotion, the refinement of *NewProcess* is the central aspect. The refinement of this operation is discussed in the next subsection.

3.12.2 Process Creation

Process creation involves:

- Adding a descriptor to the process table
- Insertion of process reference in scheduler queue (*MakeReady*)

With the exception of the null (idle) and initial processes, each process is created by some other process. The other process, the parent, must be the currently executing process, of course, when the operation is performed. This has the consequence that the *NewProcess* operation can handle errors in any way it sees fit. It also means that there is no need to obtain the identifier of the current process before doing anything else.

It should be noted that the entire operation is wrapped in an *EnterCritical*, *LeaveCritical* pair. These operations disable and enable interrupts, respectively.

$$
\begin{array}{l}
NewProcess \mathrel{\widehat=} \\
\quad EnterCritical \\
\quad (\exists\, st : PSTATE \mid st = psready \bullet \\
\qquad (AddPD[mypid!/p!, err/serr!] \land \\
\qquad InitProcessStack \\
\qquad\quad \fatsemi ((IsSysOk[err/serr!] \land MakeReady[mypid!/p?, err/serr!] \land SysOk) \\
\qquad\qquad \lor ReturnSysErr[err/terr?])) \setminus \{err\}) \\
\quad \fatsemi ExitCritical
\end{array}
$$

As far as the refinement process is concerned, this operation is the reason for our making the assumption $p? \in used$ above; every process must be created by the above operation and it ensures that $p \in used$ holds, for all newly allocated p. Below, we are able to discharge the assumption.

The last definition expands and simplifies to

$$
\begin{array}{l}
((used \subset PID \land \\
\quad (mypid! \notin used \land \\
\qquad used' = used \cup \{mypid!\} \land \\
\qquad prio' = prio \oplus \{mypid! \mapsto pr?\} \land \\
\qquad smsg' = smsg \oplus \{mypid! \mapsto nullmsg\} \land \\
\qquad wakingtime' = wakingtime \oplus \{mypid! \mapsto 0\} \land \\
\qquad InitProcessStack \land \\
\qquad state' = (state \oplus \{mypid \mapsto st?\}) \oplus \{mypid! \mapsto psready\} \land \\
\qquad ((pq = \langle\rangle \land pq' = \langle p? \rangle \land serr! = sysok)
\end{array}
$$

$$
\begin{array}{l}
\lor (((\#pq < maxs \land \\
\quad ((prio(p?) \leq prio(head\, pq) \land pq' = \langle p? \rangle \frown pq) \\
\quad \lor (prio(last\, pq) < prio(p?) \land pq' = pq \frown \langle p? \rangle) \\
\quad \lor (\exists s_1, s_2 : \mathrm{seq}\, PID \mid s_1 \neq \langle\rangle \land s_2 \neq \langle\rangle \land s_1 \frown s_2 = pq \bullet \\
\qquad prio(last\, s_1) < prio(p?) \land \\
\qquad prio(p?) \leq prio(head\, s_2) \land \\
\qquad pq' = s_1 \frown \langle p? \rangle \frown s_2)) \land \\
\quad serr! = sysok)) \\
\quad \lor serr! = schedqfull)) \\
\quad \lor serr! = pdinuse)) \\
\lor serr! = ptabful)
\end{array}
$$

The *NewProcess* operation is called by the initial process to create processes. The precondition is

$$\mathrm{pre}\, NewProcess \mathrel{\widehat{=}} used \neq PID \land \#pq < maxs$$

The first conjunct is derived from $used \subset PID$, note.

Again, some of the components do not refine. This implies that the refinement process should be in terms of

$$AddPD \mathbin{⨾} MakeReady$$

This expands into

$$
\begin{array}{l}
AddPD ⨾ \\
\quad SetStateToReady \land \\
\quad \exists \Delta PRIOQ \bullet \\
\qquad \Phi SCHED \land MakeReady
\end{array}
$$

This is a refinement and the refinement of *MakeReady* has already been undertaken. Furthermore, the refinement of *MakeReady* in this context involves the substitution of a value ($p?$) whose priority is not affected by that operation. It appears logical, therefore, to concentrate on the composition

$$AddPD \mathbin{⨾} SetStateToReady$$

It should be noted that $mypid! \in used$, so *SetStateToReady* is valid in this case.

The *InitProcessStack* is a low-level operation that is hardware-specific. On the Intel IA32 processor, for example, this operation would first simulate a procedure call (so that any parameters can be passed to the new process); next, it would push a dummy flags register (set to denote interrupted code), followed by a word containing the offset of the code segement in a table (the TSS), then the entry point of the process; the eight 0s (one per register) are then pushed onto the stack and the operation is ready. On other machines, this operation would be different, hence the reason for merely stating its specification in English. (But note that we *could* specify it formally—all of the concepts are readily amenable to formalisation.)

3.12.3 Process Management

Here, we deal with

- Self-suspension
- Sleep
- Termination

All process-management operations are performed by the currently executing process. This has the consequence that any errors must be handled either by the process itself or just left for something else to pick them up. In addition, the operations must be wrapped inside the operations that disable and then enable interrupts. The reason for this is that the operation must be atomic as far as other processes are concerned.

As will be seen, a useful property of both *EnterCritical* and *ExitCritical* is that they can be omitted when calculating preconditions. The reason for this is that they only affect the *after* state. Here, again, is the definition of *EnterCritical*, by way of example:

$$\begin{array}{|l} \hline \textit{EnterCritical} \\ \Delta HW \\ \hline intflg' = on \\ \hline \end{array}$$

The predicate of this schema reduces to *true* when existentially quantified and then simplified.

The *SuspendSelf* operation suspends its caller. It is the *SuspendMe* operation wrapped in the interrupt disable/enable operations.

$$\begin{aligned} &SuspendSelf \mathrel{\widehat=} \\ &\quad EnterCritical \\ &\quad \fatsemi SuspendMe \\ &\quad \fatsemi ExitCritical \end{aligned}$$

Given the property of the interrupt-flag manipulation operations, we can express the precondition immediately

$$\text{pre}\ SuspendSelf \mathrel{\widehat=} \text{pre}\ SuspendMe$$

The critical-section operations do not refine (or, more correctly, refine to themselves), so *SuspendSelf* refines to *SuspendMe*. The *SuspendMe* operation, however, is defined as the composition of *SCHED* operations (which refine to themselves) and *SCHED* operations defined in terms of promotion. This implies that the refinement of the *PRIOQ* operations has already been performed, so there is nothing left to be done here.

The *SendSelfToSleep* operation puts the caller to sleep for a period determined by a parameter to the operation.

$$
\begin{array}{l}
SendSelfToSleep \mathrel{\widehat=} \\
\quad EnterCritical \\
\quad \fatsemi ((CurrentProcessId[c/p!] \land \\
\qquad\qquad TimeNow[t/tn!] \land \\
\qquad\qquad SendMeToSleep[c/p?, t/tnow?]) \setminus \{c, t\} \\
\qquad \fatsemi SchedNext) \\
\quad \fatsemi ExitCritical
\end{array}
$$

The precondition is given by the next definition

$$\mathrm{pre}\ SendSelfToSleep \mathrel{\widehat=} \mathrm{pre}\ SendMeToSleep \land \mathrm{pre}\ SchedNext$$

The precondition can be written thus because its components contain disjoint sets of variables.

The definition again involves components that do not refine, so refinement should concentrate on

$$
\begin{array}{l}
(CurrentProcessId[c/p!] \land \\
\qquad TimeNow[t/tn!] \land \\
\qquad SendMeToSleep[c/p?, t/tnow?]) \setminus \{c, t\} \\
\quad \fatsemi SchedNext
\end{array}
$$

Since *TimeNow* does not refine any further, this can be simplified to

$$
\begin{array}{l}
(CurrentProcessId[c/p!] \land SendMeToSleep[c/p?, tnow/tnow?]) \setminus \{c\} \\
\quad \fatsemi SchedNext
\end{array}
$$

where the substitution (not strictly Z) $[tnow/tnow?]$ merely substitutes the current value of the clock from the global variable. (The precondition of *TimeNow* is *true*, in any case.)

We begin with

$$(CurrentProcessId[c/p!] \land SendMeToSleep[c/p?, tnow/tnow?]) \setminus \{c\}$$

but this is just a substitution instance of *SendMeToSleep* and this operation has already been refined.

When a process is terminated by some external agency (but not an error—this kernel is too simple) or by calling *TerminateSelf*, its state has to be set to *psterm*.

$$
\begin{array}{l}
SetProcessStateToTerminated \mathrel{\widehat=} \\
\quad \exists\, st : PSTATE \mid st = psterm \bullet \\
\qquad SetProcState[st/st?]
\end{array}
$$

This expands into

SetProcessStateToTerminated

$$
\begin{array}{l}
\Delta PTAB \\
p? : PID \\
\hline
state' = state \oplus \{p? \mapsto psterm\}
\end{array}
$$

The termination operation is now defined. Clearly, it is only called by the currently executing process. In this system, it is not possible for one process directly to terminate another. Each process is responsible for freeing the resources it holds.

$$
\begin{array}{l}
TerminateSelf \mathrel{\widehat{=}} \\
\quad EnterCritical \\
\qquad \mathbin{⨾}((CurrentProcessId[c/p!] \land \\
\qquad\quad SetProcessStateToTerminated[c/p?]) \\
\qquad\quad \mathbin{⨾}DelPD[c/p?]) \setminus \{c\} \\
\qquad \mathbin{⨾}SchedNext
\end{array}
$$

This is

$$
\begin{array}{|l}
\hline
\textit{TerminateSelf} \\
\Xi SCHED \\
\Delta PTAB \\
serr! : SYSERR \\
\hline
\exists c : PID : PTAB \bullet \\
\quad curr = c \land \\
\quad (state'' = state \oplus \{c \mapsto psterm\} \land \\
\qquad c \in used \land \\
\qquad used' = used \setminus \{c\} \land \\
\qquad serr! = sysok) \\
\quad \lor serr! = unusedpd \\
\mathbin{⨾}SchedNext \\
\hline
\end{array}
$$

This is equivalent to

$$
\begin{array}{l}
\exists PTAB \bullet \\
\quad state'' = state \oplus \{curr \mapsto psterm\} \land \\
\quad (curr \in used \land \\
\qquad used' = used \setminus \{curr\} \land \\
\qquad serr! = sysok) \\
\quad \lor serr! = unusedpd \\
\mathbin{⨾}SchedNext
\end{array}
$$

and to

$$
\begin{array}{|l}
\hline
\textit{TerminateSelf} \\
\Delta PTAB \\
serr! : SYSERR \\
\hline
((state' = state \oplus \{curr \mapsto psterm\} \land curr \in used \land used' = used \setminus \{curr\} \land \\
\quad serr! = sysok) \\
\lor serr! = unusedpd) \\
\mathbin{⨾}SchedNext \\
\hline
\end{array}
$$

The precondition can be written as

$$\text{pre } \mathit{TerminateSelf} \mathrel{\widehat=} \mathit{curr} \in \mathit{used} \land \text{pre } \mathit{SchedNext}$$

or as

$$\begin{array}{l}
\text{pre } \mathit{TerminateSelf} \mathrel{\widehat=} \\
\quad \mathit{curr} \in \mathit{used} \land \\
\quad \mathit{curr} = \mathit{iprc} \\
\quad \lor\ \mathit{sq}.\mathit{pq} = \langle\rangle \\
\quad \lor\ (\mathit{state}(\mathit{curr}) \neq \mathit{psready} \lor \mathit{state}(\mathit{curr}) \neq \mathit{psrunning} \\
\qquad \lor\ \mathit{prio}(\mathit{head}\ \mathit{sq}.\mathit{pq}) < \mathit{prio}(\mathit{curr}))
\end{array}$$

The operation refines as follows. It can be seen that the definition involves components that can not be further refined. This suggests that the refinement be of

$$\begin{array}{l}
\mathit{SetProcessStateToTerminated}[\mathit{curr}/p?] \\
\fatsemi \mathit{DelPD}[\mathit{curr}/p?]
\end{array}$$

The refinement of *SchedNext* is that of a promotion, so it can be removed from the process.

First, the following operation is required.

$$\begin{array}{|l}
\multicolumn{1}{l}{\mathit{SetProcessStateToTerminated1}} \\
\hline
\Delta \mathit{PTAB} \\
p? : \mathit{PID} \\
\hline
\mathit{state1}' = \mathit{state1} \oplus \{p? \mapsto \mathit{psterm}\} \\
\hline
\end{array}$$

$$\begin{array}{l}
\mathit{TerminateSelf1} \mathrel{\widehat=} \\
\quad \mathit{EnterCritical} \\
\qquad \fatsemi ((\mathit{CurrentProcessId}[c/p!] \land \\
\qquad\quad \mathit{SetProcessStateToTerminated1}[c/p?]) \\
\qquad\quad \fatsemi \mathit{FreePID1}[c/p?]) \setminus \{c\} \\
\qquad \fatsemi \mathit{SchedNext1}
\end{array}$$

The inner composition expands into, after use of the one-point rule, is

$$\begin{array}{l}
\mathit{state1}' = \mathit{state} \oplus \{\mathit{curr} \mapsto \mathit{psterm}\} \land \\
((\mathrm{dom}\ \mathit{freech} = \varnothing \land \\
\quad \mathit{freech}' = \mathit{freech} \cup \{\mathit{curr} \mapsto \mathit{nullpid}\} \land \\
\quad \mathit{endfree}' = \mathit{curr} \land \\
\quad \mathit{hdfree}' = \mathit{curr} \land \\
\quad \mathit{serr}! = \mathit{sysok}) \\
\lor\ (\mathit{curr} \notin \mathrm{dom}\ \mathit{freech} \land \\
\quad \mathit{freech}' = (\mathit{freech} \oplus \{\mathit{endfree} \mapsto \mathit{curr}\}) \cup \{\mathit{curr} \mapsto \mathit{nullpid}\} \land \\
\quad \mathit{endfree}' = \mathit{curr} \land \\
\quad \mathit{serr}! = \mathit{sysok})) \\
\lor\ \mathit{serr}! = \mathit{usedpd}
\end{array}$$

In this kernel, process can change their priority. The following is the definition of this operation.

$$
\begin{array}{l}
ChangeMyPriority \mathrel{\widehat=} \\
\quad EnterCritical \\
\qquad \mathbin{\raise 0.6ex\hbox{\oalign{\hfil$\scriptscriptstyle \mathrm{o}$\hfil\cr\hfil$\scriptscriptstyle \mathrm{9}$\hfil}}}(CurrentProcessId[c/p!] \land SetProcPrio[c/p?]) \setminus \{c\} \\
\quad \mathbin{\raise 0.6ex\hbox{\oalign{\hfil$\scriptscriptstyle \mathrm{o}$\hfil\cr\hfil$\scriptscriptstyle \mathrm{9}$\hfil}}} ExitCritical
\end{array}
$$

This definition expands into the following schema:

$$
\begin{array}{|l}
\hline
\textit{ChangeMyPriority} \\
\Delta HARDWARE \\
\Delta PTAB \\
pr? : PPRIO \\
\hline
EnterCritical \\
⨾(\exists c : PID \bullet \\
\qquad c = curr \land \\
\qquad prio' = prio \oplus \{c \mapsto pr?\}) \\
⨾ExitCritical \\
\hline
\end{array}
$$

which simplifies, using the one-point rule, to

$$
\begin{array}{|l}
\hline
\textit{ChangeMyPriority} \\
\Delta HARDWARE \\
\Delta PTAB \\
pr? : PPRIO \\
\hline
EnterCritical \\
⨾prio' = prio \oplus \{curr \mapsto pr?\} \\
⨾ExitCritical \\
\hline
\end{array}
$$

The refinement of this operation has already been undertaken. It is the refinement of *SetProcPrio* (with the substitution of *curr* for *p?*).

Its first refinement is

$$
\begin{array}{|l}
\hline
\textit{ChangeMyPriority1} \\
\Delta HARDWARE \\
\Delta PTAB1 \\
pr? : PPRIO \\
\hline
EnterCritical \\
⨾prio1' = prio1 \oplus \{curr \mapsto pr?\} \\
⨾ExitCritical \\
\hline
\end{array}
$$

The second refinement of *ChangeMyPriority* is

ChangeMyPriority2

$\Delta HARDWARE$
$\Delta PTAB2$
$pr? : PPRIO$

$EnterCritical$
$\fatsemi prio2' = prio2 \oplus \{curr \mapsto pr?\}$
$\fatsemi ExitCritical$

One way for a process to obtain is identifier is by calling the following operation:

$MyProcessId \mathrel{\widehat=}$
$\quad EnterCritical$
$\qquad \fatsemi CurrentProcessId$
$\quad \fatsemi ExitCritical$

This expands into

MyProcessId

$\Delta HARDWARE$
$\Xi SCHED$
$p! : PID$

$EnterCritical$
$\quad p! = curr$
$\fatsemi ExitCritical$

This schema does not refine. The reason for this is that *SCHED* does not refine (although its component priority queue does).

3.12.4 Inter-process Communication and Synchronisation

This consists of semaphore operations:

- Allocate and intialise semaphores in semaphore table
- Wait
- Signal
- Deallocate semaphore

As noted above, it is always the current process that calls these operations. The use of *curr* is already handled in the semaphore operations *WaitSema* and *SignalSema* but not in the operations to allocate and deallocate semaphores in the semaphore table.

$AllocateSemaphore \mathrel{\widehat=}$
$\quad EnterCritical$
$\qquad \fatsemi AllocSema$
$\quad \fatsemi ExitCritical$

Apart from being wrapped in the interrupt flag operations, this operation is just *AllocSema*. It refines to *AllocSema*1 and its precondition is

$$\text{pre}\ AllocateSemaphore \mathrel{\widehat{=}} \text{pre}\ AllocSema$$

$$\begin{array}{l} DeallocateSemaphore \mathrel{\widehat{=}} \\ \quad EnterCritical \\ \qquad \mathbin{⨾} ReleaseSema \\ \quad \mathbin{⨾} ExitCritical \end{array}$$

This refines to *ReleaseSema*1 for reasons similar to that mentioned above. The precondition is, trivially,

$$\text{pre}\ DeallocateSemaphore \mathrel{\widehat{=}} \text{pre}\ ReleaseSema$$

The wait and signal operations on semaphores are, here, those defined in terms of the semaphore table. As will be remembered, wait and signal are provided by the semaphore table as promoted operations. There is no need to refine these operations because the semaphore table's refinement already takes care of them in the sense that the refinement of the table is independent of the refinement of the semaphore operations proper.

$$\begin{array}{l} SemaphoreWait \mathrel{\widehat{=}} \\ \quad EnterCritical \\ \qquad \mathbin{⨾} STWaitSema \\ \quad \mathbin{⨾} ExitCritical \end{array}$$

The precondition is unaffected by the locking operations

$$\text{pre}\ SemaphoreWait \mathrel{\widehat{=}} \text{pre}\ SemaWait$$

$$\begin{array}{l} SemaphoreSignal \mathrel{\widehat{=}} \\ \quad EnterCritical \\ \qquad \mathbin{⨾} STSignalSema \\ \quad \mathbin{⨾} ExitCritial \end{array}$$

$$\text{pre}\ SemaphoreSignal \mathrel{\widehat{=}} \text{pre}\ SemaSignal$$

The message operations

- Send synchronous message
- Receive synchronous message

are supported.

First, the send operation.

$$
\begin{array}{l}
SendSMsg \mathrel{\widehat=} \\
\quad EnterCritical \\
\qquad \fatsemi (CurrentProcessId[c/p!] \land \\
\qquad\qquad MakeMessage[c/sndr?] \land SendASynchMsg[c/p?, m/m?]) \setminus \{c, m\} \\
\quad \fatsemi ExitCritical
\end{array}
$$

Ignoring the critical-section operations (they refine to themselves, in any case), this partially expands into

$$
\begin{array}{|l}
\text{--- } SendSMsg \text{ ---} \\
\Delta HARDWARE \\
\Delta SCHED \\
dest? : PID \\
payload? : MDATA \\
\hline
\exists\, c : PID;\ m : MSG \mid c = curr \land m = mkmsg(curr, dest?, payload?) \bullet \\
\qquad SendASynchMsg[c/p?, m/m?] \\
\hline
\end{array}
$$

This particular schema expands into

$$
\begin{array}{|l}
\text{--- } SendSMsg \text{ ---} \\
\Delta PTAB \\
\Delta SCHED \\
dest? : PID \\
payload? : MDATA \\
serr! : SYSERR \\
\hline
(dest? \in used \land \\
\quad ((state(dest?) = psreceiving \land \\
\qquad ((smsgs(dest?) = nullmsg \land \\
\qquad\quad smsgs' = smsgs \oplus \{dest? \mapsto mkmsg(curr, dest?, payload?)\} \land \\
\qquad\quad state' = state \oplus \{curr \mapsto pssending, dest? \mapsto psready\} \land \\
\qquad\quad ((pq = \langle\rangle \land curr' = dest?) \\
\qquad\quad \lor ((\#pq < maxs \land \\
\qquad\qquad (prio(dest?) \leq prio(head\ pq) \land curr' = dest?) \\
\qquad\qquad \lor (((prio(last\ pq) < prio(dest?) \land \\
\qquad\qquad\qquad pq' = (tail\ pq) \frown \langle dest? \rangle) \\
\qquad\qquad\quad (\exists\, s_1, s_2 : \mathrm{seq}\, PID \mid s_1 \neq \langle\rangle \land s_2 \neq \langle\rangle \land s_1 \frown s_2 = pq \bullet \\
\qquad\qquad\qquad prio(last\ s_1) < prio(dest?) \land \\
\qquad\qquad\qquad prio(dest?) \leq prio(head\ s_2) \land \\
\qquad\qquad\qquad pq' = (tail\ s_1) \frown \langle dest? \rangle \frown s_2)) \land \\
\qquad\qquad\quad curr' = head\ pq) \land \\
\qquad\quad prev' = curr \land serr! = sysok) \\
\qquad\quad \lor serr! = schedqfull))) \\
\qquad \lor serr! = procalreadyhasmsg))
\end{array}
$$

$\lor$ *serr*! = *destinationnotrcving*))
$\lor$ *serr*! = *badmsgdestination*

This is merely a substitution instance of the predicate of *SendASynchMsg*, so the refinement is identical to that of *SendASynchMsg*.

pre *SendSMsg* $\widehat{=}$ *SendASynchMsg*

Next, the receive operation.

$RcvSMsg \mathrel{\widehat{=}}$
$\quad EnterCritical$
$\qquad \fatsemi (CurrentProcessId[c/p!] \land ReceiveSynchMsg[c/p?]) \setminus \{c\}$
$\quad \fatsemi ExitCritical$

The *RcvSMsg* schema is a substition instance of *ReceiveSynchMsg*, so it has already been refined.

pre *RcvSMsg* $\widehat{=}$ *ReceiveSynchMsg*

Finally, an operation that first puts the calling process to sleep for a specified time and then tries to receive a message.

3.12.5 Clock Operations and the Clock ISR

In this section, we include the operations of the clock and the system operation *FindAndWake* an operation that is invoked on every clock tick.

The clock is intended as an interrupt-service routine that is executed whenever there is a clock interrupt. On activation, the time-denoting variables are updated and the list of waiting processes is searched to determine whether there are any processes to activate. These operations are performed when interrupts are disabled, so there is no need to put them in a critical section.

$SystemClockOps \mathrel{\widehat{=}}$
$\quad UpdateTIMESINCEBOOT$
$\quad \fatsemi (TimeNow[now/tn!] \land UpdateClockTime[now/t?] \land$
$\qquad FindAndWake[now/now?]) \setminus \{now\}$

If an interrupt-service routine is required, here it is:

CLOCKISR $\widehat{=}$ *SystemClockOps*

The expansion of the definition of *SystemClockOps* is the following schema. This is again a case in which promotion does much of the work; the rest is handled by the fact that simple variables refine to themselves.

SystemClockOps

$\Delta TIMESINCEBOOT$
$\Delta CLOCKTIME$
$\Delta SLEEPERS$
$\Delta SCHED$

$$
\begin{array}{l}
tnow' = tnow + ticklength \\
\exists\, now : TIME \mid now = tnow' \land \\
\quad ((now \bmod tickspersec = 0) \land \\
\quad\quad ((secs + 1 \bmod 60 = 0 \land \\
\quad\quad\quad secs' = 0 \land \\
\quad\quad\quad ((mins + 1 \bmod 60 = 0 \land \\
\quad\quad\quad\quad mins' = 0 \land \\
\quad\quad\quad\quad hrs' = hrs + 1) \\
\quad\quad\quad \lor\ mins' = mins + 1)) \\
\quad\quad \lor\ secs' = secs + 1)) \land \\
\quad slps \neq \varnothing \land \\
\quad (\forall\, p : PID \mid p \in slps \land 0 < waitingtime(p) \leq now \bullet \\
\quad\quad slps' = slps \setminus \{p\} \land \\
\quad\quad waitingtime' = waitingtime \oplus \{p \mapsto 0\} \land \\
\quad\quad MakeReady[p/p?])
\end{array}
$$

This simplifies to

$$
\begin{array}{l}
((tnow + ticklength \bmod tickspersec = 0) \land \\
\quad ((secs + 1 \bmod 60 = 0 \land secs' = 0 \land \\
\quad\quad ((mins + 1 \bmod 60 = 0 \land mins' = 0 \land hrs' = hrs + 1) \\
\quad\quad \lor\ mins' = mins + 1)) \\
\quad\quad \lor\ secs' = secs + 1)) \land \\
slps \neq \varnothing \land \\
(\forall\, p : PID \mid p \in slps \land 0 < waitingtime(p) \leq tnow + ticklength \bullet \\
\quad slps' = slps \setminus \{p\} \land \\
\quad waitingtime' = waitingtime \oplus \{p \mapsto 0\} \land \\
\quad MakeReady[p/p?])
\end{array}
$$

3.12.6 Final Remarks

Some operations defined in this section cannot be further refined (e.g., the stack initialisation operation) but others can and their refinement has been outlined in this section. It is now an easy step to translate the resulting schemata results into executable code. We have, with this, concluded the refinement of the first kernel.

4

The Separation Kernel

The next refinement is of a *Separation Kernel.* The Separation Kernel is an architecture introduced by John Rushby as an architecture of cryptographic and other secure applications [11].

The purpose of this chapter is to describe the architecture and to outline its refinement.

4.1 Basic Architecture

The architecture of the Separation Kernel is simple. It is a single-processor model of a distributed system in which all user processes are separated in time and space from each other. In a distributed system, the execution of each process takes place in a manner independent of any other. Processes can wait for data inputs, particularly inputs from communications channels. For the remainder of the time, the component processes execute at rates independent of all others. There is, in a distributed system, temporal separation between the execution of one process and all other processes. Separation in space means that the processes constituting a distributed system each have their own disjoint address spaces. If two address spaces are disjoint, it is not possible for one process directly to write to the address space of any other process.

The Separation Kernel is based on these two fundamental observations. Separation in time results from the fact that no two processes can be active at exactly the same time. Furthermore, if processes communicate using asynchronous channels, no synchronisation points are required, so processes can proceed at their own rate. Separation in space results from the fact that processes are allocated their own disjoint address spaces.

Temporal separation can be enforced by the system's scheduler and by a message-passing system. On a uni-processor system, the scheduler ensures that only one process executes at any time and executions are interleaved in time. The length of time during which any process will be executing (be active) depends upon the scheduling algorithm and, as will be seen, the algorithm proposed by Rushby is particularly simple. In addition, the use of asynchronous messages means that processes do not synchronise during the exchange of messages, although they are permitted to wait for responses or results to be returned. Even in the case of waiting for a response, the waiting state depends upon the algorithms used to implement processes, not upon the underlying system.

Spatial separation can be enforced by segmentation. Most processors supporting segmented address spaces also have mechanisms for detecting and reacting to attempts by one process to access the segments of another. On the Intel IA32 and IA64 machines, for example, attempts to cross segment boundaries causes a hardware exception; a handler can be provided to handle the exception by, for example, killing the offending process. Each process is, therefore, allocated one or more segments. Should a process, either by error or through malice, attempt to address a location in another process' segments, the hardware should cause an exception to be raised. This permits the kernel to detect such illegal accesses and to perform some action.

The original proposal for the Separation Kernel was included the stipulation that a round-robin scheduler would be adequate. The round-robin scheme can be used in real-time applications because of its simplicity; it can also be used to simulate distributed systems because processes only enter the queue when they are ready to execute. Temporal separation is supported by the fact that, under pure round-robin, there is no *a priori* limit to the length of the period during which a process can execute. In many systems, timeslicing is used to share the processor between processes; each process is permitted to execute for a defined period of time and, when this period is exhausted, the process is suspended and another continues its execution. The property that round-robin scheduling allows processes to execute for indefinite periods must be qualified. Processes execute until such time as they are no longer able to continue and at such a time, they must relinquish the processor. Processes relinquish the processor either on a purely voluntary basis by executing a voluntary suspension operation or by executing some other operation whose definition includes the an operator that suspends the caller. The primitive that sends messages might suspend the caller, for example.

It should be clear that the kernel must reside in an address space that is disjoint from all user address spaces. This ensures that the kernel is protected against malicious processes. Furthermore, it is also separated in time because, by definition, it executes only when processes do not. In order to enforce the spatio-temporal separation of the kernel, it is essential to define a clean interface between it and user processes.

4.2 Extending the Architecture

The Separation Kernel defines a basic and simple set of mechanisms for managing secure applications. It makes a distinction between trusted software (the kernel) and untrusted software (applications in user processes). The architecture requires some extension in order to include devices such as communications lines, printers and so on.

The US National Security Agency has produced an extension to the Separation Kernel architecture [10] so that device handling can be included. This introduces the concept of "trusted" code into the system. The context in which trusted code is introduced is the following. The document [10] assumes that the kernel proper is formally specified and that its properties are therefore well understood. Because it is formally specified, it is completely trusted. User processes are completely untrusted; this is because they are not under the control of the developers of the kernel and are assumed not to have been formally constructed. There is no control, it is assumed, over the content of user processes. Device processes (drivers and associated support code) require greater access to kernel facilities and might have to do such things as allocating their own storage, directly accessing the scheduler queues, and so on. This has the implication that devices should only be introduced into a secure system if they are trusted to a much greater extent than user code. The production of device-related code must be carefully controlled. Ideally, this code would be constructed using formal methods. One reason for assuming that it is not so constructed is the range of possible hardware that any implementation of the Separation Kernel can control (this is quite reasonable—it is a constraint adopted for the work in reported in this book and was also adopted in our [4]). A second reason is that the NSA probably do not believe that device-handling code *can* be constructed formally—our opinion is at variance with theirs (and we have unpublished cases that tend to support our position). No matter what the reason, it is important that device-handling code should be trusted.

It is important, then, to support device-handling code. This kind of code needs to be fast and it needs access to low-level facilties. One way to support device-handling is to make the kernel open. This subverts the whole project. Instead, it is better to define and formally construct an interface to the kernel for use by device-handling code. The interface should only give device code access to a miminal set of services. In particular, it should define operations that

- Pass parameters from and to requesting user processes.
- Allow device-handling processes to suspend themselves.
- Cause device-handling processes to become active (i.e., to enter the scheduler's queue of processes ready to execute).

In addition, it should be possible to determine whether the services requested by user processes correspond to what is possible.

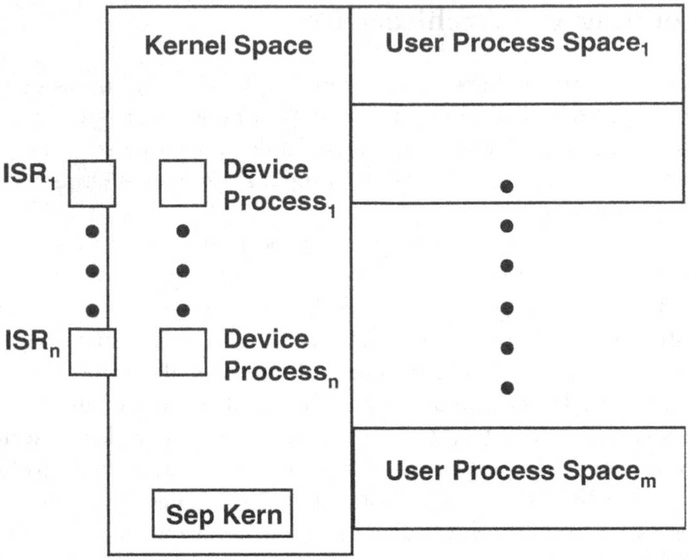

Fig. 4.1. *Devices and interfaces in the Separation Kernel.*

This is the approach adopted in this book. A set of operations is defined that provide exactly those capabilities listed above. In addition, devices are represented by "device numbers" as far as user processes are concerned. The kernel maps device numbers to actual devices, thus decoupling device (service) naming from the devices themselves (it also allows for some flexibility in the kernel). Some might object that device numbers are a low-level representation. The reply is that user processes use library calls to request such services; the bottom level of such libraries will use device numbers, not the higher levels and not user code.

4.3 Summary

The Separation Kernel can be summarised as follows

- A segmented main store that is supported by the processor hardware.
- A round-robin scheduling régime.
- Natural-break scheduling by user and device processes.
- A well-defined set of interfaces for device-handling processes.
- A well-defined interface for user processes (see Figure 4.2).

The internal organisation of our Separation Kernel can be seen in Figure 4.2.

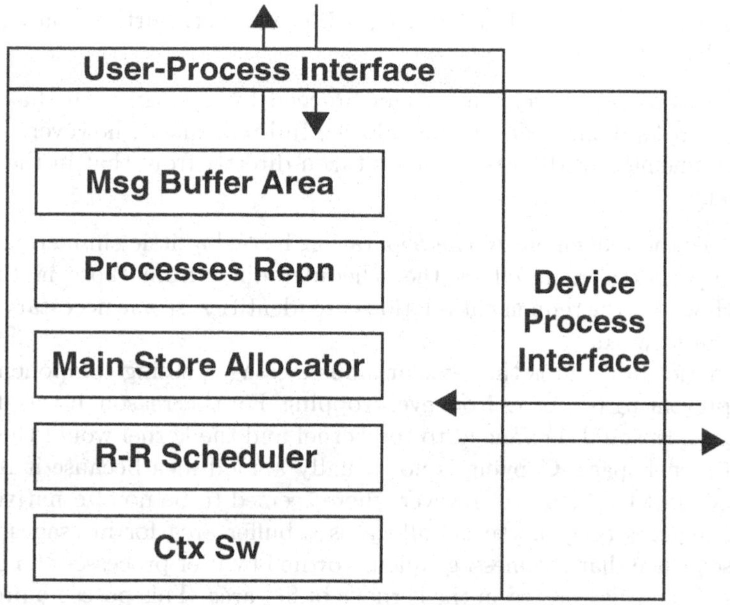

Fig. 4.2. *The internal organisation of our Separation Kernel.*

4.4 An Overview of the Formal Specification

The purpose of this section is to describe in outline the formal specification of the Separation Kernel that is included in this book. In particular, it outlines the structures included in the kernel and attempts to make clear the assumptions upon which the major decisions were made.

The first thing to note is that a number of components are the same in the Separation Kernel and in the simple kernel that precedes it in this book. Firstly, the process table's general format is identical in both cases; the two tables contain slightly different information but the representations are the same in both cases. Second, the primary data structure used by the Separation Kernel's scheduler is a pair of FIFO queues. The round-robin scheduling régime only requires a simple FIFO for its implementation. Processes enter the queue at the end and progressively move to the head; when a process reaches the head of the queue, it is ready to execute. The Separation Kernel requires two FIFOs in its scheduler: one for user processes and one for device processes (device-handling processes, that is). The reason for this is that device processes run at a higher priority than user processes. This specification uses a synchronous I/O model. For present purposes, it is assumed that device processes are concerned with input and output operations, so the model seems appropriate. This choice has the consequence that device processes can be scheduled in a strictly FIFO manner. Further consequences of these decisions are:

- The process table's refinement can proceed by analogy with that in the first kernel's refinement. We include the full refinement, however.
- The refinement of the FIFO can be taken directly from that in the earlier kernel.

This makes the refinement of the Separation Kernel a little simpler.

The operations required by the scheduler differ from those in the first kernel. However, the refinement relations are identities, so the necessary proofs are straightforward.

The major problem is the asynchronous message-passing component. One issue is preventing processes from evesdropping. For this reason, it was decided that messages would be handed to the kernel and the kernel would then *copy* them to kernel space. Copying is not usually a good idea because it requires space and time to perform. However, there seemed to be no alternative. This decision requires that the kernel allocates a buffer area for messages. It has the consequence that the message queues owned by user processes can contain *pointers* to messages stored in the kernel's buffer area. This poses no problems from the specification viewpoint but it does require some form of pointer-dereference operation is required when handing the message to the destination when it is to be read. It is also necessary to have a mechanism for deleting the store occupied by a message when it is no longer required. It is clear that such deletion cannot be left to user processes (for one thing, it provides an appealing way to crash the system).

The low-level message operations are implemented using a type that represents the buffer space itself (essentially a vector of storage elements, say bytes) together with storage-management operations. The latter is provided by the same mechanisms that is used to allocate the large chunks of store that hold processes and their data and stack areas. The difference between the two is some renaming and the scales upon which the two instances act. This is another case in which we were able to re-use specifications and refinements in the development of a new specification.

In both cases, the storage manager uses tables that are separate from the store that is managed. Some might object to this. The two could be conflated to form a single module. This would require a number of type-transfer functions, as well as other very low-level operations. There is much detail in this work[1] that does not add much to the overall presentation. There is another reason. In the case of the main store allocator, the aim is to have separate segments that are allocated from a pool that, in essence, belongs to no-one. We do not want anything to reside in the main store that could be used by a malicious process. The separation of store from its description

[1] This statement is based on experience. We have attempted this very conflation in other, unpublished, work.

achieves this, even at a cost. All the pointers and size annotations in the scheme adopted here are in a space that is formally specified and under the control of formally specified operations; there is no data in places where other processes can manipulate them.

The design of the Separation Kernel should ensure security. As stated, user processes cannot be trusted, while device processes can. Trust can be maintained by ensuring that certain development methods be followed and that development is done by trusted persons under appropriate supervision. However, as far as the specification and its refinement are concerned, this has a number of consequences. First, an interface must be defined to support device processes. A device process is a device driver and requires access to a set of kernel functions and to fixed chunks of main store that it and its associated ISR use to hold data during transfer.

The kernel operations are mostly those supporting processes but a security "feature" of this specification is that device processes are known by a *device number*, a small numeric code that denotes a device process (and associated device); device numbers are allocated when the system is configured. Furthermore, device processes do not have external identifiers; instead, their device number serves as their identifier. Message passing between device processes is not permitted, but there is the requirement that user processes be able to send data to and receive data from device processes; this impacts upon the interface presented by device processes.

The specification contains a separate module that implements the interface required by device processes. The aim of this module is to provide the minimum set of operations required by device processes in order to do their job. This set of operations is also required to isolate the kernel from device processes so that the latter are required

1. To know as little possible about the kernel and its operations, and
2. To make the task of interfacing device processes as simple as possible.

It is assumed that there is some way to map main store in the kernel segment so that shared memory can be allocated; if this is not possible, it is relatively easy to introduce another storage manager, one distinct from the others employed in this system (for security reasons).

As is the case with the other kernel, there are low-level operations that require the direct use of machine-level operations. As before, there are the context-switch and interrupt-related operations to be specified. There are also ISRs to be specified. The approach adopted here is different from that in the other kernel. In particular, it is assumed that the Separation Kernel will execute on the Intel IA32/64 range of processors. This permits us to exploit the task-management instructions provided by them. Furthermore, there a problems with the management of a segmented store. The hardware instructions solve these problems for us[2].

[2] In the current case, we have not examined the implications of porting it to another hardware architecture such as the MIPS or ARM.

5

A Separation Kernel

This chapter is concerned with the specification and refinement of a Separation Kernel. This, as described in the last chapter, is a type of kernel that was specifically designed for cryptographic and other secure applications.

The specification and refinement in this chapter relies to a certain extent on the existence of components that were specified and refined in the chapter on the simple kernel (Chapter 3). In particular, the queue types used to define the Separation Kernel's round-robin scheduler were specified in full in Chapter 3. The process representation employed in this chapter is related to that used for the earlier exercise.

The abstraction relations in this refinement are all identities (which is not at all unusual). This allows the refinement process to be shortened somewhat, for, once the abstraction relation has been identified, it is possible immediately to write out the refinements of the various operations. Furthermore, since the relationship between specification and refinement is that of identity, there is, strictly speaking, no need to engage in a proof. Below, we do present proofs, mainly for new state spaces or for state spaces that are markedly different from those in the previous refinement; we believe that these proofs are worth doing and recording as a safety check (they are, in any case, almost entirely straightforward). We are therefore permitted to reduce the length of the current chapter by the omission of much immediately derivable material.

5.1 Basic Types

We need to define the main types to be used by the Separation Kernel. The reader will find the majority of the types familiar from Chapter 3.

First, a type that will take the place of explicit truth values:

$YESNO ::= yes \mid no$

The type for process identifiers is very much as in the previous exercise.

$PID \mathrel{\widehat=} minpid \mathinner{\ldotp\ldotp} maxpid$
$GPID \mathrel{\widehat=} \{nullpid\} \cup PID$

In this specification, the *nullpid*, null process value is also required.

$$
\begin{array}{|l}
nullpid : \mathbb{N} \\
\hline
\forall p : PID \bullet \\
\qquad nullpid < p
\end{array}
$$

This last definition might need a bit of a tweak.

Since this is a secure kernel, it is necessary to have a naming scheme for user processes. These names are intended to be unrelated to process identifiers. The simplest form of user identifier is to use a natural number to denote each process. It is assumed that the supply of natural numbers is large enough to suit the needs of the user.

$UPID \mathrel{\widehat=} \mathbb{N}$

We need to distinguish between user and device processes for scheduling purposes.

$PTYPE ::= uproc \mid dproc$

The reason for this is that the scheduler maintains two queues: one for user processes and one for device processes. Device processes are always at a higher priority than user processes.

Device processes are assumed to be trusted code that controls peripheral devices. They reside within the kernel's address space and are independent of user processes.

Devices are identified by a unique number (the "device" or "service" number).

$$
\begin{array}{|l}
mindev, maxdev : \mathbb{N} \\
\hline
mindev < maxdev
\end{array}
$$

These two values determine the type *DEVNO*:

$DEVNO == mindev \mathinner{\ldotp\ldotp} maxdev$

All Separation Kernel processes are in a unique state at any time. The Separation Kernel has fewer types than the one in Chapter 3.

$$
\begin{array}{lcl}
PSTATE & ::= & psterm \\
& \mid & psrunning \\
& \mid & psready \\
& \mid & psdevwait \\
& \mid & pswtgdev
\end{array}
$$

The last value of *PSTATE* denotes the state in which a device process is waiting for a request from a user process or when it is waiting for a device to return data to it.

The *ADDR* type defines addresses. Addresses must be between 0 and the maximum address supported by the particular processor being used (or some other *a priori* limit).

$ADDR == nulladdr \mathrel{..} maxaddr$

$$
\begin{array}{|l}
nulladdr : \mathbb{N} \\
maxaddr : \mathbb{N} \\
\hline
nulladdr = 0 \\
nulladdr < maxaddr
\end{array}
$$

The following type

$[PSU]$

denotes the *Primary Storage Unit.* On some machines, this is 8 bits, while on others it is 16-, 32- or 64-bits. It is the unit by which main store is addressed and is used in the specification of storage mechanisms.

$[MSG]$

$[MSGDATA]$

$$
\begin{array}{|l}
nullmsg : MSG
\end{array}
$$

Although there is no use put to the following, it is still useful to include it as a reminder that messages containing no data are also possible.

$$
\begin{array}{|l}
nullmsgdata : MSGDATA
\end{array}
$$

User processes communicate with the Separation Kernel using structures that look rather like messages (even though they are not handled like messages—a somewhat more direct method is used). Each "message" has a single opcode to denote its function. The type to which opcodes belong is *SYSOPCODE*:

$$
\begin{array}{lcl}
SYSOPCODE & ::= & newuproc \\
 & | & suspself \\
 & | & termself \\
 & | & sndmsg \\
 & | & gotmsgs \\
 & | & gotmsgfromsrc \\
 & | & nextmsg \\
 & | & nextmsgfromsrc \\
 & | & devrequest
\end{array}
$$

Finally, we still need the error type. Here it is:

$$
\begin{aligned}
SYSERR ::= & \; sysok \\
| & \; unusedpd \\
| & \; pdinuse \\
| & \; ptabfull \\
| & \; emptyqueue \\
| & \; nospaceinstore \\
| & \; blocklocerror \\
| & \; badblockaddr \\
| & \; msgqfull \\
| & \; emptymsgq \\
| & \; nomsgsfrom \\
| & \; calleridentmismatch \\
| & \; mainstorefull \\
| & \; badmsgdest?? \\
| & \; nodevreply \\
| & \; baddevnum \\
| & \; badcallerid
\end{aligned}
$$

In this kernel, the latest error is stored in a global variable. The variable is the state component of the following schema:

$ERRV$

$serr : SYSERR$

This variable is updated by various kernel operations and could be inspected by user processes. At present, the user-level operation required to inspect *serr* is not provided; its inclusion is a simple matter, though.

The error variable is initially set to *ok*:

$ERRVInit$

$ERRV'$

$serr' = sysok$

The error variable is set by the following operation

$SetSysErr$

$\Delta ERRV$
$e? : SYSERR$

$serr' = e?$

and is read by the next one

$$
\begin{array}{|l}
\hline
\textit{SysErr} \\
\Xi ERRV \\
e! : SYSERR \\
\hline
e! = serr \\
\hline
\end{array}
$$

We define an abbreviation for recording the fact that an operation has gone according to plan.

$SysOk \mathrel{\widehat=} (\exists\, e : SYSERR \mid e = sysok \bullet SetSysErr[e/e?])$

5.2 Hardware Issues

In the case of the Separation Kernel, we are aiming our specification *mostly* at the Intel IA32/64 architectures in uni-processor versions *only* (we could run on a multi-core by executing on one processor only but this will still complicate our assumptions and require some additional machinery).

The IA32 architecture supports tasking by providing appropriate instructions and data formats. In particular, it has a structure called a *TSS* (*Task Structure Segment*) which contains all the registers of a process (including its segment registers).

Since we are aiming at an IA32 implementation, it will be necessary to refer to TSSs from within this specification, it is necessary to define a type

$[TSS]$

A few functions need to be defined:

$$
\begin{array}{|l}
tss\_stacktop : TSS \rightarrow ADDR \\
tss\_stackseg : TSS \rightarrow ADDR
\end{array}
$$

The first returns a pointer to the top of the current stack (often the ESP registers on the Intel IA32), the second returns the start address (the base) of the segment in which the stack resides.

The TSS must be pointed to by the process descriptor. It is necessary to define the TSS table, together with allocation and deallocation operations. We sketch them only.

$$
\begin{array}{|l}
\hline
\textit{HW} \\
\vdots \\
tsstab : \mathrm{seq}\ TSS \\
\vdots \\
\hline
\end{array}
$$

We assume an operation *AllocateTSS* that allocates the TSS table in main store; we also assume that *AllocateIDT* is defined—this is the operation to allocate the IDT (interrupt vector) in main store.

The *AllocateProcTSS* operation allocates a TSS when a new process is allocated.

$$
\begin{array}{|l}
\hline
\textit{AllocateProcTSS} \\
\Delta HW \\
\vdots \\
tss! : TSS \\
\hline
\vdots \\
\hline
\end{array}
$$

When a process terminates, its TSS must be returned to the pool. This is the outline of the deallocation operation that returns a process' TSS to the free pool.

$$
\begin{array}{|l}
\hline
\textit{DeallocateTSS} \\
\Delta HW \\
p? : PID \\
tss? : TSS \\
\hline
\vdots \\
\hline
\end{array}
$$

The process table must refer to TSS:

$$
\begin{array}{|l}
\hline
\textit{PTAB} \\
\vdots \\
tss : PID \rightarrowtail\!\!\!\!\!\rightarrow TSS \\
\hline
\mathrm{dom}\, tss = used \\
\forall p : PID \bullet \\
\qquad p \in \mathrm{dom}\, tss \Leftrightarrow ptype(p) = uproc \\
\hline
\end{array}
$$

(We assume that device processes have a TSS.)

The context switch proper now handled by a single instruction and can be defined as

$$
\begin{array}{|l}
\hline
\textit{ContextSwitch} \\
\Delta HARDWARE \\
outproc? : PID \\
\hline
\mathtt{jmp}\ tss(outproc?) \\
\hline
\end{array}
$$

This will automatically switch between the currently running process and *outproc?*. The IA32/64 processor records the identity of the suspended process (however, it will be recorded by software).

The IA32 makes the combination of interrupts and context switches natural. Therefore, the context-switching mechanism will be specified as interrupt driven. To do this, an interrupt number is allocated for the context switch operation and an ISR that acutally performs the context switch (by calling the *ContextSwitch* operation, in particular), must be defined. Inside the kernel, an operation to cause an interrupt must be defined.

First, we define the interrupt type. As far as we are concerned, interrupts are just small positive integers:

$$
\begin{array}{|l}
minint, maxint : \mathbb{N} \\
\hline
minint < maxint
\end{array}
$$

$$INTNO == minint \mathrel{..} maxint$$

The operation of causing a software interrupt is performed by the following operation:

$$
\begin{array}{|l}
\textit{RaiseInterrupt} \\
\hline
\Delta HW \\
ino? : INTNO \\
\hline
intno' = ino?
\end{array}
$$

The number of the interrupt that causes system termination is (partially) defined as

$$
\begin{array}{|l}
killintno : INTNO
\end{array}
$$

The operation to cause *killintno* is

$$
\begin{array}{l}
RaiseKillInterrupt \mathrel{\widehat=} \\
\quad \exists\, ino : INTNO \mid ino = killintno \bullet \\
\qquad\quad RaiseInterrupt[ino/ino?]
\end{array}
$$

Below, more will be said on the content of the ISR that must service this interrupt.

Finally, we define the number of the interrupt that will cause the context switch

$$
\begin{array}{|l}
ctxtswintno : INTNO
\end{array}
$$

The operation that causes this interrupt is the following

$$
\begin{array}{l}
CTXTSW \mathrel{\widehat=} \\
\quad \exists\, ino : INTNO \mid ino = ctxtswintno \bullet \\
\qquad\quad RaiseInterrupt[ino/ino?]
\end{array}
$$

There is very little else to say about context switches because the IA32 handles the rest. It switches registers between TSSs when context switches occur. This is very pleasant for IA32 users; for users of other processors, more work will have to be done.

5.3 Security Exits and Return Values

In this kernel design, the information returned to users is deliberately minimal. This is so that malicious users can infer as little as possible about what has happened.

In some cases of error, the kernel halts and all processes are killed. This can occur, for example, if an attempt is made to create more processes than there are slots in the process table or if a segmentation fault occurs. The kernel kill prints a message stating "Kernel halted. Security violation?". This requires the types

$$
\begin{aligned}
CHAR == & \text{`}a\text{'} \mathrel{..} \text{`}z\text{'},\\
& \text{`}A\text{'} \mathrel{..} \text{`}Z\text{'},\\
& \text{`}0\text{'} \mathrel{..} \text{`}9\text{'},\\
& \text{`}.\text{'}, \text{`},\text{'}, \text{`}\backslash n\text{'}, \text{`}?\text{'}
\end{aligned}
$$

(where '\n' is the newline character, as in C; other characters can be assumed as required) and

$$STRING == \operatorname{seq} CHAR$$

The printing is effected by the following operation

$$
\begin{array}{|l}
\hline
\textit{PrintKMsg} \\
\hline
km? : STRING \\
\hline
kprint(km?) \\
\hline
\end{array}
$$

It is assumed that there is some mechanism outside of the kernel that can print a string on some screen or send it elsewhere. The *kprint* operation is not further specified. It is hardware dependent.

Next, we define a mechanism which will halt the processor and kill all current processes. It should do this when a fatal error occurs. The operation is to be called from an ISR that is executed as a result of some piece of code raising the *killintno* interrupt. This interrupt is raised to signal the fatal error.

The kernel kill operation requires the *DeleteAllProcesses* operation defined over the process table (*PTAB*). It also sets the current process to the idle process.

$$
\begin{aligned}
& KillKernel \mathrel{\widehat{=}} \\
& \quad (IDLEPROCESSIdent[ip/p!] \land \\
& \qquad UpdateCurrentProcess[ip/p?]) \setminus \{ip\} \\
& \quad \mathbin{⨾} DeleteAllProcesses \\
& \quad \mathbin{⨾} (\exists\, msg : STRING \mid msg = \text{“}Kernel\ halted.\ Security\ violation?\text{''} \bullet \\
& \qquad PrintKMsg[msg/km?])
\end{aligned}
$$

This definition expands into the following schema.

$$
\begin{array}{|l}
\multicolumn{1}{l}{\textit{KillKernel}} \\
\hline
\Delta PTAB \\
\hline
\exists\, ip : PID \bullet \\
\quad ip = ipid \land \\
\quad curr' = ip \land \\
\quad prev' = curr \land \\
\quad used' = \varnothing \land \\
\quad (\exists\, msg : STRING \mid msg = \text{“}\textit{Kernel halted. Security violation?}\text{''} \bullet \\
\qquad kprint(msg)) \\
\hline
\end{array}
$$

The *KillKernel* schema can then be simplified and we obtain (using the one-point rule):

$$
\begin{array}{|l}
\multicolumn{1}{l}{\textit{KillKernel}} \\
\hline
\Delta PTAB \\
\hline
curr' = ipid \\
prev' = curr' \\
used' = \varnothing \\
kprint(\text{“}\textit{Kernel halted. Security violation?}\text{''}) \\
\hline
\end{array}
$$

The *KillKernel* operation is intended to constitute a generic ISR. This ISR is executed whenever a lethal (or in the present case, *any*) error is encountered. For simplicity, as well as to demonstrate the paranoia principle, this specification and its refinement treats *all* errors as possible indications that something untoward has happened, so the *KillKernel* operation is invoked for every error.

5.4 The Process Table

The process table is very similar to that used by the first system.

First, the error schemata are defined.

$$
\begin{array}{l}
UnusedPD \mathrel{\widehat=} \\
\quad (\exists\, e : SYSERR \mid e = unusedpd \bullet \\
\qquad SetSysErr[e/e?]) \land \\
\quad RaiseKillInterrupt
\end{array}
$$

When it is detected that a process identifier has already been allocated, the error is raised by the following schema:

$$
\begin{array}{l}
PDInUse \mathrel{\widehat=} \\
\quad (\exists\, e : SYSERR \mid e = pdinuse \bullet \\
\qquad SetSysErr[e/e?]) \land \\
\quad RaiseKillInterrupt
\end{array}
$$

If an attempt to allocate more process identifiers than there are slots in the process table, the following schema is used to report the error.

$$
\begin{array}{l}
PTABFull \mathrel{\widehat=} \\
\quad (\exists\, e : SYSERR \mid e = ptabfull \bullet \\
\qquad SetSysErr[e/e?]) \land \\
\quad RaiseKillInterrupt
\end{array}
$$

5.4.1 Top Level

This specification organises the process table as a collection of arrays. At the top level, the arrays are modelled as partial functions whose domain is almost always *PID*, the type of process identifiers. The reader will see that the process table, again called *PTAB*, is somewhat more complex than the one used in Chapter 3. In particular, the need to provide user-oriented identifiers for user processes introduces the *nextupid*, *extpid* and *pidext* variables. The variables *devmap*, *devrqs* and *devrpy* are used to support device processes. The remainder of the variables are common to user and device processes.

$$
\begin{array}{l}
\textbf{PTAB} \\
\hline
nextupid : UPID \\
extpid : UPID \rightarrowtail\!\!\!\!\rightarrow PID \\
pidext : PID \rightarrowtail\!\!\!\!\rightarrow UPID \\
used : \mathbb{F}\, PID \\
tss : PID \rightarrowtail\!\!\!\!\rightarrow TSS \\
devmap : DEVNO \rightarrowtail\!\!\!\!\rightarrow PID \\
state : PID \rightarrowtail\!\!\!\!\rightarrow PSTATE \\
ptype : PID \rightarrowtail\!\!\!\!\rightarrow PTYPE \\
msgq : PID \rightarrowtail\!\!\!\!\rightarrow MSGQ \\
devrqs : PID \rightarrowtail\!\!\!\!\rightarrow MSG \\
devmsg : PID \rightarrowtail\!\!\!\!\rightarrow (GPID \times MSG) \\
devrpy : PID \rightarrowtail\!\!\!\!\rightarrow MSG \\
cdseg : PID \rightarrowtail\!\!\!\!\rightarrow SDESC \\
dsseg : PID \rightarrowtail\!\!\!\!\rightarrow SDESC \\
\hline
\exists\, devs, uprocs : \mathbb{F}\, PID \mid \\
\qquad\qquad devs = \{p : PID \mid p \in used \land ptype(p) = dproc\} \land \\
\qquad\qquad uprocs = \{p : PID \mid p \in used \land ptype(p) \neq dproc\} \bullet \\
\qquad used = \mathrm{dom}\, state \land \\
\qquad used = \mathrm{dom}\, ptype \land \\
\qquad uprocs = \mathrm{dom}\, cdseg \land \\
\qquad uprocs = \mathrm{dom}\, dsseg \land \\
\qquad\qquad used = \mathrm{dom}\, tss \land \\
\qquad \mathrm{ran}\, devmap = dprocs \land \\
\qquad uprocs = \mathrm{dom}\, msgq \land
\end{array}
$$

$$
\begin{array}{l}
\quad dprocs = \mathrm{dom}\ devrqs \land \\
\quad dprocs = \mathrm{dom}\ devmsg \land \\
\quad dprocs = \mathrm{dom}\ devrpy \\
\mathrm{ran}\ extpid = uprocs \\
\mathrm{dom}\ pidext = uprocs \\
pidext = extpid^{-1} \\
\forall d : DEVNO \bullet \\
\quad d \in \mathrm{dom}\ devmap \Rightarrow \\
\quad \exists_1 p : PID \bullet \\
\qquad p = devmap(d)
\end{array}
$$

The invariant of this schema is somewhat more complex than in the corresponding one in Chapter 3. This is because some components relate only to device processes. For example, device processes have device numbers, which are stored in the *devmap* variable, while the identifiers user processes are given to identify themselves and other processes are stored in *pidext* and *extpid*. Note that these two functions are mutually inverse. The *pidext* map translates internal process identifiers to external ones, while *extpid* performs the inverse operation. We decided to have two functions to make the operations more explicit.

The various components will be explained in more detail when the relevant operations are defined.

We can define *free* as:

$$PID \setminus used = free$$

This is the same as in Chapter 3, so proofs involving used and free identifiers will be the same here as they were there.

The initialisation operation for this version of $PTAB$ is scarcely more complex than the other one. The difference is that the external process identifier source, *nextupid*, must be initialised to 1.

PTABInit

$$
\begin{array}{l}
PTAB' \\
\hline
used' = \varnothing \\
nextupid' = 1
\end{array}
$$

The following is a schema that is true when the *internal* process identifier, $p?$, is an element of *used*.

UsedPID

$$
\begin{array}{l}
\Xi PTAB \\
p? : PID \\
\hline
p? \in used
\end{array}
$$

The next schema defines a predicate. The interpretation and justification for this schema is the same in this case as in the previous one.

$$
\begin{array}{|l}
\hline
\textit{GotFreePIDs} \\
\Xi PTAB \\
\hline
used \subset PID \\
\hline
\end{array}
$$

In this kernel, process identifiers are allocated by a non-deterministic operation, called *AllocPID*. This operation is the same as in the previous specification.

$$
\begin{array}{|l}
\hline
\textit{AllocPID} \\
\Delta PTAB \\
p! : PID \\
\hline
p! \notin used \\
used' = used \cup \{p!\} \\
\hline
\end{array}
$$

In this kernel, however, we do not want user processes to have any knowledge of the workings of the kernel. One aspect of this is that we do not want user processes to know what their process identifier (an element of *PID*) is. This is achieved by allocating another identifier, an element of *UPID*, which can be used by user processes. This requires translation between *PID* and *UPID* at various points in the kernel but this is a small price for privacy. The operation to allocate an element of *UPID* is defined by the following schema.

$$
\begin{array}{|l}
\hline
\textit{AllocUPID} \\
\Delta PTAB \\
u! : UPID \\
\hline
u! = nextupid \\
nextupid' = nextupid + 1 \\
\hline
\end{array}
$$

The operation is, itself, quite simple. The current value of *nextupid* is used as the external process identifier. The counter, *nextupid*, is then incremented by one.

The following schema defines an operation that adds an external identifier to the *extpid* external identifier mapping table.

$$
\begin{array}{|l}
\hline
\textit{AddProcUPID} \\
\Delta PTAB \\
p? : PID \\
u? : UPID \\
\hline
extpid' = extpid \oplus \{u? \mapsto p?\} \\
\hline
\end{array}
$$

When a user process is created, the following operation is used to generate the two identifiers associated with it.

$$
\begin{array}{l}
NewUPIDForProcess \mathrel{\widehat=} \\
\quad AllocPID \land \\
\qquad AllocUPID \land \\
\qquad AddProcUPID[p!/p?, u!/u?]
\end{array}
$$

The definition of *NewUPIDForProcess* expands into the following schema:

$$
\begin{array}{|l}
\multicolumn{1}{l}{\text{— } NewUPIDForProcess \text{ —}} \\
\Delta PTAB \\
u! : UPID \\
\hline
p! \notin used \\
used' = used \cup \{p!\} \\
u! = nextupid \\
nextupid' = nextupid + 1 \\
extpid' = extpid \oplus \{u! \mapsto p!\} \\
\hline
\end{array}
$$

The kernel allows two kinds of process to be created: user and device processes. The type *PTYPE* has two elements, one denoting user processes, the other denoting device processes. The type of each process is stored in *ptype*. The operation to add the type of a new process is defined thus:

$$
\begin{array}{|l}
\multicolumn{1}{l}{\text{— } SetProcType \text{ —}} \\
\Delta PTAB \\
p? : PID \\
pt? : PTYPE \\
\hline
ptype' = ptype \cup \{p? \mapsto pt?\} \\
\hline
\end{array}
$$

The operation to allocate user-process identifiers (if there are any free), an external identifier and record the type of the new process (if it can be created) is defined by the following formula. The operation has the same name as the similar operation in the first specification, namely *AddPD*.

$$
\begin{array}{l}
AddPD \mathrel{\widehat=} \\
\quad ((GotFreePIDs \land \\
\qquad\qquad NewUPIDForProcess[uu!/u!] \land \\
\qquad\qquad SetProcType[p!/p?] \land \\
\qquad\qquad SysOk) \\
\quad \lor PTABFull
\end{array}
$$

The *AddPD* operation expands into:

$$
\begin{array}{|l}
\multicolumn{1}{l}{\text{— } AddPD \text{ —}} \\
\Delta PTAB \\
\Delta HW \\
\Delta ERRV
\end{array}
$$

$$
\begin{array}{l}
p! : PID \\
u! : UPID \\
pt? : PTYPE \\
\hline
(used \subset PID \land \\
\quad p! \notin used \land \\
\quad used' = used \cup \{p!\} \land \\
\quad u! = nextupid \land \\
\quad nextupid' = nextupid + 1 \land \\
\quad extpid' = extpid \oplus \{u! \mapsto p!\} \land \\
\quad ptype' = ptype \cup \{p! \mapsto pt?\} \land \\
\quad serr' = sysok) \\
\lor (serr' = ptabfull \land intno' = killintno)
\end{array}
$$

The *AddPD* operation is very important, so its precondition has to be calculated. It is:

$$
\begin{array}{l}
\text{pre}\, AddPD \mathrel{\widehat{=}} \\
\quad used \subset PID \land \\
\quad p! \notin used
\end{array}
$$

This formula implies

$$\text{pre}\, AddPD \mathrel{\widehat{=}} used \subset PID$$

We can prove a useful result at this stage.

Theorem 58. *$AddPD \Rightarrow p! \notin free'$. In other words, $p!$ is not a free process identifier in the after state of AddPD.*

PROOF. The predicate contains the conjunct $used' = used \cup \{p!\}$. By the definition of *used*, $free = PID \setminus used$, so if $p! \in used'$, $p! \notin free'$ for the equation implies $free \setminus \{p!\} = PID \setminus (used \cup \{p!\})$ since the set of all identifiers is fixed. □

We need to define an operation that sets the initial values for process attributes. This operation will be used when a process is created.

$$
\begin{array}{l}
\text{— } AddPDESC \text{ —} \\
\Delta PTAB \\
p? : PID \\
st? : PSTATE \\
\hline
state' = state \cup \{p? \mapsto st?\}
\end{array}
$$

An operation is required to create the idle process. This process does not have a *UID* since it cannot be accessed outside the kernel. Even though it resides in the kernel, the idle process is still regarded as a user process (this is really just a matter of choice—it could equally be a device process).

$$
\begin{array}{l}
AddIdleProcess \mathrel{\widehat=} \\
\quad \exists\, pt : PTYPE;\ st : PSTATE \mid pt = uproc \land st = psready \bullet \\
\qquad AllocPID[ip!/p!] \land \\
\qquad AddPDESC[ip!/p?, st/st?] \\
\qquad SetProcType[ip!/p?, pt/pt?]
\end{array}
$$

This definition expands to:

$$
\begin{array}{|l}
\hline
\textit{AddIdleProcess} \\
\Delta PTAB \\
p! : PID \\
\hline
\exists\, pt : PTYPE;\ st : PSTATE \mid pt = dproc \land st = psready \bullet \\
\quad ip! \notin used \land \\
\quad used' = used \cup \{ip!\} \land \\
\quad state' = state \cup \{ip! \mapsto st\} \land \\
\quad ptype' = ptype \cup \{ip! \mapsto pt\} \\
\hline
\end{array}
$$

Removing the existential quantifier using the one-point rule, the following is obtained:

$$
\begin{array}{|l}
\hline
\textit{AddIdleProcess} \\
\Delta PTAB \\
ip! : PID \\
\hline
ip! \notin used \\
used' = used \cup \{ip!\} \\
state' = state \cup \{ip! \mapsto psready\} \\
ptype' = ptrype \cup \{ip! \mapsto dproc\} \\
\hline
\end{array}
$$

The next schema defines the operation that translates an external user process identifier, an element of *UPID*, and translates it into an element of *PID*.

$$
\begin{array}{|l}
\hline
\textit{PIDforUPID} \\
\Xi PTAB \\
u? : UPID \\
p! : PID \\
\hline
p! = extpid(u?) \\
\hline
\end{array}
$$

The following is the definition of the operation that deallocates a process identifier. It is similar to the one in the earlier specification and its justification is also similar.

FreePID

$$\Delta PTAB$$
$$p? : PID$$

$$used' = used \setminus \{p?\}$$

On termination, the external identifier of a process must be cancelled. This schema defines the operation.

DelProcUPID

$$\Delta PTAB$$
$$p? : PID$$

$$extpid' = extpid \lhd \{p?\}$$

We need an operation to remove a process' external identifier when it is terminated. This schema defines that operation.

DelExtPD

$$\Delta PTAB$$
$$p? : PID$$

$$extpid' = extpid \lhd \{p?\}$$

To delete a user process, the following is required:

$$DelUserPD \mathrel{\widehat{=}} DelExtPD \land FreePID$$

This operation expands into

$$\Delta PTAB$$
$$p? : PID$$

$$extpid' = extpid \lhd \{p?\}$$
$$used' = used \setminus \{p?\}$$

By calculation, the precondition of this operation is just *true*. This does not seem adequate, so we define

$$\text{pre}\ DelUserPD \mathrel{\widehat{=}} p? \in used$$

Sometimes, it is necessary to terminate *all* processes and to do it as quickly as possible. The following operation deletes all the information about processes.

DeleteAllProcesses

$$\Delta PTAB$$

$$used' = \varnothing$$

This operation is used (gleefully!) by the ISR that responds to lethal errors.

Operations to access and set various process attributes are defined in the next few schemata. The structure of these schemata is relatively simple and their interpretation should be immediate.

ProcType

$$\Xi PTAB$$
$$p? : PID$$
$$pt! : PTYPE$$

$$pt! = ptype(p?)$$

ProcState

$$\Xi PTAB$$
$$p? : PID$$
$$st! : PSTATE$$

$$st! = state(p?)$$

SetProcState

$$\Delta PTAB$$
$$p? : PID$$
$$st? : PSTATE$$

$$state' = state \oplus \{p? \mapsto st?\}$$

pre *SetProcState* $\widehat{=}$ $p? \in used$

Note that this is implied by the invariant.

$$SetStateToReady \mathrel{\widehat{=}}$$
$$\exists st : PSTATE \mid st = psready \bullet$$
$$SetProcState[st/st?]$$

$$SetStateToRunning \mathrel{\widehat{=}}$$
$$\exists st : PSTATE \mid st = psrunning \bullet$$
$$SetProcState[st/st?]$$

$$SetStateToTerminated \mathrel{\widehat{=}}$$
$$\exists st : PSTATE \mid st = psterm \bullet$$
$$SetProcState[st/st?]$$

Because all of the *SetState* operations are similar, only *SetStateToReady* is expanded here.

$$\begin{array}{l}
\textit{SetStateToReady} \\
\hline
\Delta PTAB \\
p? : PID \\
\hline
state' = state \oplus \{p? \mapsto psready\}
\end{array}$$

(The remainder can be obtained by an obvious substitution.)

The reader is warned that a significant number of operations, those dealing with device processes, are not included in this subsection. The missing class of operation is defined in the section dealing with device processes. The refinement of the device-process operations is directly analogous to the process whose documentation now begins.

5.4.2 Refinement One

Having defined the process table and the general operations that act upon it, the refinement can begin. The first step is to define the refined process table and its initialisation schema; then the abstraction relation is defined.

This first refinement corresponds closely to that of the *PTAB* in the first specification. The strategy is exactly the same as in that case, namely that the set of free process table entries (denoted by process identifiers) should be implemented as a chain through a vector, called *next*, that maps process identifiers to process identifiers. As a first step, *used* is replaced by a free chain mapping. In addition, we require that all the partial functions that initially specified the various attributes of processes should be refined to functions whose domains are *PID* and whose codomains are the sets defining each attribute type (e.g., for *state*, we want a function $PID \rightarrow PSTATE$). This second goal is achieved at this stage in the refinement. The first goal is only partially reached; it will require a second step to refine to the representation in which *next* is used.

Now, it should be clear that this refinement strategy is identical to that used in the refinement documented in Chapter 3 of this book. The representation of the process tables in this and in the other case are extremely close (sets and partial functions). For this reason and for reasons given after the abstraction relation has been stated, most of the refinement proofs that would normally be associated with refinement steps are omitted from this chapter.

$$\begin{array}{l}
\textit{PTAB1} \\
\hline
hdfree, endfree : GPID \\
freech : PID \rightarrowtail\!\!\!\!\!\rightarrow GPID \\
nextupid1 : UPID \\
extpid1 : UPID \rightarrow PID \\
pidext1 : PID \rightarrow UPID \\
devmap1 : DEVNO \rightarrow PID \\
tss1 : PID \rightarrow TSS \\
state1 : PID \rightarrow PSTATE
\end{array}$$

$$
\begin{array}{l}
ptype1 : PID \rightarrow PTYPE \\
msgq1 : PID \rightarrow MSGQ \\
devrqs1 : PID \rightarrow MSG \\
devmsg1 : PID \rightarrow (GPID \times MSG) \\
devrpy1 : PID \rightarrow MSG \\
cdseg1 : PID \rightarrow SDESC \\
dsseg1 : PID \rightarrow SDESC \\
\hline
hdfree = nullpid \Leftrightarrow endfree = nullpid \\
hdfree = nullpid \Leftrightarrow \operatorname{dom} freech = \varnothing \\
(hdfree \neq nullpid \Rightarrow \\
\qquad \operatorname{dom} freech \neq \varnothing \land \\
\qquad hdfree \in \operatorname{dom} freech \land \\
\qquad endfree \in \operatorname{dom} freech \land \\
\qquad freech(endfree) = nullpid)
\end{array}
$$

The initialisation schema is much as one would expect.

$$
\begin{array}{l}
\textbf{PTAB1Init} \\
PTAB1' \\
\hline
hdfree' = minpid \\
endfree' = maxpid \\
\forall p : PID \bullet \\
\qquad (p = maxpid \Rightarrow freech'(p) = nullpid) \land \\
\qquad (p < maxpid \Rightarrow freech'(p) = p + 1) \\
nextupid1' = 0
\end{array}
$$

$$
\begin{array}{l}
\textbf{UsedPID1} \\
\Xi PTAB1 \\
p? : PID \\
\hline
p? \in \operatorname{dom} freech
\end{array}
$$

$$
\begin{array}{l}
\textbf{GotFreePIDs1} \\
\Xi PTAB1 \\
\hline
hdfree \neq nullpid
\end{array}
$$

$$
\begin{array}{|l}
\hline
\textit{AllocPID1} \\
\Delta PTAB1 \\
p! : PID \\
\hline
p! = hdfree \\
freech' = freech \ntriangleleft \{p!\} \\
hdfree' = next(hdfree) \\
\hline
\end{array}
$$

$$
\begin{array}{|l}
\hline
\textit{AllocUPID1} \\
\Delta PTAB1 \\
u! : UPID \\
\hline
u! = nextupid1 \\
nextupid1' = nextupid1 + 1 \\
\hline
\end{array}
$$

$$
\begin{array}{|l}
\hline
\textit{AddProcUPID1} \\
\Delta PTAB1 \\
p? : PID \\
u? : UPID \\
\hline
extpid1' = extpid1 \oplus \{u? \mapsto p?\} \\
\hline
\end{array}
$$

$$
\begin{array}{l}
NewUPIDForProcess1 \mathrel{\widehat=} \\
\quad AllocPID1 \land \\
\quad\quad AllocUPID1 \land \\
\quad\quad AddProcUPID1[p!/p?, u!/u?]
\end{array}
$$

The definition of *NewUPIDForProcess1* expands into the following schema:

$$
\begin{array}{|l}
\hline
\textit{NewUPIDForProcess1} \\
\Delta PTAB1 \\
p! : PID \\
u! : UPID \\
\hline
p! = hdfree \\
freech' = freech \ntriangleleft \{p!\} \\
hdfree' = next(freech) \\
u! = nextupid1 \\
nextupid1' = nextupid1 + 1 \\
extpid1' = extpid1 \oplus \{u! \mapsto p!\} \\
\hline
\end{array}
$$

$$
\begin{array}{|l}
\hline
\textit{SetProcType1} \\
\Delta PTAB1 \\
p? : PID \\
pt? : PTYPE \\
\hline
ptype1' = ptype1 \oplus \{p? \mapsto pt?\} \\
\hline
\end{array}
$$

$$
\begin{array}{l}
AddPD \mathrel{\widehat=} \\
\quad ((GotFreePIDs1 \land \\
\qquad\qquad NewUPIDForProcess1[uu!/u!] \land \\
\qquad\qquad SetProcType1[p!/p?] \land \\
\qquad\qquad SysOk) \\
\quad \lor PTABFull
\end{array}
$$

The *AddPD1* operation expands into:

$$
\begin{array}{|l}
\hline
\textit{AddPD1} \\
\Delta PTAB1 \\
\Delta ERRV \\
\Delta HW \\
p! : PID \\
u! : UPID \\
pt? : PTYPE \\
\hline
(hdfree \neq nullpid \land \\
\quad p! = hdfree \land \\
\quad freech' = freech \lhd \{p!\} \land \\
\quad hdfree' = next(freech) \land \\
\quad u! = nextupid1 \land \\
\quad nextupid1' = nextupid1 + 1 \land \\
\quad extpid1' = extpid1 \oplus \{u! \mapsto p!\} \land \\
\quad ptype1' = ptype1 \oplus \{p! \mapsto pt?\} \land \\
\quad serr' = sysok) \\
\lor (serr' = ptabfull \land intno' = killintno) \\
\hline
\end{array}
$$

The *AddPD1* operation is very important, so its precondition has to be calculated. It is:

$$
\begin{array}{l}
\mathrm{pre}\, AddPD1 \mathrel{\widehat=} \\
\quad hdfree \neq nullpid
\end{array}
$$

This formula implies

$$\mathrm{pre}\, AddPD1 \mathrel{\widehat=} used \subset PID$$

We need to refine the operation that sets the initial values for process attributes. It is as follows:

$$
\begin{array}{|l}
\hline
\textit{AddPDESC1} \\
\Delta PTAB \\
p? : PID \\
st? : PSTATE \\
\hline
state1' = state1 \oplus \{p? \mapsto st?\} \\
\hline
\end{array}
$$

$$
\begin{array}{l}
AddIdleProcess1 \mathrel{\widehat=} \\
\quad \exists\, pt : PTYPE;\ st : PSTATE \mid pt = uproc \land st = psready \bullet \\
\qquad AllocPID1[ip!/p!] \land \\
\qquad AddPDESC1[ip!/p?, st/st?] \\
\qquad SetProcType1[ip!/p?, pt/pt?]
\end{array}
$$

$$
\begin{array}{|l}
\hline
\textit{PIDforUPID1} \\
\Xi PTAB1 \\
u? : UPID \\
p! : PID \\
\hline
p! = extpid1(u?) \\
\hline
\end{array}
$$

The following schemata define operations on the free chain. They are identical to those in the previous refinement.

$$
\begin{array}{|l}
\hline
\textit{EmptyFreeChain1} \\
\Xi PTAB1 \\
\hline
\mathrm{dom}\, freech = \varnothing \\
\hline
\end{array}
$$

The *AddNewLastFreechain* schema defines an operation that adds an element to the end of the free chain.

$$
\begin{array}{|l}
\hline
\textit{AddNewLastFreechain} \\
\Delta PTAB1 \\
p? : PID \\
\hline
freech' = freech \oplus \{endfree \mapsto p?\} \\
\hline
\end{array}
$$

The *AddFreechainLast* schema defines an operation that maps the last element of the free chain to *nullpid*.

$$
\begin{array}{|l}
\hline
\textit{AddFreechainLast} \\
\Delta PTAB1 \\
p? : PID \\
\hline
freech' = freech \cup \{p? \mapsto nullpid\} \\
\hline
\end{array}
$$

The *SetFCHead* operation sets the value of *hdfree*.

$$
\begin{array}{|l}
\hline
\textit{SetFCHead} \\
\Delta PTAB1 \\
p? : PID \\
\hline
hdfree' = p? \\
\hline
\end{array}
$$

Analogously, *SetFCLast* sets the value of *endfree*.

$$
\begin{array}{|l}
\hline
\textit{SetFCLast} \\
\Delta PTAB1 \\
p? : PID \\
\hline
endfree' = p? \\
\hline
\end{array}
$$

The following is the definition of the operation that deallocates a process identifier. It is similar to the one in the earlier specification and its justification is also similar.

$$
\begin{array}{l}
FreePID1 \mathrel{\widehat=} \\
\quad (((EmptyFreeChain1 \land \\
\qquad\qquad AddFreechainLast \land SetFCLast \land SetFCHead) \\
\quad \lor (UsedPID1 \land \\
\qquad\qquad (AddNewLastFreechain \mathbin{;} AddFreechainLast) \land SetFCLast)) \land \\
\qquad SysOk) \\
\quad \lor UnusedPID
\end{array}
$$

This can be transformed by distribution of *SysOk*. The transformation is justified by the propositional calculus theorem $(p \lor q) \land r \Leftrightarrow (p \land r) \lor (q \land r)$. The use of this theorem occurs frequently and can be used both to expand a schema by producing copies of conjuncts and to contract them by reducing multiple occurrences of a conjunct to a single one.

$$
\begin{array}{l}
FreePID1 \mathrel{\widehat=} \\
\quad ((EmptyFreeChain1 \land \\
\qquad\qquad AddFreechainLast \land SetFCLast \land SetFCHead \land SysOk) \\
\quad \lor (UsedPID1 \land \\
\qquad (AddNewLastFreechain \mathbin{;} AddFreechainLast) \land SetFCLast \land SysOk)) \\
\quad \lor UnusedPID1
\end{array}
$$

This definition can then be expanded into the schema that follows. A small amount of simplification has been performed on the schema, it should be noted. Very often, when expanding definitions into schemata, we will take the opportunity to engage in some simplification; we will, though, outline the transformations employed unless they are obvious.

$$
\begin{array}{l}
\hline
\textit{FreePID1} \\
\Delta PTAB1 \\
\Delta ERRV \\
\Delta HW \\
p? : PID \\
\hline
((\mathrm{dom}\, freech = \varnothing \land \\
\quad freech' = freech \cup \{p? \mapsto nullpid\} \land \\
\quad endfree' = p? \land \\
\quad hdfree' = p? \land \\
\quad serr' = sysok) \\
\lor (p? \notin \mathrm{dom}\, freech \land \\
\quad freech' = (freech \oplus \{endfree \mapsto p?\}) \cup \{p? \mapsto nullpid\} \land \\
\quad endfree' = p? \land \\
\quad serr' = sysok)) \\
\lor (serr' = usedpd \land intno' = killintno) \\
\hline
\end{array}
$$

On termination, the external identifier of a process must be cancelled. This schema defines the operation.

$$
\begin{array}{l}
\hline
\textit{DelProcUPID1} \\
\Delta PTAB1 \\
p? : PID \\
\hline
extpid1' = extpid1 \lhd \{p?\} \\
\hline
\end{array}
$$

We need an operation to remove a process' external identifier when it is terminated. This schema defines that operation.

$$
\begin{array}{l}
\hline
\textit{DelExtPD1} \\
\Delta PTAB1 \\
p? : PID \\
\hline
extpid1' = extpid1 \lhd \{p?\} \\
\hline
\end{array}
$$

To delete a user process, the following is required:

$$DelUserPD1 \mathrel{\widehat=} DelExtPD1 \land FreePID1$$

This operation expands into

$$
\begin{array}{l}
\hline
\Delta PTAB1 \\
\Delta ERRV \\
\Delta HW \\
p? : PID \\
\hline
extpid1' = extpid1 \lhd \{p?\} \\
\end{array}
$$

$$
\begin{array}{l}
((\mathrm{dom}\, freech = \varnothing \land \\
\quad freech' = freech \cup \{p? \mapsto nullpid\} \land \\
\quad endfree' = p? \land \\
\quad hdfree' = p? \land \\
\quad serr' = sysok) \\
\lor (p? \notin \mathrm{dom}\, freech \land \\
\quad freech' = (freech \oplus \{endfree \mapsto p?\}) \cup \{p? \mapsto nullpid\} \land \\
\quad endfree' = p? \land \\
\quad serr' = sysok)) \\
\lor (serr' = usedpd \land intno' = killintno)
\end{array}
$$

By calculation, the precondition of this operation is just *true*. This does not seem adequate, so we define

$$\mathrm{pre}\, DelUserPD1 \mathrel{\widehat=} p? \notin freech$$

Sometimes, it is necessary to terminate *all* processes and to do it as quickly as possible. The following operation deletes all the information about processes.

DeleteAllProcesses1

$$
\begin{array}{l}
\Delta PTAB1 \\
\hline
hdfree' = nullpid \\
\mathrm{dom}\, freech' = \varnothing
\end{array}
$$

This operation is used by the ISR that responds to lethal errors. Its precondition is *true*, so it can be applied at any time!

ProcType1

$$
\begin{array}{l}
\Xi PTAB1 \\
p? : PID \\
pt! : PTYPE \\
\hline
pt! = ptype(p?)
\end{array}
$$

ProcState1

$$
\begin{array}{l}
\Xi PTAB1 \\
p? : PID \\
st! : PSTATE \\
\hline
st! = state(p?)
\end{array}
$$

$$
\begin{array}{|l}
\hline
\textit{SetProcState}1 \\
\Delta PTAB1 \\
p? : PID \\
st? : PSTATE \\
\hline
state' = state \oplus \{p? \mapsto st?\} \\
\hline
\end{array}
$$

$\text{pre } SetProcState1 \mathrel{\widehat=} p? \in used$

Note that this is implied by the invariant.

$$
\begin{array}{l}
SetStateToReady1 \mathrel{\widehat=} \\
\quad \exists\, st : PSTATE \mid st = psready \bullet \\
\qquad SetProcState1[st/st?]
\end{array}
$$

$$
\begin{array}{l}
SetStateToRunning1 \mathrel{\widehat=} \\
\quad \exists\, st : PSTATE \mid st = psrunning \bullet \\
\qquad SetProcState1[st/st?]
\end{array}
$$

$$
\begin{array}{l}
SetStateToTerminated1 \mathrel{\widehat=} \\
\quad \exists\, st : PSTATE \mid st = psterm \bullet \\
\qquad SetProcState1[st/st?]
\end{array}
$$

Because all of the *SetState1* operations are similar, only *SetStateToReady1* is expanded here.

$$
\begin{array}{|l}
\hline
SetStateToReady1 \\
\Delta PTAB1 \\
p? : PID \\
\hline
state1' = state1 \oplus \{p? \mapsto psready\} \\
\hline
\end{array}
$$

We now give the abstraction schema. The difference between the schema as presented here and the one in the previous refinement is that the current one has more process attributes to relate. The "structural" components (those dealing with the existence of processes) are the same in both cases.

$$
\begin{array}{|l}
\hline
AbsPTAB1 \\
PTAB \\
PTAB1 \\
\hline
\operatorname{dom} freech = PID \setminus used \\
\operatorname{dom} freech \cap used = \varnothing \\
nextupid1 = nextupid \\
\forall p : PID \bullet p \in used \Leftrightarrow pidext(p) = pidext1(p) \\
\forall p : PID \bullet p \in used \Leftrightarrow extpid(pidext(p)) = extpid1(pidext1(p)) \\
\forall p : PID \bullet p \in used \Leftrightarrow state(p) = state1(p)
\end{array}
$$

$$\forall p : PID \bullet p \in used \Leftrightarrow ptype(p) = ptype1(p)$$
$$\forall p : PID \bullet p \in used \Leftrightarrow msgq(p) = msgq1(p)$$
$$\forall p : PID \bullet p \in used \Leftrightarrow pidext(p) = pidext1(p)$$
$$\forall p : PID \bullet p \in used \land ptype(p) \neq dproc \Leftrightarrow cdseg(p) = cdseq1(p)$$
$$\forall p : PID \bullet p \in used \land ptype(p) \neq dproc \Leftrightarrow dsseg(p) = dsseg1(p)$$
$$\forall p : PID \bullet p \in used \land ptype(p) = dproc \Leftrightarrow devrqs(p) = devrqs1(p)$$
$$\forall p : PID \bullet p \in used \land ptype(p) = dproc \Leftrightarrow devrpy(p) = devrpy1(p)$$
$$\forall p : PID \bullet p \in used \land ptype(p) = dproc \Leftrightarrow devmsg(p) = devmsg1(p)$$
$$\forall d : DEVNO \bullet devmap(d) \in used \Leftrightarrow devmap1(d) = devmap(d)$$

This schema is yet another identity (and this is usual). This implies that we can compute the operations we require for $PTAB1$, using those defined for $PTAB$. It also implies that the refinement proofs must be straightforward. We give the initialisation theorem as an example proof.

Next, we state and prove the initialisation theorem for $PTAB1$. This is the only proof in this section. It is included to demonstrate to the reader that the abstraction relation is sensible. The other proofs could be included but they are all relatively straightforward. (The interested reader might like to compare this abstraction relation with the parallel one in Chapter 3 and thus gain an idea of what the proofs are like.)

Theorem 59. $\forall PTAB'; PTAB1' \bullet PTAB1Init \land AbsPTAB1 \Rightarrow PTABInit$

PROOF. The universal implies that $\mathrm{dom}\, freech' = PID$ since $PID \setminus used' = freech'$. We have $PID \setminus used = PID$, so $used' = \varnothing$, $\mathrm{dom}\, freech' \neq \varnothing$ for $hdfree \neq endfree \neq nullpid$.

By $AbsPTAB1'$, $nextupid' = nextupid1' = 1$. □

5.4.3 Refinement Two

The second refinement of $PTAB$ is the subject of this subsection. The new $PTAB2$ schema is given immediately.

$PTAB2$

$$freehd, freelst : GPID$$
$$next : PID \rightarrowtail GPID$$
$$nextupid2 : UPID$$
$$extpid2 : UPID \rightarrow PID$$
$$pidext2 : PID \rightarrow UPID$$
$$devmap2 : DEVNO \rightarrow PID$$
$$state2 : PID \rightarrow PSTATE$$
$$tss2 : PID \rightarrow TSS$$
$$ptype2 : PID \rightarrow PTYPE$$
$$msgq2 : PID \rightarrow MSGQ$$
$$devrqs2 : PID \rightarrow MSG$$

$$
\begin{array}{l}
devmsg2 : PID \rightarrow (GPID \times MSG) \\
devrpy2 : PID \rightarrow MSG \\
cdseg2 : PID \rightarrow SDESC \\
dsseg2 : PID \rightarrow SDESC \\
\hline
freehd = nullpid \Leftrightarrow freelst = nullpid \\
freehd = nullpid \Rightarrow next^*(\!|\ \{freehd\}\ |\!) = \varnothing \\
freehd \neq nullpid \Leftrightarrow \\
\quad \forall p : PID \bullet \\
\quad\quad p = freehd \Rightarrow nullpid \in next^+(\!|\ \{freehd\}\ |\!) \\
freehd \neq nullpid \Leftrightarrow \\
\quad \forall p : PID \bullet \\
\quad\quad p = freelst \Rightarrow next(freelst) = nullpid \\
freehd \neq nullpid \Rightarrow \exists_1\, k : \mathbb{N} \bullet next^k(freehd) = nullpid
\end{array}
$$

The reader should compare this with the corresponding schema in the refinement of the other kernel in this book. It will be seen that the two are quite similar. We make use of the similarity in the remainder of this subsection.

We immediately present the abstraction schema.

$$
\begin{array}{l}
\textit{AbsPTAB2} \\
\hline
PTAB1 \\
PTAB2 \\
\hline
freehd = hdfree \\
freelst = endfree \\
freehd \neq nullpid \Rightarrow \\
\quad next^*(\!|\ \{freehd\}\ |\!) \setminus \{nullpid\} = \mathrm{dom}\, freech \\
\mathrm{dom}\, freech = \varnothing \Leftrightarrow freehd = freelst \land freehd = nullpid \\
freehd \neq nullpid \Leftrightarrow \forall p : PID \bullet p \in \mathrm{dom}\, freech \Rightarrow next(p) = freech(p) \\
\mathrm{dom}\, freech \subseteq \mathrm{dom}\, next \\
\mathrm{ran}\, freech \subseteq \mathrm{ran}\, next \\
\forall p : PID \bullet \\
\quad p \in \mathrm{dom}\, freech \Leftrightarrow next(p) = freech(p)
\end{array}
$$

Again, this is similar to the corresponding schema in Chapter 3. With the exception of the relationships between the domain and codomain of *freech* and *next*, the other conjuncts are identities. We can treat the predicate of this schema as if it were an identity. This has what, by now, should be familiar consequences for the conduct of the refinement.

We state the initialisation schema (it is quite obvious):

$$
\begin{array}{l}
\underline{\quad PTAB2Init \quad} \\
PTAB2' \\
\hline
freehd' = minpid \\
freelst' = maxpid \\
\forall p : PID \bullet \\
\quad p = maxpid \Rightarrow next'(p) = nullpid \land \\
\quad p < maxpid \Rightarrow next'(p) = p + 1
\end{array}
$$

The schemata defined at this level can be translated with ease into a programming language, so there is no more to be done here.

5.5 Process Queues

This section contains the refinement of the FIFO queue type used to implement the process queues manipulated by the Separation Kernel's scheduler. The type is identical to that defined in Chapter 3. This means that we can import all refinements and proofs *intact* from that earlier exercise and use them in the current context. This clearly saves us a little work; it also serves to shorten this book a little.

We will state the single error schema required by the process queue type. It is

$$
\begin{array}{l}
ProcessQueueEmpty \mathrel{\widehat{=}} \\
\quad (\exists e : SYSERR \mid e = emptyqueue \bullet \\
\quad\quad SetSysErr[e/e?]) \land \\
\quad RaiseKillInterrupt
\end{array}
$$

5.5.1 Top Level

This is a relatively straightforward specification of a FIFO queue. It uses a sequence as its basic container structure.

The state schema is the following.

$$
\begin{array}{l}
\underline{\quad PROCESSQUEUE \quad} \\
procs : \mathrm{seq}\, PID
\end{array}
$$

As was the case with the previous example, it is possible to include *PTAB* in the *PROCESSQUEUE* schema, thus making *used* a visible component. This would permit the invariant to include $\mathrm{ran}\, procs \subseteq used$. Equally, the sequence type could be declared as being an *injective* sequence. This would imply that elements can appear only once. In this case, as in the last, we prefer not to take these measures. We can prove that only elements of *used* can be in *procs* since only elements of *used* can execute on the processor.

Furthermore, it is not necessary to use an injective sequence. The reason for this is that when a process is in the scheduler's queue, it cannot be executed and cannot, therefore, be placed on the scheduler's queue; necessarily, each process identifier occurs in *procs* exactly once.

The initialisation operation is the obvious one.

$$\begin{array}{|l}
\textit{PROCESSQUEUEInit} \\ \hline
\textit{PROCESSQUEUE}' \\ \hline
\textit{procs}' = \langle\,\rangle \\ \hline
\end{array}$$

The test for queue emptiness is equally obvious.

$$\begin{array}{|l}
\textit{IsEmptyPROCESSQUEUE} \\ \hline
\Xi \textit{PROCESSQUEUE} \\ \hline
\textit{procs} = \langle\,\rangle \\ \hline
\end{array}$$

New elements are enqueued at the *back* of the queue (it is a FIFO queue). This is captured by the following schema.

$$\begin{array}{|l}
\textit{EnqueuePROCESSQUEUE} \\ \hline
\Delta \textit{PROCESSQUEUE} \\
p? : \textit{PID} \\ \hline
\textit{procs}' = \textit{procs} \frown \langle p? \rangle \\ \hline
\end{array}$$

The head of the queue is the first element or *head procs*, since $\textit{head procs} = \textit{procs}(1)$ iff $\textit{procs} \neq \langle\,\rangle$. The next schema defines the basic operation; the condition on the queue will be imposed at a later time.

$$\begin{array}{|l}
\textit{TheHeadOfPROCESSQUEUE} \\ \hline
\Xi \textit{PROCESSQUEUE} \\
p! : \textit{PID} \\ \hline
p! = \textit{head procs} \\ \hline
\end{array}$$

The above operation is not useful. It must test for the empty queue. This extension is made in the following definition.

$$\begin{array}{l}
\textit{HeadOfPROCESSQUEUE} \mathrel{\widehat=} \\
\quad (\textit{IsNonEmptyPROCESSQUEUE} \land \\
\qquad \textit{TheHeadOfPROCESSQUEUE} \land \\
\qquad \textit{SysOk}) \\
\quad \lor \textit{ProcessQueueEmpty}
\end{array}$$

The definition expands into:

$$
\begin{array}{l}
\textit{HeadOfPROCESSQUEUE} \\
\hline
\Xi PROCESSQUEUE \\
\Delta ERRV \\
\Delta HW \\
p! : PID \\
\hline
(procs \neq \langle\rangle \land \\
\quad p! = head\ procs \land \\
\quad serr' = sysok) \\
\lor (serr' = emptyqueue \land intno' = killintno)
\end{array}
$$

When a process is removed from the queue, it is removed from the head. The following schema defines this operation. It is the obvious specification, taking the tail of the queue and assigning it to the after state of the queue ($procs'$):

$$
\begin{array}{l}
\textit{DelHeadOfPROCESSQUEUE} \\
\hline
\Delta PROCESSQUEUE \\
\hline
procs' = tail\ procs
\end{array}
$$

A dequeue can only take place when the queue is not empty. The operation to perform the dequeue is totalised by the addition of checks. It is

$$
\begin{array}{l}
DequeuePROCESSQUEUE \mathrel{\widehat=} \\
\quad (IsNotEmptyPROCESSQUEUE \land \\
\qquad HeadOfPROCESSQUEUEU \land \\
\qquad DelHeadOfPROCESSQUEUE \land \\
\qquad SysOk) \\
\quad \lor ProcessQueueEmpty
\end{array}
$$

This compound operation expands into:

$$
\begin{array}{l}
\textit{DequeuePROCESSQUEUE} \\
\hline
\Delta PROCESSQUEUE \\
\Delta ERRV \\
\Delta HW \\
p! : PID \\
\hline
(procs \neq \langle\rangle \land \\
\quad p! = head\ procs \land \\
\quad procs' = tail\ procs \land \\
\quad serr' = sysok) \\
\lor (serr' = emptyqueue \land intno' = killintno)
\end{array}
$$

This is all there is to the queue type used by the scheduler. The round robin scheduling algorithm requires a strict FIFO queue. This is what has been presented.

5.5.2 Refinement

The refinement of this type follows that in the *PROCESSQUEUE* section of the first kernel. The proofs are not repeated here.

It should be noted that the *DEVPROCQUEUE* type is defined in the next section. Type *DEVPROCQUEUE* is another FIFO queue type whose elements are elements of *PID*. The *DEVPROCQUEUE* type is defined in terms of renaming components of *PROCESSQUEUE*. The refinement proofs for *DEVPROCQUEUE* are identical to those for *PROCESSQUEUE*, so they may safely be omitted.

5.6 The Scheduler

The separation kernel is intended to model a distributed sytem. This implies that the scheduler can be very simple.

The original paper on Separation Kernels, [10], specifies the round-robin scheduling algorithm. A problem can arise when high-priority devices need to be included in the system. To solve this, the scheduler is specified as two queues. One queue is used to schedule user-level processes. The second queue is used to schedule device processes. The device process queue has higher priority than the one for scheduling user processes.

It is necessary to begin by defining a separate queue type for device processes. This is required so that the names of device and process queue components and operations do not clash. We continue by defining new queue types and operations by renaming those defined for FIFO queues. Note that name substitutions must be performed in order to ensure that the new queue type does not contain names that clash with any existing (or to be defined) types.

$$DEVPROCQUEUE \mathrel{\widehat=} PROCESSQUEUE[devs/procs]$$

$$DEVPROCQUEUEInit \mathrel{\widehat=} PROCESSQUEUEInit[devs/procs]$$

$$IsEmptyDEVPROCQUEUE \mathrel{\widehat=} IsEmptyPROCESSQUEUE[devs/procs]$$

$$EnqueueDEVPROCQUEUE \mathrel{\widehat=} \\ \quad EnqueuePROCESSQUEUE[devs/procs, devs'/procs', dp?/p?]$$

$$DequeueDEVPROCQUEUE \mathrel{\widehat=} \\ \quad DequeuePROCESSQUEUE[devs/procs, devs'/procs', dp!/p!]$$

To assure the reader that this is proper, the above operations are now expanded so that their full definition can be seen.

First, there is the queue type schema:

$$\begin{array}{|l} \hline DEVPROCQUEUE \\ \hline devs : \mathrm{seq}\, PID \\ \hline \end{array}$$

The device queue is initialised by the following operation:

$$
\begin{array}{|l}
\hline
\textit{DEVPROCQUEUEInit} \\
\textit{DEVPROCQUEUE}' \\
\hline
\textit{devs}' = \langle\,\rangle \\
\hline
\end{array}
$$

The emptiness of the device queue is tested by the following operation:

$$
\begin{array}{|l}
\hline
\textit{IsEmptyDEVPROCQUEUE} \\
\Xi \textit{DEVPROCQUEUE} \\
\hline
\textit{devs} = \langle\,\rangle \\
\hline
\end{array}
$$

The enqueue operation for device processes is defined by the following schema:

$$
\begin{array}{|l}
\hline
\textit{EnqueueDEVPROCQUEUE} \\
\Delta \textit{DEVPROCQUEUE} \\
\textit{dp}? : \textit{PID} \\
\hline
\textit{devs}' = \textit{devs} \frown \langle \textit{dp}? \rangle \\
\hline
\end{array}
$$

The dequeue operation expands to the following:

$$
\begin{array}{|l}
\hline
\textit{DequeueDEVPROCQUEUE} \\
\Delta \textit{DEVPROCQUEUE} \\
\Delta \textit{ERRV} \\
\Delta \textit{HW} \\
\textit{dp}! : \textit{PID} \\
\hline
(\textit{devs} \neq \langle\,\rangle \land \\
\quad \textit{dp}! = \textit{head devs} \land \\
\quad \textit{devs}' = \textit{tail devs} \land \\
\quad \textit{serr}' = \textit{sysok}) \\
\lor (\textit{serr}' = \textit{emptyqueue} \land \textit{intno}' = \textit{killintno}) \\
\hline
\end{array}
$$

Finally, the scheduler schema can be defined. This schema contains variables to represent the currently executing process, the previously executed process, the identifier of the idle process and two FIFO queues, one each for user and device processes. The schema is:

$$
\begin{array}{|l}
\hline
\textit{SKSCHED} \\
\textit{curr}, \textit{prev} : \textit{PID} \\
\textit{ipid} : \textit{PID} \\
\textit{devq} : \textit{DEVPROCQUEUE} \\
\textit{procq} : \textit{PROCESSQUEUE} \\
\hline
\end{array}
$$

It should be noted that the user-process queue is just an unmodified copy of *PROCESSQUEUE*.

Upon seeing this definition, it should be clear that promotion is to be used in the definition of the scheduler, just as it was in the case of the previous one. This is a natural method for the specification of the scheduler (it also cuts down the work to be done in refining it to executable code).

The associated initialisation schema is the next one to be defined.

$$
\begin{array}{|l}
\hline
\textit{SKSCHEDInit} \\
SKSCHED' \\
p? : PID \\
\hline
curr' = minpid \\
prev' = minpid \\
ipid' = p? \\
devq' = \theta DEVPROCQUEUEInit \\
procq' = \theta PROCESSQUEUEInit \\
\hline
\end{array}
$$

Note that the initialisation of the two FIFO queues, *devq* and *procq* uses the θ notation.

The component *ipid* is the identifier of the idle process (sometimes called the "null" process). This is just a process that does nothing; it is there to absorb processor time in when there is nothing else to do. It can be implemented as a simple loop, such as:

```
while true do
   skip
od
```

The next few schemata define operations that manipulate the scalar variables in the scheduler's schema. Their names are chosen so that they indicate function. The names of the variables are identical to those in the previous specification, so the reader can refer to the previous scheduler for explanation, should it be required.

$$
\begin{array}{|l}
\hline
\textit{IDLEPROCESSIdent} \\
\Xi SKSCHED \\
p! : PID \\
\hline
p! = ipid \\
\hline
\end{array}
$$

$$
\begin{array}{|l}
\hline
\textit{RunningProcess} \\
\Xi SKSCHED \\
p! : PID \\
\hline
p! = curr \\
\hline
\end{array}
$$

$$
\begin{array}{|l}
\hline
\textit{SetRunningProcess} \\
\Delta SKSCHED \\
p? : PID \\
\hline
curr' = p? \\
\hline
\end{array}
$$

$$
\begin{array}{|l}
\hline
\textit{PreviouslyRunningProcess} \\
\Xi SKSCHED \\
p! : PID \\
\hline
p! = prev \\
\hline
\end{array}
$$

$$
\begin{array}{|l}
\hline
\textit{SetPreviousProcess} \\
\Delta SKSCHED \\
p? : PID \\
\hline
prev' = p? \\
\hline
\end{array}
$$

The final operation in this set is a little more complex. It is defined as the composition of other schemata:

$$
\begin{array}{l}
\textit{UpdateCurrentProcess} \mathrel{\widehat{=}} \\
\quad \textit{SetRunningProcess} \land \\
\quad (\textit{RunningProcess}[p/p!] \land \textit{SetPreviousProcess}[p/p?]) \setminus \{p\}
\end{array}
$$

It expands into a simple schema that can be simplified to give the following schema:

$$
\begin{array}{|l}
\hline
\Delta SKSCHED \\
p? : PID \\
\hline
curr' = p? \\
prev' = curr \\
\hline
\end{array}
$$

The scheduler, *SKSCHED*, is defined in terms of promotion. The promoted components are the user- and device-process queues. The promotion schema is defined in the obvious fashion as follows.

$$
\begin{array}{|l}
\hline
\Phi SKSCHED \\
\Delta SKSCHED \\
\Delta DEVPROCQUEUE \\
\Delta PROCESSQUEUE \\
\hline
devq = \theta DEVPROCQUEUE \\
devq' = \theta DEVPROCQUEUE' \\
procq = \theta PROCESSQUEUEInit \\
procq' = \theta PROCESSQUEUEInit' \\
\hline
\end{array}
$$

We can now define the promoted operations. Again, names are chosen to indicate function. We have little to say about these definitions. The operations correspond to those defined for device queues and are defined in a fashion similar to them.

$$\begin{array}{l} IsEmptyUSERPROCESSQUEUE \mathrel{\widehat=} \\ \quad \exists\, \Delta PROCESSQUEUE \bullet \\ \qquad \Phi SKSCHED \wedge IsEmptyPROCESSQUEUE \end{array}$$

$$\begin{array}{l} EnqueueUSERPROCESSQUEUE \mathrel{\widehat=} \\ \quad \exists\, \Delta PROCESSQUEUE \bullet \\ \qquad \Phi SKSCHED \wedge EnqueuePROCESSQUEUE \end{array}$$

$$\begin{array}{l} DequeueUSERPROCESSQUEUE \mathrel{\widehat=} \\ \quad \exists\, \Delta PROCESSQUEUE \bullet \\ \qquad \Phi SKSCHED \wedge DequeuePROCESSQUEUE \end{array}$$

$$\begin{array}{l} IsEmptyDEVICEQUEUE \mathrel{\widehat=} \\ \quad \exists\, \Delta DEVPROCQUEUE \bullet \\ \qquad \Phi SKSCHED \wedge IsEmptyDEVPROCQUEUE \end{array}$$

$$\begin{array}{l} EnqueueDEVICEPROCESS \mathrel{\widehat=} \\ \quad \exists\, \Delta DEVPROCQUEUE \bullet \\ \qquad \Phi SKSCHED \wedge EnqueueDEVPROCQUEUE \end{array}$$

$$\begin{array}{l} DequeueDEVICEQUEUE \mathrel{\widehat=} \\ \quad \exists\, \Delta DEVPROCQUEUE \bullet \\ \qquad \Phi SKSCHED \wedge DequeueDEVPROCQUEUE \end{array}$$

The operation that enqueues a user process in the user process ready queue is defined as follows:

$$\begin{array}{l} MakeReady \mathrel{\widehat=} \\ \quad SetStateToReady \wedge EnqueueUSERPROCQUEUE \end{array}$$

It is possible to strengthen this definition, making it more secure. The definition of *MakeReady* would look something like:

$$
\begin{array}{l}
MakeReady \mathrel{\widehat{=}} \\
\quad (KnownPID \land \\
\qquad (IsUserPID \land \\
\qquad\quad SetStateToReady \land \\
\qquad\quad EnqueueUSERPROCQUEUE \land \\
\qquad\quad SysOk) \\
\qquad \lor NotUserPID) \\
\quad \lor UnknownPID
\end{array}
$$

This would be a much more secure operation. However, it would require additional checks, *KnownPID* and *IsUserPID*, whose execution might incur unacceptable amounts of additional time (*KnownPID* must search the free chain in *PTAB*). The use of this operation (which requires the definition of additional schemata) remains an option but it is one with which we do not continue.

Next, the operation to place a device process on the ready devices queue, *devq*, is defined:

$$
\begin{array}{l}
ReadyDeviceProcess \mathrel{\widehat{=}} \\
\quad SetStateToReady \land EnqueueDEVPROCQUEUE
\end{array}
$$

This expands and simplifies to:

$$
\begin{array}{|l}
\Delta PTAB \\
\Delta SKSCHED \\
\Delta PROCESSQUEUE \\
\hline
state' = state \oplus \{p? \mapsto psready\} \\
devs' = devs \frown \langle p? \rangle
\end{array}
$$

The operation is now defined that executes the idle process at times when the scheduler determines that there is nothing else to do.

$$
\begin{array}{l}
RunIdleProcess \mathrel{\widehat{=}} \\
\quad (IDLEPROCESSIdent[i/p] \land \\
\qquad SetStateToRunning[i/p?] \land \\
\qquad UpdateCurrentProcess[i/p?]) \setminus \{i\}
\end{array}
$$

This expands and simplifies to:

$$
\begin{array}{|l}
\Delta PTAB \\
\Delta SKSCHED \\
\Delta PROCESSQUEUE \\
\hline
state' = state \oplus \{ip \mapsto psrunning\} \\
curr' = ip \\
prev' = curr
\end{array}
$$

It is sometimes necessary for a process to be removed from the scheduler queue in which it currently resides. When this happens, the process is said to be *unreadied.* Unreadying can occur when, for example, the current process makes a request for an I/O operation. I/O operations require time to complete and a device process must be scheduled, data transferred and the requesting process must be notified and then put back into the scheduler's queue. This is the most common case of unreadying and is, probably the only case relevant to the Separation Kernel. In other cases, a process that is not currently running is identified and removed from the queue. It is considered that, in the configuration of the Separation Kernel defined in this chapter, that this will not be a frequent operation; the case is included in the schema defining the unready operation, however.

In the operations specified here, an *unready* operation will not be used. Instead, use will be made of the fact that it is the current process that is performing the operation that requires the current process to be suspended. Nevertheless, the provision of the operation is useful because it provides a clean operation that can be employed by device processes (which are not specified in detail in this book).

It is also expected that device processes will never be unreadied. Therefore, the following definition is of the operation to remove user-level processes from the scheduler. If the process is the currently executing one, another process must be selected to execute. If the process to be unreadied is not yet executing (and is, therefore, in the user-process queue), it is merely removed from the queue and the current process continued.

$$
\begin{array}{l}
SKMakeUnready \mathrel{\widehat=} \\
\quad (RunningProcess[r/p!] \land \\
\qquad (IsEmptyUSERPROCESSQUEUE \land RunIdleProcess \mathbin{;} CTXTSW) \\
\qquad \lor (DequeueUSERPROCESSQUEUE[n/p!] \land \\
\qquad\quad SetStateToRunning[n/p?] \land \\
\qquad\quad UpdateCurrentProcess[n/p?] \mathbin{;} CTXTSW) \setminus \{n\}) \setminus \{r\}
\end{array}
$$

The main scheduling operation is the following:

$$
\begin{array}{l}
SKSchedNext \mathrel{\widehat=} \\
\quad (IsEmptyDEVICEQUEUE \land \\
\qquad (IsEmptyUSERPROCESSQUEUE \land RunIdleProcess \mathbin{;} CTXTSW) \\
\qquad \lor (DequeueUSERPROCESSQUEUE[n/p!] \land \\
\qquad\quad SetStateToRunning[n/p?] \land \\
\qquad\quad UpdateCurrentProcess[i/p?] \mathbin{;} CTXTSW) \setminus \{n\}) \\
\quad \lor (DequeueDEVICEQUEUE[d/p!] \land \\
\qquad SetStateToRunning[d/p?] \land \\
\qquad UpdateCurrentProcess[d/p?] \mathbin{;} CTXTSW) \setminus \{d\}
\end{array}
$$

Notice that *SKSchedNext* always stores in *prev* the identifier of the process that was current in its before state. After simplification, this operation can be written as

$$
\begin{array}{|l}
\hline
\Delta SKSCHED \\
\hline
(devq = \langle\rangle \wedge \\
\quad (procq = \langle\rangle \wedge \\
\quad\quad curr' = ip \wedge prev' = curr \wedge \\
\quad\quad state' = state \oplus \{ip \mapsto psrunning\} \fatsemi CTXTSW) \\
\quad \vee (state' = state \oplus \{head\ procq \mapsto psrunning\} \wedge \\
\quad\quad procq' = tail\ procq \wedge \\
\quad\quad curr' = head\ procq \wedge prev' = prev \fatsemi CTXTSW)) \\
\vee (devq' = tail\ devq \wedge \\
\quad state' = state \oplus \{head\ devq \mapsto psrunning\} \wedge \\
\quad curr' = head\ devq \wedge prev' = curr \fatsemi CTXTSW) \\
\hline
\end{array}
$$

Since this is such an important operation, its precondition must be calculated.

pre $SKSchedNext \mathrel{\widehat=} true$

The requeue operation just puts an unreadied process back onto the appropriate queue in the scheduler. Requeueing occurs, for example, when a user process has received data from a device request (e.g., received a data buffer from an input device). There are two versions of this operation, one each for user and device processes. Here, initially, is the requeue operation for user processes.

$RequeueUserProcess \mathrel{\widehat=}$
$\quad (SKSchedNext \fatsemi MakeReady)$

This definition expands into

$$
\begin{array}{|l}
\hline
RequeueUserProcess \\
\Delta SCHED \\
p? : PID \\
\hline
\exists procq'' : \mathrm{seq}\ PID;\ curr'', prev'' : PID;\ state'' : PID \pfun PSTATE \bullet \\
\quad ((devq = \langle\rangle \wedge \\
\quad\quad (procq = \langle\rangle \wedge \\
\quad\quad\quad curr' = ip \wedge prev' = curr \wedge \\
\quad\quad\quad state'' = state \oplus \{ip \mapsto psrunning\} \fatsemi CTXTSW) \\
\quad\quad \vee (state' = state \oplus \{head\ procq \mapsto psrunning\} \wedge \\
\quad\quad\quad procq'' = tail\ procq \wedge \\
\quad\quad\quad curr' = head\ procq \wedge prev' = curr \fatsemi CTXTSW)) \\
\quad \vee (devq' = tail\ devq \wedge \\
\quad\quad state'' = state \oplus \{head\ devq \mapsto psrunning\} \wedge \\
\quad\quad curr' = head\ devq \wedge prev' = curr \fatsemi CTXTSW)) \\
\quad \wedge procq' = procq'' \frown \langle p? \rangle \\
\quad \wedge state' = state'' \oplus \{p? \mapsto psready\} \\
\hline
\end{array}
$$

The operation deals only with user processes, so only that part of *SKSchedNext* is affected by simplification (this is also the reason for the omission of *devq* in the enclosing existential quantifier). The simplified operation is

$$
\begin{array}{l}
\textit{RequeueUserProcess} \\
\hline
\Delta SCHED \\
p? : PID \\
\hline
(devq = \langle\rangle \land \\
\quad (procq = \langle\rangle \land curr' = ip \land prev' = curr \land \\
\quad\quad state' = state \oplus \{ip \mapsto psrunning, p? \mapsto psready\} \land \\
\quad\quad procq' = \langle p? \rangle \\
\quad\quad {}_{9}^{\circ} CTXTSW) \\
\quad \lor (state' = state \oplus \{head\ procq \mapsto psrunning, p? \mapsto psready\} \land \\
\quad\quad procq' = (tail\ procq) \frown \langle p? \rangle \land \\
\quad\quad curr' = head\ procq \land prev' = curr \\
\quad\quad\quad {}_{9}^{\circ} CTXTSW)) \\
\lor (devq' = tail\ devq \land \\
\quad state' = state \oplus \{head\ devq \mapsto psrunning\} \land \\
\quad curr' = head\ devq \land prev' = curr \\
\quad {}_{9}^{\circ} CTXTSW) \\
\hline
\end{array}
$$

This is another important operation, so its precondition is calculated.

$$\text{pre } \textit{RequeueUserProcess} \mathrel{\widehat{=}} true$$

The requeue operation for device processes is now defined. Uses of this operation will be seen when the device-process interface is defined. The device-requeue operation is analogous to that for user processes, as can be seen from its definition.

$$
\begin{array}{l}
\textit{RequeueDeviceProcess} \mathrel{\widehat{=}} \\
\quad (\textit{SKSchedNext} \ {}_{9}^{\circ}\ \textit{ReadyDeviceProcess})
\end{array}
$$

The reader will undoubtedly notice the considerable similarity between the definiton of this operation and the corresponding one for user processes. The definition of *RequeueDeviceProcess* expands to

$$
\begin{array}{l}
\textit{RequeueDeviceProcess} \\
\hline
\Delta SKSCHED \\
p? : PID \\
\hline
\exists\, devq'' : seqPID;\ curr'', prev'' : PID;\ state'' : PID \twoheadrightarrow PSTATE \bullet \\
\quad (devq = \langle\rangle \land \\
\quad\quad (procq = \langle\rangle \land \\
\quad\quad\quad curr' = ip \land prev' = curr \land \\
\quad\quad\quad state'' = state \oplus \{ip \mapsto psrunning\} \ {}_{9}^{\circ}\ CTXTSW) \\
\quad\quad \lor (state'' = state \oplus \{head\ procq \mapsto psrunning\} \land \\
\quad\quad\quad procq' = tail\ procq \land
\end{array}
$$

$$
\begin{array}{l}
\qquad\qquad curr' = head\ procq \land prev' = curr \fatsemi CTXTSW)) \\
\lor\ (devq'' = tail\ devq \land \\
\qquad state'' = state \oplus \{head\ devq \mapsto psrunning\} \land \\
\qquad curr' = head\ devq \land prev' = curr \fatsemi CTXTSW) \\
\fatsemi \\
\qquad devq'' = devq \frown \langle p? \rangle \land \\
\qquad state' = state'' \oplus \{p? \mapsto psready\}
\end{array}
$$

Simplification of the above schema yields the following:

$$
\begin{array}{l}
\textit{RequeueDeviceProcess} \\
\Delta SKSCHED \\
p? : PID \\
\hline
(devq = \langle\rangle \land \\
\qquad devq' = \langle p? \rangle \land \\
\qquad (procq = \langle\rangle \land \\
\qquad\qquad curr' = ip \land prev' = curr \land \\
\qquad\qquad state' = state \oplus \{ip \mapsto psrunning, p? \mapsto psready\} \\
\qquad\qquad \fatsemi CTXTSW) \\
\qquad \lor\ (state' = state \oplus \{head\ procq \mapsto psrunning, p? \mapsto psready\} \land \\
\qquad\qquad procq' = tail\ procq \land \\
\qquad\qquad curr' = head\ procq \land prev' = curr \\
\qquad\qquad \fatsemi CTXTSW)) \\
\lor\ (devq' = (tail\ devq) \frown \langle p? \rangle \land \\
\qquad state' = state \oplus \{head\ devq \mapsto psrunning, p? \mapsto psready\} \land \\
\qquad curr' = head\ devq \land prev' = curr \fatsemi CTXTSW)
\end{array}
$$

Again, the precondition is required and is, therefore, calculated:

$$\text{pre } \textit{RequeueDeviceProcess} \mathrel{\widehat{=}} true$$

5.7 Storage Pools

The Separation Kernel requires storage allocation to be performed in a number of places:

- In main store when processes are allocated. This operation consists of allocating the store and partitioning it into the required number of segments (2 in the current scheme).
- Inside the kernel, to allocate buffer space for inter-process messages.

The same operations can be used to implement storage allocation in both contexts. Although this might not be ideal, due to the fact that the allocator was originally specified for the allocation and deallocation of small buffers and might not be optimal when operating on larger chunks of store, it shows how one specification can be employed in a number of contexts.

The error schemata are defined before the operations, as is our convention. There are 3 schemata.

The *NoSpace* operation sets the error varible when all the space in the pool has been allocated (this is probably going to be a rarely used operation).

$$\begin{array}{l} NoSpace \mathrel{\widehat=} \\ \quad (\exists\, e : SYSERR \mid e = nospaceinstore \bullet \\ \qquad SetSysErr[e/e?]) \land \\ \quad RaiseKillInterrupt \end{array}$$

5.7.1 Top Level

The top-level specification now follows. The specification introduces a state space (called *STOREPOOL*), its initialistion schema and the following operations:

- An allocation operation.
- A deallocation operation.
- A scavenge operation that is called periodically to merge any isolated free blocks.

The storage-freeing operation specified in this section is relatively naive. The basic idea behind it is that it merges blocks whenever possible. However, due to the fact that the order in which deallocation requests occur is unrelated to that in which blocks were allocated, it is possible for isolated blocks to be left in the pool. These isolated blocks count as storage leaks and must be collected and merged with other blocks. For this reason, the scavenge operation is included.

Before defining the operations, it is necessary to define a type.

The *MD* type is the *Memory Descriptor* type. It consists of the address of the start of a block of storage and the size of the block in bytes. An element of *MD* represents a block of storage.

$$MD = ADDR \times \mathbb{N}_1$$

It is necessary to define three operations: one to construct elements of *MD* (*mkmd*), one to access the address of the block (*mdaddr*) and one to access the block's size (*mdsz*). The definitions are simple and are as follows:

$$
\begin{array}{|l}
mkmd : ADDR \times \mathbb{N}_1 \to MD \\
mdaddr : MD \to ADDR \\
mdsz : MD \to \mathbb{N}_1 \\
\hline
\forall a : ADDR; \ sz : \mathbb{N}_1 \bullet \\
\qquad mkmd(a, sz) = (a, sz) \\
\forall m : MD \bullet \\
\qquad mdaddr(m) = fst \ m \\
\qquad mdsz(m) = snd \ m
\end{array}
$$

Next, the definition of the storage pool schema is given; it is called *STOREPOOL*:

$$
\begin{array}{|l}
\textit{STOREPOOL} \\
\hline
freebs : \mathrm{seq}\, MD \\
maxfree : \mathbb{N}_1 \\
alloc : \mathbb{N} \\
psize : \mathbb{N}_1 \\
scavthresh : \mathbb{N} \\
scavcnt : \mathbb{N} \\
\hline
(freebs = \langle\rangle \wedge alloc = psize) \\
\vee \ (freebs \neq \langle\rangle \wedge \\
\qquad \sum_{i=1}^{i=\#freebs} mdsz(freebs(i)) + alloc = psize) \\
\hline
\end{array}
$$

The schema is composed of the following components:

- *freebs*: A sequence of memory descriptors. The descriptors point into the area of storage that is to be operated upon. Elements of this sequence denote the free blocks in the storage area; initially, there is just one descriptor in the sequence.
- *maxfree*: The maximum number of free blocks permitted in the storage pool.
- *alloc*: The number of bytes currently allocated in the storage pool.
- *psize*: The size of the storage area in bytes.
- *scavthresh*: The scavenge threshold (see below).
- *scavcnt*: The scavenge count (see below).

The initialisation operation is as follows:

$$
\begin{array}{|l}
\textit{STOREPOOLInit} \\
\hline
STOREPOOL' \\
mf? : \mathbb{N}_1 \\
ba? : ADDR \\
ps? : \mathbb{N}_1
\end{array}
$$

$$
\begin{array}{|l}
scthrsh? : \mathbb{N} \\
\hline
maxfree' = mf? \\
psize' = ps? \\
alloc' = 0 \\
freebs' = \langle mkmd(ba?, ps?) \rangle \\
scavthresh' = scthrsh? \\
scavcnt' = 0 \\
\hline
\end{array}
$$

The amount allocated is set to 0 ($alloc' = 0$) and the various sizes are also set by input variables. The scavenger-related variables are set (see below).

The interesting part is the assignment to *freebs'*. A single element of type *MD* is assigned to the sequence. The *MD* element is composed of the start address of the storage pool (i.e., a pointer to the start of the pool), *ba*?, and the size of the pool in bytes, *ps*?. Initially, the storage pool is completely unallocated, so this memory descriptor correctly describes the initial situation.

The following operation checks that there is sufficient space left in the buffer pool and there are sufficient blocks remaining, it also tests that there is a block whose size is at least that requested.

$$
\begin{array}{|l}
\multicolumn{1}{l}{\_\_ CanAllocateBlock \_\_} \\
\Xi STOREPOOL \\
rqsz? : \mathbb{N}_1 \\
\hline
alloc + rqsz? \leq psize \\
\#freebs < maxfree \\
\exists i : 1 \mathinner{\ldotp\ldotp} \#freebs \bullet \\
\qquad mdsz(freebs(i)) \geq rqsz? \\
\hline
\end{array}
$$

The basic block allocation operation is now given.

$$
\begin{array}{|l}
\multicolumn{1}{l}{\_\_ AllocBlk \_\_} \\
\Delta STOREPOOL \\
rqsz? : \mathbb{N}_1 \\
a! : ADDR \\
\hline
\exists i : 1 \mathinner{\ldotp\ldotp} \#freebs \bullet \\
\qquad (mdsz(freebs(i)) = rqsz? \land \\
\qquad\qquad freebs' = freebs \rhd \{freebs(i)\} \land \\
\qquad\qquad alloc' = alloc + rqsz? \land \\
\qquad\qquad a! = mdaddr(freebs(i))) \\
\qquad \lor (mdsz(freebs(i)) > rqsz? \land \\
\qquad\qquad freebs' = \\
\qquad\qquad\qquad freebs \oplus \{i \mapsto \\
\qquad\qquad\qquad\qquad mkmd(mdaddr(freebs(i)) \\
\qquad\qquad\qquad\qquad\qquad +rqsz?, mdsz(freebs(i)) - rqsz?)\} \land
\end{array}
$$

$$
\begin{array}{l}
alloc = alloc + rqsz? \land \\
a! = mdaddr(freebs(i)))
\end{array}
$$

The operation works by iterating over the free blocks in *freebs*. If there is a block of identical size, it is returned; if there is a block of size greater than that requested, it is split into two.

The *AllocBlk* operation is important, so its precondition is calculated.

$$
\begin{array}{l}
\text{pre } AllocBlk \mathrel{\widehat{=}} \\
\quad \exists\, i : 1 \mathrel{..} \#freebs \bullet \\
\quad\quad mdsz(freebs(i)) \geq rqsz?
\end{array}
$$

The block-freeing operation is as follows. It works by iterating over the free blocks, looking for a block that starts immediately after or immediately before the one being freed. If there is no such block in the storage pool, the one being freed is added to the end of the *MD* list in *freebs*.

$$
\begin{array}{l}
\textbf{FreeBlk} \\
\hline
\Delta STOREPOOL \\
a? : ADDR \\
sz? : \mathbb{N}_1 \\
\hline
(\exists\, i : 1 \mathrel{..} \#freebs \bullet \\
\quad (mdaddr(freebs(i)) = a? + sz? \land \\
\quad\quad alloc' = alloc - sz? \land \\
\quad\quad freebs' = freebs \oplus \{i \mapsto mkmd(a?, mdsz(freebs(i)) + sz?)\}) \\
\quad \lor (mdaddr(freebs(i)) + mdsz(freebs(i)) = a? \land \\
\quad\quad alloc' = alloc - sz? \land \\
\quad\quad freebs' = \\
\quad\quad\quad freebs \oplus \{i \mapsto mkmd(mdaddr(freebs(i)), mdsz(freebs(i)) + sz?)\}) \\
\quad \lor (freebs' = freebs \frown \langle mkmd(a?, sz?)\rangle \land \\
\quad\quad alloc' = alloc - sz?)
\end{array}
$$

This operation's precondition is also required.

$$
\text{pre } FreeBlk \mathrel{\widehat{=}} true
$$

Finally, a block-scavenging operation is defined. This reduces the store as far as possible to a single block. This requires the following function

$$
\begin{array}{l}
mergemds : MD \times MD \rightarrow MD \\
\hline
\forall\, m_1, m_2 : MD \bullet \\
\quad mergemds(m_1, m_2) = mkmd(mdaddr(m_1), mdsz(m_1) + mdsz(m_2))
\end{array}
$$

The block scavenger operation is applied on a periodic basis. It iterates over the storage pool and tries to merge blocks wherever possible.

$$
\begin{array}{l}
\textit{BlockScavenge} \\
\hline
\Delta STOREPOOL \\
\hline
\forall i : 1 \mathrel{..} \# freebs \bullet \\
\quad \forall j : 1 \mathrel{..} \# freebs \mid i \neq j \bullet \\
\qquad [mdaddr(freebs(i)) + mdsz(freebs(i)) = mdaddr(freebs(j)) \land \\
\qquad\quad \exists freebs'' : \mathrm{seq}\, MD \bullet \\
\qquad\qquad freebs'' = freebs \rhd \{freebs(j)\} \land \\
\qquad\qquad freebs' = freebs'' \oplus \{i \mapsto mergemds(freebs(i), freebs(j))\}] \\
\qquad \lor [mdaddr(freebs(j)) + mdsz(freebs(j)) = mdaddr(freebs(i)) \land \\
\qquad\quad \exists freebs'' : \mathrm{seq}\, MD \bullet \\
\qquad\qquad freebs'' = freebs \rhd \{freebs(i)\} \land \\
\qquad\qquad freebs' = freebs \oplus \{j \mapsto mergemds(freebs(j), freebs(i))]
\end{array}
$$

The *BlockScavenge* operation's precondition must be calculated. It is:

$$
\begin{array}{l}
\mathrm{pre}\ BlockScavenge \mathrel{\widehat=} \\
\quad \forall i : 1 \mathrel{..} \# freebs \bullet \\
\qquad \forall j : 1 \mathrel{..} \# freebs \mid i \neq j \bullet \\
\qquad\quad mdaddr(freebs(i)) + mdsz(freebs(i)) = mdaddr(freebs(j)) \\
\qquad\quad \lor mdaddr(freebs(j)) + mdsz(freebs(j)) = mdaddr(freebs(i))
\end{array}
$$

The scavenger is triggered by a "scavenge counter". This counter is incremented when a deallocation is performed. It is:

$$
\begin{array}{l}
\textit{IncFreeCnt} \\
\hline
\Delta STOREVEC \\
\hline
scavcnt' = scavcnt + 1
\end{array}
$$

After a block scavenge operation is performed, the counter should be cleared. The following operation defines it:

$$
\begin{array}{l}
\textit{ClearFreeCnt} \\
\hline
\Delta STOREVEC \\
\hline
scavcnt' = 0
\end{array}
$$

When the scavenge counter reaches the threshold, the next operation, a predicate, is true.

$$
\begin{array}{l}
\textit{ShouldScavenge} \\
\hline
\Delta STOREVEC \\
\hline
scavcnt = scavthresh
\end{array}
$$

The specification is now complete and the refinement can start.

5.7.2 Refinement One

This is the first level of refinement.

Initially, a *nullmd* must be defined. It is clear that it should be the following unique definition:

$$nullmd : MD$$

$$nullmd = mkmd(0, 0)$$

The first refinement of the *STOREPOOL* schema is the following:

STOREPOOL1

$freebs1 : 1 \mathinner{..} maxfblocks \rightarrow MD$
$maxfblocks : \mathbb{N}_1$
$nextm : \mathbb{N}_1$
$alloc1 : \mathbb{N}$
$psize1 : \mathbb{N}$
$scavthresh1 : \mathbb{N}$
$scavcnt1 : \mathbb{N}$

$(nextm = 1 \land alloc1 = psize1)$
$\lor (nextm > 0 \land \sum_{i=1}^{i=nextm-1} mdsz(freebs1(i)) + alloc1 = psize1)$

The biggest difference between this schema and the one in the specification is that *freebs* is to be related to *freebs*1, whose type is $1 \mathinner{..} maxfblocks \rightarrow MD$, not seq *MD*.

Note that the variable *nextm* has been introduced. This variable is used to indicate the next element of *freebs*1 into which an *MD* can be stored. The *nextm* variable is used only when deallocating variables.

STOREPOOLInit1

$STOREPOOL1'$
$mf? : \mathbb{N}_1$
$ba? : ADDR$
$ps? : \mathbb{N}_1$
$scthrsh? : \mathbb{N}$

$maxfblocks' = mf?$
$psize1' = ps?$
$alloc1' = 0$
$nextm' = 2$
$freebs1'(1) = mkmd(ba?, ps?)$
$scavthresh1' = scthrsh?$
$scavcnt1' = 0$

The initialisation schema is as one would expect. The principle behind it is identical.

The next schema corresponds directly to the one in the specification.

$$
\begin{array}{l}
\textit{EnoughSpace1} \\
\hline
\Xi \mathit{STOREPOOL} \\
rqsz? : \mathbb{N}_1 \\
\hline
alloc1 + rqsz? \leq psize1
\end{array}
$$

The following schema also corresponds directly to *CanAllocateBlock*:

$$
\begin{array}{l}
\textit{CanAllocateBlock1} \\
\hline
\Xi \mathit{STOREPOOL1} \\
rqsz? : \mathbb{N}_1 \\
\hline
alloc1 + rqsz? \leq psize1 \\
nextm \leq maxfblocks \\
\exists i : 1 \mathinner{\ldotp\ldotp} nextm - 1 \bullet \\
\qquad mdsz(freebs1(i)) \geq rqsz?
\end{array}
$$

The allocation operation is now defined. It is also very close to the original specification, the differences being due to the different representation of the free block list.

$$
\begin{array}{l}
\textit{AllocBlk1} \\
\hline
\Delta \mathit{STOREPOOL1} \\
rqsz? : \mathbb{N}_1 \\
a! : ADDR \\
\hline
\exists i : 1 \mathinner{\ldotp\ldotp} nextm - 1 \bullet \\
\qquad (mdsz(freebs1(i)) = rqsz? \land \\
\qquad\qquad alloc1' = alloc1 + rqsz? \land \\
\qquad\qquad a! = mdaddr(freebs1(i)) \land \\
\qquad\qquad nextm' = nextm - 1 \land \\
\qquad\qquad \forall j : i \mathinner{\ldotp\ldotp} nextm - 2 \bullet \\
\qquad\qquad\qquad freebs1' = freebs1 \oplus \{j \mapsto freebs1(j + 1)\}) \\
\qquad \lor (mdsz(freebs1(i)) > rqsz? \land \\
\qquad\qquad alloc1' = alloc1 + rqsz? \land \\
\qquad\qquad a! = mdaddr(freebs1(i)) \land \\
\qquad\qquad freebs1' = \\
\qquad\qquad\qquad freebs1 \oplus \{i \mapsto \\
\qquad\qquad\qquad\qquad mkmd(mdaddr(freebs1(i)) + rqsz?, \\
\qquad\qquad\qquad\qquad\qquad mdsz(freebs1(i)) - rqsz?)\})
\end{array}
$$

The deallocation operation's schema refines to the following schema:

FreeBlk1

$$\Delta STOREPOOL1$$
$$a? : ADDR$$
$$sz? : \mathbb{N}_1$$

$$
\begin{array}{l}
(\exists i : 1 \mathrel{..} nextm - 1 \bullet \\
\quad (mdaddr(freebs1(i)) = a? + sz? \land \\
\qquad alloc1' = alloc1 - sz? \land \\
\qquad freebs1' = freebs1 \\
\qquad\quad \oplus \{i \mapsto mkmd(a?, mdsz(freebs1(i)) + sz?)\}) \\
\quad \lor (mdaddr(freebs1(i)) + mdsz(freebs1(i)) = a? \land \\
\qquad alloc1' = alloc1 - sz? \land \\
\qquad freebs1' = \\
\qquad\quad freebs1 \oplus \\
\qquad\qquad \{i \mapsto mkmd(mdaddr(freebs1(i)), mdsz(freebs1(i)) + sz?)\}) \\
\lor (freebs1' = freebs1 \oplus \{nextm \mapsto mkmd(a?, sz?)\} \land \\
\quad nextm' = nextm + 1 \land \\
\quad alloc1' = alloc1 - sz?)
\end{array}
$$

The different representation of the free list is quite clear from a comparison of this schema with the original specification.

Finally, the block scavenger's first refinement now follows:

BlockScavenge1

$$\Delta STOREPOOL$$

$$
\begin{array}{l}
\forall i : 1 \mathrel{..} nextm - 1 \bullet \\
\quad \forall j : 1 \mathrel{..} nextm - 1 \mid i \neq j \bullet \\
\qquad [mdaddr(freebs1(i)) + mdsz(freebs1(i)) = mdaddr(freebs1(j)) \land \\
\qquad\quad nextm' = nextm - 1 \land \\
\qquad\quad \exists freebs1'' : 1 \mathrel{..} maxfblocks \rightarrow MD \bullet \\
\qquad\qquad freebs1'' = freebs1 \mathbin{\rhd\!\!\!\!-} \{freebs1(j)\} \land \\
\qquad\qquad freebs1' = freebs1'' \oplus \{i \mapsto mergemds(freebs1(i), freebs1(j))\}] \\
\qquad \lor [mdaddr(freebs1(j)) + mdsz(freebs1(j)) = mdaddr(freebs1(i)) \land \\
\qquad\quad nextm' = nextm - 1 \land \\
\qquad\quad \exists freebs1'' : 1 \mathrel{..} maxfblocks \rightarrow MD \bullet \\
\qquad\qquad freebs1'' = freebs1 \mathbin{\rhd\!\!\!\!-} \{freebs1(i)\} \land \\
\qquad\qquad freebs1' = freebs1 \oplus \{j \mapsto mergemds(freebs1(j), freebs1(i))]
\end{array}
$$

$$
\begin{array}{l}
\text{pre } BlockScavenge \mathrel{\widehat{=}} \\
\quad \forall i : 1 \mathrel{..} nextm - 1 \bullet \\
\qquad \forall j : 1 \mathrel{..} nextm - 1 \mid i \neq j \bullet \\
\qquad\quad mdaddr(freebs1(i)) + mdsz(freebs1(i)) = mdaddr(freebs1(j)) \\
\qquad\quad \lor mdaddr(freebs1(j)) + mdsz(freebs1(j)) = mdaddr(freebs1(i))
\end{array}
$$

The refined scavenge count operations are now given.
First, the operation to increment the scavenge count.

$$
\begin{array}{l}
\textit{IncFreeCnt1} \\
\hline
\Delta STOREVEC1 \\
\hline
scavcnt1' = scavcnt1 + 1
\end{array}
$$

It is identical to the original specification, as is the schema to clear the scavenge count.

$$
\begin{array}{l}
\textit{ClearFreeCnt1} \\
\hline
\Delta STOREVEC1 \\
\hline
scavcnt1' = 0
\end{array}
$$

The schema defining the operation that determines whether a block scavenge should occur is also identical to the specification:

$$
\begin{array}{l}
\textit{ShouldScavenge1} \\
\hline
\Delta STOREVEC1 \\
\hline
scavcnt1 = scavthresh1
\end{array}
$$

That these 3 operations are identical to the specification should not come as too much of a surprise, for all 3 schemata perform simple operations on scalar variables. In each case, the variable name is different but operation is the same. This suggests how the abstraction relation will be defined. It is to this relation that we now turn.

The abstraction relation is defined by the following schema.

$$
\begin{array}{l}
\textit{AbsSTOREPOOL1} \\
\hline
STOREPOOL \\
STOREPOOL1 \\
\hline
alloc1 = alloc \\
psize1 = psize \\
maxfblocks = maxfree \\
\#freebs = nextm - 1 \\
\forall i : 1 \mathinner{..} \#freebs \bullet \\
\qquad freebs1(i) = freebs(i) \\
scavcnt1 = scavcnt \\
scavthresh1 = scavthresh
\end{array}
$$

The abstraction relation is an identity. The scalar variables are just renamed and so their refinement is not terribly interesting. The most interesting conjunct (if there is *anything* interesting about this relation, it is so straightforward) are:

$\#freebs = nextm - 1 \forall i : 1 \mathrel{..} \#freebs \bullet$
$\quad freebs1(i) = freebs(i)$

Here, the relationship between the index of the next free element of *freebs*1 and the length of *freebs* is defined. The *nextm* variable always points to the next element of *freebs*1 that can be used to store an *MD*; this corresponds to the next element after the end of *freebs*, so must be equal to $nextm - 1$.

The other conjunct relates the two free block lists. It states that all descriptors in the two representations of the list are identical.

Theorem 60.

$$\forall STOREPOOL'; STOREPOOL1' \bullet$$
$$STOREPOOLInit1 \land AbsSTOREPOOL1' \Rightarrow STOREPOOLInit$$

PROOF. It is immediate from the abstraction relation that $maxfblocks' = maxfree = mf?$, $alloc1' = alloc' = 0$ and $psize' = psize1' = ps?$.

The abstraction relation states that $nextm' = \#freebs' + 1$, so $nextm' = 2$ implies that $\#freebs = 1$, which, in turn, implies that $freebs' = 1$. The predicate of the abstraction relation requires that $freebs1'(i) = freebs'(i)$ for all $i \in 1 \mathrel{..} \#freebs'$ (or, equivalently $i \in 1 \mathrel{..} nextm' - 1$. Since $nextm' = 2$, $nextm' - 1 = 1$ and $freebs1'(1) = freebs'(1)$ ($= head\, freebs'$) and $freebs1'(1) = mkmd(ba?, ps?) = freebs'(1)$.

Finally, since $scavcnt1 = scavcnt$ and $scavthresh1 = scavthresh$, the proof is done. □

Theorem 61. $\forall STOREPOOL; STOREPOOL1; rqsz? : \mathbb{N}_1 \bullet pre\, AllocBlk \land AbsSTOREPOOL1 \Rightarrow pre\, AllocBlk1$

PROOF. The precondition of *AllocBlk* is

$$\exists i : 1 \mathrel{..} \#freebs \bullet mdsz(freebs(i)) \geq rqsz?$$

and that of *AllocBlk*1 is

$$\exists i : 1 \mathrel{..} nextm - 1 \bullet mdsz(freebs1(i)) \geq rqsz?$$

By the predicate of *AbsSTOREPOOL*1, $nextm = \#freebs + 1$, so $\#freebs = nextm - 1$. Since $1 \leq i \leq \#freebs$ (or, equivalently, $1 \leq i \leq nextm - 1$), by the abstraction relation, $freebs(i) = freebs1(i)$. The remainder is immediate. □

Theorem 62.

$$\forall STOREPOOL; STOREPOOL'; STOREPOOL1; STOREPOOL1';$$
$$rqsz? : \mathbb{N}_1; s! : ADDR \bullet$$
$$pre\, AllocBlk \land$$
$$AbsSTOREPOOL1 \land$$
$$AbsSTOREPOOL1' \land$$
$$AllocBlk1$$
$$\Rightarrow AllocBlk$$

PROOF. First, that the ranges of the quantifiers are identical can be seen from the following. By the predicate of $AbsSTOREPOOL1$, $nextm = \#freebs + 1$, so $\#freebs = nextm - 1$. Next, by the same predicate, $alloc = alloc1$, so $alloc1 + rqsz? = alloc + rqsz?$, while the predicate of $AbsSTOREPOOL1'$ requires that $alloc' = alloc1'$, so $alloc1 + rqsz? = alloc + rqsz? = alloc1' = alloc'$.

For the reason that $1 \leq i \leq nextm - 1$, or equivalently that $1 \leq i \leq \#freebs$, $freebs1(i) = freebs(i)$ and $freebs1'(i) = freebs'(i)$ by the predicates of the two abstraction schemata. From this, it can be inferred that $mdsz(freebs1(i)) = rqsz? = mdsz(freebs(i))$, $mdsz(freebs1(i)) > rqsz?$ implies $mdsz(freebs(i)) > rqsz?$ and $mdaddr(freebs1(i)) = mdaddr(freebs(i))$. A consequence of the last is that $a! = mdaddr(freebs1(i)) = mdaddr(freebs(i))$.

All that remains is the equivalence of $\forall j : i \mathinner{..} nextm - 2 \bullet freebs1' = freebs1 \oplus \{j \mapsto freebs1(j+1)\}$ and $freebs' = freebs \rhd \{freebs(i)\}$ (the update in the second disjunct is a simple consequence of the abstraction relations and the range condition, $1 \leq i \leq \#freebs$). It should be clear that $freebs1'(i) = freebs1(i+1)$; that is, $freebs1' = freebs1 \rhd \{freebs1(i)\}$ and the abstraction relations permit the proof to be completed. □

Theorem 63.

$$\forall STOREPOOL; STOREPOOL1; a : ADDR; sz? : \mathbb{N}_1 \bullet$$
$$pre\ FreeBlk \land AbsSTOREPOOL1 \Rightarrow pre\ FreeBlk1$$

PROOF. Trivial. □

Theorem 64.

$$\forall STOREPOOL; STOREPOOL'; STOREPOOL1; STOREPOOL1';$$
$$a : ADDR; sz? : \mathbb{N}_1 \bullet$$
$$pre\ FreeBlk \land$$
$$AbsSTOREPOOL1 \land$$
$$AbsSTOREPOOL1' \land$$
$$FreeBlk1$$
$$\Rightarrow FreeBlk$$

PROOF. The quantifier range $1 \mathinner{..} nextm - 1$ is equivalent, by the predicate of $AbsSTOREPOOL1$, to $1 \mathinner{..} \#freebs$ since $nextm = \#freebs + 1$.

The rest of the proof divides into three cases. However, in all cases, the equation $alloc1' = alloc1 - sz?$ occurs. By the predicate of the abstraction relation, $AbsSTOREPOOL1$, $alloc1 = alloc$ and by the predicate of $AbsSTOREPOOL1'$, $alloc1' = alloc'$, so $alloc1' = alloc1 - sz? = alloc - sz? = alloc'$.

It should be noted that in all three cases, $1 \leq i \leq nextm - 1$, by the predicate of the abstraction relation $AbsSTOREPOOL1$, is equivalent to $1 \leq i \leq \#freebs$, so i is always in range. This has the implication, by the predicates

of the two abstraction relations, that $freebs(i) = freebs1(i)$ and $freebs'(i) = freebs1'(i)$.
Case 1. $mdaddr(freebs1(i)) = a? + sz?$. By the above remarks, this is clearly equivalent to $mdaddr(freebs(i)) = a? + sz?$. The update of $freebs1$ follows (RHS) from the fact that i is in the range $1 \mathrel{..} nextm - 1$ or, equivalently, to $1 \mathrel{..} \#freebs$ and (LHS) from the fact that $freebs1'(i) = freebs'(i)$, $1 \leq i \leq nextm - 1$.
Case 2. Similar to Case 1.
Case 3. First, it is clear that $nextm - 1 = nextm' = \#freebs' = \#freebs - 1$, since, by $AbsSTOREPOOL1$, $nextm = \#freebs{+}1$ and, by $AbsSTOREPOOL1$, $nextm' = \#freebs' + 1$. Finally, letting m denote $mkmd(a?, sz?)$,

$$
\begin{aligned}
& freebs1' \\
& \quad = freebs1 \oplus \{nextm \mapsto m\} \\
& \quad = freebs \oplus \{nextm \mapsto m\} \\
& \quad = freebs \oplus \{\#freebs + 1 \mapsto m\} \\
& \quad = freebs \cup \{\#freebs + 1 \mapsto m\} \\
& \quad = freebs \frown \langle m \rangle \\
& \quad = freebs'
\end{aligned}
$$

where, $nextm = \#freebs + 1$. The equivalence of the first and last lines is a consequence of $AbsSTOREPOOL1'$. The fourth to sixth lines are justified by the fact that $nextm = \#freebs + 1$ and $\#freebs + 1 \notin \operatorname{dom} freebs$, so $freebs \oplus \{\#freebs{+}1 \mapsto m\} = freebs \cup \{\#freebs{+}1 \mapsto m\}$; it is also the case that $(freebs \cup \{\#freebs{+}1 \mapsto m\})(\#freebs) = last\ freebs$, while $(freebs \cup \{\#freebs \mapsto m\})(\#freebs + 1) = m$ or $last\ freebs' = m$; therefore, $freebs' = freebs \frown \langle m \rangle$.
□

Theorem 65.

$$
\begin{aligned}
& \forall STOREPOOL;\ STOREPOOL1 \bullet \\
& \quad pre\ BlockScavenge \land AbsSTOREPOOL1 \Rightarrow pre\ BlockScavenge1
\end{aligned}
$$

PROOF. Since, by the abstraction relation, $1 \leq i, j \leq next - 1$ iff $1 \leq i, j \leq \#freebs$, $freebs(i) = freebs1(i)$ and $freebs(j) = freebs1(j)$. The remainder is trivial. □

Theorem 66.

$$
\begin{aligned}
& \forall STOREPOOL;\ STOREPOOL';\ STOREPOOL1;\ STOREPOOL1' \bullet \\
& \quad pre\ BlockScavenge \land \\
& \qquad AbsSTOREPOOL1 \land \\
& \qquad AbsSTOREPOOL1' \land \\
& \qquad BlockScavenge1 \\
& \quad \Rightarrow BlockScavenge
\end{aligned}
$$

PROOF. By the predicates of $AbsSTOREPOOL1$ and $AbsSTOREPOOL1'$ and by the fact that, given $AbsSTOREPOOL1$, $1 \leq i, j \leq next - 1$ iff $1 \leq i, j \leq \#freebs$, $freebs(i) = freebs1(i)$ and $freebs(j) = freebs1(j)$ and, furthermore, $freebs'(i) = freebs1'(i)$ and $freebs'(j) = freebs1'(j)$. The result then follows using the definition of *mergemds*. □

The rest of the refined operations are trivially related to the top-level specification and the associated proofs are also trivial (simple identities), so they are omitted.

5.8 Raw Storage

The last section dealt with a storage allocator. The current section deals with the storage itself. The specification is quite obvious.

First, the necessary error schema is defined. It sets the error variable whenever an attempt to address a block fails.

$$\begin{aligned}
&BlockLocError \mathrel{\widehat=} \\
&\quad (\exists\, e : SYSERR \mid e = blocklocerror \bullet \\
&\qquad SetSysErr[e/e?]) \land \\
&\quad RaiseKillInterrupt
\end{aligned}$$

The specification requires the definition of a new type, *PSU*:

$[PSU]$

This is the *Primary Storage Unit.* On some machines it is a byte and on others it is a 16-, 32- or 64-bit word.

5.8.1 Top level

The schema representing raw storage is as follows:

$$\begin{array}{|l}
\hline
STOREVEC \\
\hline
sv : 1 \mathinner{\ldotp\ldotp} svsize \rightarrow PSU \\
svsize : \mathbb{N}_1 \\
startaddr : ADDR \\
scavcnt : \mathbb{N} \\
scavthresh : \mathbb{N}_1 \\
\hline
\end{array}$$

The store proper is represented by sv. The size of the store (in terms of PSU) is given by $svsize$. The store starts at address $startaddr$. The remaining two variables are used for storage management.

This schema can be directly implemented as code, as, indeed, can the operations defined over it. There is no refinement required in the case of $STOREVEC$ and its associated operations.

The initialisation operation is given by the schema:

$$
\begin{array}{|l}
\hline
\textit{STOREVECInit} \\
\hline
\textit{STOREVEC}' \\
ps? : \mathbb{N}_1 \\
sa? : \textit{ADDR} \\
\hline
svsize' = ps? \\
startaddr' = sa? \\
\hline
\end{array}
$$

The following schema defines a predicate that is true when the address, *loc*?, plus the block size, *sz*?, is within the storage area being modelled.

$$
\begin{array}{|l}
\hline
\textit{CanStoreBlock} \\
\hline
\Xi \textit{STOREVEC} \\
loc? : \textit{ADDR} \\
sz? : \mathbb{N}_1 \\
\hline
startaddr \leq loc? \\
loc? + sz? \leq startaddr + svsize \\
\hline
\end{array}
$$

The next schema defines an operation that copies a block of store from one location to another.

$$
\begin{array}{|l}
\hline
\textit{CopyBlock} \\
\hline
\Delta \textit{STOREVEC} \\
v? : 1 \mathrel{..} sz? \rightarrow \textit{PSU} \\
loc? : \textit{ADDR} \\
sz? : \mathbb{N}_1 \\
\hline
\exists\, a : 1 \mathrel{..} svsize \mid a = startaddr - loc? \bullet \\
\quad \forall\, i : 1 \mathrel{..} sz? \bullet \\
\qquad sv' = sv \oplus \{a + (i - 1) \mapsto v?(i)\} \\
\hline
\end{array}
$$

The entire block is passed as *v*? and the destination address is passed as *loc*? and its size is passed as *sz*?.

The *CopyBlock* operation is unsafe in the sense that it performs no checks that the address and size passed to it are correct in the sense that the start and end of the block are inside the storage area to which the block is to be copied.

$$
\begin{array}{l}
\textit{StoreBlock} \mathrel{\widehat{=}} \\
\quad (\textit{CanStoreBlock} \land \textit{CopyBlock} \land \textit{SysOk}) \\
\quad \lor \textit{BlockLocError}
\end{array}
$$

The definition expands into

$$
\begin{array}{|l}
\hline
\textit{StoreBlock} \\
\Delta STOREVEC \\
\Delta ERRV \\
\Delta HW \\
v? : 1 \mathrel{..} sz? \rightarrow PSU \\
loc? : ADDR \\
sz? : \mathbb{N}_1 \\
\hline
(startaddr \leq loc? \land \\
\quad loc? + sz? \leq startaddr + svsize \land \\
\quad (\exists a : 1 \mathrel{..} svsize \mid a = startaddr - loc? \bullet \\
\qquad \forall i : 1 \mathrel{..} sz? \bullet \\
\qquad\quad sv' = sv \oplus \{a + (i - 1) \mapsto v?(i)) \land \\
\quad serr' = sysok) \\
\lor (serr' = blocklocerror \land intno' = killintno) \\
\hline
\end{array}
$$

The following operation is a checking operation. It returns a block of storage that has been stored in the vector. The returned block is bound to $v!$ and its size is $sz?$; the address at which the block starts in the storage vector is $addr?$.

$$
\begin{array}{|l}
\hline
\textit{StoredBlock} \\
\Xi STOREVEC \\
\Delta ERRV \\
\Delta HW \\
addr? : ADDR \\
sz? : \mathbb{N} \\
v! : 1 \mathrel{..} sz? \rightarrow PSU \\
\hline
(startaddr \leq addr? \land \\
\quad addr? + sz? \leq startaddr + svsize \land \\
\quad (\exists v : 1 \mathrel{..} sz? \rightarrow PSU \bullet \\
\qquad (\forall i : 1 \mathrel{..} sz? \bullet \\
\qquad\quad v(i) = sv(addr? + i)) \land \\
\qquad\quad v! = v) \land \\
\quad serr' = sysok) \\
\lor (serr' = badblockaddr \land intno' = killintno) \\
\hline
\end{array}
$$

The simplification is omitted because it will be used in the expansion and simplification of the next schema.

5.8.2 Message Buffering

This subsection contains the definitions required to turn the storage vector just defined into an area of store that can be used to represent a buffer pool suitable for use by a message-passing system. The basic definitions are performed by renaming existing components.

First, we define the storage area for messages. This is done in terms of renaming, using the *STOREVEC* state schema and its associated operations. Note that renaming, in effect, provides us with a new copy of *STOREVEC*.

It is necessary for the reader to remember that the definitions that follow are of the storage area *only*. The storage-management operations will be defined at this subsection.

$$MSGSTORE \mathrel{\widehat=} STOREVEC[mv/sv, mvsize/svsize, mstartaddr/startaddr,\\ mscavcnt/scavcnt, mscavthresh/scavthresh]$$

$$MSGSTOREInit \mathrel{\widehat=} STOREVECInit\\ [MSGSTORE'/STOREVEC', mps?/ps?, msa?/sa?]$$

$$CanStoreMsg \mathrel{\widehat=} CanStoreBlock[MSGSTORE/STOREVEC]$$

$$StoreMsg \mathrel{\widehat=} StoreBlock[MSGSTORE/STOREVEC]$$

$$StoredMsg \mathrel{\widehat=} StoredBlock[MSGSTORE/STOREVEC]$$

In these definitions, as in the ones that occur at the end of this subsection, it is assumed that the substitution of the name of the new state schema (*MSGSTORE*) for the basic one (*STOREVEC*) also substitutes the appropriate state variables, thus renaming the variables. This convention applies to *CanStoreMsg*, *StoreMsg* and *StoredMsg*.

The operation to delete stored messages must perform checking. It is defined as:

$$\begin{array}{l} DeleteStoredMsg \mathrel{\widehat=} \\ \quad (\exists\, sz : \mathbb{N} \mid sz = msgsz(msgat(a?)) \bullet \\ \quad\quad (StoredMsg[a?/addr?, m/v!, sz/sz?] \land \\ \quad\quad\quad FreeMsg)) \\ \quad ⨾ (IncMsgFreeCnt \land \\ \quad\quad ((ShouldScavengeMsgs \land MsgScavenge) ⨾ ClearMsgFreeCnt)) \end{array}$$

After expansion and simplification, this operation can be transformed into

$$
\begin{array}{|l}
\hline
\textit{DeleteStoredMsg} \\
\Delta MSGSTORE \\
\Delta STOREPOOL \\
\Delta ERRV \\
\Delta HW \\
a? : ADDR \\
\hline
(startaddr \leq a? \land \\
\quad a? + msgsz(msgat(a?)) \leq startaddr + svsize \land \\
\quad (\forall i : 1 \mathinner{\ldotp\ldotp} msgsz(msgat(a?)) \bullet \\
\qquad v!(i) = sv(a? + i)) \land \\
\quad FreeMsg \\
\quad \fatsemi (scavcnt = scavthresh - 1 \land \\
\qquad MsgScavenge \land \\
\qquad scavcnt' = 0) \\
\quad serr' = sysok) \\
\lor (serr' = badblockaddr \land intno' = killintno) \\
\hline
\end{array}
$$

Since it is known that *FreeBlk*1 is a proper refinement of *FreeBlk* and that *BlockScavenge*1 properly refines *BlockScavenge*, and noting that *STOREVEC* does not refine any further, the above can immediately be refined to

$$
\begin{array}{|l}
\hline
\textit{DeleteStoredMsg} \\
\Delta MSGSTORE \\
\Delta STOREPOOL1 \\
\Delta ERRV \\
\Delta HW \\
a? : ADDR \\
\hline
(startaddr \leq a? \land \\
\quad a? + msgsz(msgat(a?)) \leq startaddr + svsize \land \\
\quad (\forall i : 1 \mathinner{\ldotp\ldotp} msgsz(msgat(a?)) \bullet \\
\qquad v!(i) = sv(a? + i)) \land \\
\quad FreeMsg1 \\
\quad \fatsemi (scavcnt = scavthresh - 1 \land \\
\qquad MsgScavenge1 \land \\
\qquad scavcnt' = 0) \\
\quad serr' = sysok) \\
\lor (serr' = badblockaddr \land intno' = killintno) \\
\hline
\end{array}
$$

The remaining storage-area operations are defined as follows. In these and the next set of definitions, the renaming convention we described above is assumed.

$IncMsgFreeCnt \mathrel{\widehat=} IncFreeCnt[MSGSTORE/STOREVEC]$
$ShouldScavengeMsgs \mathrel{\widehat=} ShouldScavenge[MSGSTORE/STOREVEC]$
$ClearMsgFreeCnt \mathrel{\widehat=} ClearFreeCnt[MSGSTORE/STOREVEC]$

The next set of operations deal with storage management. The state space is called *MSGPOOL* and corresponds to *STOREPOOL*. The same renaming convention is assumed here as for *MSGSTORE*.

$$
\begin{aligned}
&MSGPOOL \mathrel{\widehat=} STOREPOOL[msgbs/freebs, mgfree/maxfree,\\
&\qquad msgalloc/alloc, mpsize/psize,\\
&\qquad mscavthresh/scavthresh, mscavcnt/scavcnt]\\
&MSGPOOLInit \mathrel{\widehat=} STOREPOOLInit[MSGPOOL/STOREPOOL,\\
&\qquad mmf?/mf?, mba?/ba?, mps?/ps?, mscthrsh?/scthrsh?]\\
&CanAllocateMsg \mathrel{\widehat=} CanAllocateBlock[MSGPOOL/STOREPOOL]\\
&AllocMsg \mathrel{\widehat=} AllocBlk[MSGPOOL/STOREPOOL]\\
&FreeMsg \mathrel{\widehat=} FreeBlk[MSGPOOL/STOREPOOL]\\
&MsgScavenge \mathrel{\widehat=} BlockScavenge[MSGPOOL/STOREPOOL]
\end{aligned}
$$

5.9 Message Queues

The separation kernel is intended as a simulation of a distributed system. In distributed systems, asynchronous message passing is the norm.

The specification begins, as usual, with the error schemata.

Each process has a message queue. If the queue becomes full and an attempt is made to enqueue another message, the following schema is used.

$$
\begin{aligned}
&MessageQueueFull \mathrel{\widehat=}\\
&\quad (\exists e : SYSERR \mid e = msgqfull \bullet\\
&\qquad SetSysErr[e/e?]) \land\\
&\quad RaiseKillInterrupt
\end{aligned}
$$

If an attempt is made to dequeue a message from an empty message queue, the following operation is used to signal the error.

$$
\begin{aligned}
&EmptyMessageQueue \mathrel{\widehat=}\\
&\quad (\exists e : SYSERR \mid e = emptymsgq \bullet\\
&\qquad SetSysErr[e/e?]) \land\\
&\quad RaiseKillInterrupt
\end{aligned}
$$

This message-passing system allows processes to ask for messages from a designated source. The following schema sets the error variable when there are no messages from the designated source.

$$
\begin{aligned}
&NoMessagesFrom \mathrel{\widehat=}\\
&\quad (\exists e : SYSERR \mid e = nomsgsfrom \bullet\\
&\qquad SetSysErr[e/e?]) \land\\
&\quad RaiseKillInterrupt
\end{aligned}
$$

5.9.1 Top Level

The specification can now be undertaken. Basically, the requirement is that a FIFO queue of message structures is to be specified. The specification that follows differs from many others in an important aspect. Instead of operating on message-representing structures, this specification consists of schemata defining operations over message *pointers*. The queue is, here, a queue of pointers to messages and the dequeue operation returns a *pointer* to a message; clearly, the enqueue operation adds a *pointer* to a message to the queue. This has the implication that we must, at some stage, specify the way in which messages are stored.

The following function creates a message. It requires the source and destination process identifiers and some data.

$$mkmsg : PID \times (PID \times MSGDATA)$$

$$\forall\, src, dest : PID;\; data : MSGDATA \bullet$$
$$\quad mkmsg(src, dest, data) = (src, (dest, data))$$

The length of message payloads (the data component) is given by the first of the following two functions. The second function returns the length of the message header; for any system, this function should be a constant.

$$msgpayloadlen : MSG \rightarrow \mathbb{N}$$
$$msghdrlen : MSG \rightarrow \mathbb{N}_1$$

The *message header* is composed of the source and destination slots (it might also contain the length of the payload). The header imposes a fixed overhead on messages and will always be the same.

These two functions are not further specified.

Given the structure of a message as a product, it is possible to give definitions for the functions that return the source, destination and data components of a message:

$$msgsrc : MSG \rightarrow PID$$
$$msgdest : MSG \rightarrow PID$$
$$msgdata : MSG \rightarrow MSGDATA$$

$$\forall\, m : MSG \bullet$$
$$\quad msgsrc(m) = fst\ m$$
$$\quad msgdest(m) = fst(snd\ m)$$
$$\quad msgdata(m) = snd(snd\ m)$$

The address of a message structure is given by the following (partially-defined) function:

$$msgaddr : MSG \rightarrow ADDR$$

The total size of the message is the size of the payload plus the size of the header. It is computed by the following function.

$$msgsz : MSG \rightarrow \mathbb{N}_1$$

$$\forall m : MSG \bullet \quad msgsz(m) = msgpayloadlen(m) + msghdrlen(m)$$

Below, the *MPTR* type is defined. It is the type of message pointers. The *msgat* function takes a message pointer and returns the message that is located at that address; if the pointer is null, *msgat* returns the null message. Other than that, the function is not further defined.

$$msgat : MPTR \rightarrow MSG$$

$$\forall mp : MPTR \bullet \quad msgat(nullmptr) = nullmsg \quad \ldots$$

$$msgToPSU : MSG \rightarrow \operatorname{seq} PSU$$
$$PSUsToMsg : \operatorname{seq} PSU \rightarrow MSG$$

These two functions are just type-changing functions or casts.

$$msz : MSG \rightarrow \mathbb{N}$$

$$\forall m : MSG \bullet \quad msz(m) = \begin{cases} 0, & \text{if } m = nullmsg \\ msgsz(m), & \text{otherwise} \end{cases}$$

We need to get down to the byte level in this specification and its refinement.

$$BYTE == 0 \,..\, 255$$

$$msgtobytes : MSG \rightarrow \operatorname{seq} BYTE$$

This is used by the copy operation.

The message pointer type is a subset of *ADDR*:

$$MPTR \subset ADDR$$

The null message pointer:

$$nullmptr : MPTR$$

Message queues are implemented by a slot in the *PTAB*. The definition at the top level is the following.

$$\begin{array}{|l}
\hline
\textit{PTAB} \\
\ldots \\
msgq : PID \rightarrowtail\!\!\!\!\!\!+ MSGQ \\
\ldots \\
\hline
\mathrm{dom}\ msgq = used \\
\hline
\end{array}$$

The usual constraint is imposed upon the domain of *msgq*.

In the following, the subscript, M, is used. In the schema, all components of *PTAB* that do not relate to *msgq* are assumed constant. This differentiates this schema from all others.

$$\begin{array}{|l}
\hline
\Phi PTAB_M \\
\Delta PTAB \\
\Delta MSGQ \\
p? : PID \\
\hline
\theta MSGQ = msgq(p?) \\
msgq' = msgq \oplus \{p? \mapsto \theta MSGQ'\} \\
\hline
\end{array}$$

The message queue proper is defined by the following schema. Note that there is a limit to the size of the queue. The queue obeys the FIFO discipline and there can be duplicates; a simple sequence is the obvious representation.

$$\begin{array}{|l}
\hline
MSGQ \\
mq : \mathrm{seq}\, MPTR \\
maxms : \mathbb{N}_1 \\
\hline
\# mq \leq maxms \\
\hline
\end{array}$$

The initialisation schema is defined in the obvious manner.

$$\begin{array}{|l}
\hline
MSGQInit \\
MSGQ' \\
mm? : \mathbb{N}_1 \\
\hline
maxms' = mm? \\
mq' = \langle\, \rangle \\
\hline
\end{array}$$

The schema that follows defines the operation that answers the question: is there enough space in the queue for a new message?

$$\begin{array}{|l}
\hline
CanEnqueueMsg \\
\Xi MSGQ \\
\hline
\# mq < maxms \\
\hline
\end{array}$$

The enqueue operation simply adds a new message to the end of the queue:

EnqueueMsg

$\Delta MSGQ$
$mp? : MPTR$

$mq' = mq \frown \langle mp? \rangle$

As with process queues, the dequeue operation is decomposed into obtaining the queue head and removing it. The complete operation is given by the following schema:

DelMSGQHd

$\Delta MSGQ$
$mp! : MPTR$

$mp! = head\ mq$
$mq' = tail\ mq$

GotMsgs

$\Xi MSGQ$

$mq \neq \langle\rangle$

This is a predicate which is true if there are any messages left in the queue.

GotMsgsFromSrc

$\Xi MSGQ$
$src? : PID$

$\exists i : 1 \mathrel{..} \#mq \bullet$
$\quad msgsrc(msgat(mq(i))) = src?$

This is a predicate which is true when the message queue is not empty and there is at least one message from process *src*?. This is the first point where the fact that the entries of the *mq* FIFO are message pointers becomes important.

In addition to *GotMsgsFromSrc*, there is the *NextMsgFromSrc* operation. It is used when there are messages and at least one is from the destination specified by *src*?. The message is returned as *mp*!.

NextMsgFromSrc

$\Delta MSGQ$
$src? : PID$
$mp! : MPTR$

$\exists i : 1 \mathrel{..} \#mq;\ q_1, q_2 : \mathrm{seq}\ MPTR \bullet$
$\quad \exists m : MPTR \mid m = mq(i) \bullet$
$\qquad q_1 \frown \langle m \rangle \frown q_2 = mq \land$

$$
\begin{array}{l}
\quad q_1 \frown q_2 = mq' \land \\
\quad msgsrc(msgat(mq(i))) = src? \land \\
\quad mp! = m \land \\
\quad (\forall j : 1 \mathrel{..} i-1 \bullet \\
\qquad msgsrc(msgat(mq(j))) \neq src?)
\end{array}
$$

The precondition is clearly

$$
\begin{array}{l}
\text{pre } NextMsgFromSrc \mathrel{\widehat=} \\
\quad mq \neq \langle\rangle \land \\
\quad \exists\, m : MSG \mid m \in \operatorname{ran} mq \bullet \\
\qquad msgsrc(msgat(m)) = src?
\end{array}
$$

The operation to add a message to the queue is defined as follows:

$$
\begin{array}{l}
AddMsg \mathrel{\widehat=} \\
\quad \exists\, sz : \mathbb{N} \mid sz = msgsz(m?) \bullet \\
\qquad (CanAllocateBlock[sz/rqsz?] \land \\
\qquad\quad ((CanEnqueueMsg \land \\
\qquad\qquad AllocMsg[sz/rqsz?, m/a!] \land \\
\qquad\qquad (\exists\, v : 1 \mathrel{..} \mathbb{N}_1 \to PSU;\ sz : \mathbb{N}_1 \\
\qquad\qquad\qquad \mid v = msgToPSU(m?) \land sz = msgsz(m?) \bullet \\
\qquad\qquad\quad StoreMsg[v/v?, m/loc?, sz/sz?]) \land \\
\qquad\qquad EnqueueMsg[m/mp!] \land \\
\qquad\qquad SysOk) \\
\qquad\quad \lor MessageQueueFull)) \setminus \{m\} \\
\qquad \lor NoSpace
\end{array}
$$

The operation checks whether a buffer can be allocated (if not, the operation aborts—why continue when the store cannot be allocated?); if it can, the operation tests that there is space left in the destination process' message queue. Next, the message is allocated a buffer and stored; it is then enqueued.

The schema for the operation expands and simplifies to:

$$
\begin{array}{l}
\textit{AddMsg} \\
\hline
\Delta MSGQ \\
\Delta ERRV \\
\Delta HW \\
m? : MSG \\
\hline
(alloc + msgsz(m?) \leq psize \land \#freebs < maxfree \land \\
\quad (\#mq < maxms \land \\
\qquad ((\exists\, i : 1 \mathrel{..} \#freebs \bullet \\
\qquad\quad msgsz(freebs(i)) \geq msgsz(m?) \land \\
\qquad\quad (mdsz(freebs(i)) = msgsz(m?) \land \\
\qquad\qquad freebs' = freebs \lhd \{freebs(i)\} \land
\end{array}
$$

$$
\begin{array}{l}
\quad\quad alloc' = alloc + msgsz(m?) \land \\
\quad\quad mq' = mq \frown \langle mdaddr(freebs(i)) \rangle \land \\
\quad\quad startaddr \leq mdaddr(freebs(i)) \land \\
\quad\quad mdaddr(freebs(i)) + msgsz(m?) \leq startaddr + svsize \land \\
\quad\quad \forall j : 1 \mathrel{..} msgsz(m?) \bullet \\
\quad\quad\quad sv' = sv \oplus \{(startaddr - mdaddr(freebs(i))) + (j - 1) \\
\quad\quad\quad\quad\quad \mapsto msgToPSU(m?)(j)\}) \\
\quad \lor (mdsz(freebs(i)) > msgsz(m?) \land \\
\quad\quad freebs' = freebs \oplus \{i \mapsto \\
\quad\quad\quad mkmd(mdaddr(freebs(i)) + msgsz(m?), \\
\quad\quad\quad\quad mdsz(freebs(i)) - msgsz(m?))\} \land \\
\quad\quad alloc' = alloc + msgsz(m?) \land \\
\quad\quad mq' = mq \frown \langle mdaddr(freebs(i)) \rangle \land \\
\quad\quad startaddr \leq mdaddr(freebs(i)) \land \\
\quad\quad mdaddr(freebs(i)) + msgsz(m?) \leq startaddr + svsize \land \\
\quad\quad \forall j : 1 \mathrel{..} msgsz(m?) \bullet \\
\quad\quad\quad sv' = sv \oplus \{(startaddr - mdaddr(freebs(i))) + (j - 1) \\
\quad\quad\quad\quad \mapsto msgToPSU(m?)(j)\})) \land \\
\quad\quad serr' = sysok) \\
\quad \lor (serr' = msgqfull \land intno' = killintno) \\
\lor (serr' = nospaceinstore \land intno' = killintno))
\end{array}
$$

The precondition must be calculated. It is:

$$
\begin{array}{l}
\text{pre } AddMsg \mathrel{\widehat=} \\
\quad alloc + msgsz(m?) < psize \land \#mq < maxms \land \\
\quad (\exists i : 1 \mathrel{..} \#freebs \bullet msgsz(freebs(i)) \geq msgsz(m?)) \land \\
\quad\quad startaddr \leq mdaddr(freebs(i)) \land \\
\quad\quad mdaddr(freebs(i)) + msgsz(m?) \leq startaddr + svsize
\end{array}
$$

The *NextMsg* operation is, basically, a dequeue operation. It tests that there are messages in the queue and returns the head. If there are no messages, *EmptyMessageQueue* is used).

$$
\begin{array}{l}
NextMsg \mathrel{\widehat=} \\
\quad (GotMsgs \land DelMSGQHd \land SysOk) \lor EmptyMessageQueue
\end{array}
$$

The operation expands into

$$
\begin{array}{l}
\underline{\quad NextMsg \quad} \\
\Delta MSGQ \\
\Delta ERRV \\
\Delta HW \\
mp! : MPTR \\
\hline
(mq \neq \langle\rangle \land mp! = head\ mq \land mq' = tail\ mq \land serr' = sysok) \\
\lor (serr' = emptymsgq \land intno' = killintno)
\end{array}
$$

The precondition is

$$\text{pre}\ NextMsg \mathrel{\widehat=} mq \neq \langle\,\rangle$$

The following is similar to *NextMsg* but, instead of returning just the head, it returns the first element of the queue that is from the designated source. The operation performs the relevant checks.

$$NextMessageFromSource \mathrel{\widehat=} ((GotMsgsFromSrc \land NextMsgFromSrc \land SysOk) \lor NoMessagesFrom$$

The definition expands into

$$\begin{array}{l}
\textbf{NextMessageFromSource} \\
\hline
\Delta MSGQ \\
\Delta ERRV \\
\Delta HW \\
src? : PID \\
mp! : MPTR \\
\hline
(\exists i : 1 \mathinner{\ldotp\ldotp} \#mq \bullet \\
\quad msgsrc(msgat(mq(i))) = src?) \land \\
\quad (\exists i : 1 \mathinner{\ldotp\ldotp} \#mq;\ q_1, q_2 : \mathrm{seq}\, MPTR \bullet \\
\qquad \exists m : MPTR \mid m = mq(i) \bullet \\
\qquad\quad q_1 \frown \langle m \rangle \frown q_2 = mq \land \\
\qquad\quad q_1 \frown q_2 = mq' \land \\
\qquad\quad msgsrc(msgat(mq(i))) = src? \land \\
\qquad\quad mp! = m \land \\
\qquad\quad (\forall j : 1 \mathinner{\ldotp\ldotp} i - 1 \bullet \\
\qquad\qquad msgsrc(msgat(mq(j))) \neq src?)
\end{array}$$

This can be simplified as follows. First, the two outer quantifiers have the same range and matrix, so they can be merged. Next, the one-point rule can be applied to remove *mp*!.

$$\begin{array}{l}
\textbf{NextMessageFromSource} \\
\hline
\Delta MSGQ \\
\Delta ERRV \\
\Delta HW \\
src? : PID \\
mp! : MPTR \\
serr! : SYSERR \\
\hline
(\exists i : 1 \mathinner{\ldotp\ldotp} \#mq;\ q_1, q_2 : \mathrm{seq}\, MPTR \bullet \\
\quad q_1 \frown \langle mp! \rangle \frown q_2 = mq \land \\
\quad q_1 \frown q_2 = mq' \land \\
\quad msgsrc(msgat(mp!)) = src? \land \\
\quad (\forall j : 1 \mathinner{\ldotp\ldotp} i - 1 \bullet \\
\qquad msgsrc(msgat(mq(j))) \neq src?)
\end{array}$$

The precondition must be calculated for this important operation.

$$
\begin{array}{l}
\text{pre } \mathit{NextMessageFromSource} \mathrel{\widehat=} \\
\quad \exists\, i : 1 \mathrel{..} \#mq \bullet \\
\qquad \mathit{msgsrc}(\mathit{msgat}(mq(i))) = \mathit{src}? \land \\
\quad\ \neg\, (\exists\, j : 1 \mathrel{..} i - 1 \bullet \\
\qquad\quad \mathit{msgsrc}(\mathit{msgat}(mq(j))) = \mathit{src}?)
\end{array}
$$

This concludes the specification. We now turn to its refinement.

5.9.2 Refinement One

We immediately state the refined version of the message queue type. Note that, by use of promotion, we are separating the development of the queue type from that of the process table.

$$
\begin{array}{|l}
\hline \mathit{MSGQ1} \\
mq1 : 1 \mathrel{..} \mathit{maxmsgs} \rightarrow \mathit{MPTR} \\
\mathit{maxmsgs} : \mathbb{N}_1 \\
\mathit{mnxt} : \mathbb{N} \\
\hline
\mathit{mnxt} \leq \mathit{maxmsgs} + 1 \\
\hline
\end{array}
$$

The refined message queue type differs from the original in that the former uses a function to represent the queue; the original used a sequence. The domain of the function is an subrange of the naturals, so the function represents a vector. The variable, *mnxt*, is the index of the next free element of the vector, $mq1$.

The initialisation schema is exactly as one might expect.

$$
\begin{array}{|l}
\hline \mathit{MSGQInit1} \\
\mathit{MSGQ1}' \\
mm? : \mathbb{N}_1 \\
\hline
\mathit{maxmsgs}' = mm? \\
\mathit{mnxt}' = 1 \\
\hline
\end{array}
$$

The predicate determining whether there are free elements of $mq1$, the message queue, is now defined in terms of indices:

$$
\begin{array}{|l}
\hline \mathit{CanEnqueueMsg1} \\
\Xi \mathit{MSGQ1} \\
\hline
\mathit{mnxt} \leq \mathit{maxmsgs} \\
\hline
\end{array}
$$

Equally, the predicate determining whether there are messages in the queue is definded in terms of the *mnxt* index.

$$
\begin{array}{|l}
\hline
\textit{GotMsgs1} \\
\Xi MSGQ1 \\
\hline
mnxt > 1 \\
\hline
\end{array}
$$

The enqueueing operation consists of assigning a message (pointer) to the next free element of $mq1$ and then incrementing $mnxt$, the end pointer, by one.

$$
\begin{array}{|l}
\hline
\textit{EnqueueMsg1} \\
\Delta MSGQ1 \\
mp? : MPTR \\
\hline
mq1' = mq1 \oplus \{mnxt \mapsto mp?\} \\
mnxt' = mnxt + 1 \\
\hline
\end{array}
$$

Removal of a message consists of copying the first element, then copying the vector down one element; finally, the insertion point is moved down one position.

$$
\begin{array}{|l}
\hline
\textit{DelMSGQHd1} \\
\Delta MSGQ1 \\
mp! : MPTR \\
\hline
mp! = mq1(1) \\
\forall i : 1 \mathrel{..} mnxt - 2 \bullet mq1' = mq1 \oplus \{i \mapsto mq1(i + 1)\} \\
\hline
\end{array}
$$

The next operation is the refinment of *GotMsgsFromSrc*. At any time, there are only $mnxt - 1$ elements in $mq1$ (when there are no elements, $mnxt = 1$).

$$
\begin{array}{|l}
\hline
\textit{GotMsgsFromSrc1} \\
\Xi MSGQ1 \\
src? : PID \\
\hline
\exists i : 1 \mathrel{..} mnxt - 1 \bullet msgsrc(msgat(mq1(i))) = src? \\
\hline
\end{array}
$$

The following operation corresponds to *NextMsgFromSrc*. The two universals can be accounted for as follows. The second moves all elements from the one selected for output down one position (so that the hole produced by selecting a message is healed). The first is part of the condition: the selected message is the first in the queue from the source specified by *src?*.

$$
\begin{array}{l}
\textit{NextMsgFromSrc1} \\
\hline
\Delta MSGQ1 \\
src? : PID \\
mp! : MPTR \\
\hline
\exists i : 1 \mathinner{\ldotp\ldotp} mnxt - 1;\ m : MPTR \mid m = mq1(i) \bullet \\
\quad msgsrc(msgat(m)) = src? \land \\
\quad (\forall j : 1 \mathinner{\ldotp\ldotp} i - 1 \bullet msgsrc(msgat(mq1(j))) \neq src?) \land \\
\quad (\forall j : i + 1 \mathinner{\ldotp\ldotp} mnxt - 1 \bullet mq1' = mq1 \oplus \{j - 1 \mapsto mq1(j)\}) \land \\
\quad mp! = m
\end{array}
$$

This schema easily simplifies to:

$$
\begin{array}{l}
\textit{NextMsgFromSrc1} \\
\hline
\Delta MSGQ1 \\
src? : PID \\
mp! : MPOTR \\
\hline
\exists i : 1 \mathinner{\ldotp\ldotp} mnxt - 1 \bullet \\
\quad mp! = mq(i) \land \\
\quad msgsrc(msgat(mp!)) = src? \land \\
\quad (\forall j : 1 \mathinner{\ldotp\ldotp} i - 1 \bullet \\
\qquad msgsrc(msgat(mq1(j))) \neq src?) \land \\
\quad (\forall j : i + 1 \mathinner{\ldotp\ldotp} mnxt - 1 \bullet \\
\qquad mq1' = mq1 \oplus \{j - 1 \mapsto mq1(j)\})
\end{array}
$$

The *AddMsg1* operation corresponds to *AddMsg*:

$$
\begin{array}{l}
AddMsg1 \mathrel{\widehat=} \\
\quad \exists sz : \mathbb{N} \mid sz = msgsz(m?) \bullet \\
\qquad (CanAllocateBlock[sz/rqsz?] \land \\
\qquad\quad ((CanEnqueueMsg1 \land \\
\qquad\qquad AllocMsg1[sz/rqsz?, m/a!] \land \\
\qquad\qquad (\exists v : 1 \mathinner{\ldotp\ldotp} \mathbb{N}_1 \rightarrow PSU;\ sz : \mathbb{N}_1 \\
\qquad\qquad\qquad \mid v = msgToPSU(m?) \land sz = msgsz(m?) \bullet \\
\qquad\qquad\quad StoreMsg[v/v?, m/loc?, sz/sz?]) \land \\
\qquad\qquad EnqueueMsg1[m/mp!] \land \\
\qquad\qquad SysOk) \\
\qquad\quad \lor MessageQueueFull)) \setminus \{m\} \\
\qquad \lor NoSpace
\end{array}
$$

After expansion and simplification, it is

AddMsg1

$$
\begin{array}{l}
\Delta MSGQ \\
\Delta ERRV \\
\Delta HW \\
m? : MSG \\
\hline
(alloc1 + msgsz(m?) \leq psize1 \land nextm \leq maxfblocks \land \\
\quad (mnxt \leq maxmsgs \land \\
\quad\quad ((\exists i : 1 \mathinner{\ldotp\ldotp} nextm - 1 \bullet \\
\quad\quad\quad msgsz(freebs1(i)) \geq msgsz(m?) \land \\
\quad\quad\quad (mdsz(freebs1(i)) = msgsz(m?) \land \\
\quad\quad\quad\quad (\forall j : i \mathinner{\ldotp\ldotp} nextm - 1 \bullet \\
\quad\quad\quad\quad\quad freebs1' = freebs1 \oplus \{j \mapsto freebs1(j + 1)\}) \land \\
\quad\quad\quad\quad alloc1' = alloc1 + msgsz(m?) \land \\
\quad\quad\quad\quad mq1' = mq1 \oplus \{nextm \mapsto mdaddr(freebs1(i))\} \land \\
\quad\quad\quad\quad nextm' = nextm + 1 \land \\
\quad\quad\quad\quad startaddr \leq mdaddr(freebs1(i)) \land \\
\quad\quad\quad\quad mdaddr(freebs1(i)) + msgsz(m?) \leq startaddr + svsize \land \\
\quad\quad\quad\quad \forall j : 1 \mathinner{\ldotp\ldotp} msgsz(m?) \bullet \\
\quad\quad\quad\quad\quad sv' = sv \oplus \{(startaddr - mdaddr(freebs1(i))) + (j - 1) \\
\quad\quad\quad\quad\quad\quad\quad \mapsto msgToPSU(m?)(j)\}) \\
\quad\quad\quad \lor (mdsz(freebs1(i)) > msgsz(m?) \land \\
\quad\quad\quad\quad freebs1' = freebs1 \oplus \\
\quad\quad\quad\quad\quad \{i \mapsto \\
\quad\quad\quad\quad\quad\quad mkmd(mdaddr(freebs1(i)) + msgsz(m?), \\
\quad\quad\quad\quad\quad\quad\quad mdsz(freebs1(i)) - msgsz(m?))\} \land \\
\quad\quad\quad\quad alloc1' = alloc1 + msgsz(m?) \land \\
\quad\quad\quad\quad mq1' = mq1 \oplus \{nextm \mapsto mdaddr(freebs1(i))\} \land \\
\quad\quad\quad\quad nextm' = nextm + 1 \land \\
\quad\quad\quad\quad startaddr \leq mdaddr(freebs(i)) \land \\
\quad\quad\quad\quad mdaddr(freebs1(i)) + msgsz(m?) \leq startaddr + svsize \land \\
\quad\quad\quad\quad \forall j : 1 \mathinner{\ldotp\ldotp} msgsz(m?) \bullet \\
\quad\quad\quad\quad\quad sv' = sv \oplus \{(startaddr - mdaddr(freebs1(i))) + (j - 1) \\
\quad\quad\quad\quad\quad\quad\quad \mapsto msgToPSU(m?)(j)\})) \land \\
\quad\quad\quad\quad serr' = sysok) \\
\quad \lor (serr' = msgqfull \land intno' = killintno)) \\
\lor (serr' = nospaceinstore \land intno' = killintno))
\end{array}
$$

The precondition is calculated:

$$
\begin{array}{l}
\text{pre}\ AddMsg1 \mathrel{\widehat{=}} \\
\quad alloc1 + msgsz(m?) < psize1 \land \\
\quad mnxt < maxmsgs \land \\
\quad (\exists i : 1 \mathinner{\ldotp\ldotp} nextm - 1 \bullet msgsz(freebs1(i)) \geq msgsz(m?)) \land \\
\quad\quad startaddr \leq mdaddr(freebs1(i)) \land \\
\quad\quad mdaddr(freebs1(i)) + msgsz(m?) \leq startaddr + svsize
\end{array}
$$

Operation *NextMsg1* corresponds to *NextMsg*:

$$NextMsg1 \mathrel{\widehat=} (GotMsgs1 \land DelMSGQHd1 \land SysOk) \lor EmptyMessageQueue$$

This definition expands into:

$$\begin{array}{l}
\textit{NextMsg1} \\
\hline
\Delta MSGQ1 \\
\Delta ERRV \\
\Delta HW \\
mp! : MPTR \\
\hline
(mnxt > 1 \land \\
\quad mp! = mq1(1) \land \\
\quad (\forall i : 1 \mathinner{..} mnxt - 2 \bullet mq1' = mq1 \oplus \{i \mapsto mq1(i+1)\}) \land \\
\quad serr' = sysok) \lor (serr' = emptymsgq \land intno' = killintno)
\end{array}$$

The precondition of this operation is

$$\text{pre } NextMsg1 \mathrel{\widehat=} mnxt > 1$$

The *NextMessageFromSrc1* operation corresponds to *NextMessageFromSrc*. The definition is

$$NextMessageFromSrc1 \mathrel{\widehat=} ((GotMsgsFromSrc1 \land NextMsgFromSrc1 \land SysOk) \lor NoMessagesFrom$$

The definition expands to

$$\begin{array}{l}
\textit{NextMessageFromSrc1} \\
\hline
\Delta MSGQ1 \\
\Delta ERRV \\
\Delta HW \\
src? : PID \\
mp! : MPOTR \\
\hline
((\exists i : 1 \mathinner{..} mnxt - 1 \bullet \\
\quad msgsrc(msgat(mq1(i))) = src?) \land \\
(\exists i : 1 \mathinner{..} mnxt - 1;\ m : MPTR \bullet \\
\quad m = mq(i) \land mp! = m \land \\
\quad msgsrc(msgat(mp!)) = src? \land \\
\quad (\forall j : 1 \mathinner{..} i - 1 \bullet \\
\qquad msgsrc(msgat(mq1(j))) \neq src?) \land \\
\quad (\forall j : i + 1 \mathinner{..} mnxt - 1 \bullet \\
\qquad mq1' = mq1 \oplus \{j - 1 \mapsto mq1(j)\})) \land \\
\quad mnxt' = mnxt - 1 \land
\end{array}$$

$$
\begin{array}{l}
\quad\quad serr' = sysok) \\
\lor (serr' = nomsgsfrom \land intno' = killintno)
\end{array}
$$

This schema can be simplified to produce

$$
\begin{array}{|l}
\hline
NextMessageFromSrc1 \\
\Delta MSGQ1 \\
\Delta ERRV \\
\Delta HW \\
src? : PID \\
mp! : MPOTR \\
\hline
(\exists i : 1 \mathrel{..} mnxt - 1 \bullet \\
\quad mp! = mq1(i) \land \\
\quad msgsrc(msgat(mp!)) = src? \land \\
\quad (\forall j : 1 \mathrel{..} i - 1 \bullet \\
\quad\quad msgsrc(msgat(mq1(j))) \neq src?) \land \\
\quad (\forall j : i + 1 \mathrel{..} mnxt - 1 \bullet \\
\quad\quad mq1' = mq1 \oplus \{j - 1 \mapsto mq1(j)\})) \land \\
\quad mnxt' = mnxt - 1 \land \\
\quad serr' = sysok) \\
\lor (serr' = nomsgsfrom \land intno' = killintno) \\
\hline
\end{array}
$$

The precondition is

$$
\begin{array}{l}
\mathrm{pre}\ NextMessageFromSrc1 \mathrel{\widehat=} \\
\quad \exists i : 1 \mathrel{..} mnxt - 1 \bullet \\
\quad\quad msgsrc(msgat(mq1(i))) = src? \land \\
\quad\quad \neg (\exists j : 1 \mathrel{..} i - 1 \bullet \\
\quad\quad\quad msgsrc(msgat(mq1(i))) = src?)
\end{array}
$$

Finally, the abstraction relation is defined.

$$
\begin{array}{|l}
\hline
AbsMSGQ1 \\
MSGQ \\
MSGQ1 \\
\hline
maxmsgs = maxms \\
mnxt = \#mq + 1 \\
\forall i : 1 \mathrel{..} \#mq \bullet \\
\quad mq(i) = mq1(i) \\
\hline
\end{array}
$$

There should be no surprises here!

Theorem 67.

$$
\begin{array}{l}
\forall MSGQ'; MSGQ1' \bullet \\
\quad MSGQ1Init \land AbsMSGQ1 \Rightarrow MSGQInit
\end{array}
$$

PROOF. By the abstraction relation, $maxmsgs' = maxms'$, so $mm? = maxmsgs' = maxms'$. The abstraction relation also states that $mnxt = \#mq + 1$, so $mnxt' = 1 = \#mq + 1 = 0 + 1$, from which it follows that $mq' = \langle\rangle$. □

Theorem 68.

$$\forall MSGQ;\ MSGQ1;\ m? : MSG$$
$$\quad pre\ AddMsg \land AbsMSGQ1 \land AbsSTOREPOOL1 \Rightarrow pre\ AddMsg1$$

PROOF. The preconditions are:

$$\begin{array}{l} \text{pre } AddMsg \mathrel{\widehat=} \\ \quad alloc + msgsz(m?) < psize \land \\ \quad \#mq < maxms \land \\ \quad (\exists i : 1\,..\,\#freebs \bullet msgsz(freebs(i)) \geq msgsz(m?)) \land \\ \quad startaddr \leq mdaddr(freebs(i)) \land \\ \quad mdaddr(freebs(i)) + msgsz(m?) \leq startaddr + svsize \end{array}$$

and

$$\begin{array}{l} \text{pre } AddMsg1 \mathrel{\widehat=} \\ \quad alloc1 + msgsz(m?) < psize1 \land \\ \quad mnxt \leq maxmsgs \land \\ \quad (\exists i : 1\,..\,nextm - 1 \bullet msgsz(freebs1(i)) \geq msgsz(m?)) \land \\ \quad startaddr \leq mdaddr(freebs1(i)) \land \\ \quad mdaddr(freebs1(i)) + msgsz(m?) \leq startaddr + svsize \end{array}$$

It should be noted that the $STOREVEC$ component cannot be subjected to refinement. Therefore, there is an identity relation between the components of $STOREVEC$ in the two preconditons.

The abstraction relation states that $psize = psize1$, $alloc = alloc1$ and that $maxmsgs = maxms$. It also states that $mnxt = \#mq + 1$. This permits the inferences that $alloc + msgsz(m?) < psize \Leftrightarrow alloc1 + msgsz(m?) < psize1$ and $\#mq < maxms \Leftrightarrow mnxt \leq maxmsgs$.

The range of the quantifier is $1\,..\,\#freebs$ and by the abstraction relation for $STOREPOOL$, $\#freebs = nextm - 1$, and that abstraction relation also states that $\forall i : 1\,..\,\#freebs \bullet freebs(i) = freebs1(i)$x, so it follows that

$$\begin{array}{l} msgsz(freebs(i)) \geq msgsz(m?) \\ \quad \Leftrightarrow msgsz(freebs1(i)) \geq msgsz(m?) \end{array}$$

$mdaddr(freebs(i)) = mdaddr(freebs1(i))$ and, finally, that

$$\begin{array}{l} mdaddr(freebs(i)) + msgsz(m?) \leq startaddr + svsize \\ \Leftrightarrow mdaddr(freebs1(i)) + msgsz(m?) \leq startaddr + svsize \end{array}$$

□

Theorem 69.

$\forall\, MSGQ;\ MSGQ';\ MSGQ1;\ MSGQ1';\ m? : MSG\ \bullet$
$pre\ AddMsg\ \wedge$
$\quad AbsMSGQ1\ \wedge$
$\quad AbsMSGQ1'\ \wedge$
$\quad AbsSTOREPOOL1\ \wedge$
$\quad AbsSTOREPOOL1'\ \wedge$
$\quad AddMsg1$
$\Rightarrow AddMsg$

PROOF. The abstraction relations states that $alloc = alloc1$, $maxfree = maxfblocks$ and $\#freebs = nextm - 1$. This permits the inference that $alloc + msgsz(m?) = alloc1 + msgsz(m?)$ and $\#freebs < maxfree$ implies that $nextm \leq maxfblocks$. The relation also states that $\#mq = mnxt - 1$, so $mnxt \leq maxmsgs$ implies $\#mq < maxms$. The same relation permits the inference that $nextm - 1 = \#freebs$, so the bound variable of the outer existential quantifier is in range and it can be inferred that $freebs(i) = freebs1(i)$ (for the reason that $\forall\, i : 1\,..\,\#freebs \bullet freebs(i) = freebs1(i) \Rightarrow \exists\, i : 1\,..\,\#freebs \bullet freebs(i) = freebs1(i)$). This permits the inference that $mdsz(freebs(i)) = mdsz(freebs1(i))$ and $mdaddr(freebs(i)) = mdaddr(freebs1(i))$. Most of the remainder of the proof follows immediately.

The only point of note is

$$\forall\, j : i\,..\,nextm - 1 \bullet$$
$$\quad freebs1' = freebs1 \oplus \{j \mapsto freebs1(j+1)\}$$

This clearly removes $freebs1(i)$ from $freebs1$ and corresponds directly to $freebs' = freebs \rhd \{freebs(i)\}$. In support of this claim, the following reasoning is offered. The above formula implies that $freebs1'(i) = freebs1(i+1)$, so $freebs1(i)$ is no longer an element of $freebs1'$. By the equivalence of $freebs'$ and $freebs1'$ required by $AbsSTOREPOOL1'$, $freebs(i)$ cannot be an element of $freebs'(i)$, so $freebs' = freebs \rhd \{freebs(i)\}$. □

Theorem 70.

$\forall\, MSGQ;\ MSGQ1\ \bullet$
$\quad pre\ NextMsg \wedge AbsMSGQ1 \Rightarrow pre\ NextMsg1$

PROOF. The preconditions are as follows:

$$\text{pre}\ NextMsg \mathrel{\widehat{=}} mq \neq \langle\,\rangle$$

and

$$\text{pre}\ NextMsg1 \mathrel{\widehat{=}} mnxt > 1$$

By the abstraction relation, $mnxt = \#mq + 1$, so if $mq = \langle\,\rangle$, $mnxt = 1$ since $\#\langle\,\rangle = 0$. If $mq \neq \langle\,\rangle$, $\#mq > 0$, so $mnxt > 1$. □

Theorem 71.

$$
\begin{array}{l}
\forall\, MSGQ;\ MSGQ';\ MSGQ1;\ MSGQ1';\ mp! : MPTR;\ \bullet \\
\quad pre\ NextMsg \wedge \\
\qquad AbsMSGQ1 \wedge \\
\qquad AbsMSGQ1' \wedge \\
\qquad NextMsg1 \\
\quad \Rightarrow NextMsg
\end{array}
$$

PROOF. By the previous result, $mnxt > 1$ implies $mq \neq \langle\rangle$. Since 1 is in range as an index of $mq1$, the predicate of $AbsMSGQ1$ permits the inference that $mq1(1) = mq(1)$ and $mq(1) = head\ mq$ by the definition of *head*; so, $mp! = mq1(1) = head\ mq$.

The quantified formula $\forall\, i : 1 \mathinner{..} mnxt \bullet mq1' = mq1 \oplus \{i \mapsto mq1(i+1)\}$ translates $mq1$ one position downwards with the result that $mq1'(1) = mq1(2)$ and so on. This is the removal of the first element of $mq1$ which, as noted in the last paragraph is equivalent to $head\ mq$. The removal of the head of a sequence is the result of the *tail* operation and it is clear that the universally quantified formula is equivalent to $mq' = tail\ mq$. □

Theorem 72.

$$
\begin{array}{l}
\forall\, MSGQ;\ MSGQ1;\ src? : PID\ \bullet \\
pre\ NextMessageFromSource \wedge AbsMSGQ1 \Rightarrow pre\ NextMessageFromSource1
\end{array}
$$

PROOF. The preconditions are:

$$
\begin{array}{l}
\text{pre } NextMessageFromSource \mathrel{\widehat=} \\
\quad \exists\, i : 1 \mathinner{..} \#mq\ \bullet \\
\qquad msgsrc(msgat(mq(i)) = src? \wedge \\
\qquad \neg\, (\exists\, j : 1 \mathinner{..} j-1\ \bullet \\
\qquad\quad msgsrc(msgat(mq(j))) = src?)
\end{array}
$$

and

$$
\begin{array}{l}
\text{pre } NextMessageFromSource1 \mathrel{\widehat=} \\
\quad \exists\, 1 \mathinner{..} mnxt - 1\ \bullet \\
\qquad msgsrc(msgat(mq1(i))) = src? \wedge \\
\qquad \neg\, (\exists\, j : 1 \mathinner{..} i-1\ \bullet \\
\qquad\quad msgsrc(msgat(mq1(i))) = src?)
\end{array}
$$

By the abstractin relation, $mnxt = \#mq - 1$, so $\#mq = mnxt - 1$. From this, the equivalence of ranges of the outer quantifiers can be inferred. This equivalence also permits us to infer that $\forall\, i : 1 \mathinner{..} \#mq \bullet mq(i) = mq1(i))$ and, then, that $msgsrc(msgat(mq(i))) = msgsrc(msgat(mq1(i)))$ for $1 \leq i \leq \#mq$.
□

Theorem 73.

$$\begin{array}{l} \forall MSGQ;\ MSGQ';\ MSGQ1;\ MSGQ1';\ src? : PID;\ mp! : MPTR \bullet \\ \quad pre\ NextMessageFromSource \land \\ \qquad AbsMSGQ1 \land \\ \qquad AbsMSGQ1' \land \\ \qquad NextMessageFromSource1 \\ \quad \Rightarrow NextMessageFromSource \end{array}$$

PROOF. First of all, it is necessary to observe that $mnxt - 1 = \#mq$ is a simple consequence of $AbsMSGQ1$, so it can be inferred that the outermost quantifier ranges are equivalent. This also permits the inference that $\forall i : 1 \mathinner{..} \#mq \bullet mq(i) = mq1(i)$ and that $msgsrc(msgat(mq(i))) = msgsrc(msgat(mq1(i)))$ for $1 \leq i \leq \#mq$; in particular, if $1 \leq i \leq \#mq$ and $j < i$, this identity also holds. It also permits the inference that

$$\begin{array}{l} \forall j : i + 1 \mathinner{..} mnxt - 1 \bullet \\ \quad mq1' \\ \qquad = mq1 \oplus \{j - 1 \mapsto mq1(j)\} \\ \qquad = mq \oplus \{j - 1 \mapsto mq1(j)\} \\ \qquad = mq \oplus \{j - 1 \mapsto mq(j)\} \\ \qquad = mq' \end{array}$$

The equivalence of $mq1'$ and mq' is assured by the condition in $AbsMSGQ1'$ that $\forall i : 1 \mathinner{..} \#mq' \bullet mq'(i) = mq1'(i)$; the remainder of the steps are justified by the equivalence noted above.

Finally, it can be seen that if $msgsrc(msgat(mq1(i))) = src?$, $mq1$ is divided into three segments: an initial segment $(1 \leq j < i)$, the segment consisiting only of $mq1(i)$ and a final segment whose indices are in the range $i+1 \leq j \leq mnxt-1$. The last range, in mq, is $i+1 \leq j \leq \#mq$. Since mq and $mq1$ coincide by the $AbsMSGQ1$, it is possible to write mq as $q_1 \frown \langle mq(i) \rangle \frown q_2$, where $q_1(j) = mq(j)$ for $1 \leq j < i$, and $q_2(j) = mq(j)$ for $i + 1 \leq j \leq \#mq$. The quantifier $\forall j : i + 1 \mathinner{..} mnxt - 1 \bullet mq1' = mq1 \oplus \{j - 1 \mapsto mq1(j)$ clearly removes $mq1(i)$ from $mq1$. From this, it can be concluded that $mq' = q_1 \frown q_2$. To verify this, $mq1'(i) = mq1(i + 1)$ and $mq'(i) = mq(i + 1) = head\ q_2$; by the abstraction relation, $head\ q_2 = mq1(i + 1)$. □

This module is now at a level where implementation is possible.

5.10 Kernel Interface – User Processes

5.10.1 Auxilliary Operations

$$\begin{array}{l} VerifyCallerIdent \mathrel{\widehat=} \\ \quad (RunningProcess[c/p!] \land PIDforUPID[c/p!]) \setminus \{c\} \end{array}$$

or

$$\begin{array}{|l}
\hline
\textit{VerifyCallerIdent} \\
\Xi PTAB \\
u? : UPID \\
\hline
curr = extpid(u?) \\
\hline
\end{array}$$

$$\begin{array}{l}
\textit{InsufficientMainStore} \mathrel{\widehat=} \\
\quad (\exists\, e : SYSERR \mid e = mainstorefull \bullet \\
\qquad SetSysErr[e/e?]) \land \\
\quad RaiseKillInterrupt
\end{array}$$

$$\begin{array}{l}
SEGMENTS \mathrel{\widehat=} \\
\quad STOREPOOL[frees/freebs, maxsgs/maxfree, \\
\qquad\qquad allocs/alloc, spsize/psize, spaddr/paddr]
\end{array}$$

$$\begin{array}{l}
SEGMENTSInit \mathrel{\widehat=} STOREPOOLInit[frees/freebs, maxsgs/maxfree, \\
\qquad\qquad allocs/alloc, spsize/psize, spaddr/paddr]
\end{array}$$

$$AllocateSegment \mathrel{\widehat=} AllocBlk[frees/freebs, maxsgs/maxfree, allocs/alloc]$$

$$FreeSegment \mathrel{\widehat=} FreeBlk[frees/freebs, maxsgs/maxfree, allocs/alloc]$$

$$CanAllocateSegment \mathrel{\widehat=} CanAllocateBlock[allocs/alloc, frees/freebs]$$

The following is just a convenience

$$SegmentTableInit \mathrel{\widehat=} SEGMENTSInit$$

For present purposes, it is assumed that segmentation is aimed at the output of the GNU C compiler, which requires two segments. One segment is the code segment (also called the "text" segment and is assumed to be read-only), the other is the combined stack and data segment. In the latter segment, the stack is assumed to grow downwards from the top, while data is allocated upwards from the bottom.

The size of the code segment is *codesz* and that of the combined stack and data segment is *dssize*. The descriptors returned are *sd*! for the stack segment and *ds*! for the other segment.

The descriptors are *sd*? for the stack segment and *ds*? for the combined segments.

It is also necessary to declare some store to be used as a message pool. This entails the allocation of a *STOREVEC* and a *STROREPOOL*; the *STOREPOOL*, however, must be distinct from the segment table just described.

5.10.2 Initialisation

This subsection deals with system initialisation for non-device processes.

The first task is to define the operations on segments in main store. To do this, it is necessary to define the type for segment descriptors. Segment descriptors are composed of an address (the start of the segment) and a size (the size of the segment in some units—bytes seem the most appropriate).

$$SDESC == ADDR \times \mathbb{N}$$

The size (the second component) must admit zero so that the null process can be represented.

Given this type definition, it is useful to have a constructor function for segment descriptors, just as we had for storage descriptors (type *MD*).

$$mksdesc : ADDR \times \mathbb{N} \rightarrow SDESC$$

$$\forall a : ADDR; \ s : \mathbb{N} \bullet \\ \quad mksdesc(a, s) = (a, s)$$

The constructor function just creates pairs.

It is also useful to have accessor functions, one for each component.

$$segaddr : SDESC \rightarrow ADDR \\ segsize : SDESC \rightarrow \mathbb{N}$$

$$\forall s : SDESC \bullet \\ \quad segaddrs(s) = fst\ s \\ \quad segsize(s) = snd\ s$$

The first accessor returns the segment's start address, while the second returns the size.

The process table is expanded by two components: one to record code segment information and one to record data and stack segment information. The code segment information is stored in *cdseg* and that for the combined data and stack segement is stored in *dsseg*. Clearly there must be one segment of each type for every process (the idle, or null, process must have zero segments, recall for the reason that it does not have any data, does not consume a stack, nor does it have a code segment—the code for the idle process is a part of the kernel).

PTAB

$$\vdots \\ cdseg : PID \rightarrow\!\!\!\!\!\!\rightarrow SDESC \\ dsseg : PID \rightarrow\!\!\!\!\!\!\rightarrow SDESC$$

$$
\begin{array}{|l}
\ldots \\
\hline
\vdots \\
\hline
\end{array}
$$

The segment usage of the GNU C compiler is assumed (it uses two segments, one for code and one for data and the stack—the stack resides at the top of the data segment and grows downwards towards the area in which data is stored). The invariant for *cdseg* (the code segment) and that for the combined stack and data segment, *dsseg*, is the same.

The operation to set the code segment information for a process is defined by the following schema:

$$
\begin{array}{|l}
\textit{SetCodeSegInfo} \\
\hline
\Delta PTAB \\
p? : PID \\
a? : ADDR \\
sz? : \mathbb{N} \\
\hline
cdseg' = cdseg \cup \{p? \mapsto mksdesc(a?, sz?)\} \\
\hline
\end{array}
$$

Segments are allocated only once, so any data that is set remains in the process table until its owning process is deleted.

In a similar fashion, the combined stack and data segment information for a new process is set by the following schema:

$$
\begin{array}{|l}
\textit{SetStackDataSegInfo} \\
\hline
\Delta PTAB \\
p? : PID \\
a? : ADDR \\
sz? : \mathbb{N} \\
\hline
dsseg' = dsseg \cup \{p? \mapsto mksdesc(a?, sz?)\} \\
\hline
\end{array}
$$

The next two schemata use the accessor functions defined for segment descriptors and apply them to the segments of a process. This first schema returns the descriptor for the code segment.

$$
\begin{array}{|l}
\textit{CodeSegAddr} \\
\hline
\Xi PTAB \\
p? : PID \\
a! : ADDR \\
\hline
a! = segaddr(cdseg(p?)) \\
\hline
\end{array}
$$

The second schema returns the combined segment for the named process.

$$\begin{array}{|l}
\hline
\textit{StackDataSegAddr} \\
\Xi PTAB \\
p? : PID \\
a! : ADDR \\
\hline
a! = segaddr(dsseg(p?)) \\
\hline
\end{array}$$

The following operation sets the registers up ready for the context switch to the intial process. The most important part of this consists of setting the registers to default or dummy values so that they can be switched into the processor's registers. The entry point of the initial process must be specified as the address at which to start the execution of the initial process when swapped onto the processor.

$$\begin{array}{l}
SwitchToFirstProcess \mathrel{\widehat=} \\
\quad CreateDummyRegs \\
\quad \mathbin{;} \cdots
\end{array}$$

The idle process must be created. The kernel contains the code that implements this process. The code has to be made into a process. First, a process identifier (*PID*) must be created using *AddIdleProcess*. Next, the segments must be created. As noted above, each segment has a zero start address (represented by *nulladdr* and has a size of 0. The segment information must be stored in the process table.

$$\begin{array}{l}
CreateIdleProcess \mathrel{\widehat=} \\
\quad AddIdleProcess \land \\
\quad AllocateProcTSS \land \\
\quad \land (\exists na : ADDR; nsz : \mathbb{N} \mid na = nulladdr \land nsz = 0 \bullet \\
\qquad SetCodeSegInfo[ip!/p?, na/a?, nsz/sz?] \\
\qquad\quad \mathbin{;} SetStackDataSegInfo[ip!/p?, na/a?, nsz/sz?])
\end{array}$$

The *CreateIdleProcess* operation is required so that the scheduler can be initialised. It is now possible to define the *SKInitSys* operation, the operation that represents the initialisation of the system proper.

$$\begin{array}{l}
SKInitSys \mathrel{\widehat=} \\
\quad AllocateGDT \land AllocateIDT \land AllocateTSSs \land \\
\quad InitDevNums \land \\
\quad PTABInit \land \\
\quad SegmentTableInit \land \\
\quad MSGSTOREInit \land \\
\quad MSGPOOLInit \land \\
\quad ((SKCreateNullProcess[ip/ip!] \land SKSCHEDInit[ip/p?]) \setminus \{ip\} \\
\quad \mathbin{;} SKCreateAndRunInitialProcess)
\end{array}$$

First, the process table is initialised to empty and the segment table is also initialised to empty. The storage area for messages is allocated and initialised, as is the descriptor space. Next the idle (null) process is created and its data stored in the process table. The scheduler is then initialised and the identifier of the idle process is stored in the variable in the scheduler. Finally, the initial process is created and its data stored in the process table. The intial process is then executed.

5.10.3 Process Management

The process management operations must be defined. These operations handle such matters as segment allocation and process creation. The operations in this section deal with *user* processes only.

The segment allocation operation is defined as follows:

$$
\begin{array}{l}
AllocateSegments \mathrel{\widehat=} \\
\quad \exists\, totsize : \mathbb{N}_1 \mid totsize = cdssize? + stkdsize? \bullet \\
\qquad (CanAllocateSegment[totsize/rqsz?] \land \\
\qquad\quad AllocateSegment[totsize/rqsz?, csaddr!/c!] \land \\
\qquad\quad stkaddr! = csaddr! + cdssize? \land \\
\qquad\quad SysOk) \\
\qquad \lor InsufficientMainStore
\end{array}
$$

The definition expands into:

$$
\begin{array}{|l}
\multicolumn{1}{l}{\textit{AllocateSegments}} \\
\Delta STOREPOOL \\
\Delta ERRV \\
\Delta HW \\
cdssize?, stkdsize? : \mathbb{N} \\
csaddr!, stkdaddr! : ADDR \\
\hline
\exists\, totsize : \mathbb{N}_1 \mid totsize = cdssize? + stkdsize? \bullet \\
\quad (totsize + alloc \leq psize \land \\
\qquad (\#frees < maxsgs \land \\
\qquad (\exists\, i : 1 \mathinner{\ldotp\ldotp} \#frees \bullet mdsz(frees(i)) \geq totsize) \land \\
\qquad AllocateSegment[totsize/rqsz?, csaddr!/a!] \land \\
\qquad stkaddr! = csaddr! + cdssize? \land \\
\qquad serr' = sysok) \\
\quad \lor (serr' = mainstorefull \land intno' = killintno)
\end{array}
$$

The primitive for creating new processes is as follows:

$$
\begin{array}{l}
SKNewProcess \mathrel{\widehat{=}} \\
\quad (AllocSegments[totsize?/rqsz?, csaddr/csaddr!, stkdaddr/stkdaddr] \land \\
\quad (\exists pt : PTYPE \mid pt = uproc \bullet AddPD) \\
\qquad \fatsemi SetCodeSegInfo[cdssize?/sz?, csaddr/a?] \\
\qquad \fatsemi SetSetDataSegInfo[stkdsize?/sq?, stkdaddr/a?])) \\
\qquad \fatsemi AllocateProcTSS \land AddPD \\
\qquad \fatsemi InitDevReply \\
\qquad \fatsemi ClearMsgQ \\
\qquad \fatsemi Clear \qquad \fatsemi MakeReady[p!/p?] \\
\qquad \land SysOk) \setminus \{csaddr, stkdaddr\}
\end{array}
$$

First, the segments for the new process are allocated. The segment information is then stored in *PTAB* and the process is made ready (added to the scheduler's ready queue).

The *UPID* for each process is returned to the newly created process, while the *PID* is retained by the kernel and never revealed to an untrusted process.

The expansion of *SKNewProcess* is quite long and can be transformed by the use of the distributive rule for $\land$ over $\lor$.

Register values need to be set before the process can run. All the information is, though, present.

When a request to create a new process is made, it must be made by some process or other. In the basic model, it should be the initial process but it is possible to arrange for other processes to have the ability to create child processes. Whatever approach is adopted, the identity of the creating process must be verified. If verification succeeds, *SKNewProcess* is called to create the process in *PTAB* and add it to the ready queue. The operation is defined as follows:

$$
\begin{array}{l}
USKNewProcess \mathrel{\widehat{=}} \\
\quad (VerifyCallerIdent \land \\
\qquad SKNewProcess[p/p!] \setminus \{p\}) \\
\quad \lor BadCallerIdent
\end{array}
$$

Creating a processes is only half the story. It is necessary to create and execute an initial process just so that there is something to which a half context switch can be made. The initial process can be put to many uses, one of which is as the ancestor of all processes in the system. For present purposes, the initial process in this specification just serves as a place to which context can be switched.

$$
\begin{array}{l}
CreateAndRunInitialProcess \mathrel{\widehat{=}} \\
\quad (SKNewProcess[fp/p!] \fatsemi RunFirstProcess[fp/p?]) \setminus \{fp\}
\end{array}
$$

The *RunFirstProcess* operation assumes that no other processes are executing. It must be executed during the low-level initialisation operation. If this condition is violated, process switches will fail. The operation basically sets up the stack with registers that can be popped when the first context switch occurs; in order for the first context switch not to fail, the stack have the contents the hardware expects. Since we are not using the process stack for intermediate register storage, the stack need only to be initialised to the entry point of the initial process and the flags register (F register on the IA32).

The operation can be approximated by the following:

SetupFirstProcess

$p? : PID$
$ep? : ADDR$
$flgs? : WORD$

$push\_stack(p?, ep?)$
$push\_stack(p?, flgs?)$

SetHWTSS

ΔHW
$\Xi PTAB$
$p? : PID$

$hwtss' = tss(p?);$

$$RunFirstProcess \mathrel{\widehat=} (SetupFirstProcess \mathbin{⨾} SetHWTSS) \mathbin{⨾} ContextSwithc$$

Processes must be able to suspend themselves. The basic idea adopted for the Separation Kernel is that *natural-break* scheduling should be employed. This has the implication that each process, by and large, determines for itself when it should be suspended. The self-suspending operation is defined by the next schema:

$$SKSuspendSelf \mathrel{\widehat=} (RequeueUserProcess \mathbin{⨾} SwitchContext)$$

This operation is then wrapped inside a check on the identity of the requesting process, as follows:

$$USKSuspendSelf \mathrel{\widehat=} (VerifyCallerIdent \land SKSuspendSelf) \lor BadCallerIdent$$

The last action a process takes is to terminate itself. The following schema defines this operation.

$$SKTerminateSelf \mathrel{\widehat=} ((RunningProcess[c/p!] \land SetStateToTerminated[c/p?] \land FreeCodeSegment[c/p?] \land FreeSDSegment[c/p?] \land (DelProcUPID \mathbin{⨾} DelPD[c/p?]) \setminus \{c\}) \mathbin{⨾} SKSchedNext)$$

For security, it must be wrapped inside an identity test.

$USKTerminateSelf \mathrel{\widehat{=}}$
$\quad (VerifyCallerIdent \land SKTerminateSelf)$
$\quad \lor BadCallerIdent$

5.10.4 Message Passing

The operations in this subsection are mostly those defined above. The main difference is that what is defined here is part of the system call's handling code.

In the definition of message-passing operations at the interface between the kernel and user processes, promotion is extensively employed. The reader will remember that in the section in which the message-passing primitives were defined, the $\Phi PTAB_M$ schema was defined but not used; it is in the definition of the following operations that this schema finds its use. It is necessary to recall that promotion has the useful property that the refinement of the contained and containing state spaces can proceed independently. Because of this, the refinement of the operations in this section requires little or no extra work here.

When sending a message, the user process (or libary routine) has the following interface

UsrSendMsgI

$\vdots$

$dest? : UPID$

$data? : MSGDATA$

$\vdots$

At the interface to the message-passing subsystem, user processes only communicate identifiers as elements of *UPID*, not as elements of *PID*. The interface operation for sending a message can be defined as

$\vdots$

$dest? : UPID$
$data? : MSGDATA$
$result! : YESNO$

$\vdots$

Inside the module handling message passing, a translation scheme will need to be employed. Note first that the above schema does not actually construct a message object, while the message-queueing operations do. This provides an opportunity, as follows.

First, assume that the following is called *after* the verification of the caller (or *src*?, that is).

```
— TranslateMessageAddrs ————————————————————
  ΞPTAB
  src?, dest? : UPID
  data? : MSGDATA
  m! : MSG
————————————
  ∃ srcpid, destpid : PID •
      PIDforUPID[src?/u?, srcpid/p!] ∧
      PIDforUPID[dest?/u?, destpid/p!] ∧
      ∃ m : MSG •
          msgsrc(m) = srcpid ∧
          msgdest(m) = destpid ∧
          msgdata(m) = data? ∧
          m! = m
————————————————————————————————————
```

This operation could be implemented as a pair of assignments if the number of bits required to store elements of *PID* $\leq$ the number of bits required to store elements of *UPID*.

On the output side, there is the need to translate a message structure into a form that can be understood by a user process.

```
— MSGToUserData ————————————————————
  ΞPTAB
  src! : UPID
  dest! : UPID
  data! : MSGDATA
  m? : MSG
————————————
  src! = pidext(msgsrc(m?))
  dest! = pidext(msgdest(m?))
  data! = msgdata(m?)
————————————————————————————————————
```

In order for this operation to work properly, it is essential that the outputs are placed on the *user-process stack.*

Using this approach, it is possible to define the remaining user-level operations.

When a message is sent, the user interface passes objects of type *UPID* as well as the message payload (the message data, an object of type *MSGDATA*). It is necessary to translate the *UPID* objects to objects of type *PID* and to create an object of type *MSG*.

$$
\begin{array}{l}
\textit{TranslateMsgAddrs} \\
\hline
\Xi PTAB \\
src?, dest? : UPID \\
data? : MSGDATA \\
m! : MSG \\
\hline
\exists\, srcpid, destpid : PID \bullet \\
\quad PIDforUPID[src?/u?, srcpid/p!] \wedge \\
\quad PIDforUPID[dest?/u?, destpid/p!] \wedge \\
\quad \exists\, m : MSG \bullet \\
\qquad msgsrc(m) = srcpid \wedge \\
\qquad msgdest(m) = destpid \wedge \\
\qquad msgdata(m) = data? \wedge \\
\qquad m! = m \\
\hline
\end{array}
$$

This schema simplifies to:

$$
\begin{array}{l}
\hline
\Xi PTAB \\
src?, dest? : UPID \\
data? : MSGDATA \\
m! : MSG \\
\hline
msgsrc(m!) = extpid(src?) \\
msgdest(m!) = extpid(dest?) \\
msgdata(m!) = data? \\
\hline
\end{array}
$$

The object, $m!$, will have to be stored using *AddMsg*; meanwhile, it remains on the stack. This causes no problems because *AddMsg* allocates dynamic storage for the message and only requires that the message take the form of a record or structure.

Promotion is used to define the basic operations, as observed when defining the message queue type. The *SendToProcess* operation adds a message to the destination process/

$$
\begin{array}{l}
SendToProcess \mathrel{\widehat{=}} \\
\quad \exists\, \Delta MSGQ \bullet \Phi PTAB_M \wedge AddMsg
\end{array}
$$

The full send-message primitive is defined as:

$$
\begin{array}{l}
USKSendMsg \mathrel{\widehat{=}} \\
\quad (VerifyCallerId \wedge \\
\qquad (\exists\, m_u : MSG;\ sz : \mathbb{N}_1;\ d : PID \mid sz = msgsz(m_u) \bullet \\
\qquad\quad PIDforUPID[dest?/u?, d/p!] \wedge \\
\qquad\quad TranslateMsgAddrs[u?/src?, m_u/m!] \wedge \\
\qquad\quad SendToProcess[d, m_u/m?, sz/rqsz?] \wedge \\
\qquad\quad SysOk)) \\
\quad \vee\ BadCallerIdent
\end{array}
$$

This is the interface operation. It verifies the caller's identity.

The data in a message has to be extracted so that it can be handed to the destination process. the following operation does this.

$$
\begin{array}{|l}
\hline
\textit{MSGToUserData} \\
\Xi PTAB \\
src! : UPID \\
dest! : UPID \\
data! : MSGDATA \\
datalen! : \mathbb{N} \\
m? : MPTR \\
\hline
src! = pidext(msgsrc(msgat(m?))) \\
dest! = pidext(msgdest(msgat(m?))) \\
data! = msgdata(msgat(m?)) \\
datalen! = msgpayload(msgat(m?)) \\
\hline
\end{array}
$$

This operation is a surrogate boolean. It is used to return a value to user processes attempting to determine whether they have messages (or messages from a stated source) in their message queue.

$$
\begin{array}{|l}
\hline
\textit{UReturnYes} \\
resp! : YESNO \\
\hline
resp! = yes \\
\hline
\end{array}
$$

$$
\begin{array}{|l}
\hline
\textit{UReturnNo} \\
resp! : YESNO \\
\hline
resp! = no \\
\hline
\end{array}
$$

The operation that tests for the presence of messages in its message queue is now defined. This is a promoted operation.

$$
\begin{array}{l}
ProcessHasMsgs \mathrel{\widehat=} \\
\quad \exists \Delta MSGQ \bullet \Phi PTAB_M \land GotMsgs
\end{array}
$$

The interface primitive for the *GotMsgs* predicate is the following:

$$
\begin{array}{l}
USKGotMsgs \mathrel{\widehat=} \\
\quad (VerifyCallerIdent \land \\
\qquad (PIDforUPID[p/p!] \land \\
\qquad\quad ((ProcessHasMsgs[p/p?] \land UReturnYes) \lor UReturnNo) \setminus \{p\} \\
\qquad SysOk) \\
\quad \lor BadCallerIdent
\end{array}
$$

This operation can be called from a user process.

The operation to return the next message in the queue is now defined by promotion.

$$
\begin{array}{l}
NextMsgForProcess \mathrel{\widehat=} \\
\quad \exists \Delta MSGQ \bullet \Phi PTAB_M \land NextMsg
\end{array}
$$

The user-interface level operation for getting the next message is defined as

$$
\begin{array}{l}
SKNextMsg \mathrel{\widehat=} \\
\quad (VerifyCallerIdent \land \\
\qquad (PIDforUPID[p/p!] \land \\
\qquad\quad (\exists mp : MPTR \bullet \\
\qquad\qquad ((NextMsgForProcess[mp/mp!] \land MSGToUserData[mp/m?]) \\
\qquad\quad {}_9^\circ DeleteStoredMsg[mp/addr?]) \\
\qquad\quad \land SysOk)) \\
\quad \lor BadCallerIdent
\end{array}
$$

As can be seen from the definition of the message queue type, processes can determine whether there are any messages from a given source in its input message queue.

$$
\begin{array}{l}
ProcessHasMsgsFromSrc \mathrel{\widehat=} \\
\quad \exists \Delta MSGQ \bullet \\
\qquad \Phi PTAB_M \land GotMsgsFromSrc
\end{array}
$$

The operation that can be invoked from a user interface is the following:

$$
\begin{array}{l}
SKProcessHasMsgsFromSrc \mathrel{\widehat=} \\
\quad (VerifyCallerIdent \land \\
\qquad (PIDforUPID[src?/u?, srcpid/p!] \land \\
\qquad\quad PIDforUPID[destpid/p!] \land \\
\qquad\quad (ProcessHasMsgsFromSrc[destpid/p?, srcpid/src?] \land UReturnYes) \\
\qquad\quad \lor UReturnNo)) \setminus \{srcpid, destpid\} \\
\quad \lor BadCallerIdent
\end{array}
$$

Promotion is used to define the actual operation.

$$
\begin{array}{l}
NextMsgForProcessFromSrc \mathrel{\widehat=} \\
\quad \exists \Delta MSGQ \bullet \\
\qquad \Phi PTAB_M \land NextMsgFrom
\end{array}
$$

The operation actually to get the next message is defined below.

$$
\begin{array}{l}
SKNextMsgFrom \mathrel{\widehat=} \\
\quad (VerifyCallerIdent \land \\
\qquad (PIDforUPID[src?/u?, srcpid/p!] \land \\
\qquad\quad PIDforUPID[destpid/p!] \land \\
\qquad\quad (\exists mp : MPTR \bullet \\
\qquad\qquad SKNextMsgFromSrc[destpid/p?, srcpid/src?, mp/mp!] \land \\
\qquad\qquad MSGToUserData[mp/m?]) \\
\qquad\quad \mathbin{⨟} DeleteStoredMsg) \setminus \{srcpid, destpid\}) \\
\quad \lor BadCallerIdent
\end{array}
$$

5.11 Devices—Trusted Code

Devices are *trusted* processes. In this design, trust only goes so far. Devices are *not* permitted full access to the kernel and have to respect a well-defined interface.

It would be extremely expensive to have each device process occupy its own set of segments. It is more convenient to have them reside in the same address space as the kernel. It would be preferable for each device not to have a stack but, inevitably, many will.

Device processes are expected never to terminate. For simplicity, it is assumed that, should it be necessary to replace a driver, the system must be shut down and rebooted with the new driver configured.

There are two main parts:

1. activation as a result of a user-process request, and
2. activation as a result of the device becoming ready or having data ready to read.

The links between device processes, the devices they control and the processes that require their services must be provided. The relationship between the device process and the physical device is a matter of addressing; each physical device has its own set of reserved addresses, so this is not an issue. This alone requires device processes either to be constructed of

- a component that operates on the physical device, and
- a component that handles requests from user processes and that passes data back to user processes (when required).

This separation of concerns is attractive.

Clearly, there must be an ISR to handle interrupts generated by the physical device's interface. The ISR can cause a component of the device process to execute. One way to do this is to use a semaphore. A second way is for the ISR to send a message. The message need not be anything involved because it merely denotes the availability of the device for writing or the availability of data for reading.

On the other side, user processes must make a request to the device process. The user process might then wait for the request to be serviced (e.g., when it is a request for data) or might continue (e.g., when the request is to write data). Synchronous protocols for writing might also be employed in which the servicing entity returns a sucess code to the user process. A synchronous interface can be implemented using the standard message-passing operations.

For the time being, it is assumed that the low-level device interface consists of an ISR and a set of addresses plus a piece of code that interfaces to the command bits in that address set. It is assumed that the code can be directly accessed by the device process.

A simple solution at the bottom level for reads is that the ISR hands a pointer to the newly input buffer to the device process, then places the device process on the device ready queue and causes a reschedule.

The device process, on the other hand, has made the device request and has passed any parameters to the device. Immediately thereafter, the device process suspends. Upon resumption, the device process reads the contents of the buffer passed to it by the ISR and passes the associated data or result code to the requesting user process.

This assumes that requests can be serviced in a simple FIFO manner and that the ISR knows the identifier of the device process. It also assumes that the device interface can be directly addressed by the device process. The second assumption suggests that:

- The device process resides in the same address space as the device-manipulating code. This implies that the device process resides in the kernel's address space.
- There must be some kind of buffer space inside the kernel to hold the data passed to and from devices.
- The interface to device processes can be effected via a mapping table. This has the implication that all devices are configured before the system is started. This scheme also permits the user-process interface to be extended to include a (polymorphic) *DeviceCall* operation. Furthermore, this scheme is in line with the general approach adopted here that user processes access the kernel and its services *only* by means of a well-defined and relatively small set of operations.

Storing device processes in the kernel's address space is just a convenience to avoid an expensive segment swap; it is also necessary for most processors allow only a limited number of physical segments. In this specification, only physical segmentation is assumed for the reason that it does not involve any secondary storage. Swapping between main and secondary storage could provide a security hole for the malicious; the assumption also has speed advantages.

Placing device processes in the kernel address space does not imply that they have complete access to the kernel. Even for device processes, *all* kernel operations are in terms of a small, well-defined set of processes. There is the chance that a device process could write to kernel data structures but this is an inevitable risk that the design implies. However, an assumption is that device processes are trusted not to operate in malicious ways. It would be far better to avoid this but, as noted above, it would require each device process to reside in its own, totally separate, address space. This, in turn, would require an address-space swap when entering the kernel, an operation that is somewhat costly on most machines (*inter alia*, it involves saving the entire context of the calling process). The introduction of virtual store appears to solve some of the problems. Again, as noted above, swapping processes between main store and some form of backing store is attractive but is costly and also opens up the possibility of attack.

The current scheme also appears to keep the design as simple as possible. It is our belief, based upon experience with similar and other software, that the simpler the software the easier it is to maintain and the easier it is to protect.

Some processors (e.g., Intel IA32) have instructions to support context switches. On the IA32, a jump or call instruction can be used to switch between address spaces. It is attractive to employ instructions such as these whenever possible on the grounds of potential speed improvement (although the IA32 switching times are about the same for all methods). By placing device processes in the same address space, the address-space switch is no longer required; this might require an additional piece of code to switch device contexts.

There is another issue that must be discussed. By permitting device processes to reside in the kernel's address space, the possibility of concurrency within that address space is opened up. This is particularly the case when prioritised interrupts are supported by the hardware. For simplicity, it will be assumed that all devices have the same interrupt priority (this is not uncommon and is assumed in many portable operating systems). Higher priority interrupts (hardware and software error conditions *except* segmentation violations) can be handled in the normal way and are orthogonal. Under this assumption, there is no contention between device processes and between device processes and ordinary ones. The scheduler's organisation only permits *either* a device or a user process to execute at any time.

It is first necessary to define a collection of operations that deal directly with the data structures relating to device processes. We will begin with a state-setting operation.

$$
\begin{array}{l}
SetDevProcStateToWaiting \mathrel{\widehat=} \\
\quad \exists\, st : PSTATE \mid st = pswtgdev \bullet \\
\qquad SetProcState[st/st?]
\end{array}
$$

This sets the state of a device process to *pswtgdev* when it is waiting for a request or for data from a device (the two states can be separately identifier, if so wished).

The following operation is a predicate that is true if the process identifier bound to $p?$ is that of a device process.

$$
\begin{array}{|l}
\hline
\textit{IsDeviceProcess} \\
\Xi PTAB \\
p? : PID \\
\hline
ptype(p?) = dproc \\
\hline
\end{array}
$$

When a device process is created, its device-message slot is initialised to the null message.

$$
\begin{array}{|l}
\hline
\textit{InitDeviceMsg} \\
\Delta PTAB \\
d? : PID \\
\hline
devmsg' = devmsg \cup \{d? \mapsto (nullpid, nullmsg)\} \\
\hline
\end{array}
$$

After a device process has serviced a request, it clears its device-message slot in *PTAB* by setting it to a null message.

$$
\begin{array}{|l}
\hline
\textit{ClearDevMsg} \\
\Delta PTAB \\
d? : PID \\
\hline
devmsg' = devmsg \oplus \{d? \mapsto (nullpid, nullmsg)\} \\
\hline
\end{array}
$$

When a user process makes a request to a device process, it performs an action akin to sending a message. This "device message' is stored in the *devmsg* slot corresponding to the device process.

$$
\begin{array}{|l}
\hline
\textit{SetDevMsg} \\
\Delta PTAB \\
d? : PID \\
p? : PID \\
m? : MSG \\
\hline
devmsg' = devmsg \oplus \{d? \mapsto (p?, m?)\} \\
\hline
\end{array}
$$

The following is the operation performed by a device process when it reads a request message.

$$
\begin{array}{|l}
\hline
\textit{GetDevMsg} \\
\Xi PTAB \\
d? : PID \\
m! : MSG \\
\hline
m! = snd\ devmsg(d?) \\
\hline
\end{array}
$$

The next two schemata define operations on device-process requests. The first returns the identifier of the requesting process (which can *never* be a device process)

DevRequesterId

$\Xi PTAB$
$d? : PID$
$p! : PID$

$p! = fst\ devmsg(d?)$

The next schema defines a predicate that is true when the device message for the device, $d?$, is not null.

GotDevMSg

$\Xi PTAB$
$d? : PID$

$devmsg(d?) \neq (nullpid, nullmsg)$

The following is just another name for the same operation.

$NonNullDevRq \mathrel{\widehat{=}} GotDevMsg$

Device requests cannot be made by the null process, the idle process or another device process:

ValidDevRqProcessId

$\Xi PTAB$
$rqid? : GPID$
$iprc? : PID$

$rqid? \neq nullpid$
$rqid? \neq iprc?$
$ptype(rqid?) \neq dproc$

ISRs use this operation to pass data to the associated device process.

$PassDataToDeviceProcess \mathrel{\widehat{=}}$
$\quad SetDevMsg$
$\quad ⨾ ReadyDeviceProcess$

PassDataToDeviceProcess

$\Delta PTAB$
$\Delta SKSCHED$
$\Delta PROCESSQUEUE$
$d? : PID$
$p? : PID$

$$
\begin{array}{|l}
m? : MSG \\
\hline
devmsg' = devmsg \oplus \{d? \mapsto (p?, m?)\} \\
state' = state \oplus \{d? \mapsto psready\} \\
devq' = devq \frown \langle d? \rangle
\end{array}
$$

The precondition is (notionally) required for the refinement process, so we calculated it.

$\mathrm{pre}\ PassDataToDeviceProcess \mathrel{\widehat{=}} true$

5.11.1 Device replies

When a device process has completed its operation, it sends a reply message to the requesting user process. In the case of write-only devices, the reply will consist of a return code denoting the success of the operation (it might also contain some other date, say confirmation of the number of bytes written). These device replies are stored in *PTAB* and each process has a *devrpy* entry.

The following schema defines the operation to initialise the device reply entry for a newly created process.

$$
\begin{array}{|l}
\multicolumn{1}{l}{\underline{\ InitDevReply\ }} \\
\Delta PTAB \\
p? : PTAB \\
\hline
devrpy' = devrpy \cup \{p? \mapsto nullmsg\}
\end{array}
$$

When a process has received a reply from a device process, it should copy the data to its own address space and then clear the reply entry. This schema defines the operation:

$$
\begin{array}{|l}
\multicolumn{1}{l}{\underline{\ ClearDevReply\ }} \\
\Delta PTAB \\
p? : PID \\
\hline
devrpy' = devrpy \oplus \{p? \mapsto nullmsg\}
\end{array}
$$

When a device process has completed its task, it reports the result to the requesting user process by setting a "message" in the *devrpy* table within *PTAB*. This is achieved by the operation defined by the following schema:

$$
\begin{array}{|l}
\multicolumn{1}{l}{\underline{\ SetDevReply\ }} \\
\Delta PTAB \\
p? : PID \\
m? : MSG \\
\hline
devrpy' = devrpy \oplus \{p? \mapsto m?\}
\end{array}
$$

The user process obtains device replies by means of the operation defined by the following schema:

$$
\begin{array}{l}
\textit{ReplyFromDeviceProc} \\
\hline
\Xi PTAB \\
p? : PID \\
m! : MSG \\
\hline
m! = devrpy(p?)
\end{array}
$$

Should a process be unsure about the result of a device request, the following predicate is defined.

$$
\begin{array}{l}
\textit{GotReplyFromDeviceProc} \\
\hline
\Xi PTAB \\
p? : PID \\
\hline
devrpy(p?) \neq nullmsg
\end{array}
$$

If a process does not receive a device reply when it should, it can use the following schema to notify the system of this eventuality.

$$
\begin{array}{l}
NoDeviceReply \mathrel{\widehat=} \\
\quad (\exists e : SYSERR \mid e = nodevreply \bullet \\
\quad\quad SetSysErr[e/e?]) \land \\
\quad RaiseKillInterrupt
\end{array}
$$

The operation employed by a device process to reply to a user process request is defined as:

$$
\begin{array}{l}
DevReplyToUserProc \mathrel{\widehat=} \\
\quad (GotReplyFromDeviceProc \land \\
\quad\quad (ReplyFromDeviceProc \mathbin{;} ClearDevReply) \land \\
\quad\quad SysOk) \\
\lor\ NoDeviceReply
\end{array}
$$

The condition *NoDeviceReply* should never happen!

The expansion of *DevReplyToUserProc* is

$$
\begin{array}{l}
\textit{DevReplyToUserProc} \\
\hline
\Delta PTAB \\
\Delta ERRV \\
\Delta HW \\
p? : PID \\
m! : MSG \\
\hline
(devrpy(p?) \neq nullmsg \land \\
\quad m! = devrpy(p?) \land \\
\quad devrpy' = devrpy \oplus \{p? \mapsto nullmsg\} \land
\end{array}
$$

$$serr' = sysok)$$
$$\lor (serr' = nodevreply \land intno' = killintno)$$

pre $DevReplyToUserProc \mathrel{\widehat{=}}$
$$p? \in \mathrm{dom}\ devrpy \land devrpy(p?) \neq nullmsg$$

5.11.2 Device numbers

The following is an error-reporting schema:

$BadDeviceNumber \mathrel{\widehat{=}}$
$$(\exists e : SYSERR \mid e = baddevnum \bullet$$
$$SetSysErr[e/e?]) \land$$
$$RaiseKillInterrupt$$

This schema is used when it is detected that a process is requesting a service from a device whose number is unknown to the system. Devices are known internally to the system by process identifiers (elements of *PID*); outside the kernel, user processes know them only by *device numbers* (or service numbers). When a device process is created, it is allocated a *PID* and a *DEVNO* (device number). The following operation sets the device number in the *devmap* table in *PTAB* when a device process is created.

InitDeviceNum

$\Delta PTAB$
$dno? : DEVNO$
$d? : PID$

$devmap' = devmap \cup \{dno? \mapsto d?\}$

The precondition is simply

pre $InitDeviceNum \mathrel{\widehat{=}} true$

Checking that a device number exists is done by the operation defined by the following schema:

IsKnownDeviceNumber

$\Xi PTAB$
$dno? : DEVNO$

$dno? \in \mathrm{dom}\ devmap$

Device numbers are allocated by the person who configures the system, not by the system proper. This way, the implementers of user processes as well as the system can know the device numbers that are in use.

Given a device number, $dno?$, what is the corresponding process identifier? The following schema defines this operation. The result is returned in $d!$. The operation can only be applied when it is known that $dno?$ is an element of $devmap$'s domain (is a defined device number, that is).

$$
\begin{array}{|l}
\hline
\textit{DeviceProcessId} \\
\hline
\Xi PTAB \\
dno? : DEVNO \\
d! : PID \\
\hline
d! = devmap(dno?) \\
\hline
\end{array}
$$

Device suspension. Devices are responsible for suspending themselves.

$$
\begin{array}{l}
SuspendDeviceProcess \mathrel{\widehat=} \\
\quad RequeueDeviceProcess[d?/p?]
\end{array}
$$

This operation was defined when specifying the scheduler.

5.11.3 Device process creation

Device processes must be created, usually at boot time. Unlike user processes, it is expected that device processes will not terminate until the system as a whole is shut down.

There is no need to create a user-level identifier, so the following new composition is adequate.

$$
\begin{array}{|l}
\hline
\textit{SetPDState} \\
\hline
\Delta PTAB \\
p? : PID \\
st? : PSTATE \\
\hline
state' = state \cup \{p! \mapsto st?\} \\
ptype' = ptype \cup \{p! \mapsto dproc\} \\
\hline
\end{array}
$$

The fact that device processes do not have external identifiers means that the operation to enter their basic details into the process table is a little different from the one used for user processes. The operation for device processes is:

$$
\begin{array}{l}
AddDevPD \mathrel{\widehat=} \\
\quad ((GotFreePIDs \land AllocPID) \\
\qquad \mathbin{;} SetPDState[p!/p?] \land \\
\qquad SysOk) \\
\quad \lor PTABFull
\end{array}
$$

This definition expands, after slight simplification, into

$$
\begin{array}{|l}
\hline
\textit{AddDevPD} \\
\Delta PTAB \\
\Delta ERRV \\
\Delta HW \\
p! : PID \\
st? : PSTATE \\
\hline
(used \subset PID \land \\
\qquad p! \notin used \land \\
\qquad used' = used \cup \{p!\} \land \\
\qquad state' = state \cup \{p! \mapsto st?\} \land \\
\qquad ptype' = ptype \cup \{p! \mapsto dproc\} \land \\
\qquad serr' = sysok) \\
\lor (serr' = ptabfull \land intno' = killintno) \\
\hline
\end{array}
$$

The simplification is to identify *state* with *state''* and *ptype'* with *ptype''*. This is permitted because they are only updated in the second component of the sequential composition.

$$\text{pre}\, AddDevPD \mathrel{\widehat=} used \subset PID$$

The primitive that creates a new device process is specified ass

$$
\begin{array}{l}
NewDeviceProcess \mathrel{\widehat=} \\
\quad (IsKnownDeviceNumber \land BadDeviceNumber) \\
\quad \lor (AddDevPD[d!/p!] \mathbin{;} InitDeviceNum[d!/d?] \mathbin{;} InitDeviceMsg[d!/d?] \mathbin{;} \\
\qquad InitDeviceRq[d!/d?] \mathbin{;} InitDevReply[d!/p?] \mathbin{;} \\
\qquad SetDevProcStateToWaiting)
\end{array}
$$

After merging the existentials, this definition expands into the following schema:

$$
\begin{array}{|l}
\hline
\textit{NewDeviceProcess} \\
\Delta PTAB \\
\Delta ERRV \\
\Delta HW \\
d! : PID \\
dno? : DEVNO \\
\hline
\exists devmsg'' : PID \rightarrowtail\!\!\!\!\!+ MSG;\ devrqs'' : PID \rightarrowtail\!\!\!\!\!+ MSG; \\
\qquad\qquad devrpy' : PID \rightarrowtail\!\!\!\!\!+ MSG \bullet \\
\quad (dno? \in \operatorname{dom} devmap \land serr' = baddevnum \land intno' = killintno) \\
\quad \lor (used \subset PID \land \\
\qquad d! \notin used \land used' = used \cup \{d!\} \land \\
\qquad state' = state \cup \{d! \mapsto st?\} \land ptype' = ptype \cup \{d! \mapsto dproc\} \land \\
\qquad serr' = sysok) \\
\quad \lor (serr' = ptabfull \land intno' = killintno)
\end{array}
$$

$$
\begin{array}{l}
\quad\quad \fatsemi devmap' = devmap'' \cup \{d! \mapsto dno?\} \\
\quad\quad \fatsemi devmsg' = devmsg'' \cup \{d! \mapsto nullmsg\} \\
\quad\quad \fatsemi devrqs' = devrqs'' \cup \{d! \mapsto nullmsg\} \\
\quad\quad \fatsemi devrpy' = devrpy'' \cup \{d! \mapsto nullmsg\}
\end{array}
$$

Note that the double-primed variables are only affected once and in their respective composition elements. This permits the following simplification.

$$
\begin{array}{l}
\textit{NewDeviceProcess} \\
\hline
\Delta PTAB \\
\Delta ERRV \\
\Delta HW \\
d! : PID \\
dno? : DEVNO \\
\hline
(dno? \in \operatorname{dom} devmap \land serr' = baddevnum \land intno' = killintno) \\
\lor ((used \subset PID \land d! \notin used \land used' = used \cup \{d!\} \land \\
\quad\quad state' = state \cup \{d! \mapsto st?\} \land ptype' = ptype \cup \{d! \mapsto dproc\} \land \\
\quad\quad \fatsemi devmap' = devmap'' \cup \{d! \mapsto dno?\} \\
\quad\quad devmsg' = devmsg'' \cup \{d! \mapsto nullmsg\} \land \\
\quad\quad devrqs' = devrqs'' \cup \{d! \mapsto nullmsg\} \land \\
\quad\quad devrpy' = devrpy'' \cup \{d! \mapsto nullmsg\} \land \\
\quad\quad serr' = sysok) \\
\quad\quad \lor (serr' = ptabfull \land intno' = killintno))
\end{array}
$$

The precondition of *NewDeviceProcess* is given by:

$$
\begin{array}{l}
\operatorname{pre} \textit{NewDeviceProcess} \mathrel{\widehat=} \\
\quad dno? \in \operatorname{dom} devmap \lor used \neq PID
\end{array}
$$

There is only one thing left. Some device processes will need to initialise their hardware as soon as the system boots. This has to be included as an option. Therefore, the following is added.

$$
\begin{array}{l}
\textit{NewDeviceProcessPossInitHW} \mathrel{\widehat=} \\
\quad \textit{NewDeviceProcess} \fatsemi (runatboot? = yes \land \textit{ReadyDeviceProcess}[d!/dp?])
\end{array}
$$

After a little obvious transformation and expansion, this schema expands into

$$
\begin{array}{l}
\textit{NewDeviceProcessPossInitHW} \\
\hline
\Delta PTAB \\
d! : PID \\
dno? : DEVNO \\
runatboot? : YESNO \\
\hline
(dno? \in \operatorname{dom} devmap \land serr! = baddevnum) \\
\lor ((used \subset PID \land
\end{array}
$$

$$
\begin{array}{l}
d! \notin used \wedge used' = used \cup \{d!\} \wedge \\
state' = state \cup \{d! \mapsto st?\} \wedge ptype' = ptype \cup \{d! \mapsto dproc\} \wedge \\
devmsg' = devmsg'' \cup \{d? \mapsto nullmsg\} \wedge \\
devrqs' = devrqs'' \cup \{d? \mapsto nullmsg\} \wedge \\
devrpy' = devrpy'' \cup \{d? \mapsto nullmsg\} \wedge \\
(runatboot? = yes \wedge \\
\qquad ReadyDeviceProcess[d!/dp?]) \\
\wedge\ serr' = sysok) \\
\vee\ (serr' = ptabfull \wedge intno' = killintno)
\end{array}
$$

The precondition is:

$$
\begin{array}{l}
\text{pre } NewDeviceProcessPossInitHW \mathrel{\widehat{=}} \\
\qquad dno? \in \text{dom } devmap \\
\qquad \vee\ used \neq PID
\end{array}
$$

It is now necessary to account for three things:

1. Communicating parameters to the device process;
2. Readying a device process when its associated ISR has completed;
3. Returning values to the user process that initially made the request.

It must be pointed out that a *synchronous* I/O model is assumed in this specification. The reason for this is that it is simple to specify and to implement.

It is assumed that user processes communicate with device processes via an interrupt. The ISR associated with this interrupt decodes the request and passes appropriate parameters to the device process. Until the device process has completed its operations and has returned at least a return code to the caller, the caller is suspended in a waiting state (*pswaitdev*). When the device process has completed, it must ready the requesting user process—this implies that the device process stores the identifier of the requesting process.

$$
\begin{array}{l}
SetStateToDevWait \mathrel{\widehat{=}} \\
\qquad \exists\, st : PSTATE \mid st = psdevwait \bullet \\
\qquad\qquad SetProcState[st/st?]
\end{array}
$$

It must be emphasised that this operation is intended for use by user processes *only*. Device processes have their own waiting state and setter operation.

When a device request is made, the requesting process' *PID* and device number are checked. Should either fail, an error value is returned in *serr*. The device data is passed to the device process, together with the requesting process' *PID*.

The parameters passed by the requesting process take the form of a message. The message is passed to the device process using *PassDataToDeviceProcess*. The requesting process then waits until the device process posts a message to its *devrpy* slot using *DevReplyToUserProc* and then readies the requesting process using *MakeReadyUserProcess*. The identifier of the requesting process must be checked to see that it is valid (not the null or idle process and not another device process).

The following operation is part of the handler code that activates device processes. If device requests are handled by an interrupt, the following operation will be used by the associated ISR.

$$
\begin{array}{l}
BadCallerIdent \mathrel{\widehat=} \\
\quad (\exists e : SYSERR \mid e = badcallerid \bullet \\
\qquad SetSysErr[e/e?]) \land \\
\quad RaiseKillInterrupt
\end{array}
$$

When a request is made to a device process, it must be verified and the device process activated. Verification, here, consists of verifying that there is a device process corresponding to the specified device number and that the requesting process is genuine. If the tests have been passed, the request is passed to the device process and the requesting user process' state is set to "waiting on device" (*psdevwait*). The operation is defined as follows:

$$
\begin{array}{l}
VerifyAndActivateDevProc \mathrel{\widehat=} \\
\quad (VerifyCallerIdent \land PIDforUPID[caller/p!] \land \\
\qquad\qquad IDLEPROCESSIdent[iprc/p!] \land \\
\qquad (ValidDevRqProcessId[caller/rqid?, iprc/iprc?] \land \\
\qquad\quad (IsKnownDevideNumber \land \\
\qquad\qquad (DeviceProcessId[dp/d!] \land \\
\qquad\qquad\quad ((PassDataToDeviceProcess[dp/d?, caller/p?] \\
\qquad\qquad\quad \mathbin{;} SetStateToDevWait[caller/p?]) \land \\
\qquad\qquad\quad SysOk \\
\qquad\qquad\quad \mathbin{;} SKSchedNext)) \setminus \{dp\}) \\
\qquad\qquad \lor BadDeviceNumber)) \setminus \{caller, iprc\} \\
\quad \lor BadCallerIdent
\end{array}
$$

For safety, this operation is expanded.

$$
\begin{array}{|l}
\hline
VerifyAndActivateDevProc \\
\Delta SCHED \\
\Delta PRIOQ \\
\Delta HW \\
\Delta ERRV \\
\Xi PTAB \\
u? : UPID \\
dno? : DEVNO \\
m? : MSG \\
\hline
\exists caller, iprc : PID \bullet \\
\quad (curr = extpid(u?) \land caller = extpid(u?) \land iprc = ipid \land \\
\qquad ((caller \neq nullpid \land caller \neq iprc \land ptype(caller) \neq dproc \land
\end{array}
$$

$$
\begin{array}{l}
\quad\quad (\exists\, dp : PID \bullet \\
\quad\quad\quad dno? \in \mathrm{dom}\, devmap \land dp = devmap(dno?) \land \\
\quad\quad\quad (\exists\, devq : \mathrm{seq}\, PID \bullet \\
\quad\quad\quad\quad (\exists\, state'' : PID \nrightarrow PSTATE \bullet \\
\quad\quad\quad\quad\quad devmsg' = devmsg \oplus \{dp \mapsto (caller, m?)\} \land \\
\quad\quad\quad\quad\quad state'' = state \oplus \{dp \mapsto psready\} \land \\
\quad\quad\quad\quad\quad devq'' = devq \frown \langle dp \rangle \land \\
\quad\quad\quad\quad\quad state = state'' \oplus \{caller \mapsto psdevwait\}) \land \\
\quad\quad\quad\quad\quad serr' = sysok \\
\quad\quad\quad\quad\quad \land\, SKSchedNext))) \\
\quad \lor (serr' = baddevnum \land intno' = killintno)) \\
\lor (serr' = badcallerident \land intno' = killintno))
\end{array}
$$

The expansion of this operation shows that a request to a device causes the device process to be readied on the scheduler's ready device queue (*devq*) and the requesting process is suspended. The operation also causes a reschedule.

This definition exemplifies our use of the reschedule operation instead of the *MakeUnready*. It is known that when the above is exceuted, the current process is the one that needs to be removed from the scheduling queue.

Note that device requests are a case where the currently executing process is unreadied. The requesting user process remains in a waiting state until the device process whose services it has requested has completed and placed a reply message in the requesting process' reply slot in *PTAB*.

The method by which the device process communicates with the hardware device under its control is not further specified here. Some shared memory will probably be employed for data buffering. Since this specification is not machine specific, it is impossible to decide here which methods should be used.

When the device process has obtained a reply from the hardware, it uses the following operation to return the data to the requesting user process. It then suspends itself ready for the next request.

$$
\begin{array}{l}
DevReturnDataAndSuspend \mathrel{\widehat=} \\
\quad ((DevRequesterId[rqid/p!] \land \\
\quad\quad DevReplyToUserProc[rqid/p?] \land \\
\quad\quad MakeReadyUserProcess[rqid/p?]) \setminus \{rqid\} \\
\quad\quad\quad \mathbin{;} SKSchedNext) \mathbin{;} SetDevProcStateToWaiting
\end{array}
$$

This partially expands into:

$$
\begin{array}{|l}
\hline
DevReturnDataAndSuspend \\
\Delta PTAB \\
\Delta SKSCHED \\
\Delta ERRV \\
\Delta HW \\
d? : PID
\end{array}
$$

$$
\begin{array}{|l}
m! : MSG \\
\hline
(\exists\, rqid : PID \mid rqid = fst\ devmsg(d?) \bullet \\
\quad ((devrpy(rqid) \neq nullmsg \wedge \\
\qquad m! = devrpy(rqid) \wedge \\
\qquad devrpy' = devrpy \oplus \{rqid \mapsto nullmsg\} \wedge \\
\qquad serr' = sysok) \\
\quad \vee\ (serr' = nodevreply \wedge intno' = killintno) \wedge \\
\quad MakeReadyUserProcess[rqid/p?]) \\
\fatsemi SKSchedNext \fatsemi SetDevProcStateToWaiting
\end{array}
$$

This operation can be used to return status information as well as requested data. In the case of output devices, a completion code could be returned in the message passed to the requesting user process.

$SetDeviceProcessData \mathrel{\widehat{=}}$
$\quad (DevRequestId[rqid/p!] \wedge SetDevReply[rqid/p?])$

It is now necessary to specify how the reply from the device process is handed to the requesting process. This is, basically, an architecture-specific issue but a general solution is to return the data as a message on the requesting process' stack.

In this model, when a device process makes a request to its associated hardware, it must suspend itself until the device has completed the requested operation (generally, it is assumed that the operation returns a value). When the ISR or device interface has completed, it must ready the device process so that it can perform its next operation. If the device process deals with hardware that does not require it to wait, it should immediately suspend ready for the next user request. The suspension of a device process is achieved by action of $SKSchedNext \fatsemi SwitchContext$) because this operation unconditionally schedules a new process and switches the context to it.

Because device processes are trusted, a suspension operation can be defined that does not engage in all the checking required for user processes. It is

$SelfSuspendDeviceProcess \mathrel{\widehat{=}} SKSchedNext$

The ISR needs, however, to obtain the device process' identifier; this might change between boots. However, the device number does not, so the ISR can call *DeviceProcessId* to obtain the device number.

$AwakenDeviceProcessFromISR \mathrel{\widehat{=}}$
$\quad (DeviceProcessId[d/d!] \wedge ReadyDeviceProcess[d/dp?]) \setminus \{d\}$

5.12 Process Interface to the Kernel

It is assumed that user processes, when performing a system call, place the input parameters on their stack. They will also retrieve results from the kernel from their stack. This requires that user-process stacks be accessible from within the kernel even though user-process stacks reside in segments other than the one in which the kernel resides.

Finally, device processes are trusted code and are programmed by systems programmers. It seems permissible, therefore, to provide direct access to all of the operations defined above. Moreover, there are no problems with crossing segment boundaries when device processes are active. The only issue is how a user process can activate a device process. This operation will be included in this section.

The first calls that are considered are those performing message-passing functions. They are directly called from user processes and are relatively complex to specify.

It should be noted that the above operations deal mostly with pointers to messages, not to message structures proper. In particular, this leads to two problems:

1. How to pass a message structure to the destination process. (This involves crossing address space boundaries.)
2. Deletion of the message structure after the destination has read the message.

In addition, there is the question of reclaiming all storage in the message pool. As noted above, the *FreeBlk* algorithm does not collect and merge all possible blocks but, if a block cannot be connected immediately to an existing free block, the algorithm just adds the newly freed block to the end of the free block chain. This leads to space leaks and is the reason for the definition of the block scavenging operation. The block scavenging operation is relatively expensive, so should not be called very frequently.

Of the process control operations, those that suspend and terminate their caller are intended to be called directly by a user-level process. The process creation operation is intended to be called from a library routine; the library routine will be called by the initial or some other process.

As an intermediate solution to the above problems, the following operation is defined. This operation is intended to be called from the ISR that is activated when a user process performs a system call; system calls consist of a number of operations on the user stack (essentially a conventional procedure call) followed by the raising of a dedicated interrupt. The top of the user stack is the opcode, *rqop*? (*requested operation*—an element of $SYSOPCODE$) which determines the operation to be performed by the system. Immediately underneath the opocde are the parameters to the system call. The decode routine performs the operation and returns values on the user's stack. All that is missing from the *DecodeSysCall* specification is the mechanism for accessing the user-process stack.

$$
\begin{array}{|l}
\hline
\textit{DecodeSysCall} \\
rqop? : SYSOPCODE \\
\hline
(rqop? = newuproc \land USKNewProcess) \\
\lor (rqop? = suspself \land USKSuspendSelf) \\
\lor (rqop? = termself \land USKTerminateSelf) \\
\lor (rqop? = sndmsg \land USKSendMsg) \\
\lor (rqop? = gotmsgs \land USKGotMsgs) \\
\lor (rqop? = gotmsgfromsrc \land SKProcessHasMsgsFromSrc) \\
\lor (rqop? = nextmsg \land USKNextMsg) \\
\lor (rqop? = nextmsgfromsrc \land SKNextMsgFrom) \\
\lor (rqop? = devrequest \land VerifyAndActivateDevProc) \\
\hline
\end{array}
$$

We have ignored the issue of obtaining parameters from the user process. The actual answer, of course, depends upon the processor being used. On the IA32, the parameters are on the user's stack. On interrupt, the user's stack is pointed to by the current hardware TSS register; the stack pointer is stored in the TSS; when an interrupt occurs, the stack regiser can be retrieved from the TSS. This is not the entire story because the IA32 is a segmented architecture, so a segment register has to be set up to point to the stack segment (combined stack and data segment in the present case) so that the user's stack can be addressed. When an interrupt occurs, the IA32 pushes two double words (two 32-bit quantities, i.e.) on the current stack—one is the flags (F) register, the other is the PC. Underneath these comes the parameter area that can be accessed to obtain parameter values. Once extracted, the stack can be adjusted ready to return results. Other architectures will arrange matters in a different way, it must be stressed.

When this operation has completed, the ISR returns. The reason for this is that any context switches are performed by component operations as their last operation (context switches also perform a Return From Interrupt operation as standard). For this reason, the *DecodeSysCall* operation does not assign a value to the standard error-return variable, *serr*.

As far as the user stack is concerned, the following must be emphasised:

- Input values are taken from the *user-process stack*. This resides in the *user process stack segment*, not in the kernel's address space.
- Output values are placed on the *user-process stack*, not the kernel stack.

When taking inputs and returning outputs, access to the user stack is required. This is a low-level operation programmed in assembly code. The complexity of this operation is dependent upon the architecture of the processor upon which the separation kernel runs.

The problem is not in principle difficult. Within the structure representing each process' state (in its process table), there is a slot each for its segments. The stack pointer is also stored there. Depending upon the architecture and compiler, there might also be a pointer to the user process' z*current stack* *frame*. This last pointer allows the kernel direct access to the top of the user's stack, albeit at the cost of a number of accesses to the process table and other structures.

5.13 Final Thoughts

The NSA documents [10] frequently refer to threads inside each Separation Kernel process. The specification that is refined in this chapter makes no mention of threads. The explicit inclusion of threads would increase the length of the chapter somewhat.

There is, however, no real need to include threads in this chapter because they can be included by simple modifications to the specification, in particular the mechanisms of the simple kernel specified and refined in Chapter 3 can be included in the Separation Kernel. The inclusion requires, among others, a few changes to the Separation Kernel's process table ($PTAB$). To see that this works, it is necessary to consider that the simple kernel operates in a single address space. The processes that the simple kernel supports do not require address-space manipulation when context switches occur; indeed, they resemble threads quite closely.

This is the other reason for combining the simple kernel and the Separation Kernel in this book.

6

Closing Thoughts

In this last chapter, we will try to collect some threads and review the content of this book.

First, the book contains the specification and refinement of two micro kernels. The first is suitable for use in embedded systems and the other is specifically a kernel for cryptographic systems. Each specification is relatively complete and the refinements reach the level at which executable code in a language such as C or Ada can be read off from the Z schemata.

The refinements are based on the standard Z technique as it is described in the literature (e.g., [12, 13]). The refined state schema was defined and then the abstraction relation was defined. Thereafter, the operation schemata were defined. The initialisation theorem was used as a test of the adequacy of the abstraction relation.

It was found that the abstraction relations were

- Functions;
- Identities.

These properties, in principle, permitted the calculation of all operations in the refinement and obviated all the associated proofs. We included all proofs in the first refinement so that the reader could see that they were possible (actually, quite simple). In the second refinement (that of the Separation Kernel), we included all the bottom-level proofs but had to omit those for the more complex operations (this had also to be done in a few cases in the first refinement); this was done to reduce the length of an already over-long book and so as not further to bore the reader with straightforward proofs.

The fact that we included proofs in both refinements is an indication of our position on formal methods. We consider that, even though they are strictly unnecessary, the inclusion of explicit and complete proofs is an essential part of the refinement to code. Proofs require us to examine our definitions and to reason about them. By engaging in proof, we have a guarantee that our definitions (state schemata) and relationships between them (operation schemata) are correct according to the axioms of the various theories we use. Without proof, we might as well not bother for there is no guarantee of anything—it is like sleepwalking through a formal notation, much as we sleepwalk from an informal specification to a piece of (one hopes) working code. The production of proofs forces us to think carefully and in detail about things; this is, we believe, essential.

That the abstraction relations are all identities is not a surprise to us. As we have already noted, the vast majority of the abstraction relations we have found over a very long period have been identities.

The specification of hardware poses a slight problem for us. This was because we did not want, in the case of this book, to specify any particular piece of hardware for the kernel of Chapters 2 and 3; the Separation Kernel is aimed at the Intel IA32 and 64 processors, so we could be a little more definite. In the case of the Separation Kernel, we specified the IA32/64 hardware operations at a level of detail that we felt adequate for the production of the tiny amounts of assembly code required to complete the kernel. In the case of the kernel of Chapters 2 and 3, the register-save operation was specified as operations on the process' stack; the operations correspond exactly to two IA32 instructions. In both cases, context switches are caused by a software interrupt (which is specified).

Turning to the refinement process itself, there are some points that can be made.

First, there is the fact that a specification is a conjunction of wffs. This implies that they lack structure. The lack of structure can be exploited by the distributive rules for $\wedge$ and $\vee$. However, it poses problems if one expects that what one considers to be a routine should be represented in a modular fashion; after all, standard software engineering requires us to consider routines as abstractions that are referred to by name.

This lack of structure is clear when a complex definition (i.e., a definition involving more than one operation schema) is expanded for simplification or for the calculation of a precondition. It would be highly desirable if each operation schema could be represented by a precondition (and, possibly, by a postcondition). This is not always possible because preconditions are represented by existentially quantified wffs in Z. In some cases, it is possible to separate operation schemata from the surrounding conjuncts in some cases (and we have encountered them in this book) but they must first be investigated in order to determine that such treatment is valid. The organisation of a specification as a conjunct is rarely mentioned in the literature. It has a further implication: as a specification grows in size, so do the conjunctions that result from the composition of operations.

As can be seen from the calculations in this book, it is sometimes possible to exploit substitutions as a way to handle complexity in expanded operations.

The definition of complex operations has implications other than visibility. It is to these that we now turn.

We have used simplification extensively above. In some cases, it was the simplification of simple operations; in others, it was the simplification of complex operations; in still others, it was the simplification of preconditions. We need to ask what the purpose of simplification is. In the case of the simplification of simple operations (those composed of a single schema), we have a form of optimisation. The simplified operation can be used directly in refinement or the production of code. In the case of preconditions, we are interested in the logical form of the operation; this is what simplification gives us, for a simplified precondition is at least implied by the unsimplified version (at best, it is materially equivalent). It is the case of complex operations, operations composed of more than one operation schema, that is interesting. Clearly, it is possible to view the simplification as an optimisation. In this case, the simplified version can be employed in refinement or the production of code. However, the simplification of a complex operation violates the modularity of its components (this, again, is the problem that specifications are large conjunctions).

If a simple (or less complex) operation is included in more than one complex one, and the more complex operations are simplified, it is more than possible that the boundaries of the included operations will not be respected in the formula that results from simplification. This might not appear problematic but an example shows that it poses problems.

Consider the case of a storage-allocation operation. In a complex system (such as an operating system or a virtual machine for a programming language), the allocation operation might be included in a number of complex operations. The storage-allocation operation will, almost certainly, be a complex operation defined in terms of a number of suboperations. When the storage-allocation operations is included in more complex operations, it becomes a candidate for simplification. When simplified, the storage-allocation operation's abstraction boundary will probably not be respected. While we are dealing with a mathematical abstraction, this is not a problem (it might be when manipulating the resulting wffs but that is another matter). It can become a problem when the production of code is concerned. If the simplified operations are considered the basis for refinement or code production, it is clear that we have the following to consider:

- Parts of the code that would comprise the storage-allocation operation appear in various other, more complex operations. It is possible (indeed, probable) that the entire operation *never* appears intact.
- It is possible (probable) that there will be replication of code because the simplifications will not necessarily remove the same conjuncts of the original operation.

It can be argued that the first of these two cases is not much of a problem and that it is, on the contrary, a benefit. The process of producing the final simplified operation is clearly documented and the result proved to be correct. The second case is more of a problem. In traditional software engineering, we are taught to define abstractions and to avoid destroying them; simplification is a clear case in which abstraction boundaries are broken. Furthermore, we are used, using traditional methods, not to expand code without good reason (object-oriented progamming is another case in which this principle is violated, often for what appears not to be a very good reason and could be solved if compilation and linking were more selective).

We do not agree with the position that storage chips are becoming cheaper all the time, so we can be profligate with code and data structures. This position is, in our opinion, an attempt to justify sloppy thinking. We need more thought in Computer Science and Software Engineering, not less!

Next, we have to comment on the use of deferred assumptions and implicit preconditions. In some parts of the specification, particularly those parts specifying some simpler operations over the process table, we could have guarded each operation with a test that the process identifier bound to the input variable was an element of *used*. This was something we did not do. Instead, we assumed that this was true and continued with the refinement. At the final stage, it was clear that the current process was always bound to the input variable $p?$ and, by other reasoning, it can be shown that $p? \in used$. The alternative would have been to include a check that became increasingly costly as the refinement progressed (this is something we observed in Chapter 4). We consider that waiting to discharge assumptions is a reasonable option, at least on logical grounds, even though it is, in human terms, a bit risky (one has to remember to discharge the assumption). It is part of our refinement plan to make the assumption that $p? \in used$ early on and then to discharge the assumption later on. In a case such as this, the process is harmless for the reason that we *had* to discharge the assumption later on (and the assumption was, in any case, quite harmless). There will be cases where the logical position should not be adopted for pragmatic reasons.

We also used an implicit precondition (a precondition that derives from the invariant) in order to show that the ready queue was valid. This is logically valid and appears to us to be a technique that should be adopted. The use of implicit preconditions makes the invariant more central. The refinement method, as presented in the literature, centres on the abstraction relation. However, it is essential that the invariant of the specification and that of the refinement be related by the abstraction relation for the reason that it is the invariant that determines the integrity (correctness) of an operation's effects in the sense that it defines the set of legal states (the invariant plays a much greater part in refinement in the B Method [1]). The use of the invariant does not appear to be as prominent as it might be (a proof that the invariants are so related should appear as part of the refinement process). Strictly speaking, when defining each operation schema, there should be a proof that the operation's predicate preserves the invariant; this is important for possibly interacting operations (e.g., operations defined by the composition of simpler ones).

Of course, it can be argued that the invariant is always *implicitly* present in all proofs because they universally. Our points are that this is not prominent enough and that the refinement relations should, ideally, be established between invariants in specification and refinement. quantify over state schemata.

In the construction of some proofs, we referred to invariants or to results at a higher level in the refinement process. This is, we believe, to be quite valid; it is justified by the following reasoning. The abstraction realtion should be a pair of homomorphisms: one transforming the specification into the refinement, the other performing the opposite transformation (they should be mutually inverse). The composition of homomorphisms is also be a homomorphism. If we have a specification, S, and two refinements of this specifiction, R_1 and R_2, such that R_1 is a refinement of S and R_2 is a refinement of R_1, and if $h_1 : S \rightarrow R_1$ and $h_2 : R_1 \rightarrow R_2$, there exists a $h_{1,2} : S \rightarrow R_2$. In the particular case of the refinements in this book, h_1 and h_2 are both identities, so $h_{1,2} = h_2 \circ h_1$ (with $h_2 \circ h_1 = h_2(h_1(S))$) definitely exists and is well defined.

In our second refinement, we reused components from the first and relied upon existing proofs as our guarantees of correctness. Reuse of this kind is natural in formal specification and is, we believe, superior to the reuse of executable code. One reason for this claim is that the reuse of specifications makes the assumptions about components explicit.

Is formal refinement worth the effort? If one is used to informal methods (or no methods), particularly when one does not engage in extensive documentation, formal methods will cost more in time and effort. A resistence to documentation is something that we have often encountered in so-called "real-world" contexts—it is often "justified" on cost grounds (but consider the costs of having to justify undocumented software as part of a court case). We believe that the amount of work required to produce a formal specification and its refinement is about the same as producing informal documents. Furthermore, formal methods yield connections between decisions made at one level with those as a lower level. In addition, there is the matter of testing. In our case, we have engaged in testing. This is just so we can check that the resulting code is a correct transcription (i.e., contains no transcription errors); it also serves to increase our confidence that the result is correct. In the case of the first kernel, we engaged in quite exhaustive testing just to assure ourselves that the code is correct. However, this testing is not only a way to increase confidence; it provides additional evidence that the code is correct. Fairly extensive testing appears useful in cases such as kernels where we want to be as sure as we can be that the code behaves correctly; in other cases, we might want to be assured that the code contains no transcription errors. It would, in any case, be far better to have a mechanical method for checking the result, for the process is fairly mechanical. We found, of course, that the code performs exactly as it should in all cases. (We have also to admit that we tested somewhat more thoroughly than usual when dealing with formally derived code so that we could state that it behaved correctly. We have previous experience of the correct functioning of code derived from formally refined specifications.)

To conclude this chapter and this book, one last issue must be raised: automation. We did all of the work in this book by hand (or by mouth because much of the text was dictated). It is clear that a good deal of automation should be possible. The construction of schema compositions can be mechanised with ease and would be most welcome as a way of helping with document management. The complete automation of simplification and proof does not appear within reach at the moment but it is clear that there are ways in which it can be supported. By this, we do not mean using current-generation proof assistants which can be rather hard to use and have a long learning curve, requiring the user to learn new names for methods and new notations. Of course, some of us find the production of proofs to be one of the more interesting and enjoyable aspects of formal specification—complete automation would deprive us of that pleasure. The checking that code conforms to the bottom level of refinement is also a case in which automation could assist, for example in generating verification conditions that can be related to the final stage of refinement. A moderate amount of carefully designed automation would help considerably.

We hope that this book has served to indicate that there are interesting issues raised by refinement in the large and that these issues have not been discussed much in the published literature. We hope that we have also demonstrated that the formal specification of operating system kernels is viable; in addition to the refinements in this book, our experience with our collection of components has been extremely positive.

References

1. Abrial, J.-R., *The B Book: Assigning Programs to Meanings*, CUP, 1996.
2. Bivot, Daniel C. and Cesati, Marco, *Understanding the LINUX Kernel*, O'Reilly & Associates, Sebastapol, CA, 2001.
3. Craig, I. D., *Formal Specification of Advanced AI Architectures*, Ellis Horwood, Chichester, England, 1991?
4. Craig, I. D., *Formal Models of Operating System Kernels*, Springer-Verlag, London, England, 2006.
5. Derrick, J. and Boiten, E., *Refinement in Z and Object-Z*, Springer-Verlag, London, 2001.
6. Dijkstra, E. J., *A Discipline of Programming*, Prentice-Hall, Englewood Cliffs, NJ, 1976.
7. Jones, C. B., *Systematic Software Development Using VDM*, Prentice-Hall, Englewood Cliffs, NJ, 1986.
8. Labrosse, Jean J., *MicroC/OS-II, The Real-Time Kernel*, Miller Freeman, Inc., Lawrence, KS, 1999.
9. Morgan, C. C., *Programming from Specifications*, 2nd edn., Prentice-Hall, Hemel Hempstead, England, 1994.
10. National Security Agency, Separation Kernel Documents, e.g., SSE-100-1; many others on line at `www:nsa.gov`.
11. Rushby, John, Design and Verification of Secure Systems, *ACM Operating Systems Review*, Vol. 15, No. 5, pp. 12–21, 1981.
12. Spivey, J. M., *The Z Notation: A Reference Manual*, 2nd edn., Prentice-Hall, Hemel Hempstead, 1992.
13. Woodcock, J. and Davies, J., *Using Z: Specification, Refinement and Proof*, Prentice-Hall, Hemel Hempstead, 1996.

List of Definitions

Schema: